The Healing Power of UFOs

300 True Accounts of People Healed by Extraterrestrials

Preston Dennett

The Healing Power of UFOs: 300 True Accounts of People Healed by Extraterrestrials

Blue Giant Books

Non-Fiction

ISBN 9781792986208

1. UFOs, Extraterrestrials, Aliens. 2. New Age, Metaphysical, Occult, Paranormal, Supernatural. 3. Healing, Alternative Healing, Medicine. 4. Science, Astronomy. I. Title

Cover Art by Christine Kesara Dennett. Website: www.kesara.org/

Contents

Preface

In 1996, after almost ten years of researching UFOs, my first book was published. *UFO Healings: True Accounts of People Healed by Extraterrestrials*, presented 103 cases of people who were cured of a wide variety of injuries, illnesses, conditions and diseases as the direct result of a UFO encounter. It was the first book ever published to document UFO healing cases.[1]

Following publication, I began to get letters from people across the world who had read the book and had something they wanted to share. Some wanted to thank me, others revealed their own UFO healing, and a few wrote asking me to put them in touch with the ETs so that they could get healed. (Which I can't do! I wish I could!)

More than twenty years later, this flow of letters (now emails) hasn't stopped. Although the book has been out-of-print for many years, I continue to get requests to speak on the subject. I have spoken on countless radio stations, television programs, at bookstores, conventions and UFO groups, and often afterward I am approached by still more people who claim to have been healed or helped by UFOs and extraterrestrials.

When I first began my research, I believed that UFO healings were *exceedingly* rare events. Now, however, the continuing stream of new cases has forced me to alter my opinion. I am currently convinced that UFO healings are a fairly consistent feature of UFO contact.

While the first book presented 103 cases, I have since collected more than three times that number! This new book contains more than 300 cases of UFO healings, including the original cases. Since more than twenty years have passed since publication of *UFO Healings*, I have been able to locate new information on many of the original cases. While readers of the first book may find some of the content familiar, the majority of the cases (about two-thirds) are new, and many are published here for the first time.

Introduction

Anyone who has done even the smallest amount of *objective* research into the subject of UFOs knows that UFOs are real. An overwhelming amount of evidence supports this fact. The evidence comes in many forms including eyewitness testimonies, photographs, moving films, radar returns, metal fragments, landing traces, animal reactions, medical effects, electromagnetic effect cases, implant removals, historical accounts, crash/retrieval claims, and thousands of pages of documents from many U.S. governmental institutions, not to mention other governments. The question today is not if UFOs are real. There are more important questions to answer, such as, what are they? Why are they here? Where do they come from?

The most popular theory is that UFOs are extraterrestrial in origin, though there are a number of lesser known theories. UFO experts continue to argue over the question of why UFOs are here. The prevailing opinion is that they are neither invaders nor saviors, but are simply here to study humanity.

Dozens of books are published each year that present the vast array of UFO evidence. Because of the abundance of evidence, UFO books have become specialized. There are books about abductions, the government cover-up, UFO propulsion, and more. The uninitiated skeptic is invariably overwhelmed by the huge amount of information on the subject.

UFO skeptics and believers may both find the accounts in this book difficult to believe. I understand skepticism as I used to be a UFO skeptic. It was only a bizarre series of events that led me to begin a UFO investigation I never meant to follow.

My introduction to the UFO field began in November 1986 when Captain Kenju Terauchi went public with his sighting of a

UFO while flying over Alaska. Believing the captain was lying, misperceiving or hallucinating, I made the mistake of asking my family, friends and co-workers what they thought of this ridiculous pilot.

I quickly discovered that several of the people closest to me were keeping secrets, and were having dramatic UFO encounters. Knowing how cruel skeptics could be, they kept quiet.

I had the opposite reaction and became quickly obsessed with the subject. I bought all the books I could find. I subscribed to UFO magazines, joined UFO groups, attended conventions, and began to interview everyone I could find who claimed to have had a UFO encounter. I went out into the field conducting UFO stake-outs and on-the-spot investigations. I began writing articles, and eventually books.

There are many reasons why people remain UFO skeptics. Almost without exception, the skeptic vastly underestimates the amount and quality of the evidence. Furthermore, prejudiced beliefs and preconceived notions tend to blind people to the possibility of UFOs. But there is one main reason why so many people remain UFO skeptics. UFOs are a package deal including the entire gamut of the unexplained. The skeptic is instantly confronted with stories of levitation, telepathy, movement through solid objects, poltergeists, Bigfoot, and even worse...unexplained healings.

The typical reaction is to reject the entire subject as complete nonsense. The skeptic leaves the subject in disgust, horrified that people can actually believe such lurid accounts as alien abductions.

Skepticism, unless taken to extremes, is healthy. The problem, however, is that skeptics tend to ignore the evidence that doesn't fit into their worldview. The perfect example of this happened in the 1950s, when accounts of humanoids started to appear in large numbers. Many UFO investigators rejected the stories outright. It was only after hundreds of accounts were recorded that the UFO community began to accept the reports.

The same unfortunate phenomenon occurred yet again when missing time abductions were reported. The idea that people could be taken inside a UFO and left with no memory of the event was simply too bizarre to be believed. However, as the accounts mounted, the evidence could not be ignored, and today UFO abductions are the cutting edge of UFO research.

The exact same thing happened again with UFO crash/retrievals. Though reports had circulated for decades, the vast majority were ignored or debunked by investigators. Now, however, most researchers take these accounts very seriously.

Reports of UFO healings have suffered terribly from this phenomenon, and have often been relegated to the fringe, and considered to be the most unbelievable of UFO accounts. I remember my own reaction when I first read of a UFO healing case. I just didn't believe it. My reasoning was simple. People who believe UFOs are here to cure us of our diseases must have a psycho-pathological need to believe in a higher power.

The idea that extraterrestrials are here to heal humanity of our illnesses is admittedly preposterous. If it were true, why would millions of people die each year, of cancer, heart disease and other illnesses?

But those pesky UFO healing stories wouldn't go away. They appeared in books, articles, lectures and firsthand accounts of UFO witnesses. By 1996, I had written more than forty articles on the subject of UFOs, and after reading about a few well-known accounts of UFO healings, I decided to examine the stories, and see if there was any truth to them.

If so, I planned to write a small article, as I really didn't think such cases were very common. To my surprise, I found dozens of reports, way too many to include in a single article. I had a few cases of my own to contribute. I would have to write a book, I realized. I buckled down, dug in and began some serious research. After a year, I had located more than 100 accounts, and so the original book, *UFO Healings,* was born.

The results of publication were way beyond what I had expected. I publicized the book by writing articles and excerpts and appearing on the radio. I was soon asked to speak at conventions and appear on television. Suddenly, I began to receive letters and emails from people who were eager to share their own

UFO healing experience. Nearly every time I lectured on the subject, another person would come up and share their account.

UFO Healings was my first book. I eventually went on to write more than twenty additional books, each covering various aspects of UFOs and the paranormal. The subject of UFO healings, however, remained very special to me, and it continued to be popular.

As the subject was pushed into the spotlight, more people began to pay attention. New books were published on the subject, most notably, *Celestial Healings*, by Virginia Aronson.

As the years passed, sales of *UFO Healings* slowed down and the book eventually went out-of-print. Copies became scarce and I started to get contacted by people asking for a copy as they had become too expensive to purchase from on-line bookstores. The same question was asked of me again and again. Would I put out a second book? If so, when?

The idea of a new book was something I'd considered for many years. However, I wanted to wait until I had enough new accounts to make a second book worth writing. Because most people don't have access to the first book, I also wanted to include the original cases and the new ones.

This new book contains the original cases, (with new information) plus more than 200 new accounts, making this the largest collection of UFO healing cases ever published. It is also the largest book I have ever written.

Doing the research for this book has been an awesome task, and it has radically changed my beliefs about UFOs. I discovered that there is a very fine line between an abductee (someone taken against their will aboard a UFO) and a contactee (someone invited aboard a UFO.) After studying the accounts of healings, I began to look at UFOs more as floating hospitals than anything else.

The types of healings seemed straight out of science fiction. People reported their bodies being opened and closed with lasers that left no scars. They told how various organs were removed and put back in again. They reported instantaneous cures of wounds and injuries. They reported healings of serious conditions, such as pneumonia or liver disease. They even reported healings of serious diseases, such as cancer.

I found strong parallels between the stories that seemed to exclude the possibility of hoaxes. In fact, the accounts were so consistent that it was obvious the witnesses were telling the truth.

A UFO healing can be simply defined as *a physiological improvement as the result of a UFO encounter.* Here are three typical scenarios of a UFO healing:

1. A person is awakened in their bedroom to see aliens at the foot of the bed. They are taken inside a UFO, given a physical examination and told that they are sick with a disease. The aliens tell the abductee that they will perform a cure. After being probed with various instruments, the person is returned to their bedroom. Upon examination, all traces of the disease are gone.

2. A person is hospitalized because of injury, illness or disease. While alone in the hospital room, the patient is visited by a strange doctor who says she is there to help the patient. The "doctor" holds a small instrument over the patient and may administer medicine in the form of pills. The "doctor" leaves, often as mysteriously as she arrived. The patient quickly discovers that all symptoms of ill health have disappeared.

3. A person is driving along a road when a UFO makes a close pass over the car, sending down a beam of light. The person is engulfed in the beam of light. Suddenly the UFO leaves and the person discovers that they no longer suffer from an illness, disease or injury.

These accounts are reported by all types of people from all over the world. But because healings are among the most incredible of all UFO stories, it is not too surprising that they are often ignored or given only brief mention.

Despite this overriding skepticism, many UFO researchers have made positive statements concerning the veracity of UFO healings. If not for these brave pioneers, this book would never have been written.

The first UFO researcher to pay any attention to UFO healings was Gordon Creighton, a pioneering investigator from England, editor of the *Flying Saucer Review*, and the author of the first article about UFO healings. In his 1970 FSR article, *Healing from UFOs*, Creighton wrote, "They [UFO healing cases] deserve to be placed on record and studied. If we are mindful of who it is that rules our world and controls the affairs of men, we shall not however expect such reports to make any impact in orthodox medical and scientific circles. It would break the hearts of most scientists to have to admit that such things could be true...I have written this present article because I think it is vitally--perhaps crucially--important that we do not lose our perspective. That benevolent UFO entities exist I have no shred of doubt."[1]

Budd Hopkins was (prior to his passing) perhaps the most influential UFO abduction researcher in the United States. His first book, *Missing Time*, took the UFO community by storm and propelled him to the frontlines of UFO research. At the *Triad UFO Conference* in Coronado, California, in 1994, I got ahold of the microphone after his presentation and asked him if he had received any UFO healing cases in his research. Hopkins admitted that yes, he has uncovered these types of accounts.

"The question," said Hopkins, "is whether we hear about healing cases. We do sometimes, very rarely, but they do turn up. And we don't know what to make of them. It's kind of a sad thing, because I have some abductees who have serious medical problems who wish they were being healed themselves, but are not. So, if they [the ETs] had the facilities, we wish they would do something. One of David Jacobs' clients said, 'I don't know whether I should be grateful as getting a present, or maybe it's just equipment maintenance.' So, we really don't know. Incidentally again, there's no evidence whatsoever that this is a malevolent, evil conspiracy going on in the sky against us, they're going to take us over, or anything else. I'm very optimistic about the outcome because they seem to be most interested in what I consider the most human aspects of our personality, of our lives, of some of the most lovely aspects of being human. They're interested in that. There's no evidence, however, that they're here to help us. We wouldn't perhaps have AIDS, the hole in the ozone layer and everything else if they were here to help us. So, there's no sense to this."[2]

David Jacobs Ph.D., one of the leading authorities on UFO abductions, admits that healings take place, but he is less optimistic than Hopkins. He writes, "In extremely rare cases, the aliens will undertake a cure of some ailment troubling the abductee. This is not in any way related to the contactee/Space Brother concepts of benevolent aliens coming to Earth to cure cancer. Rather, in special circumstances, it appears that the aliens feel obliged to preserve the specimen for their own purposes. As one abductee said, 'It's equipment maintenance.'"[3]

In his book, *Walking Among Us*, Jacobs writes that "...there are rare cases of young children being cured of serious illnesses and adults being cured of colds."

Despite this admission, he writes, "The aliens are not 'healers.'" He goes further and claims that "Aliens have accounted for short human lifespans; they do not cure seriously ill humans. Miracle cures might draw unwanted attention to abductees."[4]

Another leading abduction researcher is the late John Mack MD, a Pulitzer Prize-winning author whose book, *Abduction*, helped bring the subject of UFO encounters into the mainstream. In comparison to Hopkins and Jacobs, Mack takes the most benevolent viewpoint toward UFO healings. In his book he writes, "Some encounters are more sinister, traumatizing and mysterious. Others seem to bear a healing and educational intent...many abductees have experienced or witnessed healing conditions ranging from minor wounds to pneumonia, childhood leukemia, and even one case reported to me firsthand, the overcoming of muscular atrophy in a leg related to poliomyelitis."[5]

Mack writes, "Sometimes the experiencers feel that their health is being followed, especially through ano-rectal and colonic examinations ('check-ups'), and they even report healings of a vast array of minor and sometimes major conditions."[6]

Many UFO researchers have UFO healing cases in their files. While Hopkins and Jacobs felt such cases were rare, abduction researcher, Edith Fiore, Ph.D. disagrees. Writes Fiore, "One of the most interesting findings that emerged from this work was the many healings and attempts to heal on the part of the visitors...In about one-half of the cases I've been involved there have been healings due to operations and/or treatments. Sometimes the cures are permanent. At other times, the conditions recur...If you have noticed a healing or inexplicable improvement... you may have had help from the visitors."[7]

Researcher, Ardy Sixkiller Clarke uncovered several cases of UFO healings during her research into UFO encounters of indigenous peoples. She writes, "It's unknown how many people experience UFO healings."[8]

How common are UFO healings? The research on this question reveals some surprising answers.

The rarity versus frequency of UFO healings was first measured in 1987 by pioneering researcher Thomas E. Bullard, who, with his massive volume, *UFO Abductions: The Measure of a Mystery,* made an invaluable contribution to ufology. It represents one of the first objective studies of the UFO abduction complex. Out of 270 cases, Bullard reports that thirteen (about five percent), involved healings. "The other and more cheerful side of permanent aftereffects are the thirteen instances where the witness left the abduction healed of some ailment," Bullard writes. "Many of the cures appear to result from deliberate intervention, whereas the harmful effects could be accidental."[9]

The next study came in 1994. Dan Wright, a MUFON field investigator and manager of the MUFON Abduction Transcription Project, was in a good position to draw solid conclusions about the UFO phenomenon and UFO healings. According to a preliminary analysis, eleven percent of physiological effects caused by UFOs are healings. Wright writes, "Almost one-third of the subjects reported some type of physical effect as a direct result of one abduction episode or another. Nose bleeds resulted in thirteen cases, scars in twelve, half of those on a leg or knee. Curiously, in four cases, the subject was either told by an entity or separately concluded that the beings' 'reconstructive surgery' had repaired some medical problem."[10]

The most recent study of the commonality of UFO healings came in 2017 from the FREE Foundation UFO Survey, co-founded by researcher, Reinerio Hernandez. The FREE survey's results matched that of Edith Fiore, with fifty percent of respondents reporting some sort of healing as a result of their UFO experiences. Writes Hernandez, "UFO healings...have been swept under the rug...It is time that we shine a bright light on this little-known aspect of ET contact."[11]

Rare or common, UFO researchers have long been aware of this phenomenon. Ralph and Judy Blum were pioneers of UFO research and among the first to accept the reality of UFO healings. In 1974, they wrote, "Perhaps because they are as difficult to accept as contactee reports, reports of UFO-related healings are still scarce in the literature. And yet to me the possible connections between UFO light beams and paranormal healing is one of the most fascinating aspects of the phenomenon."[12]

Another respected and pioneering researcher, Leonard Stringfield, has noted the importance of UFO healing cases. In 1977 he wrote, "Healing cases on record baffle ufologists. More than a few who are looking into new realms for clues of the UFO nature and source are now seriously studying cases once dismissed as nonsense."[13]

Jacques Vallee has written nearly a dozen books about UFOs. Regarding healing cases, he says, "We find the phenomena of precognition, telepathy, and even healing are not unusual among the reports, especially when they involve close-range observation of an object or direct exposure to its lights."[14]

Another longtime researcher, author of many UFO books and editor of *UFO Universe* (now defunct) is Timothy Green Beckley, who writes, "It is a documented well-established fact that UFOs have affected or been able to alter in some way the normal healing process...Many miraculous healings have been--and are now---being reported, and in each case UFO activity is common; in some episodes, contact is made. No doubt we are dealing with an alien intelligence whose scientific methodology delves much deeper than our present-day technology can come close to duplicating."[15]

As the cases mounted, more UFO researchers began to pay attention. Brad Steiger investigated UFOs for decades and wrote several books on the subject. Of UFO healing cases, he writes, "Many percipients have reported miraculous healings, cures, even regeneration of teeth, after being touched by manifestations of UFO energy...over the years, several witnesses of UFO activity have reported rapid healings of cuts and accelerated alleviation of certain illnesses after a close encounter with some aspect of the UFO experience. What is there about contact with the UFO that can heal? Is it some electromagnetic radiation which might emanate from the object?"[16]

International UFO researcher Antonio Huneeus speculates that some of the beneficial physiological effects from UFOs may be caused by a radiation similar to microwaves. He writes, "It could well be that this microwave-like energy emitted by UFOs can heal under some circumstances, depending on such factors as intensity and proximity to the beam, and of course, intent on the part of the UFO occupants."[17]

Major George A. Filer has been in the UFO field for many decades. He served as the MUFON Eastern Regional Director, and was a regular contributor to the *MUFON UFO Journal* and is the editor of *Filer's Files*. "If anyone takes the time to examine the evidence, a person must come to the conclusion that UFOs exist," he writes. "There are other aspects of UFOs such as the advanced healing techniques reported of the UFOnauts that should be researched...Alien technology and their abilities are ahead of us by thousands of years. They have the ability to time travel, go through walls and manipulate their appearance. They are able to cloak their craft, manipulate people's thoughts, and heal diseases...I have interviewed dozens of abductees who claim they were healed by aliens using blue or green lights...My research indicates that UFOnauts use light to heal, rather than drugs...Billions are spent on drugs and virtually no research is being conducted in the medicine and treatments apparently used by the UFOnauts."

Why do the ETs heal some people and not others? Major Filer writes, "Several persons have told me of being healed during an abduction. I have a hunch that the aliens conduct their operations based on what is beneficial to them rather than for our benefit. If they have healed you, they may feel you are important to them."[18]

UFO researcher Richard L. Thompson is perhaps best-known for his massive volume, *Alien Identities,* which draws parallels between accounts in ancient India's Vedic culture and modern-day UFO accounts. His book tackles many of the paranormal aspects of ufology, including healings. "There are reports of remarkable healings connected with UFO encounters," writes Thompson. "Some of these appear to be of a mystical nature. Others are attributed to medical interventions that seem to make use of recognizable high technology...Of course, one can suggest that people imagine these ET cures because they need to explain natural cures occurring for unknown reasons. But Western Culture provides familiar mystical explanations of unusual cures (such as the grace of Jesus.) So why would someone try to explain mysterious cures by invoking even more mysterious ETs? The evidence that many UFO encounters tend to be accompanied by physical effects--injurious or beneficial--gives support to the hypothesis that these encounters are physically real. This is especially true in cases where the physical effect can be connected with the recollections of specific events occurring within a UFO."[19]

The late D. Scott Rogo was among the first UFO researchers unafraid to investigate the paranormal aspects of UFOs. Because of this, he is well aware of the healing power of UFOs. He says, "Writers and experts on healing--psychic, Christian Science and others--often overlook one fascinating area of inquiry: those cases on record where psychic healings have occurred during UFO encounters! There are many other cases on record which report that UFO percipients have found themselves healed of all sorts of complaints...In many cases, the healings seem to be linked to a mysterious light that was projected from the UFOs...There are definite parallels between these cases. The appearance of the projected light beam, the nocturnal nature of UFOs, and the unusually rapid healing all follow a consistent pattern."[20]

A strong proponent of UFO healings is Richard J. Boylan, Ph.D., author of *Close Extraterrestrial Encounters*, one of few books of its time to portray the contact experience in a positive light. During his own research, he has uncovered healing cases. "Healing procedures are sometimes performed aboard UFOs," he writes. "While the technology used is often so exotic that the human subject cannot tell what is being done or explain the equipment used, a number of humans have reported ET cures of conditions previously diagnosed by Earth doctors as needing attention. In other instances, the ETs diagnose and cure the condition during the on-board experience. Treatments and cures have been reported for conditions like ovarian cysts, coronary valve disorder, vaginal yeast infection and obstructed nasal passage."[21]

Boylan writes that healings are sometimes given during the physical exam often reported by abductees. "Sometimes the results learned from the exam are communicated to the human, particularly if some worrisome condition is identified or if the human asks why a certain procedure is necessary. The purpose of the exam appears to be for the ETs to determine the subject's physical and genetic levels and their overall health status. Occasionally an ET will communicate to the human that a medical condition needs some attention and will indicate that either the human should consult an Earth doctor about treating it or that it can and will be dealt with later. Sometimes, strong light, often colored, is shone down on the examinee for what may be phototherapy...On some visits, a medical scanning of a person is accomplished, apparently for diagnostic or follow-up purposes. Healing procedures have sometimes been conducted in bedrooms or other first-contact sites without removing the individual to a UFO."[22]

Barbara Lamb MS, MFT, CHt, has worked with more than 500 UFO experiencers and conducted more than 1,800 regressions. Not surprisingly, she has uncovered many healing cases. Writes Lamb, "...there are sometimes aliens who conduct complicated healing procedures on the abductee, such as healing cancer, blood disorders, autoimmune diseases or heart defects."[23]

Virginia Aronson, author of *Celestial Healings*, is one of very few researchers who has conducted an in-depth study of UFO healing cases. Following her own psychic healing at the hands of an experiencer, Aronson decided to look into the UFO healing phenomenon. "First, I very carefully researched the topic of medical healings associated with UFOs and/or contact with extraterrestrials or celestial beings," writes Aronson. "...[O]nce I began to read through the available scientific literature on UFO history and accounts of contact with extraterrestrials and celestial beings, I became convinced that something is going on. There are too many well-documented cases in which upstanding, intelligent, sane people have reported sighting a UFO and/or experiencing some sort of interaction with beings that are quite obviously from somewhere else, some other world. And a number of these people have reported healings, finding themselves cured of various medical conditions ranging from the most minor cuts and burns to fatal diseases such as cancer. I was intrigued and curious about these people who had experienced healing visits from other-worldly beings. Had all of these people cracked up, gone nuts, lost their minds too? I decided to find out."

Aronson, of course, came away fully convinced that people are being healed by ETs. "It was easier than I thought it would be to find such people," Aronson writes, "everyday people like ourselves, normal folk who have experienced some very abnormal things--and found themselves healed afterward...I was able to meet more than a dozen such people within a short period of time...The ET contact phenomenon is worldwide, and people all over the globe have reported experiencing ET-related healings...I see these brave, honest individuals as a representative sample of the many, many cases that have occurred throughout history, which includes a secret UFO history full of healing extraterrestrial encounters."

Aronson has speculated on the possibility that UFO healing cases might be an internally generated psychic projection and that people are being cured as a result of a psychosomatic mechanism

19

taking the guise of a UFO encounter. She also admits that it might be entirely and objectively real, and exactly what it appears to be. "If it is indeed literally true," she writes, "that is hundreds or even thousands of people have been healed of medical conditions by extraterrestrials or extradimensional forces, the discovery will be world-shattering in its effect on science and medicine."[24]

Researcher Mike Clelland, author of *The Messengers*, writes, "There are a surprising number of accounts where people tell of miraculous healings under the aegis of these alien beings. Some abductees have experienced the complete end of a serious illness directly after a UFO encounter."[25]

Australian Researcher Mary Rodwell (author of *New Human* and *Awakening*) writes, "[It's] so important for this information to be shared. I am meeting people all the time who have had such healings."[26]

Abduction researcher, Karin Hoppe Holloway, BA, CHt, writes that miraculous healings are among the "types of events to be noted" when investigating abduction cases. "Asthma, chronic viral infections, food allergies, hypoglycemia, diabetes and epilepsy have 'miraculously' been healed in some abductees."[27]

In his article, "UFOs: What We're Not Told," researcher Hugh F. Cochrane writes, "Most bizarre are the claims of miraculous physical healing and transformations experienced by those who have been targeted by beams of light from UFOs or had close encounters with these aerial objects...Those involved in these encounters often claim to have acquired heightened psychic abilities from the event and the claims of healing parallel the healing reported at religious shrines, and the remissions have been proven by physical tests and past hospital records."[28]

Chuck Weiss, an experiencer and author of the autobiographical book, *Abducted by Aliens,* has been healed by ETs on multiple occasions, and has more than a few words to say on this subject. "Spontaneous healings are a somewhat controversial subject in the UFO community," writes Weiss. "Not everyone gets them. Those who do don't like to talk about them very much, for fear of coming across as bragging. There are experiencers out there with serious medical problems that need attention who can't understand why, despite their willingness to cooperate with the ETs, they don't receive this kind of special attention."[29]

Researcher B.J. Booth points out that UFO encounters can be both negative and positive. In his article, "Do You Really Want ET to Call?" he writes, "Contact is normally in the form of an alien abduction, which is almost always a frightful, life-changing experience. We must remember, however, that there are those who claim benefit from these encounters, in the form of enlightenment, spiritual healing, and an ongoing connection with a more intelligent 'big brother.' People have claimed to have had diseases cured, emotional and mental problems alleviated, and their lives totally altered positively by these beings from beyond."[30]

Researcher Paula Johnson wrote one of the first full-length articles about UFO healings. "Documented cases are on record which show that UFO beings have the ability to cure our most deadly diseases and heal humans," she writes. "There is ample proof that the pilots of these sparkling celestial craft we call UFOs do have the ability--and have on numerous occasions--cured humans of serious ailments, including cancer...All this talk of aliens being able to cure cancer and other ailments isn't really that new. The files of various organizations are filled with similar accounts, adding weight to the notion that at least some ufonauts visit Earth on healing missions...How many UFOs are here on healing missions can't even be guessed at. It's possible that many who are being cured by aliens may not be aware of it. Others may be too timid to come forward and report their experiences."[31]

There are many other UFO researchers who are uncovering these types of cases. One investigator I contacted, who wishes to remain anonymous, had this to say about UFO healings: "I am a certified hypnotherapist and I work with abductees seven days a week. I have many cases in my files where healing has occurred but people are afraid to tell their doctors what happened to bring about the healing."

The anonymous researcher is skeptical that aliens perform the healings out of pure kindness, and says, "I have a hard time dealing with space brothers who are here to help us. These beings

21

have an agenda to follow and they are doing just that. They have not done one single healing out of the kindness of their hearts. It is for the end result they do the healings. They have put forth a lot of effort on our people, and they are not about to let us die before we have completed our mission for them. I have 160 cases that could tell you just the same thing I said, but none of these people will come forward."[32]

Leneesa, of the UFO Contact Center International (UFOCCI) has investigated UFO healing cases and has a more positive viewpoint of the alien agenda. She writes, "We have been inundated with information pertaining to the 'negative Greys.' It is my contention that this information has been purposefully slanted. There have been many instances of healings that have never been revealed to the public."[33]

Australian researcher, Bill Chalker is aware of healing cases and has remarked upon the use of light by the ETs. "I have been particularly interested in what are called 'solid light' cases, in which UFOs appear to use light in a coherent and controlled way," writes Chalker. "In some cases, the light beams from UFOs take on a seemingly solid appearance, turning corners, being used to lift things, or sometimes functioning as a transportation 'tunnel' from one place to another. I feel there very well may be scientific pay dirt in such cases. Many of these 'solid light' cases appear to have biological effects on the witnesses and abductees. Some are benign, some are not so pleasant, and others are remarkably beneficial, having what appears to be healing effects."[34]

Canadian UFO researcher Grant Cameron has authored several books about UFOs, and has written about UFO healing cases. "The concept of alien healings is rarely discussed, but it is not that uncommon," writes Cameron.

Regarding the instantaneous healing of flesh wounds, Cameron writes, "This very simple healing may point to the fact that aliens simply understand something about the operation of the body that we do not understand. The best understanding we have now of a cut healing itself is that the body knows how to do it. It appears the aliens just know how the body does it and have a way of speeding the process up. The process involves understanding and not magic."

There are many reasons that governments across the world are actively covering up UFO events, and Cameron points out that the ability of ETs and their technology to put people to sleep, to relieve pain, to cure almost any illness, condition or disease known to humanity--in a word, to heal us--could be one of the deciding factors. Healthcare is a very lucrative business and an important part of the economy, with billions of dollars spent in the U.S. alone. The pharmaceutical industry, points out Cameron, would have a very strong interest in keeping this type of technology and information secret, as would the health insurance industry. Writes Cameron, "...so don't count on the disclosure of alien healings any time soon."[35]

While the governments may not be talking, the people are. If the above UFO researchers are right, UFO healings may be rare or common, but they are not unique. They are a consistent feature of UFO encounters, one that can be ignored no longer. And although UFO investigators may disagree about the motive behind the healings, the accounts are finally being reported.

This book represents the largest collection of UFO healing accounts ever assembled. It includes accounts from all over the world, some which have never been published in book form before, and many others which are completely new and appear here for the first time. The cases reach back nearly a hundred years and are still occurring today.

As any scientists knows, no data can be ignored without sacrificing the truth. Too many people have fallen into the trap of forcing the evidence to fit their hypothesis. Objectivity has always been the foundation of good science. To complete the UFO puzzle, we will need all the pieces. Only then will have the whole picture.

With so many people from across the world being healed of such a wide variety of conditions, organizing this book has proved to be an awesome task. After much deliberation, I decided to present the cases both chronologically, from earliest to most recent, and topically, by the type of condition being healed. At the end of the book, I present a statistical and comparative analysis of

23

the accounts, providing some surprising answers about who is being healed by aliens, and why.

According to the *Center for Disease Control and Prevention,* and *Medical News Today,*[36] the top ten leading causes of death in the United States are:

1. Heart Disease
2. Cancer
3. Chronic Lower Respiratory Disease
4. Accidents
5. Stroke
6. Alzheimer's
7. Diabetes
8. Influenza and Pneumonia
9. Kidney Disease
10. Suicide

The *World Health Organization*[37], which measures deaths worldwide lists the top ten causes of death as:

1. Heart Disease
2. Stroke
3. Chronic Obstructive Pulmonary Disease
4. Lower Respiratory Infections
5. Alzheimer's
6. Cancer
7. Diabetes
8. Accidents
9. Diarrheal diseases
10. Tuberculosis

As we shall see in the pages that follow, ETs have cured people of all these conditions. And this is just the beginning. The actual list of injuries, illnesses and diseases cured is far longer.

Chapter One
Why Aliens Make Good Doctors

Since abductions became publicized in the 1960s and 1970s, they have become one of the primary focuses of UFO research. Most UFO researchers recognize UFO abductions as valid events. The nature of the event, however, remains debated. Today words such as "abductee" and "contactee" have been rejected by many researchers in favor of the less-charged word, "experiencer."

Whether against their will or not, people are being taken inside UFOs, subjected to various procedures, and then released. There are many thousands of recorded cases, but statistical studies such as the Roper Poll indicate that onboard UFO experiences likely number in the millions.

Researcher Thomas Bullard was among the first to outline the UFO contact experience and break it down into its common elements. In his study of 270 cases he found that the single most common onboard experience is a physical examination.[1]

The implication of this discovery is that the single greatest alien agenda is to learn about the human physical body. For whatever reason, ETs seem to be extremely interested in the human form.

Although there are many procedures performed upon humans aboard UFOs, the central and most consistent feature to all UFO abductions does appear to be the physical examination. In case after case, the details are the same: people report being paralyzed as they are undressed and placed on an examination table. Samples of skin, hair, nails, blood, and reproductive material are often taken. The examination may involve lights and/or various instruments that are placed on or near the body. In some cases, people report pain caused by needles or devices that are placed in virtually every orifice in the human body.

Other controversial reports are those of female abductees who experience what has come to be known as the "missing fetus syndrome," cases in which pregnant women have had their fetus taken during a gynecological procedure inside a UFO. With the aid of hypnosis, the witnesses often recall that their babies were removed from their uterus by the ETs. Males report having their sperm taken.

All of these cases have taught us many things. One fact, however, has become crystal clear. The aliens have a deep, almost obsessive, interest in the human body. Betraying this obsession is the fact that the vast majority of abductees can point to a scar or mark on their body given to them by the ETs. As one studies the accounts, a very strong medical theme becomes increasingly apparent.

But what does this mean? One conclusion is obvious. Since the aliens are so interested in the human body, since they have studied it extensively for many years, they must know a great deal about how the human body works. Given that their technology appears to be far in advance of our own, it's likely that they know more about the human body than we do! With their advanced technology and their extensive knowledge of human physiology, the conclusion is inescapable: aliens make good doctors.

But is this really true? Are their medical skills and knowledge superior to our own?

All we really know about aliens is what the people who have encountered them tell us. And in many cases, the abductee is impressed by how closely the room resembles a hospital room. In the exam room, everything is clean and spotless. The examinations are typically brief, lasting about fifteen minutes. Abductees report that the aliens do their jobs with efficiency and speed.

It's not difficult to find cases that illustrate the medical expertise of the ETs. Let us examine a few of them.

One early UFO abduction case to receive widespread publicity occurred in 1953 in Tujunga, California. The story was told in *The Tujunga Canyon Contacts*, (by Druffel and Rogo) and involves multiple abductions and, of course, the standard medical examination. During Sara Shaw's exam, one of the aliens became interested in the scars on her body. "They're looking at my lung surgery," Sara explains. "My scar from my lung surgery--that scar fascinates them--they came over to look at that scar too. They seem fascinated by that..."[2]

Sara actually used medical terms to describe the room: "They're taking me to an examining table. It's like an X-ray table."

Sara was told she was being examined. "They said--an electronic beam? Some kind of equipment to examine me. That I don't have to be afraid of it, and it isn't going to hurt me."[3]

Sammy Desmond, an abductee from Reseda, California describes the inside of the UFO into which he was taken. "It was a small room, all white, light colored and round," he says. "There was a table in the middle, and there were wall lights and things all over. The only thing I remember in the room besides the table was a huge, white, bright light in my face...it was a hospital-type skinny table."

Desmond describes his abductors' clothing using familiar medical terminology. "They had white jacket-sort of outfits, sort of like hospital uniforms."[4]

Examinations aboard UFOs are remarkably similar to exams in a doctor's office. Abductee Barbara X describes her exam: "They took a skin scraping...they looked at my bad leg...They said, 'You had an accident.' And I said, 'Yes.' They said, 'You had your female organs removed.' I said, 'Yes.'...they clipped my fingernails and a piece of my hair. They took a blood sample."[5]

The ETs are very thorough in their exams. Abductee Tom X says, "I'm inside some sort of room-like area, on a table, undressed, nude, and I don't like this at all...they touched me with instruments. And they were cold, hard, probably metallic. They were prodding and probing and poking. Something was inserted in my penis, and that was distinctly unpleasant, not painful."[6]

Well-known Massachusetts abductee, Betty Andreasson Luca has experienced many examinations at the hands of aliens. Needles have been inserted into her abdomen, her nose, her eyes and more. As she describes one incident, "They're holding some needles by my head, and I just feel some things moving in there...they're putting something sharp in my heel so it feels like they're shooting something inside me."[7]

Bob Luca (Betty's husband, also an abductee) describes the room he was taken to in familiar terms. "Looks like an operating table," he says. "Looks like a dentist's drill. It's folded up into the ceiling and there's a black thing on the end of it. I can't really draw it. But it looks like a dentist's drill. The arm comes out."[8]

The earliest publicized UFO abduction account in the United States--the case of Betty and Barney Hill of 1961--also displays a prominent medical theme. Barney Hill describes the room he was taken to aboard a UFO. "I saw a hospital room," he says. "It was pale blue, sky blue...it was spotless. I thought of everything being so clean."

Betty Hill's account is also filled with medical terms. "...the examiner opens my eyes, and looks at them with a light, and he opens my mouth, and he looks in my throat and my teeth, and he looks in my ears, and he turned my head, and he looked in this ear...they take a couple of strands of my hair...they look at my feet and they look at my hands, they look at my hands all over...and he cuts off a piece of my fingernail."

Betty's examination also involved an apparent pregnancy test using technology that was in advance of our own, but not for long. The ET examining Betty pierced her abdomen with a large needle. "I asked the leader, 'Why did they put that needle in my naval?' And he said it was a pregnancy test. I said, 'I don't know what they expected, but that was no pregnancy test here.'"

In 1961 there were no pregnancy tests performed in this manner. Today we have many medical procedures using laparoscopy, which is performed in a manner remarkably similar to what Betty reported.[9]

Budd Hopkins has done a great service to humanity by helping to bring the subject of UFO abductions under public scrutiny. One of the abductees featured in Hopkins' book, *Missing Time*, is Michael Bershad, whose account appears under the pseudonym Steven Kilburn. Bershad's examination involved the opening and probing of his back. "It's the one doctor's office I didn't have to wait to get into, I guess," Bershad joked.

Following his abduction, Bershad consulted with a professional neurosurgeon named Dr. Cooper, and explained how the aliens had stimulated certain nerves, causing certain reactions. Dr. Cooper was impressed. "He [Bershad] exactly described the motor reaction that happens when the femoral nerve is stimulated. And he has no particular knowledge of the nervous system...I'm really impressed with him. I told him that it seemed to me they just wanted to find out how he worked."[10]

Dr. David Jacobs Ph.D., has described the alien examination as being very similar to examinations done by humans. "Scabs, infections, or other body marks and changes attract their attention," he writes. "For instance, a woman who had given birth by cesarean section had new scars that drew the attention of the aliens who told her that this was not the way that *they* did it."[11]

Jacobs has investigated many cases involving highly technological medical equipment currently beyond our own capabilities. "The variety of machine examinations is great," he writes, "although the exact purpose of the machines is unknown. Most abductees think they are recording devices, much like X-ray equipment. Somehow people know that the machines are scanning them, 'taking pictures,' or making neurological measurements."[12]

Karen Morgan's case was investigated by Jacobs. She reports her unpleasant examination in her own words: "I hate this room. There's tables...this room seems more like an operating room than any of the others...I think they're going to do that physical examination again. Oh, they take off my clothes...they turn me around, and lay me down. They pull off my jeans, my underwear. They strap me onto a table."[13]

When Travis Walton (a woodcutter from Arizona) was abducted into a UFO in 1975, he looked around the room and instantly assumed he was inside a hospital. "They brought me into a hospital, I thought," says Walton. "I would let the doctors do all the worrying. I was safe for now...Maybe I was in an emergency room of some kind." Walton only realized that the hospital was actually the inside of a UFO when gray aliens entered the room.

Walton now speculates that the ETs may have been saving his life.[14]

Walton is not the only person to assume they were taken to a hospital. On June 2011, a nurse from Naples, Florida experienced a UFO abduction from her bedroom. She didn't want to talk about it because it scared her, and she insisted upon anonymity, but felt that it was important to report what happened. "I went to sleep around 10:00 p.m.," she says. "I regained consciousness in what seemed like a hospital room. The first thing I noticed was I was lying back down on what appeared to be a hospital bed. Immediately I assume I'm in a hospital. As I realized there was no way I could be in a hospital, I began to look around."

The witness soon realized she was aboard a UFO. She experienced a prolonged and complicated abduction and woke up in the morning with a scar on her foot. "I still have the physical marking left over from what they did, even to this day."[15]

The aliens' interest in medicine is once again illustrated by the following case. Noah (pseudonym) is a C6 quadriplegic, bound to his wheelchair in his Colorado Springs, Colorado home. On the evening of July 5, 2011, he woke to notice an odd "hieroglyphic-like" symbol on his right hip. Hot to the touch, it appeared almost branded into his skin. Over the next three weeks it scabbed over and began to heal.

It was a strange symbol, with one vertical line on the left side, three horizontal stacked lines in the center, three dots in a vertical line on the right, and stray markings below it. "At first my aide mentioned it," says Noah, "and I figured it was nothing until I saw it in a mirror. It was shockingly unnatural, and I felt a deep conviction it was made by intelligent design."

Noah wracked his brain. What could have caused this symbol on his hip to suddenly appear? There was nothing in his environment that could have done it. And yet there it was.

"All of a sudden in the shower it hit me," says Noah. "A 'dream' from the previous night. I remember being in a bright room or area, feeling very calm and not scared. This was induced and I was artificially numb to what I was encountering. An entity proceeded to ask me questions about my spinal cord injury...I was asked specifically about my hands, fingers and arms. Why were they as such? What was done to try and fix me? Why was one side stronger? I answered without hesitation."

What happened next Noah couldn't explain. "I was very psychologically level," says Noah. "Then I felt pain, looked at my right hand. All fingers were straight and spread. This isn't possible without lengthy splinting. Next my left hand and fingers did the same thing. This hurt, but it was good to see all the same. The entities seemed not to understand why I remained paralyzed, and I got the impression they were surprised/upset/confused as to what I can only guess they perceived to be primitive medical technology. This is all I remember from the dream...but had I not seen the mark on my skin I would never have recalled anything."[16]

Yet another case that indicates the ETs' interest in medicine was reported by UFO researcher Tina Choate of the International UFO Research Center in Scottsdale, Arizona. A woman and her husband were driving in the Gila Bend area (date not given) when they saw a large craft with a ring of blue lights around the circumference. Convinced they were seeing something unusual, they pulled off the road to observe. Their next memory was waking up to find themselves twenty miles farther along the road. Later, the woman, who was a nurse, decided to try regressive hypnosis to recover her memories of the missing time. Under hypnosis she recalled that both she and her husband were taken onboard the craft. The ETs (not described) told the nurse that they had abducted her because she had a basic understanding of the human body, and they wanted her to interface with them and learn about biochemistry and healing applications.[17]

In 1986, I investigated an abduction case in which the witness, Kelly Robinson of Reseda, California was taken involuntarily into a UFO, put on a table, examined--her arm was cut--and she was then told by the gray-type ETs that they were going to operate on her brain. "They tried to do something to my brain," she says, "and I was fighting them all the way. Subsequently, Kelly had three follow-up encounters in which she was given precognitive information about her personal life, her work and her church. "I think they're religious," she says. "They're not really out to hurt us. They're out to learn."

Kelly had a series of four or five encounters. After her final encounter, Kelly's mother, Diane had a "dream" during which she was taken into a weird round room. "The room was strange," says Diane. "It was like nothing I've ever seen before. It was not walls like we know. The walls were kind of rounded. It was different, not like a regular room. It was sort of blue, like a pastel."

In the center was a strange device, holding babies. Says Diane, "There was this round cylinder-type thing that turned around and around. There were all these babies in little compartments, like in enclosures. It was sort of like...a Christmas tree. It was narrow at the top and came down--and all these little compartments...and these babies--there was something wrong with every one of them."

Diane explained that while the babies seemed healthy, they were different. She saw one baby with a huge head and a small body. Another baby appeared to have two heads. She saw conjoined twins.

Standing next to the device was a red-haired, human-looking woman in a strange uniform. "She was in a white coat, like you would see a doctor," explains Diane. "She didn't look like a nurse because she had white tight pants on, and shoes. And she was really neat-looking. Everything was spotless--everything, like it was a germ-free environment. Everything was spotless."

The lady told Diane that "it wasn't planned this way," but that the babies "still need love." She encouraged Diane to hold the babies, which Diane refused to do.[18]

Many abductees are so conscious of the medical capabilities of the aliens that they actually call them doctors. Shane Kurz, an abductee from New York State describes what she saw inside a UFO: "There is a table. Everything is so white...those eyes, they are telling me, lie down. They are taking my arm and scratching it. It hurts. And he is putting it on wax paper or something. It is square-like and he gives it to the doctor. The doctor--I like him."[19]

Despite all the controversy surrounding UFOs, there is one thing that many UFO investigators agree upon: UFOs represent a superior technology. UFOs have demonstrated time and again that their machines are more powerful than our own. Their craft easily outdistance our fastest jets. They remove people from cars, dense suburbs, hotels and apartment buildings. They subject people to examinations and operations whose purposes we can only guess at. In addition, they often leave people with little or no conscious memory of what has happened to them.

The aliens have shown themselves to be outstanding pilots, superb hypnotists and excellent scientists. In the field of medicine, however, the extraterrestrials are unparalleled. Their medical technology and procedures are far in advance of our own. Their knowledge of the human body is also way beyond our own. This is evidenced not only by the reports from the thousands of people who have been examined aboard UFOs, but from the many accounts of healings.

Most people have little physical evidence of their encounter, except perhaps a scar. Some, however, are given more dramatic proof of alien intervention. Often the proof amazes even experienced UFO investigators.

Because of this, accounts of UFO healings have been largely hidden from public view. However, these cases clearly show that aliens have the capability to cure virtually every illness or disease known to humankind. Although the cases are not usually well-publicized, aliens have been actively curing people across the planet for at least a hundred years, perhaps longer. The evidence is in the pages that follow.

Chapter Two
Medical Evidence

When the modern age of UFOs began in the late 1940s, investigators had access to only a small amount of UFO evidence. At first, UFO investigators were largely limited to recording sightings and comparing them to other sightings. As time went on, more evidence accumulated in the form of radar returns, photographs and films, landing traces, reports of humanoids and the first abduction accounts. By the 1970s, UFO abductions were becoming more widely publicized, and since then, the focus has shifted toward studying the accounts involving close interactions with UFO occupants.

As the number of reported encounters increased, a new type of evidence began to exhibit itself. This evidence involved human physiological reactions to the close presence of a UFO. It became termed "medical evidence."

Medical evidence was quickly determined to be of profound importance, and it sometimes became the pivotal detail compelling investigators to accept the truth of a UFO witness's claims. Medical evidence, it turned out, could make or break a case.

The Mutual UFO Network (MUFON), the world's largest civilian UFO research organization today, has chapters in every state in the U.S. and several thousand members worldwide. MUFON field investigators are provided with an investigator's manual and reporting forms for UFO witnesses to complete.

One section of the manual focuses on medical effects. It lists the most common physiological effects as, "tingle or shock, dizziness, noticeable body temperature change, unexpected joint or muscle stiffness, motor skills affected (e.g. spasms or paralysis) levitation of the witness, eye irritation or impairment of sight, ear irritation or impairment of hearing, nose irritation or impairment of smell, a burning sensation or actual skin burn, skin rash, cut or gouge, headache, loss of appetite, nausea, extreme fatigue, sleep disorder, or other."

A few other effects worth mentioning that are not on the list include: menstrual disturbances, dehydration, bruises, scars, hair-loss, alien implants and possibly radiation sickness. The MUFON form also makes no mention of the few cases in which close encounters have resulted in the death of the witness, usually of symptoms that seem to parallel radiation sickness.

There is no mention whatsoever of UFO healings. In fact, field investigators are taught that the only available medical evidence is destructive. The heading under the chapter is titled, "Medical Injuries from UFO Close Encounters."

According to the manual, these injuries fall into three major categories. The first are those injuries of a temporary nature, the second are those of a chronic nature, and the third are psychological manifestations. The manual instructs investigators to obtain data on the witness's blood count, possible weight loss and urinary ketones, and advises X-rays as well as biopsies of any skin lesions.[1]

As can be seen, the medical evidence for UFOs takes many forms and at first glance, the list is scary, giving the impression that UFOs can be very dangerous.

The veracity of a UFO case depends on many forms of evidence. An investigator is generally happy to stumble upon a case with medical evidence because it can provide the smoking gun, proof that the experience actually took place.

There are now many hundreds of cases on record involving medical injuries. Let us examine some of the better-known instances to see more clearly the extent of the medical evidence for UFOs.

One well-known medical evidence case occurred in Texas in 1981. Three witnesses, Betty Cash, Vickie Landrum and Colby Landrum, all saw a UFO hovering in front of them on the road. The object emitted heatwaves and evidently other types of radiation. They also saw helicopters following or escorting the object.

Immediately afterward, all three began to suffer alarming symptoms.

Betty had a headache, neck pains, swollen and painful eyes, sunburn, nausea, vomiting, diarrhea, loss of appetite and severe hair loss. She was treated at Parkway General Hospital in Texas as a burn victim. Later she developed breast cancer. Vickie, who was slightly further way then Betty, suffered eye irritation and minor hair loss. Colby, who was the farthest away and hunkered down in the backseat, suffered only a minor first-degree burn on his face, and eye irritation.[2]

A particularly compelling example of medical injuries is the May 19, 1967 Falcon Lake, Canada case, in which prospector, Stephen Michalak, walked up to a landed UFO. The object took off unexpectedly, blasting him with heat, and setting his shirt on fire. Following the incident, Michalak experienced intense pain, a headache, and vomiting. He rushed to the hospital.

Soon after his arrival at the hospital, Michalak suffered a number of alarming symptoms including a headache, dizziness, weakness, numbness, nausea, vomiting, diarrhea, hives, swelling of the joints and hands, a burning sensation around his neck and chest, eye irritation, a peculiar body odor and fainting. He was unable to keep any food down and over the next few weeks, lost twenty-two pounds. His blood lymphocyte level decreased from a normal twenty-five to an alarming sixteen percent. Michalak was examined by more than twenty-seven doctors, and the only explanation that seemed to fit was exposure to radiation.[3]

Many similar incidents have occurred. On January 6, 1976, three friends, Louise Smith, Mona Stafford and Elaine Thomas were driving through Stanford, Kentucky when they saw a UFO and experienced a period of missing time. Immediately afterward, they suffered severe eye irritation, first-degree burns on their necks, fatigue, nausea, vomiting, diarrhea and weight loss. Under hypnosis, they recalled a frightening examination by humanoid ETs.

Louise Smith recalled being put on a table and examined. The ETs then made an exact mold of her body. She was told by the ETs that she was very important to them.

Thomas recalled being put on a table and subjected to various strange instruments, which made it difficult for her to speak or breathe.

However, it is Mona Stafford's recall that is particularly revealing. The ETs told her that they were very interested in her body and needed to do some tests. She was placed on a device which twisted her feet painfully. She was also put on a stool that seemed to undergo quick accelerations. Then they placed her on a table and proceeded to pull both her eyeballs out of their sockets. The eyeballs were placed on each cheek and remained connected to her head by various arteries and connective tissue. Stafford remained conscious during the entire episode. She was unable to observe how they performed the operation. As she says, "That power just drew them right out and laid them right there."

After a few moments, the ETs replaced Stafford's eyeballs and then returned the three women to their vehicle. The witnesses were left with only vague memories of what happened. Stafford, however, reported that her eyes were extremely painful. In the week following the encounters, she also became inexplicably paranoid about going blind. Finally, the burning sensation became so overwhelming that she sought the assistance of a physician who told her that her eyes had been exposed to "something," most likely an irritant. In fact, it was Stafford's insistence on seeking help that eventually led to their case being fully investigated.[4]

On October 16, 1957 the first reported abduction occurred to Brazilian farmer, Antonio Vilas-Boas. His abduction involved many of the standard elements and also a sexual encounter with an exotic-looking alien female. After his abduction, Boas suffered from insomnia, nausea, headaches, loss of appetite, burned and watery eyes, hives, bruises and scars. He was put under the treatment of a doctor who was unable to account for the symptoms.[5]

Cases of UFO injuries are not hard to find. On April 29, 1964, a very unusual encounter occurred in Albuquerque, New Mexico, to a young ten-year-old girl named Sharon Stull. As reported in the *Albuquerque Tribune*, Stull was at recess in the Lowell schoolyard when she and several other students noticed an egg-shaped "thing" floating high in the sky above the elementary school. While Stull says that nobody seemed to be paying much attention to the object, she kept her eye on the strange craft, which remained in place during the entire recess period. It appeared to be smaller than an airplane, and had no windows of any kind.

When recess was over, Stull returned to her class. About a half-hour later, her eyes suddenly became red, inflamed and irritated. She rinsed out her eyes, but when the symptoms worsened, Stull's teacher excused her and sent her to see the school doctor. The doctor immediately called Stull's mother, who came to the school and rushed Sharon to the nearby Batton Hospital.

Stull's injuries turned out to be severe. Her doctor diagnosed her with "membrane inflammation of both eyes and first-degree burns under the eyes and on the nose."

Doctors treated Stull, but were unable to explain the symptoms. Says Sharon's mother, Mrs. Max Stull, "They instructed me to keep her blinds drawn to protect her inflamed eyes and eyelids from light. Part of my daughter's face and nose appeared to be puffy and red. She continued to complain of burning pains."

Sharon's case became publicized and provoked an official response from Police Chief A. B. Martinez, who issued an unprecedented warning to Albuquerque residents warning them to stay away from any mysterious unidentified objects. Chief Martinez didn't reveal his own views on the subject, other than to say that UFOs "should be treated with respect and caution."

After being treated for her injuries, Sharon Stull was given dark glasses to wear while her eyes healed. For some time following the sighting, she could only read a few paragraphs before her eyes began to hurt. Eye irritation is one of the most common physiological effects resulting from a UFO encounter. However, what happened next was almost unheard of.

Four months later, the *Albuquerque Tribune* published a follow-up article on Stull's case. According to her mother, Sharon had grown five and a half inches and gained twenty-five pounds in the four weeks following the sighting. As Mrs. Stull told reporters, "A while ago she was just a child who liked to play with dolls and cut-outs. Now she is suddenly mature and grown-up, cooks meals by herself, cleans house and takes care of the younger children...Now Sharon is five feet two inches tall and weighs 110 pounds--and is still growing. My daughter has outgrown all her clothes and quickly outgrows new garments and shoes. I'm so confused I don't know what to believe...I know she definitely saw something in the sky that day, but I don't know what. It has been a nightmare for us ever since--I wish I had kept her inside that day."

According to Mrs. Stull, Sharon, herself, was unable to account for her sudden growth, saying only, "I just feel funny."[6]

Budd Hopkins has investigated several encounters involving medical injuries. One interesting case involves a man who was hospitalized because of a suspected kidney tumor. The doctors made this diagnosis due to "peculiar marks" found on his abdomen. The suspected tumor was never found. The patient neglected to tell the doctors that the marks appeared after an apparent UFO abduction.[7]

Hopkins' book, *Missing Time,* profiles the experiences of Virginia Horton. Immediately after one of her abductions, Horton was returned with a large cut. She still bears the scar. "I think my leg was cut with a scalpel," Horton said. "It was just really sharp and clean...as if somebody made a nice, clean, quick incision."[8]

On another occasion, Horton was filmed immediately after an abduction. The film clearly shows fresh blood on her blouse. The blood had come from a puncture wound caused by a nasal probe during her abduction. Incidentally, the ETs told Horton that they had abducted her because, as Horton explains, "They were celebrating and they said they wanted to share it with me because my research--or their research was--interesting."[9]

On January 3, 1979, Filiberto Cardenas of Hialeah, Florida and three friends were driving when their car mysteriously stalled. A UFO appeared overhead and Cardenas was lifted up into the UFO in full view of his friends. The UFO took off and Cardenas was deposited a few hours later several miles from where he was taken. Following the abduction, Cardenas suffered many symptoms, including insomnia, excessive thirst, excessive sexual appetite, changes in body temperature, peculiar body odor, skin abrasions and marks, headaches and eye irritation. Physicians at Jackson Memorial Hospital verified these symptoms.[10]

British researcher, Timothy Good, reports on another well-documented case involving medical injuries. In 1981, Denise Bishop observed a UFO hovering above her home in Plymouth, England. As she watched the object, a beam came out and struck her hand, with a paralyzing effect. "As soon as it hit my hand I couldn't move," Bishop said. "I was stopped dead in my tracks."

A few seconds later, the beam retracted and Bishop rushed back inside. Shortly later, she noticed that the beam had burned her hand. As she says, "On looking at it I noticed spots of blood and after watching it saw it was a burn."

A few days later, the burn had become worse, so Bishop saw a doctor, who told her that the burn was typical of injuries caused by lasers. Bishop still carries the scar where she was burned by the UFO.[11]

In 1964, eight-year-old Charles Keith Davis of New Mexico experienced extensive injures as the result of a UFO encounter. He was outside playing in his backyard when an object swooped down from the sky and covered him in a "blackish ball of fire." He was rushed to the hospital and treated for severe burns.[12]

Equally impressive is the case of James Flynn of Florida. While hiking out in the Everglades, Flynn encountered a UFO that flashed him with a beam of light. Flynn immediately lost consciousness. When he awoke, the UFO was gone, leaving him partially blind in his left eye and totally blind in his right eye. In addition, his forehead and face became red and swollen. Flynn eventually recovered, except for a partial cloudiness in his right eye.[13]

Abduction investigator John Carpenter has uncovered at least one healing case, and another involving what appears to be a bizarre medical experiment. At the *First Annual Gulf Breeze UFO Conference* in 1993, Carpenter revealed the details of an abduction case involving a young girl who was taken inside a UFO. While onboard, the lower half of her body was "cut away, taken out of the room, and a new lower half was brought in and attached to her!"

This strange procedure allegedly resulted in the teen-ager being "unusually proportioned."[14]

Roger Leir DPM is perhaps best known for his research into alien implants. However, during his research into a UFO crash in Brazil, known as the *Varginha Incident*, Leir uncovered one extremely bizarre close encounter case involving a poor Brazilian family who reside on the outskirts of the Amazon jungle.

Writes Leir, "A series of events occurred with this family that for many would seem similar to other typical alien visitation or abduction scenarios. In this case, however, the exception was that the abductors told their victim they were going to remove his eyes and this procedure would help them further the health of the world's population. The poor man totally accepted their explanation. He awoke the next morning blind. His eyes had been removed in total. He was not upset and it was only on the insistence of other family members that he consented to seek the opinion of an ophthalmologist. It will probably not come as a surprise that the doctor did not believe his story and told one of his relatives that whomever removed the eyes was a very skilled surgeon and did a magnificent job."[15]

One man was even able to receive worker's compensation after his injurious encounter with a UFO. Nightwatchman Harry Sturdevant of New Jersey was "buzzed" by a UFO. Shortly afterward, he experienced nausea and loss of his sense of smell and taste. He was unable to swallow and soon collapsed in pain, forcing him to seek medical attention. Six weeks later, a worker's compensation referee ruled in Sturdevant's favor, requiring that he be reimbursed for all medical expenses caused by his UFO encounter.[16]

Medical injury cases are occurring across the world. In South America, on the islands around Belem, there are dozens of cases involving people who have been struck by UFO beams that cause a number of alarming symptoms. Dr. Carvalho, the director of the community health center of Marajo, has verified all these symptoms, including weakness, dizziness, headaches, low blood pressure, anemia, burns, puncture wounds and hair loss. In several of these cases, the witnesses died shortly after being struck by the UFO beams.[17]

Death by UFO encounter is extremely rare, but it does happen. Probably the most well-known is that of Joao Prestes Filho of Brazil. Prestes was struck by a beam of light from a UFO, causing pain, swelling, headaches and burns. Shortly afterward, his flesh began to fall from his bones as if boiled. He was rushed to the hospital, but died before he arrived.[18]

Many other cases of UFO injuries could be listed. Richard Hall's outstanding reference book, *Uninvited Guests*, outlines more than thirty separate cases involving physiological effects of all kinds, including a few healing cases.[19]

John Schuessler's reference book, *UFO Related Human Physiological Effects* lists more than 400 cases of physiological effects. Not all of these are injuries. Writes Schuessler, "A listing of the more obvious effects of interest to UFO medical researchers includes: feelings of heat, field effects (hair stands on end,) disorientation, time loss, pain, headache, paralysis, marks on skin, burns, (first, second and third degree), lumps, bumps, growths, sores, loss of appetite, diarrhea, eye problems, hair loss/gain, tooth damage/decay, psychological problems, and paranormal effects...."

Many of the effects listed are temporary, such as paralysis. A smaller portion involve actual injuries, some serious, most minor. Of the 400 plus cases, only five involve healings. A few of the cases listed neglect to mention that a healing even took place.

Schuessler, who served as the president of MUFON, writes, "Don't expect government help. The UFO coverup has been going on so long that it is useless to believe that help is forthcoming, no matter how strong is the evidence of government involvement."[20]

In his book, *Deadly UFOs and the Disappeared*, Rob Shelsky explores cases involving UFO caused injuries and missing people, presenting a convincing argument that not all UFOs are friendly. Of healing cases, Shelsky writes, "Nor can we consider the rare abductee who say they were cured of cancer or any such thing, while being abducted, as positive evidence. First, we have absolutely no reliable data to support this claim. Secondly, the placebo effect is powerful indeed, and so if they are told they were cured they might well be cured...this does not mean the extraterrestrials necessarily accomplished such a cure."[21]

Despite the huge number of UFO encounters with medical effects, the vast majority involve no medical effects at all. Compared to the actual number of encounters, injuries are very rare.

The central issue, however, is that medical evidence of a UFO encounter can play a crucial role in determining the credibility of a case. Medical evidence is particularly important because it is often the only hard physical evidence available to the UFO researcher. Medical evidence represents a vital piece of the UFO puzzle.

Early accounts of UFO healings were slow to be recognized or researched. At first the accounts were not believed, and most received very little publicity or attention from investigators.

As time passed, however, more witnesses reported these cures. The number of cases continued to grow. Gradually UFO researchers recognized the importance of these cases and began to document them in more detail.

Today, the healing power of UFOs is a recognized feature of UFO encounters. New accounts continue to be reported each year.

The UFO healing phenomenon is incredibly complex. The cases that follow are numerous and varied. But each provides a small window into the heart of the UFO phenomenon, answering the many questions we have about ETs, who they are, where they come from, and why they are here.

What exactly is the ET agenda on our planet? As the following pages will prove, one of their agendas is to heal human beings.

Part One
Healings of Injuries

Injuries and wounds are a fact of life. Almost everyone who has lived on Earth has had the painful experience of burning themselves, sustaining a cut or bruise, straining a muscle, or worse, breaking a bone. Thankfully the body is strong enough to recover by itself from most minor injuries. Only in serious cases do we rush to the hospital for treatment.

Whatever the injury and its level of seriousness, Earth doctors are limited in their abilities to treat wounds. They can clean a wound and stitch it closed. They can apply salve to a burn, or set a broken bone. They can mitigate the pain caused by an injury. But they can't heal it. Our medical science has yet to advance to the level where a single laser-like instrument can make a cut disappear. The only known cure for a flesh wound is time. The human body repairs itself, but at a slow rate. Therefore, if we hurt ourselves, we often suffer for days, weeks or even months as the process of healing takes place.

Some people, however, have the incredible fortune of experiencing a UFO healing. Part one of this book documents seventy-six cases of injury healings, about twenty-five percent of the total number of cases.

As we shall see, the aliens are quite proficient in healing injuries of all kinds. It doesn't matter what type of wound it is, where it is on the body, whether it's minor or severe, the ETs have healed it. Cuts, wounds, bruises, burns, broken bones, head injuries--all have been healed. Injuries caused by falls, car accidents, animal attacks, assault and more are all represented.

Chapter Three
Hands and Arms

We begin our exploration into the healing power of UFOs with ten cases in which people have been healed of injuries sustained to their hands or arms. As with all the accounts in this book, the cases are presented in chronological order. We begin with the first UFO healing case on record.

CASE #001. BROKEN ARM.
In what might be the earliest UFO healing case on record, one afternoon in 1914, a young boy was riding his tricycle along a path near the town of Inveraray, Scotland, when he crashed and--he believes--broke his arm. He sat there crying for a few moments when a "little man" about two-and-a-half feet tall suddenly appeared, evidently to help him. The boy says that "somehow" the little man healed his injuries almost instantly.

Who are you? the boy asked.

The little man replied that he was a gnome. The boy said he looked more like a leprechaun, to which the man replied that no, he was a gnome.

The figure ran off when the boy's parents arrived, looking for their son. He told his parents what happened, but they didn't believe him. Years later, however, he stuck to his story, saying he broke his arm, and his injuries were healed by a "gnome."

The case was investigated by William Michael Mott, and reviewed by researchers, Albert Rosales and Patrick Gross.[1]

The above case is little-known and difficult to verify. This next one, however, remains a classic, undisputed case in mainstream ufology, and an excellent example of a UFO healing.

CASE #036. ALLIGATOR BITE.

On September 3, 1965, two police officers, Patrol Deputy Robert W. Goode and Chief Deputy Billy McCoy, were driving along Highway 36 South in Damon, Texas. The officers were returning from a high school football game. At the time, Deputy Goode was suffering from a painful although minor injury. He had been bitten hours earlier by his son's baby pet alligator and his finger was red and swollen.

Suddenly Chief Deputy McCoy saw strange lights rising from the right side of the road. McCoy pulled the patrol car off the road and pointed out the lights to Deputy Goode. When Goode looked, he also saw the lights.

At this point, the lights moved toward the police officers. They weren't able to see any detail until they were very close. Then they saw a solid mass 200 to 300 feet long, and fifty feet wide. There was a bright purple light on the left side and a blue light on the right. Goode estimated that the object was about the size of a football field as he could see the huge shadow it cast on the ground.

Suddenly the object moved over the patrol car and cast down a beam of light. "The inside of the car was lit up by the bright light," McCoy said.

When the beam struck, Goode's left arm with his injured finger was hanging outside the window. "I could feel the heat from the light," he said. "We got out of there."

The two terrified officers raced away at speeds approaching 100 miles per hour. They kept going until they were back in the city, where they pulled into a diner to discuss the incident.

It was then that Goode noticed his finger no longer throbbed with pain. "I suddenly realized it was not bothering me," he said, "and I pulled it out of the bandage. Hell, you couldn't tell I had ever been bit."

McCoy verified Goode's story. "The swelling had disappeared," McCoy said, "and the finger looked a lot better."

In a later interview McCoy elaborated: "I noticed Goode using his left hand. I said, 'Well, Bob, the only good thing about this is, it's made you forget about your finger.' He said. 'You know, it's not even sore!' So help me, he unwrapped those bandages and you could barely see those marks. There was no redness, the inflammation seemed to be gone. He threw the bandages away."

While at the diner, the two officers were accosted by two men posing as reporters from Pasadena. Before the officers could describe their sighting, the "reporters" described it in detail and told the men if they had stayed at the location, the object would have landed and they would have been invited onboard.

The two deputies decided to return to the location of the incident to see if the object was still there. To their surprise, it was. When the UFO started to move toward the police car, the officers sped away and refused to return.

They reported their sighting to the Air Force, and Major L.R. Leach of Ellington Air Force Base conducted an investigation. The results of the investigation were that the object remains unidentified. Major Leach wrote: "After talking with both officers involved in the sighting, there is no doubt in my mind that they definitely saw some unusual object or phenomenon." Officer McCoy, Leach pointed out, held a departmental position which required the supervision of more than forty-two personnel.

Following the incident, the officers received "considerable friendly ridicule" from their fellow officers. In addition, the officers were besieged by reporters and their story was told across the country. Today the account can be found in many UFO books.[2]

The healing of Deputy Goode's finger was one of the first UFO healings in the United States to receive any widespread publicity. Due to the credibility of the witnesses, the case was hard to explain away. The healing itself was evidently caused by the beam of light from the UFO. As we shall see, beams of light often play a starring role in reported cures of flesh wounds. Clearly these are not normal lights.

Some healings, however, are done without any instruments of any kind. Instead, the ETs use mind power, or hands-on healing methods, such as what happened to Richard Rylka.

CASE #049. CRUSHED FINGER.

Born in 1941 in New Jersey, contactee Richard Rylka may have received more UFO healings than any other single person on public record. Throughout his childhood, he had many UFO sightings. Sometime in the 1960s, while working for a medical firm, Rylka was instructed by his supervisor to transport a barrel of chemicals. To do this, Rylka had to operate a piece of heavy equipment called a *drum-lifter*. Heavy machinery is often dangerous, and somehow his index finger became caught in the machinery and crushed. Rylka's screams called the attention of co-workers who helped him to free his finger, which was "white and terribly distorted."

Rylka had no feeling in the finger and was unable to move it. He was rushed to the company's first aid room and the nurse told him to go to the hospital at once. He took a cab to Middlesex General Hospital in New Brunswick, New Jersey where doctors applied an ice-pack and prepared for X-rays. Rylka was alone in the emergency room when the ETs, (Koran and Nepos) appeared, and held their hands over his finger and cured him using body energies. Although the finger was numb for many months, the cure was effective enough to straighten the bone and close the broken skin. When the doctor returned, they found no signs of injury and sent him back to work.

Later, Rylka was contacted by the company nurse who had read his hospital file with disbelief. She told Rylka flat-out, "You were supposed to lose that finger." She demanded to know what happened, but Rylka remained silent about his alien friends.[3]

Another case involving the healing of a finger wound comes from UFO investigator Timothy Green Beckley. In this case, the witness was healed by mysterious methods during what appeared to be a simple sighting, but was clearly something more.

CASE #065. CUT FINGER.

At 10:15 p.m. on July 8, 1974, numerous witnesses observed a glowing object hovering over Prospect Park in Brooklyn, New York. One of the witnesses, Claudia Monteleone, the editor of a well-known financial magazine, looked up and saw a strange glow hover over an apartment building on Caton Avenue. Monteleone quickly got another witness. She pointed out the object to Brandon Blackman, who was himself a successful New York City syndicated columnist. Blackman watched as the object performed a "wobbling in a falling leaf motion," rising up and down repeatedly.

Suddenly the object zoomed closer, so that Blackman could clearly see an "illuminated compartment" beneath the craft. Eventually the craft left and he returned home. To his dismay, he couldn't find his keys and had to call the building superintendent to be admitted into his own apartment. Once inside, he came upon a bizarre mystery. Says Blackman, "I was dumbfounded to find the set of keys lying smack in the middle of the bed after entering the apartment."

There was no way the keys could have been there as he had locked the apartment when he left. Then came the final shocker. Earlier that day he had slashed his finger, which he quickly bandaged. That evening before going to bed, he removed the bandage to be confronted by another mystery. Says Blackman, "When I removed the wrapping, I discovered much to my amazement that the wound was completely healed, as though absolutely nothing at all had happened."[4]

An interesting aspect of Blackman's finger-healing is that it was done by unknown means. Blackman has no recall of being taken onboard a UFO. He didn't see any aliens. Nor was he struck by any beams of light. Instead, it appears that his healing was caused by exposure to UFO energies, or the mere presence of the UFO itself. The actual mechanism behind the healing remains a matter of speculation. Interestingly, however, this manner of healing is not unique. As we shall see, there are many other examples of healings due to the witness being in close proximity to a UFO.

Some people are healed by less mysterious means. In many cases, people are simply taken onboard a UFO and given an operation, such as the following.

CASE #080. ARM INJURY.

Sometime in the mid-1970s, contactee Anthony Champlain (pseudonym) of Florida was taken aboard a UFO and healed of an injury to his hand and arm, due to a fall. Anthony claims to be in contact with Pleiadeans. His memory of the healing event is sketchy. He recalls that both he and his friend were taken onboard a craft, examined and then he was healed. Like many people who have been healed, Anthony says a beam of light was responsible.

"It was a slow-moving beam of light," he said, describing his experience, "and it slowly hit you. And you sort of watched it. I thought, is it going to hurt?"

"No, it isn't going to hurt," a woman replied.

"What are you doing?" he asked.

"Is there some part of your body that is broken?" the woman asked.

"Yes," Anthony replied. "You're fixing it?"

"Yes," she said. "We're repairing it."

Anthony still doesn't remember exactly what happened. "To this day," he says, "I don't remember what it was they fixed. Because I kept trying to think, 'What was broken?' I can't remember what was broken. That was the funny thing about it. I remember some discussion that something was broken. And I remember that they were repairing it. But I don't remember what it was that was broken...what I do remember is that when I was lying down, I was no longer in clothes. I remember some aspects of it. She said, 'Are you ashamed?' I said, 'No,' something like that. I forget the actual details of it, but my other friend was there, and he was watching, and he was thinking, 'This guy's naked!' And she asked him, 'Are you ashamed?' And he said, 'Yes,' So I don't know. He went into another room."[5]

While many of the healing cases come from contactees and friendly human-looking ETs, the majority involve gray-type ETs and other kinds of aliens. The following case, investigated by Brad and Sherry Hansen Steiger, displays many of the typical elements of a UFO healing.

CASE #103. HAND CUT.
In 1983, a married couple who owned a farm in the midwestern United States were loading livestock in preparation for sale when the wife cut her hand. The wound became inflamed and infected, so the woman went to her doctor, who prescribed antibiotic medication. He told her that the wound would take several weeks to heal.

The next morning, she was walking outside and saw a glowing, egg-shaped craft descend from the sky toward her. Suddenly she found herself inside a brightly lit room filled with strange high-tech equipment. Three short beings wearing surgical masks surrounded her. The witness passed out. Writes Steiger, "When she awakened back in the field, she discovered that her hand was completely healed."[6]

In the above case, the witness doesn't actually remember being healed, though due to the nature of her experience, it can be reasonably assumed that the healing was done inside the UFO. Some cases, such as this next one, are equally mystifying.

CASE #162. FINGER INJURY, DENTAL HEALING.
Late one summer evening in 1990, Vasily A. of Kolva Base, Verk, in Komi, Russia was lying in bed reading while his wife slept next to him. He heard a strange popping sound and the window flew open. As he got up, he heard a humming noise. After smoking a cigarette, he closed the window and was about to go to bed when he heard a voice telling him to pick up the book and he would be able to read it "faster than before." Vasily picked up the book and found himself speed-reading it at an impossible speed. He then heard a voice which said, "We are going to examine you."

A strange whirling energy swept from his head downward. He heard voices and felt his entire body being scanned, including his organs. He felt his teeth and jaw being fixed. His little finger, which had been injured earlier, was also healed.

Vasily next found himself sitting in a chair in a very large gray room with no corners. Another woman sat next to him. She was more than six feet tall, with black eyes and a tiny nose. He saw another taller more muscular figure. One of the beings approached him and said that Vasily would be going with them. Vasily became fearful and refused.

Suddenly he found himself waking up in bed breaking free of a temporary paralysis. He looked in the mirror and saw another image of a skinny, gray being. The humming sound was still present when Vasily heard the beings speak to him telepathically. They asked him why he didn't want to go with them. Vasily found himself transported back to them where they showed him a strange engine and asked him more questions. The aliens then said they were leaving. Vasily felt a sharp pain in his solar plexus and woke up in bed. The humming sound, which had been present throughout the encounter, now faded away and Vasily went back to sleep.[7]

For some people, it is the presence of a miraculous healing that provides the evidence that they are in contact with aliens, such as in the following case.

CASE #193. PULLED ARM MUSCLE.

Beginning in January 1994, Chuck Weiss (a driver from San Francisco, California) began waking up to notice strange marks on his body. Also, he began to experience bizarre phone problems and strange ringing noises in his head. But it was what happened on the evening of February 21, 1994 that really woke Weiss up to the possibility that he was being contacted by aliens.

Weiss was working out on his exercise machine when he strained his left arm. The pain was so bad that it forced him to hold his arm tightly against his body. He sat down on the couch and was trying to decide what to do when something strange happened.

"I felt something press several times against my lower back at the base of my spine," writes Weiss. "The sensation lasted a good two or three seconds. I looked behind me. There was nothing on the couch, but then I noticed that my arm and chest no longer hurt."

Weiss was stunned. In the space of a minute, the pain disappeared completely. By this time, he was keeping a diary to catalogue the strange events. He wrote: "One minute severe pain, the next nothing! This is not natural. What's happening to me?"

Weiss's strange experiences continued, including more instances of healings.[8]

Weiss did not see any beings during his healing event. But as investigators know, UFO entities sometimes exhibit the ability to turn invisible. Cases like Weiss's are unusual. Most healing cases involve the presence of a UFO or an entity or both. The following case is typical in many ways, presenting many of the procedures often reported by abductees. What makes this case particularly unusual is that the witness was fully conscious throughout the entire experience and was able to converse extensively with the ETs. Also unusual, the witness was healed of an injury that occurred *during* his encounter.

CASE #223. HAND CUT, SHOULDER INJURY.

On September 20, 1999, a computer-specialist was working in Momoishi, Japan. It was around 2:00 a.m. and Tim (pseudonym) was taking a relaxing walk on the beach after a long twelve-hour work day. Suddenly a bright light shone down from the land alongside the beach, followed by a loud boom. The light was now rising and changing colors. Thinking there was an accident, Tim approached the light. He tried to call the police on his cellphone, but it was strangely malfunctioning. He suddenly felt a sense of danger. Filled with fear, he ran. He fell off the path and gashed his hand open.

Injured and scared, Tim decided to head back to his car. "I stood back up on my feet," he says, "but when I looked forward, no more than ten meters away, that small guy with his huge head was staring at me. My legs gave up on me at the very same moment. I was shaking so much that I couldn't even scream for help. Thinking about it now, I am not half the man I thought I was."

Tim noticed a second figure about seventy-five feet away. He was so shocked, he couldn't even think. "The worse part for me," he says, "was the staring. Those big, black, shiny eyes were so indifferent, so cold...Those eyes saw right through me."

Tim heard a voice in his head. "Come down, now," it said. "No harm will come to you. Come down, now."

Tim became scared. He held his injured hand and took a defensive position.

"No harm will come to you," the voice repeated.

"What do you want from me?" Tim asked.

"To teach," the voice replied.

"I don't understand...what do you want to teach me?"

"No harm will come to you. I am here to answer your questions. I am here to show you our ways."

"If you mean me no harm," Tim replied, "can I go home now?"

"I am no more alien to you than you are to me," the figure said. "I am here to help you, to guide you. I cannot force you to see what I want to show you."

"What will happen to me if I choose to see what you want to show me?"

"No harm will come to you. I will show you our way. I will guide you."

"Will I be allowed to go home after that?"

"Yes," the alien replied.

Tim found himself following the two figures to a small platform-like device. They were whisked upward about 100 feet into a large triangular-shaped craft.

Now inside a dark rounded room, the figures led Tim out of the room into another room with an exam table in the center. He was instructed to sit on the table. "One of them took my hand and pointed a pen-like instrument toward my wound. I felt like getting an electrical shock, so I pulled my hand away. As I looked at my wound, cleaning the blood using my shirt, it was fully closed and a small scar replaced the wound. I was amazed. Once more, it pointed the instrument on my shoulder, and the pain was gone (after the shock, of course.)"

Tim was then led through the ship, shown the control room and other things. He watched as the craft he was in, was chased by military jets. The UFO evaded the jets by darting into deep space. The beings then told Tim that humanity was at the end of a life-cycle and that only those who are capable of organizing and learning will be allowed to go through the next cycle. They told him that humanity was not ready, and would be destroyed.

Tim protested and they gave him a long explanation about their mission to teach our species. They said, "No harm will come to those who are willing to understand and learn."

The ETs told him that they had made a pact with human leaders. They gave the Earth leaders their technology. In exchange, the ETs were allowed to contact people individually as long as they agreed not to impose their presence on humanity at large. "We will help those who can be saved," they said. "No harm will come to you."

Says Tim, "We walked back to the corridor, back to the rounded room where we arrived. I was dropped about thirty kilometers away from where my car was parked...I never spoke a word about what happened that night, and I never went back to that beach alone again, especially at nighttime. This is my story. Feel free to discard it, or publish it, but do not try to locate or contact me in any way. I will not discuss this in public."[9]

The following case, reported to MUFON is a typical example of a "bedroom visitation," with a UFO healing. Once again, we see lights being used to heal.

CASE #260. HAND INJURY.

Kathryn (pseudonym) of Fresno, California reports that she and her family have experienced a wide variety of inexplicable events. Kathryn had a visitation in which she saw a figure holding a light, and then vanished. Her mother saw a cigar-shaped UFO hover directly over their home. At the same time, Kathryn and her sister (who was working in Canada) both experienced strange poltergeist-like activity. In addition to this, Kathryn reports being followed in her car by apparent strangers. Also, she was having scary dreams of hiding in panic from UFOs.

In 2010, Kathryn injured her hand. One evening she woke up "to a feeling of two beams on my body, one on my hand, and the other somewhere near my stomach."

She fell back asleep. When Kathryn woke up, she realized her hand no longer hurt. She remembered the beam of light. She now feels that it "healed me because I was having pain in that hand, which I no longer have."

Kathryn reports other healing-like encounters. "I have also had a few experiences when I could actually feel a presence and a feeling of total peace and tranquility, like they were somehow doing something to me to make me feel a good feeling."

In addition to all this, Kathryn recalls a missing time episode from her childhood. She is now considering hypnotic regression and is hoping to meet other people who have undergone similar experiences.[10]

The above cases complete the catalogue of healings of the hands and arms. The accounts reach back more than a hundred years and come from across the United States and the world. While some of the cases are better verified than others, the sheer number of them and their remarkable similarities lend credence to the reality of what is being described.

The motive behind the healings remains unclear. Some appear to be accidental, while others are clearly intentional. While a few of the above cases involve severe hand or arm injuries, most are minor, and yet the ETs still healed them. Why would ETs heal someone of a minor injury that is not likely to cause them significant discomfort or disability? Are they just being nice? Are they displaying their ability and leaving proof of contact? Are they experimenting?

These kinds of questions are difficult to answer, especially with only a small sampling of cases. But as we shall see in the following chapters, we now have a very large collection of cases.

And as we continue our exploration into the healing power of UFOs, answers to these questions and others begin to reveal themselves.

Chapter Four
Legs and Feet

One strong theme that immediately becomes apparent throughout this book is the strong similarity of the accounts. Despite separation by date and location, the healing cases corroborate each other with incredible detail. Therefore, despite the fantastical nature of the accounts, it becomes increasingly difficult to deny their veracity.

This chapter presents twenty-three cases involving people who have been healed by a UFO of injuries to their legs or feet. The first case here is also among the first ever to be publicly revealed.

CASE #010. BROKEN LEGS.

In 1952, pioneering UFO researcher Gordon Creighton interviewed Hans Klotzbach, a young German citizen. On May 25, 1948, Klotzbach stowed away on a coal train heading toward Luxembourg. Having no passport, Klotzbach hoped to enter the country illegally. His plan worked, and in the middle of the night as the train approached the frontier control station at the border, he leapt from the moving train. He landed badly and sustained "terrible injuries" to his legs. Bleeding badly and unable to walk, Klotzbach fainted.

When he awoke, he found himself in an unexpected place: the interior of a UFO. The cabin was lit up with a bright opal-blue light. He heard a voice address him in German, and give him information about upcoming cataclysmic events on Earth. The voice said that they had come upon his body as he lay dying beside the railway line, and feeling compassion for him, took him aboard and healed him. The voice continued to speak, and at some point, Klotzbach again lost consciousness.

According to Creighton, "Four days later, Hans Klotzbach came to and found himself lying on a mossy bank in a small wood just six kilometers inside Luxembourg and about ten kilometers from where he had made his jump. His trousers were thickly encrusted with dried blood and his shoes were full of dried blood. But his injured legs had been totally healed."

The case first appeared in Gordon Creighton's article, "Healing from UFOs," (in the *Flying Saucer Review*) which was the first article to address the subject of UFO healings.[1]

In the previous chapter we examined the case of "Tim" who was healed of an arm injury sustained during a UFO encounter. The vast majority of cases involve healings of injuries that had occurred prior to the encounter. However, a small number of cases involve people who were injured during their encounter, such as the following.

CASE #027. LEG INCISION.

Sometime in the late 1950s, contactee Ann Grevler of the Eastern Transvaal in South Africa encountered a landed UFO. She was subsequently invited aboard the ship and was given a tour through space.

However, prior to her invitation, the alien showed her just how advanced they were. Before her eyes, the alien made Grevler's car invisible using a "rod-like device." Believing that her car was gone and not just invisible, Grevler walked over to where her car should have been. As she did, she "gashed her leg on the invisible license plate."

The alien told her that although they could turn objects invisible using mind power, it was much easier with gadgets. The undescribed spaceman then cured Grevler using mind power alone. As the report on the case says, "...the spaceman was able to administer first aid accomplished by directing his gaze to the wound, which promptly healed."[2]

Obviously some UFO healing cases are better verified than others. Some rely solely on the testimony of one witness. Others

59

have multiple witnesses. Some involve undiagnosed conditions. Others involve conditions that have been fully documented. A well-substantiated and widely-published case comes from pioneering investigator, Jacques Vallee, and involves a gentleman, a medical doctor, who was cured of two injuries.

CASE #044. AXE WOUND ON ANKLE, PARTIAL PARALYSIS.

On November 2, 1968, in the French Alps, "Doctor X," (a physician) was awakened just before 4:00 a.m. by the cries of his infant son. He found his son looking out the window, gesticulating toward something. Looking out through the shutter, the doctor saw strange flashes of light, which he first thought were lightning.

A few minutes later, he looked out an un-shuttered window and saw two luminous discs hovering outside his home. They were white on top, red underneath, and flared brightly at regular intervals. As he watched, the two discs moved to the left, and then converged together and became one. The single object then shone a beam of light down upon the ground. After a moment, the beam swept forward and struck the doctor on the front of his body. There was a loud *bang!* And the object disappeared.

At the time of the incident, Doctor X suffered from partial paralysis of his right arm and leg. The paralysis was a result of injuries received many years earlier during the Algerian War. Before the war, the doctor was able to play the piano quite well. After the war, the paralysis rendered him unable to play the piano at all, and he also walked with a limp.

Doctor X also suffered from a recent flesh wound on his ankle. He had been chopping wood three days earlier when the axe slipped and gouged deeply into his ankle, which was still swollen and painful.

After being struck by the beam of light, the doctor was dazed and shaken. He woke his wife and told her what happened. She instantly saw that his ankle wound had "completely disappeared." The next day, Doctor X realized that he no longer suffered from any type of paralysis. He no longer walks with a limp and has taken up piano playing again.[3]

There are a number of cases in which people are healed of injuries sustained in an auto accident. Interestingly, in some of these cases (such as the following) there are indications that the ETs are aware of the accident *before* it actually happens.

CASE #047. LEG INJURIES.

As investigated by French UFO researcher, Guy Tarade, on August 11, 1969, ambulance driver Jean Migueres was driving his ambulance near Rouen, France when he heard a telepathic voice say, "Do not be afraid, nothing bad will happen to you, you will feel nothing."

Twenty minutes later, he was still driving when he saw a sixty-foot-wide metallic object shrouded in mist moving toward him. The ambulance was moving at 100 mph. At this moment, his ambulance was struck by an oncoming vehicle. Migueres hadn't seen it coming. It was a head-on collision.

While Migueres was trapped in the wreckage of his vehicle, a being "materialized" next to him, assured him that he was injured, but alive, and that he would feel no pain. "I am going to regenerate you by a procedure that is not yet known on your planet," he told Migueres. The being removed a one-inch-wide glowing, white disc from a pouch on his belt and placed it against the nape of Migueres' neck. He felt a prickling sensation move down his spinal column. The being said, "This accident was necessary for you; we will come back to see you."

Migueres suffered broken bones and serious injuries from the accident. He was rushed to the hospital. He underwent multiple operations and was declared clinically dead twice. When his gallbladder burst, the beings telepathically told him to leave the hospital. Migueres left and was put in the Montepellier Hospital near his home.

There he underwent more operations and had another near-death experience. After three weeks in the hospital, he was sent home. The beings told him he had succeeded in his mission and that "we will continue to protect you."

Unfortunately, his injuries from the accident left him unhealed. Even three years later, he was still in pain and unable to walk. Then one day, he began healing "in record time" and found himself able to walk, even without a limp. He also discovered that he had "the gift of healing." He remains in telepathic contact with the ETs and has written a book about his experiences.[4]

As we have seen, a common pattern that runs throughout this book is that the UFO healing cases are universal, occurring across the entire planet. UFOs, it appears, display no prejudice in regards to race. Some countries have produced more reports than others, but it could be that this is due to cultural issues as opposed to the actual number of cases. For example, despite its large size and population, only one case comes from China.

CASE #117. LEG INCISION.
Around midnight on March 7, 1987, a family of three from Ping Wu, in the Szechwan Province of China was awakened by a loud humming noise. The mother, father and young child went outside and saw a huge, red-orange, hat-shaped UFO hovering overhead. Suddenly all three witnesses found themselves inside the object strapped to three steel tables, being examined by bluish aliens with three apparent eyes on their forehead. At one point during the examination, one of the ETs made an incision on the child's thigh, then quickly healed it by passing a pencil-like device over it.[5]

The following case has a number of unusual elements that make it stand out from other cases. The witness was injured under unusual circumstances. He was cured in full view of another person. Also, while most cases involve the use of lights or technology, in this case the witness was healed using mind power.

CASE #164. SWOLLEN LEG.
One evening in 1990, former military officer, Mr. Moskalenko of Moscow, Russia was walking with his friend, Major Oleg Belomestnov when Moskalenko was struck by an invisible force which knocked him down and flung him off the road. His leg was injured and he became mentally disoriented. Major

Belomestnov assisted Moskalenko and as they continued to walk home, a short, thin man in black clothing stopped them and, ignoring Major Belomestnov, turned to Moskalenko and telepathically warned him of another possible "energized strike" against him.

The strange man squatted down and touched Moskalenko's swollen leg with the palm of his hand. Moskalenko felt a flash of heat, at which point the pain in his leg disappeared and Moskalenko's mental confusion cleared up.

Then events became even more bizarre. Previously Moskalenko had experienced a UFO encounter, and the strange man now questioned him about the incident, and then moments later, disappeared. Researcher Albert Rosales, perhaps best known for his multi-series volumes chronicling humanoid sightings across the world, writes that this case is one of many reports "indicating curative powers on the part of aliens or humanoids."[6]

One of the rarest types of healing is of an injury caused by an animal attack. We have already examined the case of Deputy Robert Goode who was bitten by a baby alligator. The following case involves another type of animal attack.

CASE #173. SHARK BITE ON LEG.

In January 1991, store owner, Amador Piazza Velez saw a UFO hovering over a mountain in Las Cuchara in Ponce, Puerto Rico. Unknown to Velez, there was another witness. Jose Maria Fernandez Martinez (a fisherman and the father of seven children) also saw the UFO earlier the same week as Velez. When the object remained in place for more than ten minutes, Fernandez grabbed his camera and tried to record it. At that moment, his camera malfunctioned.

Following the incident, something very strange happened. Some days earlier Fernandez had been bitten by a shark. His family and those around him saw Fernandez's wound on his lower leg, which was severe enough that everyone knew it would take a long time to heal. The morning after trying to film the UFO, Fernandez woke up to find his leg and foot healed, showing only a scar on his heel. "I cannot tell that the beings who came in the ship cured me," says Fernandez, "but something strange happened to me because my wound closed since that night."

On the same evening, Fernandez's wife, Gloria Santiago saw strange lights coming of out of the water.[7]

Because UFO healings are often relegated to the fringe of UFO research, many potentially good cases receive only brief mention. The following case is a good example, and involves a cluster of cases with multiple witnesses and healings. Despite this, the only U.S. coverage was in a small press UFO magazine, *The Missing Link*, (now defunct.)

CASE #188. KNEE INJURY.

An undated case (circa 1993) comes from researcher Helga Morrow. A boy from Tbilisi, Georgia in Russia injured his knee. While still suffering from the injury, the boy received a visit from friendly extraterrestrials who "operated" on his knee, restoring it to normal. This case is only one of several coming from the Tbilisi region.[8]

While most cases of healing involve the use of technology, some involve the use of hands-on-healing, such as this next case, from researcher, Barbara Lamb.

CASE #202. KNEE INJURY.

Matthew (of California) has had multiple encounters with ETs. On August 17, 1995, he had an encounter during which three grays entered his home. Matthew described them as having four fingers (without fingernails) and beige or gray-green skin. He found himself unable to move and understandably frightened. One of the beings told him telepathically that they would not take long.

During the visitation, one of the beings (who Matthew sensed was female) performed an apparent healing procedure. "Matthew had been suffering with an ongoing problem with his knee that was quite painful, a fact that the being seemed to be aware of," writes Lamb. "Through touch, she somehow deliberately intensified the pain in his knee to the point that he was aware of tears streaming down his face. Matthew felt she was testing his endurance to pain, but she told him that the examination was intended to diagnose his physical condition and contribute to his healing."

Interestingly, during Matthew's encounter, one of the entities retrieved pain medication from the bathroom and telepathically queried him about its use.[9]

Most UFO healings occur inside UFOs. Some occur at the location of the injury, on the road while driving, or even inside people's bedrooms. As most UFO researchers soon learn, a UFO encounter can happen virtually anywhere, even in very crowded locations. In a small number of cases, UFO healings occur in a very unexpected, but logical location: hospitals, such as the following, which comes from researcher, Virginia Aronson.

CASE #204. BROKEN LEGS.
In November of 1995, Connie Isele (of Sacramento, CA) and her friend were in a tragic automobile accident which left Isele gravely injured. At the hospital, her doctors told her that her right leg would have to be amputated. Isele, however, believed that the ETs could heal her. She had already experienced healings from them before. While in the hospital, and in desperation, she prayed to the ETs for help. Isele is convinced that they responded.

Says Isele, "It was an extraordinary feeling to wake up, alive. Out of the corner of my eye, I saw an ET, a very tall being with whom I was familiar. When I turned to look at him directly, he was no longer there." To everyone's amazement, Isele recovered quickly and her leg was saved. The doctors were so stunned, they gave her the nick-name "miracle legs."[10]

As we have seen, some cases of healings involve injuries that occurred during the UFO encounter. Sometimes the injury is accidental, other times it is inflicted upon the abductee by the ETs, such as this next case, which involves both technology and mind power. It was first revealed at the famous 1994 UFO conference at M.I.T.

CASE #207. LEG INCISION.

Erica X. is a designer for a popular New York City clothing store. She has had UFO experiences her whole life. Although she lives in a large apartment building in Manhattan, her abduction experiences continue. One particularly dramatic incident occurred in 1995. She was taken from her apartment and into a UFO, where she was examined and operated upon. After cutting open her leg, one of the aliens placed his hand over her wound and healed up the cut. Says Erica, "I was looking at this as if in shock, and then the wound in my leg kind of sealed up."

The next morning, Erica checked her leg and found a faint hairline scar, already completely healed. Erica has a medical condition which normally causes very slow healing. She has to be very careful because cuts usually take weeks or months to heal and *always* leave noticeable rough scars. This scar, however, was not only healed, it was practically invisible. For Erica, this was proof that her encounters were real, and even her doctor, she says, was impressed by the scar.[11]

Many abductees struggle to deal with their experiences. It is not unusual for witnesses to deny their abduction memories and call them dreams. However, when a healing occurs, these kinds of denials can no longer be sustained. It's not unusual for a healing to occur, providing proof to the witness that something unusual is happening to them. In this next case, a young man learned the reality of his UFO experiences following an auto accident.

CASE #206. BROKEN LEG.

Dave, a successful businessman originally from Murphys, California was five years old when he had his first encounter. The year was 1981. He was looking for his friend and went to search the garage. To his surprise, instead of his friend, he saw what he now recognizes as a gray-type ET. "I remember seeing a large head poke out from behind a tall box," Dave writes. "Nothing happened, nor was I spoken to...I tried to run away."

As he tried to flee, he noticed a strange effect: "Running away was difficult--as if I was moving in slow motion, as if time slowed down." At this point, he doesn't remember anything else. But as the years passed, he never forgot the time he saw an alien hiding behind a stack of boxes in their attached garage.

Following this event, Dave experienced a continuing series of "very vivid dreams of aliens in the house."

Then late one evening in 1991, as a freshman in high school, Dave lay in bed with his eyes closed, when he heard a strange warbling tone echoing around him. His entire body was paralyzed. The room filled with blue light. He opened his eyes, but was facing the wall and couldn't see what was going on. Says Dave, "I heard a voice that said, 'Don't move.' The voice sounded synthesized and not like it came from a being spoken through vocal chords...it also had a sinister tone to it, in my opinion."

Dave lay there for an undetermined time in a panic until the paralysis broke. He ran into his dad's room and told him what happened. It was 4:45 a.m.

In the weeks that followed, the strange tone descended upon him several times. Dave learned how to fight it off most of the time. A few times, when he was awake and lying in bed, it would get him, and he'd find himself experiencing a vivid, lucid dream-like experience with gray-type ETs. In one scenario he saw himself as a five-year-old. In another, he encountered a gray-type ET in the bathroom.

Proof that Dave was having actual contact came in 1995, following a severe car accident with his friend. "I was in the back seat of his car without my seat belt when he ran his car off the road," Dave writes.

The boys were rushed by ambulance to Memorial Hospital. Dave felt certain that his leg was broken. Thankfully, their injuries weren't life threatening. Dave's shin had been badly bruised. Other than being temporarily unable to walk, he was fine. He was bandaged up and sent home to recuperate.

That evening, he heard the warbling tone and suddenly woke up inside the dream state to find himself kicking field goals on the school football field in the middle of the night. Dave wondered to himself, what am I doing out here?

"The moment I thought this," says Dave, "I opened my eyes and I was on a table, completely paralyzed...I was in a dark room with subtle light shining on me. There were beings to the left and right of me, but my eyes couldn't move enough to see. The room was octagonal...a very flat olive green, almost a grayish olive green. There was a frosted window on each of the three walls in front of me, with silhouettes of small figures behind them, one per window. The rooms behind the frosted windows were brightly lit.

"The moment I realized what was happening," Dave continues, "I began to severely panic. In the blink of an eye, I was back in bed again, instantly. My leg was completely healed as if nothing ever happened from the accident the night before."

Unable to explain what had happened to him, Dave kept his healing secret. He did notice one pattern. Once again, the experienced ended at precisely 4:45 a.m.

In 1995 and 1996, Dave had two more experiences that began with the tone, followed by a lucid dream that seemed to transform into an actual encounter with gray-type ETs. The experiences continued throughout his life. In 2008, he had a profound experience in which he met a group of ETs, one of whom gave him gave him a lesson about how to manifest and create through the power of consciousness.[12]

In some cases, people are healed of illnesses they didn't know they had. In this next case, a man asked to be cured of an injury, which the ETs agreed to do. They then healed him of an unknown condition.

CASE #216. KNEE INJURY, KIDNEY STONES.

In June 1997, two friends were out hiking and fishing in a rural area outside of Borovye, Chelyabinsk, Russia, when they saw an egg-shaped object landed in a field. One of the friends approached and suddenly found himself inside the object with tall humanoids. He held a long conversation with them. They told him that there is no disease on their planet, and they live an average of 500 years.

At one point the witness asked the ETs, "Can you heal my leg? I suffered a knee injury and it did not heal."

The being replied, "If you like, we will help you."

The being touched a device and three robotic-type beings entered the room carrying instruments. The witness's seat transformed into a table. He was undressed and one of the ETs poured a greenish foam on the injured knee. The foam hardened, forming a cast. The witness couldn't recall what happened next. When he regained awareness, he was fully dressed and back in the chair. He touched his leg and felt no pain. His knee was flexible. He was cured!

"We have corrected your leg," said the ET. "And purified you of kidney stones."

"I didn't have any kidney pain," the witness said.

"You would've gotten sick," they replied.

After what seemed like fifteen minutes, the witness exited the craft. His friend was frantic and said that he had been missing for much longer.

The witness remembered only approaching the craft. He didn't remember anything that happened onboard until one year later. He did notice immediately that his leg was healed, and saw a peculiar pink scar. He went to his doctor who confirmed that his knee was healed.[13]

Healing cases often involve the presence of entities of various appearances. Most common are grays, human-looking ETs and praying mantis. This next case involves a being that is extremely unusual.

CASE #225. BROKEN LEGS.

In 1999, a man hiking along a cliffside path in the wilderness in the Grand Tetons, in Wyoming slipped and fell. He broke his right leg above the ankle and his left leg had a compound fracture to the femur. He woke up around dusk to find himself lying in a bush, unable to move. He had a water bottle and three energy bars.

He survived the night, but in the morning, was in too much pain to move. His right thigh was now so swollen that he had to cut his pants open. Two days later, the hiker was still waiting for help. He had consumed all his food and water and was struggling to remain conscious.

Suddenly the hiker realized that somebody was picking him up and carrying him. It was a normal-looking man. When they reached the trail, the rescuer closed his eyes. Suddenly the hiker saw a strange red glow appear around them, and he wondered if he was hallucinating. About ten minutes later, another figure approached, covered from head to toe in light blue feathers, with no other clothes. The hiker wondered if he was hallucinating again, or if the figure was wearing a costume.

The feathered being began to examine the hiker's legs. The being put his hands on the hiker's chest and closed his eyes. Again, the hiker--who was still being held by his initial rescuer--saw a red glow engulf him.

Afterward, the man released the hiker and let him stand on his own. The hiker was amazed to find that both his legs were healed, as though they had never been injured. The beings said they were friendly and were there to protect him. The hiker learned that the feathered being was female.[14]

Well-documented UFO healing cases are difficult to find. However, with hundreds of cases now on record, some definitely rise above the rest. The following case is one that is particularly well-verified, with multiple eyewitnesses, physical proof and doctor's confirmation.

CASE #244. BROKEN KNEE.

Stan Romanek exploded onto the UFO scene when he presented a remarkable video segment showing an apparent gray ET peeking into his living room in April 2003. Before then, he and his family had already experienced a wide variety of bizarre events in their home outside Denver, Colorado. But the videotape was the straw which broke the camel's back. The Romaneks finally realized that they were dealing with ETs, and Stan seemed to be the target.

The months and years that followed brought more encounters, which escalated in number and intensity. Before long, Romanek found himself with an abnormally large amount of evidence. Realizing that his case was unusual in this regard, he went public and wrote a book about his encounters. This was soon followed by another book, and also a book by his wife, Lisa.

The evidence supporting the Romanek case includes multiple independent eyewitness testimonies, photographs, moving films, landing traces and much more, including one particularly dramatic and well-verified healing.

On May 4, 2006, Romanek was painting the outside of his house. He was on the top of the ladder when it began to wobble. He tried unsuccessfully to keep his balance and fell twelve feet to the ground. As he landed, he heard his knee pop and felt excruciating pain shoot up his leg and through his body. Romanek managed to hobble into the house and tell Lisa, who rushed him to the emergency room. The news was not good: he had torn his anterior cruciate ligament and his hamstring muscle. The doctors told him that he would need reparative surgery. Romanek agreed and surgery was scheduled for next week. Meanwhile, they gave him a knee brace and painkillers, and told him not to use his leg until after surgery.

Romanek returned home and did his best to recuperate. When a weekend fishing trip presented itself, he reasoned that the trip might prove relaxing and take his mind off his many worries, and he agreed to go. It turned out to be a huge mistake. The additional activity aggravated his knee, which swelled to three times its normal size. He returned home and--still wearing the knee brace--went to bed in miserable pain.

When Romanek awoke, he discovered that it was the middle of the night and he was standing in his underwear in his living room. Lisa walked in from the garage, and was surprised to see him there. She told him the power had gone out and she had to reset the circuit breakers. They were both "sluggish and dazed" and after cleaning up a mysterious blood stain on Romanek, they returned to bed. When they woke in the morning, they discovered an eight-foot circle of swirled and crushed grass outside their home.

They stared at it in surprise. It was then that Romanek and Lisa realized that he wasn't wearing his knee brace. "What happened next was even more of a shock," writes Romanek, "but this time in a good way. Lisa asked me how my leg was feeling. Curious that it didn't seem to be hurting, I gingerly put all my weight on the injured knee. Lifting my leg, I began bending it back and forth and noticed that there was no pain, and that the swelling was completely gone...Not only was the swelling absent, but there were now five perfectly spaced holes running vertically down the right side of the knee. They appeared to be tiny puncture wounds aligned in a perfect straight line...Was it possible that I had been abducted again but this time, instead of performing some bizarre medical procedure on me, they had instead performed a useful service by repairing my damaged knee?"

Romanek photographed his leg and the landing traces. He was excited by the possibility that "our alien friends might also be helpful instead of merely annoying," and they began to search for the knee brace. They looked in the house, but there was no sign of it. They found it later that night outside "melted and fused to some spare bricks lying on the ground next to the house." Later they found more pieces scattered in the field behind the house.

"Why they had incinerated my brace was puzzling," writes Romanek. "Were they trying to make a statement--get my attention and fairly shout that they had done me a favor just in case I missed the point--or was there some other even more obscure reason? In any case, I didn't care. They had repaired my knee--instantaneously as far as I could tell--and for the first time in years I was actually thankful I had been taken!"

Romanek called the doctor and cancelled his surgery. The doctor disagreed strongly. Romanek remained firm, so the doctor insisted that Romanek come in for an examination. The doctor examined his knee and the strange puncture wounds, but was unable to provide an explanation. He told Romanek that his knee was now healthy. Writes Romanek, "I doubt if there was a more bewildered doctor in the state of Colorado."

The entire event caused Romanek to re-evaluate his relationship with his abductors. "The ETs seemed capable of healing as well as harming--although how one defined 'harm' is difficult to say. Perhaps from their perspective they are trying to help the human race--perhaps even save it--so how could I maintain with any degree of certainty that they were harming me when they abducted me?...if an advanced alien species really wanted to do us harm, it's pretty obvious they could have done so by now. And if the ETs are evil, why did they fix my knee?...A philosopher I'm not, but I can tell you that I was very grateful that they not only fixed my knee, but forced me to do some careful soul searching."[15]

It is difficult to determine why some people are being healed and others aren't. One such clue, however, becomes immediately obvious. Those who experience a lifetime of contact are more likely to experience a healing than somebody who has no history of encounters. The following case involves a man who had an encounter as a teen-ager, and later experienced a dramatic encounter with his wife and multiple other witnesses.

CASE #258. KNEE PAIN, IMPROVED VISION.

When he was sixteen years old, "Cory" was on a boy scout camping trip (location unknown, somewhere in the USA) and experienced a UFO abduction during which he was examined by gray ETs. It was a positive experience, and Cory longed to stay with the ETs. They refused but told him that they would see him again. Years later, in September 2009, Cory woke up in the middle of the night to a strange back pain. He went to the mirror and found strange marks on his back that were sore and tender. As he examined himself, he spontaneously recalled that he had just been visited by ETs. He recalled that he and his wife were both taken to a strange building with windows all around the walls. Many other people were also in the room. Outside was an unfamiliar grassy area.

Everybody suddenly evacuated the room, at which point, several UFOs appeared, including one directly over the building. The UFO emitted a brilliant beam of light. "I walked into the light," said Cory, "and it felt good; it penetrated into me and felt like a healing light, but I did not stay long in the light because it was so powerful that I felt it could burn me."

The next thing Cory knew, he was talking to a gray that was somehow disguised as a human. It was asking him a series of confusing questions and Cory felt that it was trying to hypnotize him. In an effort to break the spell, he looked away. That's when he saw that each of the other people around him also had a gray alien standing next to them. He saw a gray removing one person's eye and then replacing it. Others appeared to be undergoing various operations, though everybody seemed to be in some sort of daze. There the dream ended.

A few days later, Cory began to notice several strange symptoms. Earlier he had major surgery on both shoulders to repair damage to his joints. The surgery was a success and he was close to enjoying full range of motion again. However, both his knees suffered from the same condition and were swollen and painful. Following the experience, however, his knee pain was unaccountably gone. The only explanation Cory can find is his strange alien experience. "I believe the aliens examined my shoulders," says Cory, "and saw the types of surgeries that were done on them and did something similar with my knees. I believe that other people that I was with had similar things done to them by the aliens...I also have noticed that my vision has become better and my sense of smell is better."

Why was he healed? Cory believes it might be because he has hybrid alien children. "I have wondered about hybrid alien children," he says, "and if they have the human desire to know who their parents are, and if they come back to see their human parents. Then they may help their parent out by healing them from an illness. This, I believe, is what has happened in my case."[16]

In some cases, a witness may experience missing time but have no idea what happened. The only evidence is the healing itself. The following case involved many clues that something strange had occurred. The witness not only received a healing, but an apparent boost to his intelligence.

CASE #265. BROKEN FOOT.

Late in the early morning hours of July 23, 2012, Michael Chambliss (pseudonym) was driving from work to his friend's house to celebrate his birthday (Chambliss was turning 31 years old) when he felt a strange "warmth" in his head, and heard a voice telling him to go to his parents' home in Lehighton, Pennsylvania. He obeyed the voice and arrived around 3:30 a.m. As he exited the car, he heard a sound like a rock hitting metal.

The dogs in the house began barking frantically. Looking at the house, he was shocked to see two large red orbs of light, each containing a strange gray-type ET figure about four feet tall. Large shadows moved back and forth near the grays, who were making odd bleeping noises as though speaking to each other. It looked to Chambliss like the strange figures were trying to get in the house through an open window.

Chambliss took immediate action. He dashed inside and grabbed a stoker rod from the fireplace to chase the figures away. He turned the corner of the house and without any warning, found himself waking up from an unconscious state. He was now lying on the ground outside the house. The fireplace stoker was right next to him. He felt weak, disoriented and groggy, as though he had just been anesthetized. His clothes, he realized, were not on him correctly.

Feeling too weak to make it the short distance to the house, he stumbled into his car, where he learned that he was missing about one or two hours of time. He remained there until morning.

Following the incident, Chambliss noticed another bizarre symptom. Writes the MUFON field investigator who researched the case, "His right foot which was broken some time before the incident was now healed..."

Strangely, now his left leg hurt, though it did not appear to be broken. Chambliss doesn't remember any encounters before this, but he admits that at age eighteen, he began to dream about strange subjects like quantum physics, Einstein's theories, three-dimensional space, the Unified Field Theory and more. He now wonders if he was "watched" by ETs while growing up in his parents' home, which was located on an isolated lot, hidden inside a grove of trees.[17]

While the presence of a UFO healing would seem to indicate a positive ET agenda, this is not necessarily true. For example, consider the following case involving two sisters, one who experienced a healing, and the other who was seriously injured.

CASE #272. KNEE INJURY.
As investigated by researchers Kathleen Marden and Denise Stoner, twin sisters from Massachusetts have experienced visitations by gray-type ETs since they were children and on through adulthood.

In 2013, one of the twins was in her bedroom when the room filled with bright light, something that usually happened at the onset of an abduction experience. She became temporarily paralyzed. The next thing she knew, some time had passed and she was dropped back onto her bed. She was bleeding and had to be rushed to the hospital and treated for severe loss of blood.

Following this incident, the same twin had a fully conscious encounter during which the ETs healed her of a prior knee injury. She also found unusual fluorescent marks on her body. Her case is ongoing.[18]

One of the leading factors pointing toward the veracity of UFO healings is the extraordinarily large number of cases. The fact that most major researchers have uncovered these types of cases is clearly not a coincidence. One early and pioneering researcher, Don Worley, contributes the following case, involving someone who injured herself aboard a UFO as a result of fighting against her abductors. Her experience reveals why some ETs (despite having the technology to heal people) choose *not* to heal them of certain conditions.

76

CASE #273. LEG INJURY.

U.S. Army veteran Ruth Simmons of Alaska experienced a remarkable UFO healing after being injured aboard a UFO during an abduction. She reports being taken many times. She thinks one of the reasons she was chosen by the ETs is because "I am very strong." Despite this, the encounters are frightening and she sometimes tries to resist them.

"I was on a table in an upright or standing position," Simmons says, describing the 2013 encounter [date approximate] in which she was healed, "and around me were four little beige aliens, two tall blonds, and a dark, curly-haired man...They had secured my upper body and were attempting to secure my legs. While they were doing this a robotic arm was moving into position over my lower abdomen. I kicked my left leg up and actually impaled myself on a sharp edge that was under the robotic arm...The little beige aliens became frantic, and I got the feeling that they were distressed, like, 'She hurt herself! She hurt herself!'"

What happened next can only be described as incredible. "One of the blond aliens came," said Simmons, "and put his hand over my injury, and wiped off my leg. And then I saw that my leg was healed. But there was a scar! That is when the dark-haired man *mind-talked* to me, and told me not to worry, the scar would eventually fade away and my leg would look as it always had."

Earlier, Simmons had given birth by C-section, and now had an unsightly scar and stretch marks. During her experience, she decided to make a request.

"I asked him to get rid of my C-section and my stretch marks."

The man smiled. "I can't do that," he said.

"Why not?" Simmons inquired.

"Because people will know we are here."

"Well, what if I tell people you are here?" Simmons asked.

"Well, no one will believe you."

"Yep," said Simmons. "You are right, no one will."[19]

The following case, published here for the first time, may provide a clue about who is being healed and why. Healings involve men and women of all ages. The cases come from all over the world. Race, religion and education do not seem to be determinative factors. We already know that a history of encounters increases your chances of having a UFO healing. As the cases add up, another pattern becomes increasingly apparent: many people who report healings have professions that are helpful toward humanity, or who have the potential to help enlighten and teach humanity in some way.

CASE #278. FOOT INJURY.

"John" (pseudonym) is a highly intelligent and deeply spiritual young man from Belgium. Ever since he was a child, he knew he was different from most people. "I remember choosing this life," he says, "clear as day. Always have, always had to hide it from people. But I always knew where we come from."

One evening John and his girlfriend were in his home in Overmere, watching a crime drama on television. The first commercial break occurred at 11:20 p.m. John felt the urge to pee and ventured into the backyard to look at the stars and quickly relieve his bladder.

"It was one of those cold clear nights," John said. "I could easily see many stars out, when suddenly I noticed a dark patch, as if one spot had no stars at all. I kept my eyes on it and saw a reddish-amber glow on the bottom, which allowed me to see the shape. It was huge and silent, pretty close too. I stood there a few minutes, jaw-dropped, and went back inside because I soon got chilly. Inside, the TV is on a different channel, I find my girlfriend, she's pacing around like mad. 'Where have you been? Did you go out for a drink without me? Were you at X's house?' And I don't know what's up, but I ask for the time. She tells me that it's 12:50 (a.m.) and wants to know where I've been. Apparently, I was missing an hour and a half of time. I tried to explain, but she thought I was lying...She was a non-believer."

This is not the only unusual event in John's life. Another incident occurred in 2014. At the time he had a service job which entailed long periods of standing. Normally this wasn't a problem.

John was very active and healthy. He loved sports and often played football, or went cycling or swimming.

"I had this job for years," John says. "One day I noticed my left foot was uncomfortable and I would always lean on my right. It got worse over a few weeks, to the point where walking became an issue. My foot was swollen and it felt like either something was broken inside or infected.

"Needless to say, I called a doctor, because, well, I couldn't walk normally. He found nothing and said that maybe a recent change of shoes had caused it. I saw another doctor who specialized in sports injuries. He also found nothing, but prescribed some painkillers anyway. Because I was missing a lot of work due to this injury, I was getting new slips to stay at home every week, because we always thought that it would pass quickly."

Unfortunately, John's problem didn't pass quickly. As his foot pain continued to worsen, he finally sought out a new treatment: laser-therapy. He went to his appointments twice a week, and the treatments were expensive. Furthermore, there was no guarantee that the treatments would work.

"In fact," says John, "it just got worse. It got so bad that I didn't fit in my shoe anymore and had to use crutches to walk...to not even be able to walk, as a healthy young man, the idea of never running again--it felt as if God was playing a cruel joke on me. The constant agony, it brought me to tears."

John was at the end of his rope. He had nowhere to turn. He went to the local park, near a pond with ducks and a big tree. He had always felt the presence of nature there and felt like it was his "church." There he broke down and prayed. "I cursed God and all that was holy for taking away my ability to run...I asked the heavens to be healed...I said that for the rest of my life I would spend at least an hour and a half per day working in the name of the energy I prayed to."

John's foot remained swollen and sore. His laser therapy failed to produce any results. But it wasn't long after he prayed for a healing that he had an incredible nighttime experience. As he was sleeping, he woke up and became conscious that there were three entities in his room. His eyes were closed and he couldn't physically see them, but he sensed that there was one "doctor" and two guards. "The other two," says John, "I think they were here just to protect the 'doctor,' it felt like, or subdue me."

The doctor began to manipulate David's left foot. "This presence," David explains, "is messing with my toes, yanking them and twisting...to the point that I thought he was gonna break my toes."

John struggled to break free and wake up. Suddenly, the next thing he knows, he's waking up and it's morning.

"Before I can even open my eyes, my body leaps forward, arms outstretched to grab whoever is in the house by the neck. I see that my room is empty. I was running down the stairs, trying to find who had been in my home, seeing if the doors would be unlocked...then I realized I was *running* down the stairs. I kinda stopped midway, looked down smiling, no swelling anymore, no pain, understanding perfectly what had happened. And then looking at the doors, I was way more relaxed as if I knew they weren't going to be open...I raced down the stairs anyway, to check the doors, still with the key in the lock--locked up safely. Hmm...I was helped."

John was delighted. He felt certain that he had just been healed by ETs and he couldn't wait to see his doctor. He went that day.

"I went to see the doctor again, with a big smile on my face, and said, 'I'll no longer need laser therapy. I'm healed! But doctor, I want to tell you what happened, this weird *dream* I had...' So I told him about it."

The doctor listened to John's story and said, "The power of the laser is truly remarkable."

"That's what he took away from it," says John. Following the incident, John tried to duplicate the way his toes had been forcibly flexed and twisted, but he was unable to do so.

While the doctor was skeptical and felt that the laser was responsible for John's spontaneous healing, John feels certain that he was healed by the ETs. "I've always had a sense of being protected or time slowing down a lot when in danger."

The experience ultimately proved to have a profound effect on his life. "It feels so humbling to think that another species would not only be able to understand our pain, but take time to actually help us as well."

John didn't take his healing for granted, and worked hard to pay it forward. "I put a lot of work into theoretical physics and how energy drives matter, almost like trying to prove the living soul in all things, plants, animals, humans...Also, I wrote an equation on the curvature of the Earth, which professors in mathematics could not find a flaw in...It feels like a calling, like I owe them this to earn that healing I received. Part of me thinks 'they' knew all along what I would be working on in life. I don't want fame or wealth--only to advocate the truth and improve how we think about life. And I feel very thankful on having a 'calling' that I can work on for the rest of my days, or as long as the complexity of it all allows for a sense of wonder...Sometimes I think that the reason I feel protected or 'watched over' is because I hopefully will contribute a lot to physics regarding the souls and conscious minds in all life."

John is eager to "earn" his healing. He adores animals and works hard to save the environment. He has become more open with his spirituality and shares his point of view with others. Initially hesitant to discuss his healing, he has recently spoken of it openly.

He says, "By all means, use my healing story. We are being bottlenecked or pre-programmed to have a fear of ETs, which may result in a negative reaction when contact happens. So anything to do away with this false image of them being 'evil creatures,'--I would love to be a small part of that, honored even...My foot is still fine, BTW, for which I am thankful."[20]

A healing case revealed by the FREE study, this next encounter first appeared in the book, *Beyond UFOs*.

CASE #276. CUT ON TOE.

Alina Del Castillo had her first encounter at age three, when she saw a short glowing humanoid sitting next to her crib in her home in the United States. As a teen-ager and adult, she became very interested in UFOs and the paranormal. In 2012, Del Castillo had a close-up sighting of a silvery flying disc only about 250 feet above her.

On the morning of July 13, 2014, Del Castillo was giving herself a pedicure when she accidently cut deeply into the skin of her third left toe. She began to bleed, so she quickly washed the wound and applied bandages. She spent an active day and returned home in the evening to find her toe throbbing with pain. Not too concerned, she went to bed. However, as the night progressed, she woke up in excruciating pain. Just to touch her left foot caused agonizing pain. She realized she might have to go immediately to the emergency room.

She quickly prayed for assistance. Almost immediately a large grapefruit-sized, violet, orb of light appeared and floated toward her and stopped right in front of her face. "I then felt and saw the orb enter my shoulder," says Del Castillo, "and I felt the sensation of warm energy trickle down my body and reach my toe. It was the most incredible feeling of instantaneous relief and comfort from this horrible pain, and just like that, it was gone. I never witnessed the orb leave, but I knew that it had healed me."

Del Castillo went back to bed, and in the morning, her wound was still present, but there was no redness, swelling or pain. She reports having had previous paranormal experiences, but this was her only healing.[21]

Earlier we examined the case of Dr. X, a medical doctor who was cured of an axe-wound on his foot. This next case, from researcher Ardy Sixkiller Clarke, also involves the healing of an axe-wound on the foot. The witness is also a "medicine woman," working for the health and wellness of her community. As we shall see, there are a number of cases involving doctors.

CASE #261. AXE WOUND TO FOOT.

"Some people call me a medicine woman," says Belle (a Native American from Alaska), "but I don't like the title, medicine woman. I'm just an old woman who knows about plants."

Belle lives in a remote Alaskan village with about forty houses. Not far from the village, says Belle, is a sacred field where the "Star People," come and visit with the local population, or collect the native healing plants. Says Belle, "They are our ancestors and they care about us, but some are also scientists. They measure the levels of pollution, they examine the Earth and the plants to determine if there are poisons that are changing them."

On one occasion (date not given, circa 2000s) Belle was healed by the ETs. "I was chopping wood one day," says Belle, "and I hit my foot with the axe. It went all the way through my shoe into my foot. By the time I freed myself from the axe, my shoe was filled with blood. All my kids were at school. I tied a dishrag around my foot and tried to stop the blood. Suddenly they [the Star People] appeared and they untied the dishcloth, and with their hands they took away the pain and the bleeding. After that, I walked normal and never had any problems. There is still a scar though...the Star People saved me."[22]

As UFO researchers know, encounters can happen almost anywhere, even in the most unlikely places. The following encounter took place during a UFO conference in Irvine, California, in the luxury Irvine Hotel. By coincidence, I was a speaker at this conference, and was staying in the hotel at the time the encounter occurred. Other sightings were also reported in the same area around the same time.

CASE #284. SEPARATED ACHILLES TENDON.

On the days of September 24-27, 2015, MUFON field investigator, Thomas Michael Knox (a former Air Force officer) attended the MUFON conference in Irvine, California. In the evening, he retired to his hotel room. At the time, he had recently torn his Achilles tendon in his left leg. Doctors told him it was completely separated and that he needed surgery.

The next morning, Knox woke up to find that his leg was no longer in pain. He was healed. However, there were strange marks on his leg.

Knox's roommate in the hotel room, Melissa (pseudonym) was amazed and proceeded to tell him an incredible story. She had come into the room around 11:00 p.m. Knox was already asleep in bed. "I fell asleep quickly," says Melissa. "Around approximately midnight I was woken up and felt like I was floating out of the hotel room. I remembered standing outside of the hotel room on the rooftop looking back into the window at my roommate laying in bed. Inside the room with him I could see three gray aliens standing by his bed, holding his leg and giving him some sort of injection. I was pounding on the window yelling for him to wake up."

Melissa told Knox that he fought them, kicking and yelling. She then explained that both of them were abducted, along with several other people she recognized from the MUFON conference, some of who were well-known. Melissa and Knox were drawn up inside a cigar-shaped craft. Says Melissa, "At least seven other people were also removed from the hotel and boarded into the cigar-shaped craft. Onboard, all of us were placed in chairs which resembled beauty-salon chairs with hair-dryers above them. We were all restrained in the chairs and the parts that looked like a hair-dryer was placed over each one of our heads, and it fit very snugly."

She had the impression that the ETs were allowing the people in the chairs to transfer mental information between each other. Melissa counted at least twenty grays onboard the craft. She says that after the information-transfer procedure, some of the people were then examined. Afterward, everyone was returned to their hotel room.

Later that morning, after having flashbacks, Melissa told Knox what happened. Knox remembered nothing other than sleeping "like the dead." Together they located a black light and saw weird phosphorescent particles on Knox's leg, on her pajamas, her bed, and at various spots throughout the entire room. There were also three strange fingerprints on Knox's leg and a round red mark the size of a quarter.

84

Both Melissa and Mike Knox were amazed. Knox spoke publicly about his encounter at a later conference. Melissa reported her encounter to NUFORC.[23]

We have now examined twenty-three cases involving healing of the legs and feet. The earliest case occurred in 1952, and the latest in 2014. Again, the cases occur all across the world to all kinds of people.

The majority of the cases involve healings that profoundly benefited the witness. Victims of falls, car accidents, flesh wounds and more are all being healed. In some cases, the injuries are minor. In most of the cases, the benefit to the witness is undeniable. The evidence that ETs do care about the welfare of human beings is difficult to deny. Does this mean they are our friends? As we have seen, some of the witnesses feel this way. Others, no.

Before we make any firm conclusions one way or another, there are still many cases to examine. So far we have only touched the surface of healings of injuries. There are many more to explore.

Chapter Five
Abdomen and Chest

This chapter focuses on injuries involving the abdomen and chest. There are only a half-dozen of these cases--not a lot--and those fall into two main categories: incisions and hernias. These cases, although not particularly numerous, exhibit the same patterns we've seen in other cases.

CASE #034. HERNIA.

In 1961, a woman was picnicking with relatives on a beach in Isla Verde, Puerto Rico. Without any warning, she found that she had been abducted into a UFO. The smaller craft entered a mother ship. Inside the mother ship, the witness was taken to a room where she was cured of a painful hernia.[1]

The difficulty with labeling experiencers as contactees or abductees is typified by the following case. Denise and Bert Twiggs experienced a UFO sighting with missing time. Under hypnosis a harrowing abduction scenario was revealed. However, as time went on, the Twiggs's attitude toward their experiences changed, as did the nature of their experiences. What started out as traumatic, had become positive and benevolent. The following healing is only one of many reported by the Twiggs family.

CASE #097. ABDOMINAL INCISION.

In November 1981, Denise Twiggs of Hubbard, Oregon gave birth to her son, Christopher by caesarean section. She had planned to deliver him naturally, but unforeseen complications demanded immediate surgery. The umbilical cord was wrapped around Christopher's neck. Luckily there were no other difficulties, and Christopher was born a healthy normal baby.

Denise was disappointed to have a C-section as the recovery process is longer than with natural birth. However, Denise had alien friends who actually visited the hospital room and sped up the healing process of her incision. "...the Androme doctors visited me, giving me a helping hand with my recovery. My human doctor was amazed at how quickly I was healing."

Denise didn't tell him about her ET encounters.[2]

We have already examined a few cases in which people have been vivisected aboard a UFO and then instantly healed. The following case is a typical example of this type of procedure. Although technically there is a healing, it wouldn't be necessary if the ETs hadn't caused the incision in the first place. Instead of providing evidence of ET benevolence, these rare cases seem to show that ETs are experimenting on humans with little regard to the emotional wellbeing of their patients. At the very least, their bedside manner could use some significant improvement. This next case of a UFO-caused injury and subsequent healing comes from researcher Karla Turner Ph.D.

CASE #129. ABDOMINAL INCISION.

In October of 1988, "Fred" of New York City was abducted from a friend's apartment. His conscious memory of the event was virtually non-existent. The only indications that something had happened were a time lapse in his memory and several scratches, marks and bruises on his body. Later, he began having some dream recall of the event, and eventually underwent hypnotic regression and recovered the event in its entirety.

He remembers being taken aboard a craft. He was given a standard medical examination, and sperm was removed. While in the medical room, he saw other operations occurring. He observed one animal injected with a needle which extracted fluid from its body.

Fred also saw a nude woman lying perfectly still on a table. To his horror, he saw that the woman had a large surgical incision down the center of her chest. "She has been opened up," Fred explained, "and has a vertical incision from the top of her chest down to the groin area."

Unable to move, Fred watched the gray aliens insert their hands inside the woman's chest cavity. Fred then noticed that the woman's legs were spread-eagled with clamps around her ankles, and a "long tube-like instrument" was inserted in her vagina.

Fred had the impression that the examination of the woman, himself and the animal were part of a related experiment involving reproduction. "This was strictly surgical," Fred says.

At one point, Fred saw another gray-type alien holding a small instrument with lights on it approach the woman. The alien pointed the laser-like beam of light at the incision and healed the cut. "What he is doing to the skin, as he pulls it together, it's just sealing it up as if there wasn't any cut," Fred explains. "He uses the light, pulls the skin together, and you can't tell she was ever cut."[3]

The following undated case (circa 1980s?) comes from Major George A. Filer. It is yet another case of an incision made and healed during an abduction event.

CASE #153. CHEST INCISION.

"I had two medical doctors examine the two-foot-long horizontal scar across the chest of an abductee," writes Major George A. Filer. "They could think of no medical reason for making such a long incision on the chest of this man. However, the scar proved the incision had occurred and healed in a matter of hours by a green light. The UFOnauts used a pencil-like flashlight to make the incision and close and quickly heal the wound."[4]

Hernias can occur when the abdominal wall becomes weakened and the intestines start to protrude. It's most common among the elderly but can occur at any age. It can usually be cured with simple surgery. In the following case, a woman diagnosed with a hernia reports that she was healed as a result of her UFO contacts.

CASE #192. HERNIA.

At 4:31 a.m., January 19, 1994, Northridge, California was struck by a 6.8 earthquake. However, the night before the earthquake, nearby Topanga Canyon resident, Michelline, (pseudonym) experienced a dramatic UFO sighting over her home. She and her boyfriend saw a large diamond-shaped craft towing a smaller craft using a beam of light as a tow-rope. The craft hovered over two nearby water towers before moving slowly away. More UFO activity followed. Michelline was so shaken by the sightings, that she slept in the living room. A few hours later, the earthquake struck, devastating her home. When she inspected her bedroom, she saw that a large buffalo head sculpture had fallen onto the bed, right where she would've been sleeping.

Two weeks later, Michelline had another visitation. However, on this occasion she saw a gray alien standing next to her in her bedroom. She tried to get up but found herself paralyzed. Oddly, she felt no fear. "It kind of looked like it was a cat-face without any hair, and a combination of a skeleton face," she said. "I tried getting up and my legs would not move. After a little while, I actually had an orgasm, just sitting on the couch. The weird part was, while I was sitting there looking at this thing, I was trying to write down the things it was telling me. It was telling me that they were trying to invent ways of intercourse. They needed babies. They were just telling me a bunch of things telepathically; there would be more earthquakes. And then you know, we had all those earthquakes all over the world.

"A few weeks later," Michelline continues, "I all of a sudden had this bulge in the left side of my stomach. I had gone to the doctor, and I went to the emergency room. They wanted to do surgery. They said, 'You know, maybe it could be a hernia,' or 'We're not really sure what it is.' I didn't want to have an operation. And I decided in my head, this is going to go away. And it went away three days later.

"Three days after that, I dropped a 75-pound slate of marble on my foot. It didn't cut my foot, but you could see where there was an indentation in my foot, probably being broken. Two days later, that went away. And then about four months later, I had a miscarriage and there was nothing in the sac."

Micheline credits her sudden healing abilities to the extraterrestrials. "When I saw them," she says, "the thing that I wrote down was that I would be able to heal myself. And I would be able to heal people. If they wanted me to heal them, I would be able to heal them."[5]

This next case is a wonderful example of why ETs are healing some people and not others. In this instance, it appears that the ETs were interested in the witness's genetic make-up. The case is also compelling because the witness allowed his own name to be used, his condition was diagnosed by doctors, and the cure was also medically verified.

CASE #231. HERNIA.

In November 2000, Jim Law of Gainesville, Florida was diagnosed with an inguinal hernia. He was scheduled to undergo surgery on February 23, 2001. About one week before surgery, he woke in the middle of the night sensing a presence in the room. In a state of semi-sleep, he saw that they were gray-type ETs. They came through the wall.

Law felt a rush of fear. But the grays had visited him before, and he quickly calmed himself. He then told them that if they wanted to visit him, they needed to help him or he would make them go away. One of the beings replied, "We know of the condition you have a concern about and we will help you."

One of the beings held a shiny instrument about one-foot-long next to his hernia. Law felt nothing, but the hernia was healed.

Law asked the beings why they kept visiting him. They replied, "We are interested in you because you have genetic potential to live a long time." Law's grandfather was 106 years old and still active. Law was in the process of writing a book about him.

Law says that the grays are trying to hybridize to live on Earth, that they destroyed their planet and are a dying race.

90

Following the experience, Law was examined by doctors who found no trace of his hernia, which never returned.[6]

So closes the accounts of abdominal and chest injury healings. Compared to the total number of healing cases, there are only a few. There are enough, however, to show that ETs do have the ability to cure people of hernias and incisions. Again, the question remains, why would they heal a minor condition when our own Earth methods are capable of handling it? With so many minor conditions being healed, it becomes clear that ETs must be closely monitoring their subjects.

The ease with which the ETs are able to open and close human bodies is both disturbing and intriguing. Yes, they heal people, but in some instances, they are also making surgical incisions.

Each healing case adds another piece of the puzzle and provides additional evidence that these types of cases are real. They also bring us one step closer to understanding the ET agenda on our planet.

Chapter Six
Neck and Back

Anyone who's suffered from neck and/or back pain knows how miserable and crippling it can be. It can have a variety of causes, but is often due to injuries resulting in tissue damage among the muscles, tendons and bones that comprise the spine and neck. While in most cases, injuries will completely heal, this is not always the case. Some people live with agonizing neck and back pain due to injuries that occurred years earlier. Sometimes the damage is chronic, and the patient has no choice but to learn to live with their condition.

This chapter presents fifteen cases of healings of injuries to the neck and back. Some recount healings of minor pain, while others recount healings of serious injuries.

CASE #032. BROKEN NECK.

Jeffrey (pseudonym) of Seattle, Washington was born in 1948. When he was twelve years old, one summer evening in 1960, he was dozing in a steel-framed hammock when an accident caused him to be thrown seven or eight feet into the air. "I descended upside down and landed directly on my head," Jeffrey said. "The last thing I remember was a loud snap, a cracking sound as my head snapped onto my shoulder. That, except for the incident that I will relate next, may have been the tragic end of the story."

Jeffrey continues: "The next thing I am aware of is that I am standing up holding onto the nearby handrail. I don't remember getting up; I'm just up. Then I hear a voice in my head say, 'Look up.' So I look up. There in the sky, directly overhead are three hovering discs."

The discs were mirror-like, reflecting the darkness on one side and the setting sun on the other. They hovered in a triangular formation. The middle disc was lowest, at an estimated 120 feet.

Says Jeffrey, "I yelled at my brother, who is already looking at them. 'Chuck, look!' He saw the whole thing. He says a beam of light came out of one of them and hit me. I cannot verify that, as I was out of commission at the time."

Suddenly the discs took off. "They immediately moved in perfect silent unison, due west to the horizon in about two seconds."

While the sighting lasted only two minutes, and Jeffrey has no memory of being struck by a beam of light, he believes his neck was healed by the ETs. Whatever happened, events weren't over yet. "Shortly after that," says Jeffrey, "I had a long series of really weird nighttime events. Something came into our room almost every night for a long time. When they came I would call to my older brother, but he wouldn't wake. Then his weird experience would happen."

Ultimately, the results of the encounter proved to be beneficial. "My school performance went from poor to exceptional," Jeffrey says. "Emotional problems that I had been experiencing seemed to reconcile. My neck has never caused me any pain to this day. My brother still comments on the events of this amazing moment in our lives."[1]

One of the strange aspects about UFO healing cases is *when* they occur. In some cases, people are injured and instantly healed. In others, such as the following, they can suffer from a condition for many years before finally receiving a healing at the hands of ETs.

CASE #060. CHRONIC BACK PAIN.

In March 1973, Olga Adler (of the United States) was lying in bed suffering from "chronic back pain, making any movement, especially bending, painful and difficult."

Her eyes were closed when the room suddenly became bright. Adler was just as suddenly paralyzed. She perceived a "figure in a long, light brown robe, resembling a monk's habit, with the hood pulled up and rendering the face in deep shadows."

The figure entered through a closed door and floated across the room. At this point, the entity used an instrument to cure Adler of her chronic back pain. "In his arms," Adler says, "he held what looked like a heavy metal cylinder behind my back as I lay there on my side, and pressed it down. I could feel the bed depress with the extra weight and could see the figure leaning on it directly behind me, the face always in deep shadow. With contact of the cylinder at my back, I could feel a comfortable warmth penetrating my body and felt surrounded by a tingling sensation as electricity. The figure bent over me and held the cylinder like that for at least five minutes as I relaxed in the comforting warmth."

At this point, the figure departed through the closed door and Adler fell asleep. Upon awakening, Adler was astounded to discover that her backache was healed. "It was completely gone, and I could bend and twist and move with absolutely no pain," she said. "I believe I had been healed by some kind of spirit guide or angel."

One year later, Adler had another encounter in which the figure entered her bedroom and spoke telepathically, "Come with me--it's time to go!" Adler has vague memories of being floated outside through a closed window. From that point, she has missing time.

Researcher Mark Chorvinsky, editor of *Strange Magazine*, wrote about the case and remarked on the many strange parallels to classical accounts of the Grim Reaper, during which witnesses see a "hooded, robed, faceless entity." However, as can be seen, the above account has many details in accord with UFO accounts.[2]

In many cases, UFO abductions are traumatic events. Witnesses report being taken against their will and kidnapped into a UFO. Regardless of motive, this type of behavior is considered a crime in virtually every culture on our planet. Not surprisingly, many abductees resist being taken. Sometimes this results in injury. The ETs then proceed to abduct the witness and heal them of the injury they sustained in their attempts to resist the kidnapping. The perfect example is what happened to Sergeant Charles Moody.

CASE #070. BACK INJURY.

On the evening of August 13, 1975, USAF flight mechanic Charles Moody (who worked at Holloman AFB in New Mexico), decided to watch the Perseid meteor showers, which were active that evening. He left his home in Alamogordo and drove outside of town to watch the stars. After seeing several shooting stars, he was shocked to see one of them drop out of the sky in front of him and stop.

In a later interview, Moody described what happened: "I observed a dull metallic object that seemed to just drop out of the sky and start to hover with a wobbling motion, approximately 100 feet in front of me."

As the object moved toward him, Moody tried to start his car, but the engine mysteriously died. The object approached closely and Moody heard a high-pitched whining sound coming from the craft. Looking up, he saw oddly-shaped windows, behind which were two or three human-looking forms. Says Moody, "At this time the high-pitched sound stopped, and a feeling of numbness came over my body. The fear that I had before left me, and I felt a very peaceful calmness. The object lifted very fast. It made no sound."

After the object had departed, Moody's car started easily. As he drove home, he looked at his watch and saw that it was 2:45 a.m., at least one hour and twenty-five minutes later than it should have been.

Afterward Moody suffered from lower back pain and a strange rash on his lower body. Concerned about the missing time and his symptoms, Moody discretely contacted APRO researchers, Jim Lorenzen and Wendelle Stevens. Moody was concerned that the Air Force would hear about the incident.

Apparently they did because a few weeks later, Moody was transferred overseas, something Lorenzen had predicted would happen. Before he left, however, Moody wrote a letter to Lorenzen, explaining that his memory of the incident had returned naturally over the past few weeks, and that he now consciously recalled almost everything that had occurred onboard the craft.

Moody says that after hovering in front of him, the craft landed on the road. Two men dressed in tight fitting suits approached his car. Moody attempted to shoot at them with his revolver but suddenly felt powerless as the two strange figures pulled him out of the car and dragged him into the craft.

"The beings were about five feet tall and very much like us," Moody said, "except their heads were larger and had no hair; ears very small, eyes a little larger than ours, nose small, and the mouth had very thin lips. I would say their weight was maybe between 110-130 pounds. There was speech but their lips did not move."

The beings were dressed in featureless black, skin-tight suits, except for one of the figures whose suit was silver-white. Moody was taken to a room where one of the figures (who Moody perceived to be the leader) placed a "rod-looking device" around his body. Says Moody, "He said there had been a scuffle when they first made contact with me, and he only wanted to correct any misplacement that might have happened."

Moody was impressed by the interior of the craft, which he described as having indirect lighting and being "as clean as an operating room."

The beings were telepathic and answered Moody's questions as he formulated them in his mind. Says Moody, "I was thinking to myself, 'If only I could see the drive unit of the craft, how wonderful that would be.' The elder or leader put his hand on my shoulder and said to follow him. We went to a small room that had no fixtures and was dimly lit...The floor seemed to give way like an elevator. I guess we went down about six feet and what I saw then was a room about twenty-five feet across, and in the center was what looked like a huge carbon rod going through the roof of the room; around the rod were three what looked like holes covered with glass. Inside the glass-covered holes or balls were what looked like large crystals with two rods, one on each side of the crystal. One rod came to a ball-like top, the other came to a 'T' type top. I was told this was their drive unit, and that I could understand it if I tried."

The beings told Moody that the craft was only a small observation craft, and that they had a much larger craft which was about 400 miles above the Earth. Moody asked if he could see the main craft and was told that time was too short. They said that limited contact with humans would be made in the future, but only over a gradual period of time. They said that they are concerned about the radiation tests being conducted. They told him that radar interferes with their ability to navigate, and also that there were currently several different alien races working together. The beings then told Moody that he would not remember what had happened this evening, but that his memory would return over a period of time. Finally they said they could find him whenever they wanted and that "they would see me again."

While Moody did receive a healing of a back injury, it was an injury he sustained while being abducted.[3]

In most cases of back and neck healings, the procedure is done quickly and easily with a single instrument. In other cases, a simple beam of light seems to suffice.

CASE #076. BACK INJURY.

In 1976, Vladimir S. was sent by his family to the Molebka area, Perm Region in Ural, Russia. Non-traditional healers were known to live in this area, and eighteen-year-old Vladimir was seeking a cure for back injuries sustained in a job-related accident. His back injuries were so severe, he had to walk with a cane.

While camping with other people along the river Chosovaya, Vladimir woke one evening to urinate and saw a large, luminous, egg-shaped object rise from the river and hover in front of him. It radiated a strong heat. Through a window, Vladimir saw a humanoid with long hair. Suddenly a green beam of light shot out from the top of the object and struck Vladimir on the face, temporarily blinding him. When he could see again, the object was off in the distance, moving away. Following this incident, the witness recovered from his injuries and threw away his cane.[4]

In several cases in this book, victims of injury and disease have prayed to God, angels and spirit guides for healing, and instead found themselves being healed by ETs, such as the following case, published here for the first time.

CASE #086. BACK PAIN.

One evening around 1978, Ana M. had an experience that would change her life. Her daughter, Maria, explains what happened: "At the time, she was a single mother with three kids, working as a secretary. One day she injured her back severely and doctors said back surgery was needed. That night my mom went to bed praying intensely to her angels, that she may receive their divine healing, as she needed to work and support three children.

"My sister and I were sleeping in another room. In the early a.m. hours our bedroom was flooded with brilliant orange light, coming from the outside of our home. I was terrified! I covered my head with the blanket and prayed '*Whatever happens, please don't take me.*'

"My sister and I felt the light was emanating from a UFO. It lasted about twenty minutes, or so it seemed to us. The next morning my mom was so happy. She shared her weird dream with us.

"One man, wearing a white-silver, all-body suit (including face covering), came into her room with some scientific instrumentation around his waist. She was told telepathically to 'not be afraid.' My mom felt that she had been waiting for him. She pleaded, 'Please don't let it be painful.' And he said to 'relax.' He pressed some buttons on his instrumentation. A laser-like light felt warm to her body. She fell asleep.

"The next day she woke up completely healed from her back issues. We were all so shocked as my sister and I had seen the strange glowing light of her interplanetary healers."

Needless to say, Ana did not undergo surgery, at least not by Earth doctors. Forty years later, Ana still has no back issues.[5]

Most reported healings can be directly correlated to a specific UFO event, such as being struck by a beam of light, or being taken inside a UFO and operated upon. Other healings are enacted by mysterious means unknown to the witness. In the following case, a man suffering from chronic back pain experienced a series of encounters, leading to an inexplicable healing.

CASE #105. BACK PAIN.

In the summer of 1984, a couple (Jose Maria Arranz and Maria Zarzugaza) from Bilbao, Spain were vacationing in Villalacre, Burgos. While on vacation, they experimented with a Ouija board and began communicating with a being named "M4" who claimed to be extraterrestrial in origin.

After several conversations, M4 said he would appear before the witnesses. On September 9, 1984, the couple saw a luminous glowing figure about seven feet tall, wearing a shiny diver's suit with a cap.

Over the next month, M4 appeared no less than ten times. During the last Ouija board session, M4 said he would not appear again. Following this, Jose Maria Arranz found himself mysteriously cured of his back ailment. Later on, during their return home from vacation, the couple saw a UFO.[6]

A UFO abduction can happen anywhere. In this next case, a man was taken from a public train station.

CASE #112. BACK INJURY.

At 10:00 p.m., on May 15, 1986, Alexander Viktorovich was with two friends standing at a train station in Donetsk, Ukraine when he saw something moving next to him. He reached out and found that he had grabbed the arm of a very strange-looking man. The man was very tall, dressed in all black and had slit-like eyes. Despite this, Viktorovich felt no fear. The figure pulled him along until they were both in a foggy corridor. On the other side, Viktorovich found himself in an alien place, with exotic-looking buildings around him. He felt a strange download of information rush into him. Realizing he was very far from home, he told the strange man he needed to return. The man told Viktorovich that he knew the way.

Viktorovich found himself back in the same foggy corridor. Coming out the other side, he was in an area not far from his home. He returned to his residence and found his wife in tears. Viktorovich had been missing for three days. All he could remember is two hours, with fragmentary recall of various events.

He did notice that the acetate silk on the inside of his suit was missing, as was his watch. He also noticed that he had been healed. Writes researcher, Albert Rosales, "He had been suffering from a consistent backache and the alien had rubbed his back at one time, apparently causing the ache to disappear."[7]

While a UFO healing may sound like a singular and rare event, there is a catalogue of cases involving people reporting *multiple* healings of a wide variety of injuries, illnesses and diseases. At the top of this list is the Twiggs family. The below healing is only one of several that they have experienced as a result of UFO contact. It is almost identical to the case of Charles Moody, involving a back injury sustained during an abduction event.

CASE #146. BACK INJURY.

On October 15, 1989, Bert and Denise Twiggs of Hubbard, Oregon, woke up in their bedroom to discover several strange marks on their bodies. Because of previous extensive encounters with aliens who claimed to be from Andromeda, Bert and Denise knew what the marks meant: they had experienced a contact during the night.

Bert noticed that his back was very sore, and he wondered what had transpired during the night to cause his back pain. Both Bert and Denise decided to undergo hypnosis to recover their memories. Both easily remembered what happened.

While aboard the UFO, Bert had tripped and fallen backward against a metal support bar, injuring his back. The two of them were returned to their home, and later, the extraterrestrials made a house call to heal Bert's back. "The doctor placed a hand-held machine over the sore area," Denise said. "The machine reversed most of the damage that occurred when Bert hit his back on the metal bar. After this process was finished, they left...and Bert awoke nearly healed."[8]

One of the central questions behind the UFO healing phenomenon is: who is being healed and why? Some people are healed apparently because they are already having extensive contact. In the following case, however, the witness reports no prior UFO history. However, her transformation following her encounter may provide the answer as to why she was healed. The case is published here for the first time.

CASE #175. NECK AND BACK PAIN.
In 2017, I was contacted by a woman from Norway who wanted to share her experience of a UFO healing. Natalie (pseudonym) is a retired artist who currently works on social and environmental issues. She had seen UFOs several times, but always from a distance. On one occasion, she saw what appeared to be a star-like object high in the sky. As she studied it, suddenly six or seven star-like objects flew across the night sky in formation and at incredible speed.

While working as an art director in 1991 she suffered a severe neck and back injury. Trying to cope with the injury and work was proving to be a struggle. Shortly after this injury, Natalie experienced her first and only visitation by ETs. "I woke up one night with a terrible pain in my back, and realized that I couldn't move. I discovered my bed was surrounded by little grays. One was taller and was doing some surgery on my back. They flipped me on my back like I was a ragdoll...I was terrified. They didn't say anything; the non-communication scared me...and they left through the wall. Outside, there was a bluish light. Then I could move again, and went straight to the window. Everything looked different, even the nature. It was like looking into another dimension. Then suddenly the light was gone and everything was normal."

Natalie sat back on her bed and suddenly realized something incredible: "The amazing part was that my back pain from my injury was gone. And never came back. Whatever this was, it has healed me and made my life a lot easier. I became a lot more interested in UFOs and ETs or interdimensional beings. I also became a vegetarian and animal rights activist, and more politically active in human rights issues, environmental protection and peace activism."

Natalie has had no other UFO experiences that she can recall, but she did have one other unusual mystical experience. She was driving alone at night through a rural area when she heard a calm female voice say, "Elk could be here."

Says Natalie, "Instinctively I pulled the brakes and stopped the car as soon as I could. Out of nowhere an elk came across the road and literally jumped over the hood of my tiny Daihatsu car. I got mud from the elk's hooves on my front window. So whatever the voice came from, it saved my life."[9]

The bizarre nature of UFO healings is difficult to comprehend. Are UFOs our friends or foes? In the following case, the woman had an encounter which caused intense fear. However, she was also healed.

CASE #176. BACK PAIN.

Late one evening in 1991, a twenty-one-year-old anonymous female was driving with her sister through the outskirts of Claremont, California. For years she had suffered from intense chronic back pain. As they drove, the sisters spotted a disc-shaped craft hovering above them, sending down a beam of light. Researcher Barbara Lamb describes what happened next, "The car stopped. So they got out of the car and started running across the field. And they were followed by a beam of blue light. And the beam suddenly struck her in her lower back and she felt it radiating right through her, and felt a very, very powerful energy."

The witness was running in terror from what she thought was going to harm her. Ironically, it had the opposite effect. As Lamb says, "As a result of that, she felt that she had been healed of whatever the difficulty was, and was actually quite grateful to them."[10]

In comparison to other injuries, there seems to be a larger number of healings of back pain. The following five cases are short on details, but they show the same patterns that appear in other better documented cases.

CASE #189. BACK PAIN.
A short case with few details comes from researcher Helga Morrow who reports that a man from Tbilisi, Georgia, in Russia was operated on by friendly extraterrestrials who cured him of his chronic back pain. This is only one of many cures reported by Morrow in the Tbilisi region (circa 1993.)[11]

CASE #241. BACK PAIN.
In 2005, Terry Walters of Priestwood, in Bracknell, England was in pain from a "bad back." That is, until he experienced an alien abduction. Following his experience, his back pain was gone. As his daughter Julie Kendall writes, "...he reckoned they cured his bad back, which had baffled even top medical professionals."[12]

CASE #294. DAMAGED SPINAL CORD.
A brief undated case from the files of FREE involves a gentleman who had been having encounters his entire life. After suffering a bad industrial accident which damaged his spinal cord, the witness meditated and asked the ETs to "please fix my back."

The gentleman was taken onboard and examined. The ETs had him lie down on a table. They hooked a device to his arms and legs, controlling his movements. "To this day," says the witness, "I have no more major problems with my back."[13]

CASE #295. BACK PAIN.
Another case from FREE: "I had an abduction and the entity fixed my back...I would give it a ninety percent improvement...There is no doubt in my mind that they helped me, and I will be forever grateful to them for their help."[14]

And one more undated case from Australian researcher, Mary Rodwell, who has interviewed hundreds of abductees and researched the subject for more than twenty years.

CASE #292. BACK PAIN.

According to UFO researcher Mary Rodwell, she interviewed a lady in her sixties from Victoria, Australia. Suffering from chronic back pain, doctors told her she would likely end up in a wheelchair, but could use morphine to relieve her pain. Says Rodwell, "I did hypnosis, we discovered she went onto a craft and was healed...After she had a levitating experience, her condition was gone. She is no longer on medication...Now she's almost seventy and has more energy than her children. Part of her mission has been to prove to her family and partner that this is real. They find it difficult to believe her."[15]

So many healing cases! Because of the huge number of the cases and the striking similarities between them, and because these events have a long history and are occurring all across the world, it's clear that this is a real phenomenon. While some cases provide better evidence than others, one fact is clear: people are being healed of a wide variety of injuries by UFOs.

Chapter Seven
Head Injuries

Virtually everybody alive on Earth has had the experience of painfully bumping their head. Many people might not realize how common and dangerous head injuries can be. According to the Center for Disease Control, more than a million people suffer head injuries each year, the majority of which are sports-related. These injuries range from minor concussions to traumatic brain injury.

Despite the huge number of head injuries that occur each year, this chapter presents only three cases involving UFO healings of this kind. The first comes from researcher Edith Fiore Ph.D.

CASE #025. HEAD INJURY.

Today James X. is a successful southern California physician. He occasionally sought therapy from a psychologist because he found it useful when confronting various life issues.

During one of his sessions, he underwent hypnosis and spontaneously recalled a complex UFO abduction scenario which occurred around age eight, sometime in 1959. He recalled "being transported up on a kind of pallet. I don't understand how it happens, but I'm moving...Maybe I'm in a bubble. I'm going right inside this big thing. Just right up. It looks like your usual depiction of a spaceship, but it's going right up inside this opening."

James recalled being taken inside a strange room and put on a table. He was unable to move as various instruments were placed in his nose and ears. A dome-like contraption was placed over the top of his head. He began to feel an electrical zapping sensation and experienced some fear.

Earlier James had fallen off the jungle-gym and hit the back of his head. A huge goose-egg-sized lump appeared and his father had to take him to the hospital that night to have the lump drained. Following the incident, he suffered severe headaches.

Then one day, the headaches stopped. He never knew why. Years later, under hypnosis, James learned that the ETs fixed his head injury. "There's something on my head," he explains, "like a hemisphere over the top part of my head, and it feels like it's clamped on over my maxilla."

James watched in fascination as the aliens dissolved the lump on his head using what looked like laser beams. As he says, "They go in there and dissolve that damn clot...there's two beams, and then they cross, it creates heat at that exact location, and it takes a long time, because it dissolves that clot, gasses form, and they don't want to obstruct the blood flow."

They then injected his chest with two needles. "They're putting needles in both sides of my chest! I don't know what they're doing. I don't know why, but they've got these things in both sides. It's really strange...It feels like a clamp on my heart." Sperm samples were taken.

James was then moved through the craft on the floating pallet, and was surprised to see numerous other people encased in bubbles, floating on pallets like his. Next he was floated back into his bedroom. He reports that as a result of his encounter, he was healed of severe headaches that had been caused by a recent concussion.

In his mid-thirties, James experienced an incredible shock when the aliens returned. Just after buying his new home, he began to have bizarre recollections of strange figures in his bedroom. He discounted them until hypnosis revealed a history of encounters. Says James, "They look gray and they're maybe five feet tall. They have oval heads..."

Fiore agreed to place him under hypnosis to explore the memory. James recalled waking up to find several gray-type ETs in his bedroom. He was unable to move as he was placed on a strange "pallet" which floated him up and through the wall "...and into that big ship that's sitting out over the trees. I don't understand why people can't see that."

James was taken up a ramp and into the craft. The aliens were talking about the dangers of announcing their presence in a physical way to humanity and were interested in James' reaction. It was his job "to explain the way people think...I feel like a negotiator...I feel like I'm being interrogated."

James reports that other people were also questioned in a similar manner. He was shown some of the alien technology, such as an X-ray device that allowed them to view the inside of a body. "They're demonstrating it on somebody. First an alien and now a human...on the television screen, you can see the different energy channels, just like they're interspersed with the arteries and veins. It's like our MRI except it shows not only tissues, it shows the energy channels."

He was shown other people being operated upon and was given considerable information about the various causes of disease. They told James that he had part of their genetic material and they expressed surprise that he had survived a childhood inoculation. He was given further information and then was returned home in "a small, round-shaped craft of some kind. It's got a clear canopy in front. It's not very big....it lands in the backyard. And I am kind of led because I'm in a semi-awake state. I'm led back to my door. The doors open and they wait there while I get into bed."

James, as a physician, now realizes that the aliens were merely speeding up a process that would've occurred naturally, nevertheless, the cure of his head injury remains beyond the scope of today's medical expertise.[1]

The following case is a good example of someone who feels that their encounters are benevolent. The witness also claims to have experienced multiple healings.

CASE #091. HEAD INJURY, FOOT INJURY, PLEURISY.

Another case of a healing of a head injury comes from a man who goes by the pseudonym of "Star Traveler." Star Traveler reports that his UFO experiences have been "informative, pleasant and even funny..." One of these experiences includes the healing of a head injury. As a young boy, (1970s) he was playing soft ball when his sister accidentally struck him on the head with a baseball bat. "The baseball bat struck my skull just above my eyebrow and the flesh peeled back like the lid of a sardine can," said Star Traveler.

In the emergency room, the doctor applied a butterfly bandage and advised that he might need stiches. The next evening, Star was in his room lying in bed when he saw a bright star-like object outside his window. In the middle of the night he woke up to see two aliens with "chalk-white skin and large, black almond-shaped eyes that seemed like peaceful, glistening pools of water. They were skinny, and had large heads, thin necks and very long arms."

As he lay there, one of the figures began passing a rod-shaped instrument back and forth over his body. At first, he was frightened but then the aliens told him what they were doing. "I realized," says Star, "that they were there to heal me, and I couldn't apologize enough! They told me (telepathically) that they routinely heal 'volunteers' (those who volunteer to be of service to others before they incarnate) and ensure their health. It was their job to 'make the rounds.'"

Needless to say, Star Traveler enjoys meeting with the ETs. "I consider them my friends," he says.

A few days after the head injury, Star Traveler visited the doctor. "The physician was shocked to see that the injury was healing at an amazing rate--and that I would need no stitches."

Star Traveler says that he has been cured by the aliens on many different occasions. "They have affected many other healings for me," he says, "including healings of an impact injury to my feet, and pleurisy in my lungs. I have come to regard these interventions as a 'Zeta-Terran medical plan' that comes as a bonus for being a 'Volunteer.'"[2]

The vast majority of UFO healings occur without any outside witnesses. The following is one of only a handful of cases in which a person witnessed the healing take place. It's also rare in that the healing took place *inside* a hospital room. And while most healings are done by grays and human-looking ETs, in this case the healing was performed by the praying mantis type, also called mantids.

CASE #255. HEAD INJURY.
"My best friend was viciously attacked and left to die in 2008," writes Andrea (pseudonym) of Canada. "She barely survived the horrible attack where she was knocked unconscious after being hit on the head over and over with an object. When I saw her at the hospital, she was unrecognizable. Her beautiful face was swollen to the size of a basketball."

Andrea was devastated. She had known her friend for forty years; they had grown up together. Now, following this attack, her friend lay on her hospital bed in a drug-induced coma. Part of her skull had been removed to reduce pressure from inflammation.

Because of the delicacy of her condition, Andrea was not allowed to touch her friend. As she visited her, she would stand by her bed and meditate on healing her. When she performs a healing, Andrea feels as though she seems to be "another person, working with accuracy and knowledge that I wouldn't have in real life."

One evening, as she meditated on healing her friend, Andrea had a vision of a huge black spot on her friend's head. Out of this spot came hundreds of giant spiders. Unfortunately, her friend's condition did not appear to approve.

Andrea was in despair. She remained by her friend's bedside but was unable to help her. Finally, she reached a point of panic. She felt a sense that "something had to be done quickly."

It was at that moment that two praying mantis-type beings appeared. "All of a sudden," says Andrea, "there were two beings that appeared next to my friend. They seemed to push me aside and silently went to work on her, like skilled surgeons. They stood to her left, standing together and working furiously on my friend. I had no idea who they were, or what they were doing. I thought they looked like Praying Mantis. Never in a million years could I make this up."

Andrea had no idea that other people had reported similar ETs. At the time of the incident, she was so amazed by what was happening that she was unable to observe everything. Suddenly, she realized that the figures were doing something.

"I focused on my friend," says Andrea, "and saw her head was split wide open, like these aliens sliced it perfectly open. I saw freshly-sliced raw flesh, and these alien praying mantis were busily removing pieces of bone, rock or whatever from her brain...these two alien praying mantis worked quickly, without speaking one word."

At this point, Andrea seemed to "black out." She is unable to remember anything else about what happened. She did tell her friends about the incident, who told her that other people had also seen similar beings. They advised her to search the internet. Andrea was surprised to find many other accounts involving the same type of beings.

Andrea hoped that following the visit, her friend would be completely cured. Unfortunately, it was not to be. Says Andrea, "I'm sad to say that even with the alien healing, my friend survived only another two weeks before she died. It's just remarkable that she survived at all after her injuries. I don't know why I experienced this, but it's something I will never forget. Sincerely, and oh, yes, this is 100 percent truth, the whole story."[3]

While the head injury cases are rare, the above three cases are probably only a small sample of the actual number. Likely there are many cases of this type that haven't been reported. These cases each provide considerable information about healings. The case of James is incredibly detailed, and the fact that he is a physician himself adds a level of credibility to his story.

The case involving the praying mantis is important, not only because it exhibits some rare details, but also because it shows that even the ETs are not perfect. In the end, the patient died, indicating that ETs, despite their advanced healing technology, are not able to cure all injuries.

Star Traveler's account is interesting because the ETs revealed that the people chosen to be healed are "volunteers" dedicated to helping others, and that they perform healings "routinely." It shows that some people who are having contact experience multiple healings and believe that their relationship with ETs is entirely benevolent. As Star Traveler said, "I consider them my friends." Many of the people who have received healings feel this sense of gratitude and goodwill toward the ETs.

Chapter Eight
Body Injuries

We have already examined more than fifty cases of injuries to virtually all areas of the human body. However, here we come to the difficult task of trying to categorize UFO healings. In a number of cases, people experience multiple body injuries. If someone is healed of multiple broken bones, should these be considered separate healing events? Obviously not.

For that reason, this chapter focuses on healings involving multiple body injuries. Even though multiple healings of different parts of the body take place, each case is treated as a single healing event.

The vast majority of these fourteen cases involve vehicle accidents of some kind, while the rest are the result of falls and injuries received from assault by other humans. In a few of the cases, the witnesses believe they died as a result of their injuries and were brought back to life by the ETs. The first case is a rare early case involving a healing within an Army hospital.

CASE #009. BROKEN NOSE AND BRUISES.

In June of 1946, Allan Edwards was admitted to an Army hospital at Camp Lee, Virginia. One evening he wandered through the hospital seeking company when he spotted a very unusual-looking man. Struck by his odd appearance, Edwards walked across the room and sat down on the vacant bunk next to him. Edwards was an academically trained portrait painter, with a thorough knowledge of anatomy, and he instantly noticed several irregularities about the individual.

The man had an extremely high forehead, perfectly formed features, unusually radiant blond hair, a flawless complexion and extraordinary blue eyes "filled with great compassion." Edwards stared at the man in fascination. Suddenly Edwards was overcome with a feeling of wellbeing to the point that he felt it was a spiritual experience just to be in the man's presence.

Before he could investigate further, Edwards was called away for his own medical examination. Later that evening, he saw a young man being brought into the hospital for treatment. The young man had been beaten in a drunken brawl. He had two black eyes which were swollen shut, a badly bruised forehead and his nose appeared to be broken. The man was put in the cot next to Edwards, who now had trouble falling asleep because of the man's loud groans of pain.

The next morning, Edwards sat down for breakfast. He saw the strange-looking man on his right. Then he saw the boy who had been injured the night before, except now, he looked normal. All signs of his injuries were gone.

Says Edwards, "My eyes rested on a young lad seated at the end of the table. This was the same boy who had been brought in the night before, the one who had been so badly beaten--yet, it couldn't be. There wasn't a blemish on his face."

Who cured the boy? Edwards never found out for sure, but as he says, "I felt strongly that the man seated on my right had been responsible for this miraculous transfiguration."

Edwards had later contacts with the strange man and other ETs. In Seattle, Washington, Edwards says he was hospitalized for a respiratory ailment. He became curious about two normal and human-looking attendants who repeatedly proved their ability to read his every thought.

While in their presence at the Seattle hospital, other strange things began to happen. Edwards says he felt compelled to get up and attend to the patients, performing a type of psychic healing. "I found myself administering to them with expert hands which did not somehow seem to belong to me," he says. He was discharged shortly later, and always regrets that he didn't question the two strange hospital attendants further.[1]

A poignant example of an alien healing comes from the case files of Barbara Lamb. The healing occurred in the 1950s and involves a four-year-old girl from the United States. The details were uncovered using hypnotic regression.

CASE #028. GENITAL INJURIES.

"She had an experience at age four," says Lamb, "where she was sexually abused by her grandfather, and there was actually physical damage done to her in her genital area because of that. And fortunately the act was stopped sort of in the middle by the grandmother who discovered them. Anyway, later on that afternoon, probably an hour or so later, this lady was taken by her 'little people,' the little gray extraterrestrials, and taken aboard a spacecraft. And they did a sort of whole medical procedure on her, the little gray guys did. And there was a female [ET] too, who was a little bit larger. And the female was standing by her side on the medical table on the craft. And the female was explaining that something was done here that should not have been done, and that the other ones--the little ones--were needed to fix this, to repair this. Because they wanted to be sure that everything would be fine in later years for having babies."[2]

The following example of a UFO healing comes from an extraordinary contactee case. The healing took place in a very rural area with little exposure to the media. It's of particular interest because it illustrates how residents in this area have an interactive and benevolent relationship with UFOs, and apparently rely upon the ETs to provide medical care.

CASE #031. BODY INJURIES.

On March 10, 1960, Victor Kapetanovic (a Peruvian electrical engineer) was hunting with a local guide in the Callejon de Hauylas region--a rural area inhabited by native Peruvians. They were traveling through a local village when they came upon a family whose son had recently fallen from a cliff and now was apparently dying of his injuries. Kapetanovic was taken to see the child, who lay unmoving on the floor of the primitive hut. Says

Kapetanovic, "His swollen face had taken on a bluish color by the infections; his eyes half-closed, his mouth half-open, and with his tongue and lips swollen, [he] looked terrible."

Kapetanovic was unable to detect any pulse and realized that the boy was in a comatose state. Although the closest hospital was many miles away, Kapetanovic offered to transport the child. The boy's mother angrily refused and explained that the "Gods from the sky" would take care of her son.

Kapetanovic's guide explained that the locals are often in contact with UFO beings, whom they called the Sky Gods. Kapetanovic had recently seen many of the strange discs himself and decided to stay and see if anything would happen.

Shortly later, the sky suddenly filled with clouds. Without warning, the family began to shout and point. Kapetanovic looked and observed "an apparatus similar to a small airplane" drop out of the clouds and land silently among the herd of sheep and goats. He first thought it might be the Peruvian military until a door opened and a strange figure emerged. It was a female who looked entirely human, with white skin, except she was very short, and was dressed in a body suit unlike any Kapetanovic had seen. The strange figure floated toward them a few inches above the ground.

Kapetanovic's guide and the entire Peruvian family dropped to their knees and began to pray. The figure told them to rise up. She entered the hut, scooped up the child and carried him into the landed craft. The door to the craft closed.

After several minutes, the door opened. Says Kapetanovic, "Suddenly I saw the boy descend alone from the ladder of the ship, and upon touching the ground ran toward us, reaching down to pick up a stone, and thus showing his perfect state of health. Having seen him when he was swollen, I did not recognize him now and thought that he must be another boy, a member of the crew, perhaps. Then I waited for the reaction of the mother of the child. The little boy had not covered half the distance from the ship to us when his mother ran toward him shouting in emotion. All present embraced and gave shouts of joy."

The ET woman also exited and spoke briefly with all those present. Kapetanovic immediately approached the boy and began

115

to examine him for injuries. "Who knows how they affected this cure," said Kapetanovic, "but I could find no evidence of surgery on his arm. The boy showed no abnormality in his body." He spoke with the ET who said her name was Ivanka. She invited him aboard the ship where he saw other ETs, and was shown a screen which portrayed scenes of future events. Kapetanovic later wrote a book about his experiences.[3]

New Jersey contactee, Richard Rylka, has reported multiple healings at the hands of the ETs. His is one of many cases involving human-looking ETs and benevolent encounters. It is only one of a few cases, however, where someone was healed of otherwise fatal injuries.

CASE #051. BODY INJURIES.

In 1970, Richard Rylka of New Jersey suffered a devastating automobile accident. His body was so badly mangled, he had a near-death experience. While most people see deceased relatives when they have a near-death experience, Rylka saw his alien friends who told him that his body was so badly injured, he should be dead. They promised to heal him, and also warned him of drastic changes to his life at home and work.

All the predictions made by the aliens came true. Rylka had already been healed twice. Future healings would later occur.[4]

Swiss farmer, Eduard Meier, is without a doubt one of the most famous UFO contactees. He claims to have had contact with human-like aliens from the Pleiades. Meier's story is supported by a large amount of evidence including moving films, photos, audio recordings, landing traces, metal fragments, animal evidence, medical evidence and multiple eyewitness testimonies. Nevertheless, the case is extremely controversial.

Meier, like most contactees, has been instructed by his alien friends to tell others of his contacts. For this reason Meier has reported his experiences publicly. Like many contactees, Meier, as we shall see, has received a number of healings.

CASE #074. BODY INJURIES.

On April 3, 1976, Eduard Meier of Hinwil, Switzerland, was instructed by the aliens to travel to a certain location where a flight demonstration of the alien crafts would take place. Meier was told that he could bring his friends and also take photographs.

Unfortunately, the group was followed by unwanted human visitors who caused the demonstration to be cancelled. Meier was instructed telepathically by the aliens to depart the area. As he was leaving, he was pursued by the unwelcome visitors. In his haste to escape, he crashed his moped, damaging not only his moped, but himself. Meier fractured a rib, dislocated his shoulder, twisted his foot and suffered several abrasions.

Three days later, Meier was visited by his main ET contact, Semjase, who offered to cure his broken rib. She held a small device to the broken rib, and instructed Meier to sit between the two "poles" on the instrument. "The rib-bones will be completely regenerated after this process," she told Meier. "There will be nothing left to indicate that they had been nearly broken."

Meier felt a sudden "electrical sensation" and then nothing. He knew instantly he was cured because the pain was gone. Semjase was unable to reduce the swelling only because the correct instrument was not available at the time.

Meier's injuries and cure were verified by other witnesses. Incidentally, Meier has only one arm, having lost one in a bus accident. During one of his contacts, the aliens offered to grow him a new limb. Meier declined, fearing that people would ask too many questions.[5]

The following case is typical of someone cured of injuries as the result of a car accident. In case after case, the ETs show up immediately after the accident and cure the person of their injuries. In some cases, while they cure most of the injuries, some are left unhealed.

CASE #104. BODY INJURIES.

On the evening of February 28, 1984, an anonymous gentleman (age 27) from Farnham, England was driving his motorcycle when he collided head-on into another vehicle. The man was thrown from his motorcycle into a tree.

Before he hit the ground, the man recalled seeing a bright light in the sky above him. When he woke up, he found himself lying on a strange bed, surrounded by three even stranger beings about four and a half feet tall. The man described the beings as having gray skin, large hairless heads, and eyes with diamond-shaped pupils. The beings stood behind a raised console and told him telepathically that they were going to heal his extensive injuries.

At some point, the man lost consciousness. When he woke again, he was in the hospital. His only remaining injury was a broken arm. The case was investigated by English UFO researcher, Gordon Millington, of the Surrey Investigation Group on Aerial Phenomena (SIGAP.)[6]

While there are many cases of healings, many of them are short on details and evidence, such as the following.

CASE #111. INJURY UNDESCRIBED.

On May 9, 1986, a man from Danville, Pennsylvania experienced a missing time encounter with three other family members. At the time of the missing time incident, there was also an unexplained power failure. Following the missing time, the man reports that an injury he had suffered earlier was mysteriously healed.[7]

ETs heal a wide variety of people from all across the planet. In this next case, a high-ranking, well-known government official claims to have repeated contact and multiple healings. The case is unusual in that the witness was not only a government official, but also allowed her name to be used.

CASE #116. BODY INJURIES.

From 1975 to 1986, Dr. Rauni-Leena Luukanen-Kilde was the chief medical officer of Finnish Lapland in Finland. She was married to Svere Kilde, a Norwegian diplomat to the United

Nations. In August 1986, Luukanen had a close-up sighting of a yellow spherical object. That same year, she suffered a horrific accident in which her car was struck by a bus.

According to Luukanen, an ET appeared at the scene of the accident and began to heal her injuries. "The small ET was applying some sort of energy to my body in the area of my liver," says Dr. Luukanen. "When I got to the hospital it was determined my liver was damaged. But the aliens had prevented it from hemorrhaging and saved my life."

Two years later, in 1988, Dr. Luukanen elected to go under hypnosis and recalled the above account and many others. Following the hypnosis sessions, she began having fully conscious visitations in her home. She left her job and began researching and writing about spiritual enlightenment, life after death, government mind control and conspiracies. She claims to have had hundreds of encounters, and believes that aliens saved her life not once, but at least three times. The first was the car accident. But following that, she had an incident where she fell off her motorbike and was about to be crushed by it when a mysterious force field deflected it. On the third occasion, an elk jumped in front of her speeding car, but she was protected. "An invisible force field deflected the elk," says Luukanen, "and I was able to pass through the force field."

Luukanen says she has seen at least three different types of ETs, and has had numerous medical examinations. "I'm not afraid of these medical exams and I don't mind them," says Luukanen. "I sense that they are very positive in nature. I realize that I am part of a huge experimental project."

In 2015 Luukanen succumbed to an aggressive form of cancer. Conspiracy theorists have put forth the possibility that she may have been murdered due to her research in government conspiracies such as mind control and chem trails.[8]

The following case, personally investigated by the author, is another example of someone who received fatal injuries from a car accident and was brought back to life and cured by the ETs. Again, while they cured most of her injuries, they didn't cure them all.

CASE #122. BODY INJURIES.

Alicia Hansen (not her real name) has been having contacts for many years. In 1987 while in Atlanta, Georgia, she miraculously survived what everyone believed should have been a fatal accident. As it turned out, the accident was fatal and Alicia had literally been brought back to life by her alien contacts.

"I was in a really bad car accident," Alicia explains, "very bad." I got hit head on. I was a passenger in the car. I knocked out the side window with my face and then I went face-first through the windshield. I had to go to the emergency room and everything. They thought my neck and back were broken...I had to go through physical therapy for a year, learning how to walk again. I had a lot of internal damage done. My jaw was dislocated and all kinds of other stuff."

Despite her extensive injuries, the paramedics couldn't understand why Alicia hadn't been hurt more badly, or how she escaped from the accident with her face completely unmarked. All she remembers is waking up to find herself lying in the street. Years later, Alicia discovered the truth of what happened that night.

"I was doing a regression one night," Alicia explains, "and I saw that I had actually died in that accident. I didn't have a cut, I didn't have a scratch on my face. I knocked out two windows, and I had not a scratch. And everybody thought that was really weird...but I saw that I broke my neck, and I saw that they were doing surgery on me. They were fixing my brain stem. They were putting me back together. I saw all of that. And my face was just devastated. I saw the brain stem had been broken, damaged, and they repaired that. And my face was really cut and they just whoosh!--they fixed it. It was the weirdest thing I've ever seen. It was just healed. And I didn't have a cut, not a scratch, nothing. They left certain things, but they fixed the most important. And they were also doing something; they said my metabolism was really messed up."

Alicia doesn't understand how the aliens were able to heal her before the paramedics even arrived, however she learned from later experiences that the aliens have the ability to travel in time.

During the experience, Alicia also says that there was "an exchange of souls to some degree." She says, "I'm kind of hesitant to talk about it because I don't understand it completely yet...but the weird thing about it was when I saw this, and I saw this accident, there was some sort of exchange, like a higher part of myself changed places with myself."[9]

There are many accounts of UFOs being seen during human conflicts. However, there are only a few cases of soldiers being healed of injuries sustained during a war. The following case is a rare example. It's also a good example of how the ETs' capacity to heal is near-miraculous, but not always perfect.

CASE #123. BODY INJURIES.

In 1987, an anonymous Soviet soldier was fighting with local partisans in Afghanistan when he lost his machine gun and became severely wounded, most severely on his leg. Rather than surrender to the enemy and risk possible torture from the "Mujahideen," he decided to commit suicide with a grenade.

At that moment he saw a shiny disc-shaped object hover above him. It came lower and projected a beam of light, pulling him inside the craft.

The soldier found himself inside a bright circular room. He was no longer in any pain. Strange "people" appeared and communicated with him telepathically. They placed the soldier on a table surrounded by medical devices. Using these devices, they showed images of his organs on large screens above him.

"We can cure all your wounds," said one of the aliens, "but we cannot save your leg, so we must amputate your leg."

The soldier asked them why, with all their advanced technology, they couldn't save his leg. They told him it was beyond their capabilities and that if they did not amputate, he would not survive. The soldier blacked out.

When he awoke, he was still in the battlefield. When a medical team arrived, they were shocked to find the soldier's leg not only amputated, but almost completely healed. It appeared to them that surgery to amputate the leg must have occurred a year earlier.

The soldier said that he had been taken and healed by extraterrestrials. The medical team accused him of delirium and transported him by helicopter to a field hospital. Senior doctors there were amazed and asked the soldier what happened. The soldier repeated his story and was again not believed. Still, the doctors remained baffled. The soldier was discharged. He told his story to a friend, who reported it to investigators, Natalia and Leonid Tereteyev.[10]

This next healing is another example of aliens showing up immediately following a car accident to cure the victims of some of their injuries, but not all of them.

CASE #126. BODY INJURIES.

According to researcher Ken Pfeifer, around midnight on March 24, 1988, two friends were driving to their home on Bull Island Road in New Iberia, Louisiana when they lost control of their vehicle and flipped off the road. The driver says, "I was pinned beneath the wheel, with my hand between the wheel and the dash, with three broken ribs and a broken collar bone." The driver's friend, Michelle, broke her nose and was knocked unconscious.

The two of them were trapped in the wreck for about two or three hours until two passersby spotted them and called an ambulance. The two victims were rushed to the hospital where they learned the extent of their injuries and were nursed back to health.

One curious incident puzzled the driver. Before the accident, she was wearing her mother's ring. Afterward, it was missing. Shortly later, the driver spontaneously recalled the reason. Says the driver, "I was somehow taken from my car and into a UFO, and then later placed back into the front seat of the car.

122

My hand had been pinned between the steering wheel and the dash...A six-foot-tall alien man came and got me out of the car, got me aboard his craft by what mechanism I don't know, and cut the ring off my hand. I never got it back."

The ET was described as "six feet tall, well-shaped, with shoulder length golden-brown hair. [He] wore a white outfit with a formal Japanese-looking top, a small collar and long sleeves."

The witness believes she was given surgeries to repair her injuries sustained in the car wreck. "[They] removed some muscle tissue from my right upper arm, from shoulder to beginning of forearm. The cut was only two inches--healed without stitches--and left a very light scar. On the inside of the arm, other tissue samples were taken. The marks resulting from this were three dots in a line. Finally, a one-inch cut was made under the chin, which healed a very light almost invisible scar."[11]

A significant portion of the healing reports come from contactees, people who report friendly encounters with human-looking ETs. The contactees of the 1950s were among the first to report interaction with ETs. Some researchers remain skeptical of their accounts, while others support their validity. Although controversial, the accounts of contactees are strikingly similar to abductees in many ways, including being healed.

CASE #184. BODY INJURIES.
In January 1993, Dr. Frank E. Stranges (a reverend), drove out of Las Vegas, Nevada in order to rendezvous with ETs out in the desert. Stranges claimed to be in contact with friendly, human-looking extraterrestrials. Stranges often met with an ET named Valiant Thor who said he was from Venus.

On the way to meet Valiant Thor, Stranges was attacked by several men in a large black car. The men physically assaulted Stranges. As he says, "I was thrown to the ground and kicked over and over again." As a result of the assault, Stranges sustained numerous bruises and a badly crushed hand.

In the middle of the assault, Valiant Thor showed up and rescued Stranges from the attackers. Stranges was taken inside a

123

UFO where he was treated for his injuries. "As I lay atop the soft white table," Stranges said, "I was conscious of the beam of soft blue light that emitted from the cone-shaped instrument which was aimed first at my head, then at my solar plexus. I immediately went into a deep sleep. Upon awakening, I felt good all over."[12]

It appears that ETs are closely monitoring people or have some mechanism for knowing when an injury has occurred. In the following case, a man injured himself with a chainsaw. Not long afterward, aliens came to heal him.

CASE #186. BROKEN RIBS.
In his book, *Visitors from Hidden Realms*, researcher Brent Raynes presents an apparent UFO healing case involving a man named Ron, from Fyffe, Alabama. In 1993 the town of Fyffe was garnering national attention for waves of UFO activity, black helicopters and cattle mutilations. Ron and his family lived in the heart of the activity and spent many evenings watching the UFOs as they moved around the area, sometimes landing or diving into the waters of the Tennessee River.

While most of these were just sightings, Ron had learned long ago that aliens were a part of his life. Earlier, in Guntersville, Alabama, Ron and his brother experienced a missing time episode. Following the event, he found two identical fresh pink scars, one on each foot near the Achilles' tendon. He also began having vivid dreams about being examined by tall, slender beings.

But it was a strange event in 1993 that really got his attention. Writes Raynes, "One day, Ron was using a chainsaw to cut some trees down that were obstructing their view of the river, when a limb flew back and struck him in the chest. As a result, he had two broken ribs. One night, while in the early stages of recover from this injury, Ron was sleeping in the recliner in the living room. Around 2:00 or 3:00 a.m., he got up to use the bathroom. During this time, he would periodically cough to get 'mucus and stuff' out. He tried to do this and noticed there wasn't any pain."

"I looked and my shirt was burned," Ron explained. "Right over those two ribs. It just happened to be that my pen was in my pocket right over those two ribs...I pulled my pen out. The plastic was melted...and the ribs were healed. I never had another pain out of it."[13]

This next case is unusual in that it involves a gentleman who was cured of injuries that occurred twenty years prior. The case also enjoys the distinction of being one of the most recent in this book.

CASE #290. BODY INJURIES.

Around June of 2018, "Don," (a retired police officer from Cape Cod, Massachusetts) began to see and photograph UFOs flying around his home. Some of the photos show typical UFO craft, others look like orbs with faces and beings inside them. During this intense wave of sightings, Don was "totally disabled" and had to walk with a cane. Twenty years earlier, while on the police force, he was severely injured in a freak accident. His recovery was long and painful and required twelve major surgeries to his neck, hip, groin, both shoulders and more. For a long time, Don was confined to a wheel-chair, though he improved to being able to walk with a cane. At one point, doctors over-medicated him and Don collapsed in a full cardiac arrest. He was revived by paramedics, but remained in a coma for a short time before waking up to continue his recovery.

Due to the severity of his injuries, Don never completely healed and suffered from chronic pain, forcing him to use a cane to walk. He took thousands of milligrams of pain relievers each day.

Then the sightings began. Throughout the summer of 2018, he witnessed and photographed dozens of strange UFOs and orbs. On many occasions, he's had other witnesses with him. While some of the photos show blurry lights, others are quite striking and a few show what appear to be metallic disc-like craft.

The most amazing part of the sudden wave of sightings, Don found himself cured. Prior to the sightings, he suffered from the inability to walk freely, chronic pain, diarrhea, nausea and vomiting--all of which would sometimes leave him on the floor begging for Jesus to take his life. Now, Don feels amazing.

125

His health improvements were quick and dramatic. As he says, "I can't explain it, but I'm walking for the first time in twenty years. For the first time in twenty years, I'm not taking massive amounts of medication. For the first time in a long time, I have purpose in my life. All this is happening, as well as the UFOs flying around my house and me...In the last two weeks, I'm not only walking without a cane for the first time in twenty years, I went running for the first time in over twenty years."

He began to lose his excess weight. His strength and energy returned. His hair started growing back thick and healthy. In a short time, he soon had his "rock star hair" back.

When he went to his doctor for a check-up, she couldn't believe it. She was dumbfounded and actually broke down and wept.

Don now has more than a thousand photos and some video. He continues to photograph the objects. He has drastically reduced his pain medication and shows all signs of a full recovery.[14]

The above fourteen cases show, once again, the seemingly miraculous healing technology used by ETs. In a few of the cases, the witnesses feel that their lives were not only saved, but that they had died and were brought back to life. While Billy Meier was told that they could restore his lost limb, the soldier who lost his leg was told that his limb could not be saved. Presumably this is because we are dealing with different ETs with different levels of technological advancement.

Chapter Nine
Burns

Injuries fall into a number of different categories. This chapter focuses solely on cases of people who have been healed of burns. Compared to other types of injuries that are being healed, cures of burns are relatively rare. There are only five accounts. Ironically, it is easier to find cases of people who have been burned by a UFO than healed of a burn.

The first case is a convincing account of a UFO healing, containing not only the medical evidence, but multiple eyewitnesses and a signed affidavit from the person who was healed.

CASE #020. BURN ON HAND.

In early 1954, a wave of sightings in the Mojave Desert of California was attracting groups of flying saucer enthusiasts, including Carl Anderson, his family and friends. They set off in a convoy of three cars to Desert Hot Springs when suddenly a strange force pulled at the lead car, and the convoy began an unexpected three-mile ride down a dirt road into the desert. The group set up camp for the night.

That evening, most of the group woke up to a loud buzzing noise. Once awake, the campers found themselves unable to move. Also the tents and vehicles in which they were sleeping had become transparent, and looking outside, they saw a sixty-foot shiny silver disc complete with portholes landing near their campsite. After about fifteen minutes, the disc took off.

This was the first of many contacts for the Andersons. On October 2, 1955, Anderson again went out to Desert Hot Springs, accompanied by his wife, Stella, and their friend, Jim Stewart.

Again, their car seemed to be controlled by a mysterious force leading them to the proper location for a UFO contact.

They set up camp and waited. At around midnight, a huge UFO showed up. Says Anderson, "The great craft was now scarcely 200 feet overhead. We could now make out three round ball-like objects, equally spaced on the outer rim of the ship, from which the fluorescent glowing light appeared to emanate."

Seeing the craft descend so quickly, Anderson's wife, Stella, panicked and ran toward the car. The craft responded by climbing rapidly. Not wanting the craft to leave, Jim Stewart grabbed a flare, set it on fire and signaled the UFO.

The UFO occupants apparently got the message and quickly descended. Unfortunately, Stewart wasn't being careful, and received a severe burn on his hand from the flare. Then something amazing happened. Seconds after receiving the burn, the craft emitted a bright colorful glow and disappeared, instantly healing Stewart of his burns.

Stewart was so impressed by his experience that he left a signed affidavit, testifying: "This is to certify that I, James R. Stewart, did on or about the 2nd day of October in the year of 1955 witness a huge object hovering above me on the California desert in a remote spot south of Victorville. I also had the uncanny experience of having a severe burn which I had suffered from a burning flare, miraculously healed, as this object changed color..."[1]

Healings are not always limited to humans. There is at least one case in which a human saw an injured ET heal himself.

CASE #023. BURN ON HAND.

In 1957 and 1958, Cynthia Appleton of Aston, Birmingham in West Midlands, England, had four separate contacts with an alien entity. The alien was six feet tall, had a pale complexion, long blond hair and elongated facial features. Communicating via telepathy, the alien told Appleton that he was an extraterrestrial, and that open contact with humanity was impossible because of wars. He gave Appleton a large amount of highly technological information. Physical evidence was also left in the form of scorched marks on a newspaper where the alien stood.

During one of the contacts in February 1958, the alien accidentally burned his finger. He asked Appleton to bathe his finger in hot water, which she did. The alien then injected himself with a tube, and sprayed a jelly-like substance on his hand. The wound "healed miraculously."

Following the healing event, Appleton found a piece of the alien's skin in the bowl of water. She retrieved the piece of skin and had it analyzed by professionals using an electron microscope at Manchester University.

The investigator in charge of the case, Jenny Randles, spoke with the doctor who examined the skin. The doctor showed Randles his report which stated that the skin was not human skin, but seemed more similar in composition to animal skin. The doctor admitted that he was unable to identify the type of animal, and has declined to go public with his report.

During her contacts, the aliens also gave Appleton a method of curing cancer, which will be presented in a later chapter.[2]

In many cases, doctors have the opportunity to examine a patient both before and after a UFO healing. Almost invariably they are left baffled and confused. The following controversial contactee case is a good example.

CASE #055. BURNS ON BODY.

In 1971, southern California contactee, Dr. Fred Bell and two of his friends were victims of a crude pipe-bomb explosion. All three were injured, but Bell was thrown off his feet and onto the sidewalk where he lost consciousness. He was rushed to Laguna Memorial Hospital, in California. When he awakened, he discovered that his left hand, upper left shoulder and neck were badly burned. He also sustained a minor skull fracture and painful bruises all over his body.

Bell, however, also claims to be in contact with human-looking extraterrestrials from the Pleiades. The contacts began as a child and continued throughout his life. They have given him life-

129

saving warnings and valuable advice. They also gave him an innocuous-looking necklace called a "receptor." Bell was told that it would protect him from harm.

While alone in the hospital room, Bell felt the necklace heat up and send "marvelous energy" into his body. Within minutes, he was completely healed. His friends who were visiting him watched with disbelief. The next morning, Bell enjoyed watching the hospital physicians run a number of tests in an attempt to explain his miraculous cure.

One of the doctors told him, "This is impossible. You have no trace of the severe burns that damaged your left hand, upper left shoulder, and your neck. There is no longer evidence of a skull fracture. And what with all those bruises, eh? You were covered with bruises. Where did they disappear to?"

The doctor, Bell said, was very upset and accused him of faking his injuries. Bell did not tell the doctor about the receptor necklace, which he believes cured him using some "unknown energy."

On December 24, 1981 Bell demonstrated the proof of his contacts to a number of friends. He had been told telepathically to bring a small group of friends to a certain location near his Laguna home, so that they could witness one of the Pleiadean craft. Shortly after the group arrived, a large metallic saucer appeared, swooped low over the witnesses and sent down a shower of sparks. The craft made three passes overhead, thoroughly convincing the witnesses of the reality of Bell's contacts.[3]

The following case, published here for the first time, is the only instance of somebody healed of a sunburn. It's a remarkable account and again shows that the type of person being healed is someone doing good deeds for humanity. In this case the witness is doing profound teaching-work about human spirituality.

CASE #092. SEVERE SUNBURN.

Casey Claar was born in Las Vegas, Nevada in the mid-1960s. From a very early age she has had deeply spiritual experiences, OBEs, and ET encounters. In her life, ET and astral experiences occur concurrently and cannot be separated from each other. She consciously experiences physical contact, astral contact, and contact with the higher dimensions. She has seen various types of ETs, including grays, human-looking figures and more. She believes the ETs have been healing her and monitoring her health for most of her life.

"The most dramatic healing I have experienced--from my point of view," writes Claar, "took place when this body was fourteen [late 1970s]. I was living in Las Vegas at the time, and it was early summer. For the first time ever, my father was allowing me to go to Lake Mead with my friends for the day. It was not very good for me. I wasn't keeping a close enough eye on myself, and I returned from the full-day venture with a serious first-degree burn, full body, complicated by a second-degree burn (blisters) over a good deal of my upper half.

"I was extremely uncomfortable in my skin," says Claar. "By 6:00 p.m., I was fluxing between chills and sweats and knew this was quite serious. I knew I had to lay down and focus and not be disturbed."

After several visits from her concerned sister, Claar lay face-down on her bed and went into a deeply meditative state, moving her consciousness away from the physical body and beyond. She soon felt no pain and "went in" to the other dimensions and fell asleep.

When she woke in the morning, she had no memory of what had occurred when she went to the astral realms, which was "very unusual" for her.

"I did not surface until morning," she writes, "...when I woke...as though no time had passed, completely healed. No burn, no fever, no blisters, no scarring or peeling--no evidence at all of the night prior. Just an even, deep, dark tan, head to toe."

Although she cannot recall how the healing occurred, she feels certain that the ETs were responsible as that has been the pattern throughout her life. "When I was very young," she says, "there were also healings, from things I was too young to know about. But I was able to consciously 'shift in' always, including to the healing place."

Claar writes that the ETs have given her information about consciousness, astral travel, how to access the higher dimensions to heal herself and maintain her health. "I am being given body examinations, corrections, additions, alterations. I go astrally, etherically, and physically (at times) to the craft. Sometimes the physical body remains in the bed and work is performed right here. I am looked in on with surprising regularity. All forms of contact altering me, 'healing' me, as we might see it...I don't get sick much, or hurt. It is rare...I am helped through a good deal, taught lessons when necessary, healed/corrected when necessary. Often correction is prior to full manifestation of an effect in the physical."

Because of this type of intervention, Claar has enjoyed excellent health. She currently lives in California and runs a website forum about spirituality, astral travel and consciousness, allowing web-surfers to learn about a wide variety of esoteric subjects.[4]

This next case comes from a former southern California MUFON field investigator and medical doctor. The witness involved has been abducted on numerous occasions. Although the case does have unique elements, in most respects it fits the typical pattern of a UFO healing.

CASE #165. BURNS ON HAND AND ARM.
An anonymous southern California family has experienced countless sightings, dozens of close-up encounters and several abductions. All members of the family have had experiences, and the contacts have been ongoing for years.

Sometime in the early 1990s (date approximate), the family was driving through a remote desert area in the southwestern United States. It was a very hot day and the car overheated. The father pulled off the road and opened the hood. He then made a terrible though common mistake. While the car engine was still hot, he opened the radiator cap.

Instantly, searing hot liquid exploded out of the opening, badly burning the father's hand. The family rushed to his aid, wrapping up his hand. They quickly put more water in the radiator and drove for the nearest town. On the way there, the family was very surprised to encounter what appeared to be a hospital in the middle of the desert.

The man got out of the car and walked into the strangely located "hospital." Inside there was a nurse who said she would help him. She held his wrist and sprayed a jelly-like substance over his hand. The substance formed a layer over his hand, covering the burn. The "nurse" then instructed him not to wash his hand, and he would be fine.

By the time the family made it into town, the father's hand was completely cured. The family then realized that something strange had happened, and that the hospital was probably not what it seemed to be. They returned to the scene and were unable to locate the hospital in which the father had been cured.

The MUFON investigator who handled this case was baffled by the appearance of the hospital. He couldn't understand how aliens could convince people that they were in a hospital and not a UFO.

Actually, there are similar cases on record. One example comes from Budd Hopkins' book, *Intruders*. During one of the abductions of Kathie Davis (aka: Debbie Jordan), her only memory of the event was visiting a strange market which she thought was the local Seven-Eleven store.[5]

While the burn-healing cases are not numerous, there are enough to show that aliens have this ability. Each case also seems to show a benevolent aspect to the ETs who are performing the healing with no apparent benefit for themselves. In each case the burns were not of sufficient severity to kill the witness--some were relatively minor and would've healed naturally. And yet, the ETs intervened.

This closes the section involving healings of injuries. There are seventy-six separate cases. The people healed include men, women and children. The injuries healed range from minor to severe and include many types. Cuts, bruises, abrasions have been healed as well as incisions, puncture wounds, broken bones and internal injuries. The cases stretch back more than 100 years and come from across the world.

As the above cases illustrate, extraterrestrials are able to cure a huge variety of injuries. Another conclusion that can be easily made is that ETs must be monitoring people very closely. The fact that most of the healings occur immediately following the injury shows just how closely we are being watched.

None of the people who have been healed claim to be cured of every injury they have ever sustained. Often the witnesses are perplexed why one injury was healed and another was not. If the aliens have the ability to cure all injuries, why don't they? And why were these people cured of their injuries when other people are often injured (or even killed) with no intervention from extraterrestrials?

Unfortunately, until we have more data, these questions remain unanswered. The data shows that these cures are happening to people of all ages, races and backgrounds.

Because most people don't officially report their UFO encounters--particularly if their case involves fantastic elements such as a UFO healing--the above accounts of UFO-healed injuries almost certainly represent only a small portion of the actual number. More likely, hundreds if not thousands of cases (or more) have occurred and continue to occur.

With so many people being healed of such a wide variety of injuries, the question of whether or not these healings are actually taking place has been answered. Of course, they are. The answers as to why remain more elusive.

Part Two
Healings of Minor Illnesses and Ailments

While the healings of injuries provide a remarkable catalogue, they represent only about twenty-four percent of the actual number of cases. We have just begun to explore the healing power of UFOs.

ET healings cover virtually the entire spectrum of human medical conditions. In part two of this book, we explore sixty-seven separate cases involving a wide variety of conditions that are, in most cases, not life-threatening. Colds, flu, headaches, toothaches, stomach-aches, minor infections--most of these are easily treated, and yet, for some reason ETs sometimes find it necessary to intervene. Why ETs would fly light-years (or wherever they come from) to cure a young boy of a cold is hard to answer. But the fact is, they did...and there are many cases like this. These healing events show that no illness is considered too insignificant to receive alien medical treatment.

Again, despite the fantastic nature of these cases, they come with a large amount of evidence. Several involve very credible witnesses, professionals in the fields of law enforcement, medicine, government and more. Many of the witnesses were examined by multiple doctors and their testimonies were documented by respected researchers.

One or two cases might be considered flukes, rare outliers that almost never happen. Instead, we are flooded with cases. What is it like to visit an alien dentist or an alien eye doctor? How do ETs cure people of a cold? Why are they doing this? The answers are in the pages that follow.

Chapter Ten
Colds, Flu, Fevers and Infections

Illness is a fact of life. Nearly every one of us has suffered through a bad cold, shivered under a high fever, or struggled to recover from some type of infection or illness. While most of these are not life-threatening and can be treated at home or in the hospital, especially with the many advances of modern medicine, doctors are still unable to prevent these illnesses from occurring. There are many treatments for the common cold, but no instant cures. Modern medicine, as advanced as it has become, continues to have limitations. When surgery or drugs don't work, the options for healing through mainstream methods become limited. Often, all doctors can do is alleviate some of the symptoms.

Meanwhile, illness continues to ravage the human population. More than a trillion dollars is spent on healthcare each year. As the medical field advances, more cures are being found. Still, the cures for thousands of minor illnesses continue to elude medical professionals. And so, until the field of medical science advances further, people will continue to suffer from a wide variety of ailments. Unless, of course, they get help from another source.

This chapter documents twenty-two cases involving cures of minor infections: colds, flu, fevers, sinusitis, ear infections, yeast infections and more.

CASE #014. EAR INFECTION.

One winter in the early 1950s in New Jersey, Richard Rylka, then a young child, was playing outside in the snow with his friends. They were sleigh-riding down steep hills near their homes. While racing down the hill, Rylka was unable to steer and he crashed into a car that was driving up the hill. The driver didn't even see Rylka who was pushed under the car, thrown off the sled and knocked unconscious. By the time the driver found him, Rylka had been lying on his left side in the snow for many minutes. His left ear was badly frostbitten and he developed an ear infection which destroyed his hearing in that ear. His doctors considered performing a mastoidectomy, but instead they decided to try a new drug called penicillin.

Rylka had seen UFOs on several occasions. On a few occasions, he remembered going outside and being beamed messages from the aliens. As of yet, however, they had not visited him physically. As he recovered in the hospital, Rylka was surprised when the ETs, named Koran and Nepos, came into his hospital room for the sole purpose of healing him. The aliens were only able to affect a partial cure. Using "their own body energies" the aliens were able to get rid of the pain and the pressure. After the aliens left, Rylka was still unable to hear out of that ear. But following several more doses of penicillin, his hearing returned. This was Rylka's first visitation and first healing. Though it wouldn't be long before more followed.[1]

Jerry Wills' contact began with human-looking ETs, but it was gray aliens that actually healed him. In many cases, human-looking ETs and grays are seen at the same time.

CASE #046. FEVER.
Jerry Wills of Kentucky had his first contact with extraterrestrials in 1965, when he was twelve years old. At that time, he would stay outside night after night, watching star-like objects dart at right angles high in the sky above his house. A few months later, he had a close-up sighting of a typical flying saucer-- a hovering metallic ship with blinking colored lights.

The next year, in the same location out in the woods, he was approached by a blond-haired, blue-eyed stranger dressed in a beige jumpsuit with a silver belt. The man said his name was Zo, and that he was an extraterrestrial. So began a very complex series of contacts in which Wills was taught about science, history, philosophy, religion and other subjects. The aliens visited him three to six times a month for more than five years.

The teachings seem to have been highly effective, for Wills has invented several items including a sighting and control helmet for pilots, a virtual reality device, and a "guardian crystal" which allegedly allows its user to detect auras.

In addition to teaching him many things, Wills says that the aliens cured him when he was ill. It was nighttime around 1968 (date approximate) and Wills was in his room suffering from a high fever. In the middle of the night, the aliens came and took him inside their ship. He was surprised to see gray-type aliens. They told him telepathically to "relax and let them do their work." He was given an injection in each arm.

The next morning, Wills woke up and found that his fever was gone. He recovered completely in less than a day. Although he has not had any other cures, Willis says that he still remains in contact with his alien friends. Years later, Wills has become a psychic healer.[2]

The following case, investigated by Leonard Stringfield, illustrates one of the biggest dilemmas regarding UFO healings: why would aliens fly from light years away (or wherever they come from!), just to cure somebody of the common cold?

CASE #067. HEAD COLD.

On May 10, 1975, teen-ager, Chuck Doyle of Florence, Kentucky went outside to check his horse. Suddenly he heard a loud buzzing sound. Turning around, he saw a twenty-foot-long metallic object shaped like a "manta ray" hovering over his neighbor's garden. The object had colored lights and was emitting a green beam of light toward the ground. Chuck was so stunned by the sight that he stayed perfect still.

The beam of light began to sweep in wider circles, stopping for a moment on Chuck's pool. Then suddenly the beam swung toward him. Chuck turned to run, but he was too slow and the beam struck his entire body. "It was a straight shaft of light that didn't get wider at the bottom, like a laser," Chuck said. "then the beam came at me. When it hit me, it was like being hit by a bucket of ice-water. I felt suddenly frozen. I couldn't move."

Chuck was actually frozen in the position of trying to run away. Although he was leaning forward, he was held in position by the beam. To his surprise, a flood of strange symbols and images filled his mind. He saw mathematical equations, images of a strange planet, and a kaleidoscope of bizarre colors. Then the beam retracted and Chuck fell to the ground. The UFO disappeared with a purple flash and a loud bang. Chuck returned to his house in a state of shock.

It wasn't until he got inside that Chuck noticed something strange. Before the encounter, he had been suffering from a miserable head cold. Immediately afterward, all traces of the cold had disappeared. Chuck saw a doctor a week later, making no mention of his UFO encounter. The doctor pronounced him perfectly healthy.[3]

While most UFO healings take place onboard UFOs, some take place in very unusual locations. The following bizarre healing (originally investigated by Jan Pajak) involves multiple cures to at least four people, and took place inside a public restaurant in New Zealand. It also involves another unusual feature that turns up only very rarely: *stopping time.*

CASE #069. FLU, MIGRAINE HEADACHE.
On the afternoon of July 12, 1975, four friends (Richard, Pat, Nancy and Ross), were having lunch in a crowded coffee bar in Dunedin, New Zealand. The weather was cold and damp, and all of them were suffering from various degrees of the flu. One of them suffered from a migraine headache. There were, they estimated, about eighty people sitting at various tables around them.

As they ate together, something very strange happened. Time stopped. Everyone around them became perfectly still and unmoving, however, the four friends could still move. Richard was struck by the sight of unmoving steam above the espresso machine, and by the sight of a waitress frozen in place as she bent over an oven pulling out hotcakes.

Staring around in shock, the four of them saw a strange figure appear at the top of the stairs on the opposite side of the room, which was the only public entrance and exit to the restaurant. He appeared to be a young man about six feet tall, slender, with black wavy hair, and olive skin. He was tastefully dressed in normal clothes and seemed to have a whitish aura of light glowing around him. They watched him float down the staircase, levitate across the room to the end of the line, where customers waited for their food.

The moment the man got into the line, time began to flow normally again. The four friends watched as the people around them moved normally without any indication or awareness that something strange had just happened.

The four friends watched in amazement as the man ordered a glass of juice, sat at a nearby table, then acknowledged their attention with a smile.

The group decided to confront the man. Rather than do it at the man's table, which was difficult to access from where they were, they left the restaurant and waited by the exit for him to come out.

When he failed to appear, Richard ventured back inside only to find that he was gone. Even more surprising, the group discovered that their various flu-like symptoms, and a migraine headache, were gone.

Six weeks later, the same group of friends spotted the man at the same restaurant. He appeared at the entrance, walked lightly (and unnoticed by others) down the stairs, ordered another glass of juice, sat at a table and again smiled back at them. He was dressed the same as before, only now, his aura appeared more green than white.

This time the group was determined to confront him. When they tried, they found themselves unable to move. As if against their will, they found themselves getting up and leaving. Pat reports that she tried desperately to turn around but was unable to do so. When she finally could, she returned back shortly later, but the strange man was gone.[4]

140

Sinusitis is a well-known symptom of UFO contact. It is not unusual for people who have contact to suffer from this condition. Ironically, there are also a number of cases involving cures, such as the following well-known abduction of three people in North Dakota.

CASE #071. SINUSITIS.

On August 26, 1975, Sandra Larson, her teen-age daughter Jackie, and her daughter's boyfriend were driving near Fargo, North Dakota when they came upon UFOs and experienced missing time. Later, under hypnosis by Dr. Leo Sprinkle, she recalled that all three were taken onboard a craft where they were medically examined. "Even our heads were opened up and all parts of our brains were looked at," said Larson. "We were dissected like frogs."

At some point, one of the beings (who had metal arms and looked like mummies) stuck a scalpel-like instrument up Larson's nose. Finally they were returned.

Following the incident, Larson's sinusitis was cured. She had previously had surgery for the condition. She also felt that her awareness and intelligence had been enhanced or increased. The case is considered a classic and has been featured in more than thirty books. Following the first abduction, she had another abduction. She died on June 17, 2018 at age seventy-six.[5]

Minor infections can sometimes worsen and become quickly life-threatening. This appears to be a pattern in a number of healing cases. Infections that the witnesses initially assumed were minor, became very serious. It is then that the ETs step in to cure the condition.

CASE #102. STREPTOCOCCUS.

In the summer of 1982, thirteen-year-old "Douglas" of Willamette Valley, Oregon, was taking swimming lessons at a local public pool when he contracted an aggressive strain of Streptococcus bacteria. When his condition deteriorated, he was rushed to the local hospital, which was already overflowing with other Strep patients. Douglas's fever rose to 104 degrees, and despite antibiotic treatment, the infection spread to his kidneys, and doctors were worried he might die.

Douglas explains what happened next: "One night a creature that I at first thought was some sort of nurse came to my bedside. She wore a hooded garb like the monks of old, was round of body, and her face was this plastic-like skin...Her nose was only a V-shaped ridge. She said she had a solution to my problem, and told me to relax. Out from her left sleeve came this thing that looked like a knobby rod of brushed aluminum. She pushed the rod-like thing against me like an injection, into my left hip. I felt no needle, only something like an ice-cube being pushed against the skin."

The strange "nurse" then left and Douglas fell asleep. When he awoke the next morning, his fever had broken and his infection began to clear up. Later, his mother would also receive an even more remarkable healing by the same ETs.[6]

In a few cases, UFO healings run in families. In the following two cases, two sisters were each cured of the same condition.

CASE #132. YEAST INFECTION.

Sometime in 1988, California-based abductees, Linda and her sister, Sherri were both miraculously cured of their yeast infections. It occurred overnight, at which time Sherri had a vivid dream that she was taken onboard and healed.

Both Sherri and Linda underwent hypnosis to recall the incident. On this occasion, Linda recalled how the aliens came to take her. "They take me out the front door. There's some kind of a vehicle. It looks about the size of a car and has lots of lights, and it almost looks like glass with a bubble roof over the top. The three of us get in. They put me in the back part and we go real fast. And pretty soon we're landing in a large, large, large spaceship. It's huge! I can't believe the size. It's just huge."

Linda recalled being put on a table and cured. "They use an instrument of some kind. It looks like a big cotton ball on a stick. You know how when they take a throat culture? It's kind of like that, and they're swabbing me inside...they're cleaning it out somehow, swabbing it out. They have this jelly-like substance that looks like aquamarine blue, and it's clear, it's transparent...I told them it feels cold. They say that's to help freeze the bacteria. And then they take it out."

Linda was then given more spiritual information and was shown several other people being healed, including her sister, Sherri.

Unfortunately the cure proved to be temporary and the condition returned. It wasn't, however, her last experience with the healing power of UFOs. Later the aliens would apparently cure her of cancer. And her family, she says, have all been trained by the aliens to become psychic healers.[7]

CASE #131. YEAST INFECTION.

Under hypnosis, Linda's sister, Sherri recalled many details that confirmed Linda's memory of events. She was put on a table and a machine began to analyze her body. She was told by the aliens that they were looking to see if anything was wrong with her body. This helped to reduce her fear.

"I was lying on a table or some flat surface that seemed like it was stainless steel," says Sherri. "I don't remember any faces, but there was a doctor, or someone I perceived as a doctor, and there was some kind of machine that, I was told by mental telepathy, could analyze if there was anything wrong in my body and could also kill bacteria that wasn't good...I was being examined vaginally and it seemed like my feet were in some kind of stirrups or in something very similar to what you'd find in a doctor's office, some kind of cream was being put inside of me...It was like a cream. It was put inside of me...real deep inside of me...it was a little cold and really messy. It felt...gushy. It wasn't really cold., but I could tell that it was like a cream...they said it would take care of the yeast."

Like her sister, Sherri also saw many other people being operated upon. "I can see there's a machine over somebody, and I can see all the bones in their body through the top. It's like an X-ray, but it's fluorescent green."

She also agrees that the beings are "very loving" and totally benevolent. While both sisters did experience some fear during their recall, especially when being operated upon, both insist that the experiences are overall very positive. They both feel that they have been physically healed and given much spiritual insight by the beings. Their encounters continue. Sherri's yeast infection did not return.[8]

The Twiggs contact case is very extensive. Already we have covered a number of their healing events. The following is one more to add to the list. Flu, while usually not serious, actually kills about 3000 people annually, sometimes more.

CASE #141. FLU.

Bert and Denise Twiggs of Hubbard, Oregon had long ago discovered that they were having contact with human-like aliens from Andromeda. On July 14, 1989, Bert Twiggs was bedridden with a severe cold. Denise begged him to go to the hospital, but Bert refused, saying that he would go if he didn't feel better the next morning.

Bert went to bed, mentioning to Denise that his stomach had also begun to hurt. His cough was bad, and he had great difficulty breathing. As soon as they went to bed, they noticed strange lights in their room. These lights often appeared at the onset of an encounter. That night, they were to receive one of their most dramatic visitations.

At 4:00 a.m., Bert and Denise woke up with the memory of an alien house-call. Bert remembered the aliens arriving and being very concerned about his illness. They claimed that his condition was actually near-fatal, and that they were, in fact, saving his life. They gave him an injection on his arm and left. Only then did they allow the Twiggs to have full conscious volition. They both woke up, and Bert was not surprised to see a needle mark on his arm, exactly where he had been given the injection.

The next morning, his cold was noticeably improved, and within forty-eight hours, it was completely gone.[9]

In one of the more unusual healings on record, this case involves a man who, in addition to being healed, witnessed an impressive display of the healing power of UFOs.

Case #161. BOIL ON HAND.

On the evening of June 20, 1990, Vladimir Vasilchenko was watching TV in his home in Sochi, Russia when the TV began emitting strange noises, and the image on the screen became distorted. His dog whined and ran under the sofa. Suddenly he heard a soft hum approaching. Looking outside, he saw two beams of light hitting the ground behind his house. He heard a voice telling him to come outside. Vasilchenko went outside and saw two female figures in the beams of light. They wore gray, tight-fitting suits and large round helmets. They looked human except they had very large mouths. They appeared to be performing some type of operation or surgery on somebody who lay between them.

Vasilchenko saw that it was an old man, human-looking, except for his body appeared to be completely unformed, just an amorphous mass of flesh without legs or arms. As Vasilchenko watched, the ETs used strange-looking tools to grow limbs on the man.

Vasilchenko finally asked them who they were. One of the beings replied, "Be silent, you are interfering with our work."

Vasilchenko continued to observe until one of the beings turned and pointed to an infected boil on Vasilchenko's hand. She put her hand over the boil, then poked the boil with a hook-like instrument. She then told him to step back and remain silent.

Vasilchenko observed for a while longer, then returned inside to get a cigarette. When he returned outside, the figures and their patient were gone. He returned inside, at which point he realized that the infected boil on his hand was now completely healed.[10]

In the following case, investigated by Brad Steiger, a witness was cured of chronic sinusitis, which she had suffered from since childhood. She was also told by the ETs why they cured her, something which occurs in only a handful of cases.

145

CASE #166. SINUSITIS.

"Ann" of Chicago, Illinois, suffered from chronic sinusitis all her life, until she had an onboard UFO experience (circa early 1990s?) Ann found herself placed in a strange room where she underwent an examination at the hands of alien "doctors." She saw full-color, living X-rays projected on the wall of the room. She describes the experience in familiar terms. "The 'doctor,' who was not visible, spoke in a high-pitched, lilting, pleasant voice as I lay in a comfortable, high-tech 'dentist's chair.'"

At this point, the aliens performed a cure. "One of the alien figures standing near me placed a wand near my nose and cured my sinus condition," Ann says. "Curing my sinus problem, they said, was their gift to me of good faith."[11]

The following case is unique in that it may be the only one in which someone was cured of a harmful side-effect caused by human medication.

CASE #150. VERTIGO.

An anonymous nursing home worker from Deming, New Mexico, says that in 1989, she was suffering badly from dizziness as a side-effect of medication. The dizziness was so bad that for three months, she could only walk by holding onto furniture.

Around that time, she had a dream-like experience during which she saw four men, each four feet tall with coveralls and hoods over their faces. They were holding a "mysterious box." The witness then found herself slammed back onto her bed, and the entities were gone. She was left alone, sweating profusely in her bed. She got up and went to the bathroom. That's when she discovered that she was no longer dizzy. After she returned from the bathroom, the witness heard a heavy object strike the roof of her home and then run across it. She now believes that she experienced some type of ET visitation and that they were there to help her. Says the witness, "I think those little men took away my dizziness. I am grateful for that. I think that they will come whenever I need them."

The witness also says that she has had several UFO sightings in the past, however, as far as she knows, she has not been abducted.[12]

In 1995, I sent Dr. Richard Boylan a letter asking if he had any cases involving healings that he could discuss. The following case is one he provided. Unfortunately, the details are few.

CASE #209. YEAST INFECTION.
Writes Richard Boylan Ph.D., "I cannot release case names or identifying information. I can tell you in a general way that one woman I have dealt with had a healing of a vaginal yeast infection during an extraterrestrial encounter...." The same lady also reports a healing of cancer.[13]

The following case is a typical case of a UFO healing. With so many cases like this one, it becomes impossible to deny that ETs are sometimes here on friendly healing missions.

CASE #203. FLU.
It was the morning of September 3, 1995, and Christina (pseudonym) of Davis, California came down with the flu. She called her mother up and asked her to pick up her young child so she could get some rest. Her mother agreed, picked up Christina's child, and left Christina alone.

"I lay down on my couch," Christina says, "closed my eyes for a minute, opened them--and this being was standing over me...this being was slender, almost anorexic, [had] dark slanted oval eyes, a very slender nose, and a slender mouth."

Looking around, Christina saw that she was no longer in her home. "All I could see was white light and white walls."

The gray-type being began to speak to her. "This being didn't talk verbally," she says, "it spoke with some sort of telepathy. It told me to go to sleep, we're not going to hurt you."

The next thing Christina knew, it was morning and she was back in her home. "I woke back up feeling well, like I had no sickness at all. I think this being healed me."

147

In addition to being healed, Christina feels like the being imparted some sort of information relating to unknown "star charts" which she is still trying to understand.[14]

The single biggest determinative factor as to who is being healed and why is typified in the following case. Most people being healed have had a lifetime of encounters. While this isn't always the case, more than half of the healings occur to people who have a history of UFO contact. Yes, they are being healed. But it comes with a price.

CASE #205. FLU.

Jim Sparks, a housing developer in North Carolina, has had ET contact throughout his life. Unlike many abductees, the majority of Sparks' encounters are fully conscious, and recalled without any hypnotic regression. His experiences cover virtually the entire gamut of UFO procedures reported by various abductees, including healings.

In late 1995, Sparks contracted the flu. Over a period of a month, his condition worsened until he was suffering from coughing, fever, chills and nausea.

He was lying on the couch, feeling "like hell" when two gray aliens walked through the wall.

Anger and fear swept through him. One of the ETs projected the image of Sparks' doctor, apparently in an attempt to calm Sparks.

"What are you doing here?" Sparks asked.

"Don't you remember?" the ET asked. "I am here because of our agreement...we agreed that if ever you were to get real sick, I would come...Now I am going to examine you."

For the next few minutes, the ETs probed his body with "various instruments."

Then they stepped back and one of them said, "You have a secondary lung and throat infection as a result of the flu."

"Did you heal me? Should I go see a regular doctor, or what?"

The ETs made no response. Instead they left through the wall and Sparks passed out. "When I opened my eyes," says Sparks, "it was the next morning. I sat up on the sofa and stretched my arms. I suddenly realized I was not sick anymore. While I resist believing that the aliens would do something as helpful as healing, I cannot argue the fact that I was miraculously healed."[15]

Cases involving cures of the common cold are surprisingly numerous. The following account is typical, involving the most common type of healing ETs: gray aliens.

CASE #222. RESPIRATORY INFECTION.
"I had a severe respiratory problem in the winter of 1998," says the anonymous witness. "I had a very powerful dream of being taken to a craft by a humanoid and there being healed by a gray. I woke up coughing...I was well within two to three days. I was extremely sick and should not have recovered that quickly."[16]

If not for the fact that she had been exposed to images of ETs in the media, the following witness, who was very religious, may have concluded that she was healed by angels. Instead she decided that aliens were responsible.

CASE #230. FLU.
Sometime in the late 1990s, an elderly woman from Arkansas became very sick with the flu. Her granddaughter, Tamikea LaTrice, was a young child at the time, but she still remembers vividly what happened. One day her grandmother was sick, the next day she was healed. "My grandmother told me she was healed by extraterrestrials," says Tamikea. "It's kind of funny because my grandmother was super religious."

Her grandmother said that she found herself lying on a table. She saw her pastor there, wearing a white robe and a red stole, and there were other strange figures present. She first described them as being like "elders of the bible," but then said, "You know what they look like? What we call aliens."

149

It's a brief case, and Tamikea cannot recall any other details. Her grandmother has now passed. Today Tamikea wonders how her mother was able to reconcile her religious beliefs with her self-admitted ET encounter.[17]

What follows is a third case of a sinusitis-healing. It's also one of the rare instances in which a person asked for a healing and received it.

CASE #262. SINUSITIS.

Gwen Farrell CHT of Arizona says that she has had many benevolent encounters with ETs. Says Farrell, "Humans on this Earth have a long history of being healed by ETs, and devices are sometimes implanted into human bodies by ETs for the purpose of healing. I know this for sure because I have seen it done by ET medical teams, and that's how I came to possess my little piece of ET memorabilia."

Farrell believes that she is one of many people who have received an alien implant. "I have a long history of chronic sinus problems, aggravated by various allergens--floral and faunal--resulting in powerful headaches."

The headaches caused such severe pain and nausea that they sometimes kept her bedridden. One evening, (date not given, circa 2010?) Farrell was sitting on the couch in her living room when she made telepathic contact with her "star family"--something she had done many times before. This time, however, she asked them if they could do something to fix her painful sinusitis. "Within a moment," says Farrell, "I felt them approach and place a small device in my forehead just above and between my eyebrows. The device radiated warmth and a yellow-white light...I was told that an implant had been placed in my head and would remain there as long as I needed and wanted it. They said that the energy it radiated would prevent sinus headaches by eliminating inflammation of the tissues."

Farrell thanked them for the gift. After the experience, the frequency and severity of her sinus headaches became much less. Says Farrell, "In addition to making my life a lot easier, this experience has further convinced me of the technological abilities of the ETs, and their desire to use that technology for our benefit...How do I know for sure that it's good? I trust my people and the other healing ETs I have met and worked with...I love my implant and I'm happy to have it."[18]

ETs heal people using many different methods. Beams of light are common, as is the use of mysterious medical instruments. Surgery is sometimes used. In some cases aliens use apparent mind power. One of the rarest methods involves the use of medication, such as the following.

CASE #275. CHEST COLD.

Bus driver, Don Anderson of Utah, has had unusual UFO experiences for most of his life. As a young man he experienced repeated bedroom visitations by short beings. The visits continued throughout his life, including sightings, paranormal encounters, ET visitations, and a few onboard experiences. One of the strangest occurred in 2013, when he was fifty-three years old. He had been suffering from a persistent chest cold that just wouldn't go away. He almost never got sick, so this malingering illness was becoming increasingly worrisome. He was beginning to wonder if it might be pneumonia.

One evening he was meditating in his room when this "alien guy" appeared. The figure was almost human-looking, but had grayish skin, long hair tied up in a bun, exotic piercing eyes, and perfectly chiseled facial features. He wore a silver jumpsuit with a strange emblem on his left breast. He might have passed for human, says Anderson, except "his eyes really give him away."

"I watched him walk in," says Anderson, and it just sent shivers up my spine. It almost froze me up solid. It was really, really powerful--overwhelming."

Anderson had been visited by this being before, but never like this. Says Anderson, "He has this neon-pink vial of liquid in his hand. And he looks at me and he hands it to me, and he says, 'Drink this.'"

The vial looked like a little glass, lab beaker, containing about three ounces of the neon pink liquid. "So I drank it," says Anderson. "It was kind of a thick consistency. It didn't really have much of a taste. I just drank it really quickly."

The being took the vial and instantly vanished. Anderson was amazed, not only by the encounter itself, but by the result. "Immediately, I was better," he said. "And I never had any problems with a cold again. It's never hit me."

Anderson currently runs a website called "Shaballa," which provides deeply spiritual information to those who seek it.[19]

The following healing is one of the most recent in this book, showing that ETs are continuing to heal people on a regular basis.

CASE #289. MIGRAINE HEADACHE.

A recent example of a UFO healing occurred on December 1, 2017 in Knightsville, South Carolina. An anonymous woman was suffering from "a bad migraine," and decided to go to sleep. She was under the blanket when it happened. "I suddenly felt a finger press down on my forehead between my eyes. It wasn't a small finger."

Afraid and beginning to panic, she pulled the blanket down and reached for her phone. "When I peeked out of my blanket," the witness says, "I saw something in front of me. I could tell that there was something in front of me, but it looked like a mirage. I could see through it, but I could tell something was there...I told myself that I was seeing things and reached out my hand to prove that there was nothing there. I was wrong, and my hand grabbed onto what felt like a thin arm."

Freaked out, the witness grabbed her phone and discovered that--even though it was sitting on the charger--the phone was dead. Suddenly she found herself in a dream-state seeing a favorite TV character telling her to calm down. The witness felt at this point that she was dealing with a gray alien trying to disguise itself. She fell back into another dream.

"When I woke up again," says the witness, "I checked my phone and it was turned on, and the time was 4:00 a.m. My migraine was completely gone. The next day I felt a bit off, maybe a little traumatized. But the truth is that it was not scary. I didn't feel threatened or hurt. It just frightened me to wake up from a dream to that happening. I'm not sure how to explain it, but as soon as the finger touched my forehead, I saw in my mind's eye that it was a long grey finger, so I believe that it was a grey that visited me."

The witness wrote about her encounter in an article titled: "Healing Visitation from Grey Beings."[20]

The following undated case is yet another cure of sinusitis. The witness, Lauren Kurth, is well-known on the UFO lecture circuit. It is one of very few cases in which the ET told the witness why they healed her.

CASE #291. SINUSITIS.
When Lauren Kurth was a little girl in her home in New Zealand, she had a close-up sighting of a metallic disc. It was to be the first of many sightings and encounters throughout her life. She discovered that she was extremely sensitive to frequencies, and found she could actually feel the frequency of the planet change before a major earthquake occurred somewhere in the world.

She would often wake up with bruises and puncture marks on her body. Other times, gray-type ETs would come into her room and she would find herself paralyzed. The ETs, who call themselves Arcturans, told her that she was one of them, and that this was her first time being human. They told her that her job was to help raise her vibrational levels and those of the people around her, to help usher the planet into a new age of enlightenment.

Much of her life, Lauren suffered from sinusitis. She was always sniffling and carrying around tissues wherever she went. Then one day (date not given), she was taken onto a craft, and all that changed.

"I was taken into a craft," explains Lauren, "and I had something that some of you might think is pretty gruesome, but I had my face lasered open, and there was no blood and no pain, and they actually cleared out my sinuses for me...I actually demanded to see what was happening, and I was with the small grays and the

153

mantis and they said, they sort of argued back and forth and they said, 'No, you're not really ready to see what you're going to see.' And I said, 'Well this is my contract, and I'm in charge here, so you have to let me see what you're doing or I don't agree.' So, this is why I believe I was taken out of my body. I could actually look down on my body, and that's when I had the laser open--a big red laser came in, and no pain and no blood, and I had my nose taken back and I had my sinus cleared out."

Lauren currently works performing vibrational sound healings, which requires her to make vocal tones with her voice, something that her sinusitis was making difficult. She was surprised, however, when the ETs told her: "We cleared your sinus out so you can tone."

Following the encounter, Lauren woke up in bed and found a shiny brown burn-mark on her septum. She was, however, able to breathe clearly through her nose for the first time in years.[21]

The following case from the FREE survey is brief, but provides yet another example of the ETs' healing agenda.

CASE #296. HEADACHE.

"One day I had a bad headache...I couldn't sleep and started sobbing. Then I turned to the right and I saw a gray. He was standing by my bed. He took my headache away immediately."[22]

As we have seen, minor illnesses and ailments of many types have been cured by aliens. The cures were affected in multiple ways, but often involve the use of light beams, injections, strange alien instruments, and surgical operations. Some of the cures were verified by doctors or other credible witnesses. Despite the controversial nature of some of the accounts, the evidence that these cures take place is hard to ignore.

The question again is, why? Would ETs really travel light years to cure a person's cold? Would they really abduct somebody to cure something as minor as a yeast infection? Do they really care about a retired nurse's vertigo?

Evidently, yes. As incredible as these cases may sound, it is logical that such cures are possible. We already know that the aliens have exhibited an extraordinary knowledge of the human body. Curing human ailments appears to be a simple and routine event, often taking only minutes to perform.

Chapter Eleven
Intestinal Healings

The human body is made up of eleven organ systems that work interdependently to keep the body healthy and functional. These organ systems are integrally connected together and are vital for survival.

The stomach and intestines (large and small) are part of the human digestive system and are responsible for providing nutrients and energy to the human organism.

The list of digestive disorders is long. They range from minor conditions to life-threatening. What follows are seventeen cases of healings involving the stomach and/or intestines.

CASE #017. UNDIAGNOSED INTESTINAL HEALING.

Ellen Crystall is perhaps best-known for her book, *Silent Invasion*, which chronicled her firsthand field investigations into UFO activity primarily in the Pine Bush area of upstate New York. She was remarkably successful and was able view and photograph UFOs on multiple occasions. On at least one occasion, she saw a humanoid. Crystall began her investigations in the early 1980s after having her own sighting. However, Crystall later learned that her encounters may have started in 1952 in New Jersey, when she was only two years old, and very sick.

"I had been sick for about nine months," Crystall wrote, "but no one knew what I had. I recalled the doctors drawing outlines of my organs on my abdomen so my mother could point to the ones that were enlarging. I also remembered having to stay inside while my friends were outside playing...I asked my mother, 'What happened when I was sick? How old was I? What was going on?' She told me I was about one when I started getting sick, but nobody knew why. She gave me a long account of how I got sicker and sicker...no one knew what I had except to say that my stomach was enlarged and very upset...my parents and the doctor feared I might die because I was so much sicker. I said to my mother, 'Then what?' She replied, 'One day in April, you were perfectly fine.' It was very strange, she said. One day I was deathly ill and overnight I was completely better. She never figured it out."

Years later, Crystall was told by a psychic that she was healed by aliens who had hovered outside her home and affected a cure. The psychic provided other information that was accurate, such as the color of Crystall's house and the date of the illness.

Unfortunately, the aliens did not cure Crystall of pancreatic cancer. In 2002, at age fifty-two, after a long battle, Crystall succumbed to the disease.[1]

This next case involves a witness who had no known prior history of UFO encounters, but ended up having an experience in which he was taken to an undersea alien UFO base, eventually becoming a full-fledged contactee.

CASE #081. INTESTINAL DISEASE.
According to Swedish researcher, Alve Holmquist, his friend "Henry" suffered for years from a disorder of the large intestines which caused him considerable pain. He had the condition his entire life, and as time progressed, it worsened to the point that Henry feared he would soon die.

Henry decided to travel to the Canary Islands, which enjoyed a much warmer climate, in the hopes of improving his health. In March of 1978, he was in a rented home on the westernmost of the Canary Islands when an apparent earthquake struck. He ran outside and saw three strange lights hovering over the nearby ocean. They emitted a powerful beam of light downward and then disappeared.

Three days later, Henry was in his bedroom when a bright, glowing figure entered. The figure asked him if he had seen anything unusual lately. Henry described his recent UFO encounter. The figure replied that the lights were his craft, and that they had come to prevent the earthquake from causing damage to the island. He also told Henry, "I come to help you with your debilitating illness" and said he would return in a few days.

As predicted, a few days later, Henry was alone in his room when three figures--including the first ET--appeared. They walked up to his bed and proceeded to perform a healing on him. According to Henry, his pain instantly disappeared "as if by magic." The ETs explained that they had a base on the ocean floor, and offered to give Henry a tour. He accepted and was taken to the underwater base. According to Henry, he was taken to a dome which held--he was told--some 15,000 inhabitants. The ETs said they had a total of seven bases, and that their mission on Earth was to save humanity from destroying itself with technology. Henry says he had numerous visits with the ETs, eventually even visiting their planet.[2]

Of all the healing entities, the grays are the most common. Second to the grays, however, are human-looking ETs, such as in the following case.

CASE #163. STOMACH PAIN.
In 1987, Tatyana Grigorevna Gavrilina of Tula, Russia, had her first UFO encounter. But it was her second encounter on November 25, 1990 that changed her life. At this time, she was suffering from stomach pains. She had gone to bed as usual, but woke up when someone entered her bedroom. She saw a female, human-looking figure wearing a silver suit. Gavrilina made a sign of the cross over her body. But the woman stared at her, moved her hand palm-up toward Gavrilina, who now felt her entire body being penetrated by some sort of energy "beam." Gavrilina felt her head become numb, then her hands, and lost consciousness.

When she woke up, Gavrilina found herself sitting on a chair in an unfamiliar oval-shaped room. Several silver-suited men and women stood or sat around her. She saw a table and a strange control panel with computer-like screens. She felt lethargic and had to fight to stay awake.

Suddenly she found herself lying down on the table. One of the women told her telepathically, "Now I will check your health, examine your body, starting at the ankles." The woman used a strange device to shine a light on Gavrilina's feet and legs. Gavrilina saw one of the male figures holding a chart with a diagram and what appeared to be Gavrilina's name. She became fearful and concerned that the aliens were studying her like some sort of specimen.

The woman turned off the device and told Gavrilina that her knees were healthy but that her stomach was "in bad shape."

"Can you cure it?" Gavrilina asked them.

"To cure it, you will have to cover your eyes with the branches of a tree," the woman responded telepathically. Gavrilina was confused. She didn't understand the response, and she lost consciousness.

When she woke, she was back in the seat she had first found herself. One of the silver-suited figures handed her a box with domino-sized objects in them. The ETs told her it was "sugar fruit jelly" and that she should eat it. Gavrilina put a piece of the food in her mouth. She felt a sharp pain in her stomach. One of the figures walked over to the control panel and started pressing buttons. Gavrilina heard a loud ringing noise and lost consciousness. When she woke up, she was back in her home. The pain in her stomach was now gone.[3]

While most of the cases come from the witnesses themselves, in some instances, the information comes from an outside observer who actually watched the healing take place. The following two healings are one of several healings witnessed by one person.

CASE #134. ULCER.

California abductee, "Linda," who was cured of a yeast infection in 1988, recalls seeing many other humans aboard the UFO being operated upon by aliens. She saw one man strapped to a table with a narrow metal instrument hovering over his midsection. When Linda asked what was wrong with the man, they

159

told her that he had a stomach ulcer. They were curing the ulcer by generating energy and directing it to the proper location."[4]

CASE #135. INTESTINAL WORMS.

During a 1988 encounter, California abductee Linda saw another healing take place aboard the UFO. She saw a young girl being examined on a table by the aliens. They performed the standard physical examination and discovered that the girl suffered from intestinal worms. To cure the girl, they injected her abdomen. "It looks like a big syringe in the stomach," Linda explains. "They put salve in and carried her off the table."[5]

While most of the healings involve conditions that the witness is already aware of, this is not always the case. In the following case, the witness had no idea he was sick, until the ETs first diagnosed him, and then performed a healing.

CASE #167. INTESTINAL ILLNESS.

Bob Rylance of England had his first experience at age twelve when he woke up paralyzed and sensed a presence in his room. Afterward, he spoke to his mother who comforted him, and told him that she had also experienced the same thing.

He grew up and married, but continued to experience occasional episodes during which he would hear strange noises, experience odd floating sensations, or wake up with unexplained marks on his body. On a few occasions, he clearly recalled "little guys" coming into his room and taking him away into a small room for examination, sperm extraction or other procedures. One of these occasions involves an apparent healing.

One evening (circa early 1990s) Rylance found himself in the hands of his "little guys" onboard a craft. Instead of simply examining him, they placed a triangular grill on his stomach and appeared to be performing some type of procedure. For the first time during his encounters, Rylance felt physical pain.

The aliens spoke to him telepathically and said that the instrument was being placed on his body "to cure a diseased part of your stomach."

Tony Dodd, one of England's leading UFO researchers investigated the case and writes, "Bob's case is interesting because of the telepathic knowledge he was given that aliens were curing him when they placed the triangular grill on his stomach and caused him pain. He had no knowledge that he was ill. I have heard, from a completely separate case, a similar story."[6]

Contactees Bert and Denise Twiggs of Hubbard, Oregon, have received many cures from their alien friends from Andromeda. In fact, each member of the family has been cured at one time or another.

CASE #168. COLITIS.
Oregon-based contactee, Denise Twiggs suffered from severe colitis, which caused a section of her intestines to bleed and become badly inflamed.
At some point, (early 1990s?) her condition became aggravated enough that Denise was taken aboard the ship, presumably into the examination room, where, she says, "...they removed a section of my intestines which had been ulcerated by colitis."[7]

The following missing time encounter, researched by MUFON field investigator, L. Flechtner, contains many unusual elements, including a healing.

CASE #196. INTESTINAL ILLNESS.
It was 10:00 p.m. on July 12, 1994, and twenty-one-year-old, Jay (pseudonym), began walking to his friend's house in Williamsburg, Kentucky, about three miles away. It was a warm night, and as Jay walked down the street, a small pick-up truck came down the road. Hoping to hitch a ride, Jay stuck out his thumb. The truck pulled over. The two people inside offered to let Jay ride inside. Jay accepted the ride, but jumped into the back of the pickup instead.
Almost immediately, things became strange. "As the truck moved down the road, I looked up at the stars and saw a line of

stars," Jays explains. "Then one of the stars moved. It was like it had been hiding among the other stars. The star moved and zigzagged, and I said, *'I see you!'* I don't remember anything after that, except then being in a field with an orange craft about twenty feet in front of me."

With no memory of how he had come to be standing in a strange field, Jay examined the craft, which had a Saturn-like appearance. The actual body of the craft was almond-shaped, but it had "a wide, orange, glowing ring around it." It looked to be about the size of a semi-truck standing on end. It hovered a few inches above the ground. The pickup truck and the two people inside it were gone.

"Would you please heal me?" Jay immediately asked.

Jay explains: "I had been sick with stomach problems, and a lot more."

He recalls only bits and pieces of what happened next. "Somebody or something--I don't remember--gave me a liquid, just enough to cover my tongue, and said, *swallow.* I don't remember seeing any entity or the container the liquid came in. I did swallow the liquid, and it reminded me of a spoon, metallic tasting."

It seemed that about fifteen seconds had passed when Jay found himself in a different place. "The next thing I knew," Jay says, "I was disoriented and walking on the road again. It took me a bit to realize I was headed home."

Arriving home, Jay discovered that forty-five minutes had passed. As he reviewed what happened and realized how strange it was, he felt goosebumps and surges of adrenaline. Otherwise he felt normal.

Jay then discovered something amazing. He had no more symptoms of his intestinal illness. He was healed.

However, he soon discovered something else; the ETs had made other changes with Jay that now made his life challenging. "The good thing I was cured," Jay says, "and have never been sick a day in my life, not even a headache. The one bad side effect of the encounter is that I am so empathetic that I am housebound. I am so handicapped I cannot go out in crowds. I feel every strong emotion from other people."

Also, more than twenty years after the incident, Jay still wonders what happened to the two other people in the pick-up truck who gave him a ride on that fateful night.[8]

The following well-documented case is a good illustration of the advanced technology of the ETs. It involves what appears to be a life-saving operation. In this case, the ETs bedside manner was favorable as they communicated with the witness that they were trying to heal him.

CASE #198. INTESTINAL ILLNESS.

"David," an American electrical engineer, was abducted from his bedroom on September 12, 1994. He had no memory of the abduction at all. The only clue was a large triangular bruise on his abdomen. Doctors were baffled. David eventually elected to undergo regressive hypnosis during which he recalled being taken out of his room by gray aliens in robes, and up into a triangular-shaped craft. He was put onto a table and examined. David had the sense that they had an important job to do. "There seems to be an urgency right now for what they're doing," David says. "There is something very wrong with me...they're worried...very worried. Like they're showing me images of myself dead...with blood coming out of my mouth. Some sort of urgency!"

During this time, David felt the aliens performing complex surgery on his abdomen. "I feel like something is being pulled...uh...open. Like my abdominal area is being stretched. It's very hot like being under a very intense lamp. They don't want me to see anything. I feel a dull pain...I'm paralyzed. I'm motionless. It's like I'm stuck to a large magnet...and you couldn't move a finger if you tried...There's a hand on my forehead, covering my eyes...holding me. I feel almost as if something is stretched over it, there's no pain now, no pain whatsoever. It's just a weird feeling. Kind of like the skin is being stretched. There's no pain whatsoever...it's like the pain is being totally blocked."

David had experienced UFO encounters before and was always left feeling anxious. This encounter gave him hope. As UFO investigator C. Leigh Culver, who researched the case, writes,

"Before this episode, David had experienced some intestinal difficulties and he felt as though the beings had helped him with this in some way."[9]

While contactees are more likely than the average person to experience the healing power of UFOs, so are *friends* of contactees. Sometimes, just associating with a contactee can increase your chances of being healed, such as what happened to Craig Campobasso.

CASE #250. BOWEL OBSTRUCTION.
Craig Campobasso, a casting agent from southern California, is the author of the book, *Autobiography of an Extraterrestrial: I am Thyron*, and the screenplay adaptation of *Stranger at the Pentagon*, a book by Frank Stranges, detailing his own contacts with a human-looking ET by the name of Valiant Thor.

Stranges has reported his own healings at the hands of these human-like ETs. Campobasso was soon to become part of a very exclusive group of people: friends of contactees who receive a healing from the ETs.

While working on the film, Stranges and Campobasso became good friends, and Campobasso began to have vivid lucid dreams during which he would speak with Valiant Thor.

Earlier while writing his own book, Campobasso had dreamed about a woman who had a strong healing energy. He started dreaming about her again along with Valiant Thor and learned that her name was "Teal," and that she was a member of Valiant Thor's crew, and in fact vice-commander of the ship.

Campobasso learned of this connection when Stranges returned from one of his contacts and said, "That woman Teal said to say Hi."

One day, a few years later, (circa 2007) Campobasso suffered severe intestinal pain which increased to the point that he knew something was very wrong. He told nobody except one close friend, who drove him to the doctor. The doctor took one look at him and called an ambulance, which transported Campobasso directly to the hospital.

Campobasso was diagnosed with a severe bowel obstruction and was scheduled for immediate emergency surgery the following morning. As he lay sleeping in the hospital room that evening, something strange happened. Says Campobasso, "I woke up in my sleep and I could feel bubbles going through my intestines, and I saw and felt this woman again in my mind. When I woke up in the morning Dr. Frank Stranges was sitting at my bedside, and he said, "Teal called me early this morning, and told me that she fixed you up last night."

Campobasso knew that he had been healed. Nevertheless, doctors arrived and performed X-rays. All traces of the bowel obstruction were gone.[10]

As we shall see, the aliens are able to cure conditions which human doctors have labeled as chronic. It appears that the true definition of chronic is not "incurable," but rather, "incurable by humans." It's also well-verified in that the condition had been previously diagnosed and could not be faked. Neither could the cure. Once again, it's the healing itself that proves the validity of the case.

CASE #247. CROHN'S DISEASE.

In the mid-1990s, Chris Bledsoe of North Carolina was a highly successful house-builder with a thriving business, a wife and four children when his life was turned upside down by a devastating diagnosis. Feeling persistent intestinal pain and discomfort, Bledsoe sought medical attention. The news was bad: he had Crohn's Disease, an immune deficiency causing pain and inflammation of the intestinal system. If left untreated, it can cause a wide variety of symptoms. The causes are not fully understood, and there is no known cure. Bledsoe's condition deteriorated and he became so weak that he could no longer work and was forced to sell his house-building business. He was taking more than a dozen prescription medications a day.

"It's a debilitating disease," Bledsoe says. "You can't eat anything, nothing. It zaps the life out of me, basically it's like a cancer...For years, fourteen or fifteen years, I was very sick. I mean very, very sick, to where I took heavy loads of medication daily...If I missed a pill in the morning, I knew it within an hour or two."

On January 8, 2007, Bledsoe, his seventeen-year-old son, Chris Jr., and three adult friends from Bledsoe's business all decided to go fishing along the Cape Fear River not far from his home.

Bledsoe was too weak to go on the river and fish, so he stayed on land and walked around. He walked up a small hill overlooking the river when he saw two bright globes of light hovering in the sky. Bledsoe became scared and tried to hide. Suddenly a third ball of light appeared. He felt as though the objects were looking at him.

At this point, he lost track of time and experienced a memory lapse. Without knowing how he got there, he found himself jogging back to the river. When he arrived, he discovered that his three friends were frantic. Bledsoe thought he had been gone about fifteen minutes; in fact, it was five hours.

Bledsoe asked where his son, Chris Jr. was, and the men explained he had left two hours ago looking for him. They went hiking around and found Chris Jr. crying. He said that he had been paralyzed and held in place by two small creatures with large eyes.

They all hiked back to camp and began to talk about what happened. Suddenly one of the men pointed to the sky and told everyone to look up. At that moment, they all saw a group of eight or nine star-like objects high in the sky drop down from a high altitude and land in the forest outside their camp.

The men panicked, dropped everything and ran for their truck. As they raced away, a gray appeared and running on all fours, chased the truck. They sped up and the creature disappeared. But as they came over a crest in the road, they came upon one of the objects blocking their path.

There was a trailer alongside the road which had been occupied as they drove in. Now it appeared empty. One of the men knocked on the door to be sure, but nobody answered. At this point, gunfire came from somewhere as though somebody was shooting at the UFO, which now rose and departed. The men got back in the truck and raced home.

The UFOs appeared again, following them home. Bledsoe dropped the men off at their homes. One of the men said that he saw one of the creatures lurking in his backyard. When Bledsoe and his son finally arrived home, their ordeal continued. They encountered more gray-type ETs outside their home, accompanied by a seven-foot-tall humanoid creature. Terrified to stay in their own home, they fled to a hayfield about four miles away and slept there.

Researcher Grant Cameron writes: "It was at that point that Chris realized that he had forgotten his Crohn's medication in the house. He, however, did not feel sick anymore, especially considering it had been many hours since he had last taken a pill. He would take no more pills from that day on. The incurable Crohn's was gone."

Says Bledsoe, "I walked up on these crafts, and from that point on I've never had another [symptom], not one symptom!...I have not taken one pill since. That's the great thing...I was healed that day."

Bledsoe's encounters continued, and he says he has been given messages by the ETs to share with humanity. Bledsoe was also given prophecies of upcoming disasters, at least two of which have already occurred: an earthquake in Baja California on September 25, 2012, and Hurricane Sandy that same year.[11]

The following case is richly detailed and well-documented and seems to reveal many of the patterns exhibited in other cases, all of which point toward the alien agenda of not only healing people, but teaching them how to heal.

CASE #252. COLITIS.

On January 12, 2008, the Voronezhskiy family of Dubno, in the Rovno region of Ukraine experienced a remarkable encounter. The family consisted of 34-year-old Vladimir (a martial arts instructor and professional wrestler), his 29-year-old wife, Olga, and their three children, Vanessa (age 9), Angelica (age 8), and Arthur (age 1.) At this time, Olga suffered from chronic colitis which caused pain in her stomach area.

On that day, Vanessa and Angelica came home from a trip to the store saying that they had seen a "flying star." Their mother said they probably saw a satellite or plane, but the girls said the object was flashing colored lights, and insisted that their parents come outside and see it for themselves.

Vladimir and Olga went outside and saw the strange object, high in the sky over the nearby river. It moved and changed shapes. Olga took a picture of it on her cell phone and they went inside.

That evening in the middle of the night Vladimir was woken by a bright orange light illuminating the interior of their house. He tried to wake Olga, but she told him to go back to sleep. Then their daughter Angelica rushed into the room and woke up her mother.

Olga immediately woke up Vladimir and told him to look up. All three of them saw that the ceiling of their bedroom had disappeared or had become completely transparent. Hovering directly overhead was a huge disc-shaped craft.

Dressed in their bedclothes, Vladimir and Olga ran outside. Both found themselves paralyzed. Olga felt herself being pulled upward. Vladimir saw his wife rising to the sky and tried to catch her, but found himself suddenly inside a strange white room with his wife.

About a dozen short humanoids appeared around them. They had large heads, smooth gray skin and three fingers on each hand. They wore tight coveralls and face-masks. The only thing they could see were large black eyes. One entity was six feet tall, about twice the height of the others.

Olga was put in a chair similar to one seen in a gynecological office. Vladimir jumped up to protect his wife, but hit an invisible barrier. "What's going on?" he asked the figures.

"Nothing terrible," they replied telepathically. "Soon you will be back home."

"I'm not satisfied with that," he answered. The aliens tried to approach him several times, but Vladimir used his martial arts techniques to keep them away. Speaking telepathically with a mixture of Ukrainian and Russian, they spoke to him, asking him why he resisted. They then placed four metal rods into his chest area, rendering him totally unable to move.

Lying on the table, Olga watched as the aliens mysteriously opened up a wide incision into her abdomen. She could see the inside of her body as they poked around at various organs using strange pincer-like instruments. During this time, the figures spoke to her telepathically, calming her, asking her if she felt any pain. "We wouldn't do you any harm," they said. "We just want to look."

Olga was struck by their polite bedside manner. Afterward, they sewed her stomach up as mysteriously as they opened it. No trace of the incision was visible.

One of the ETs spoke with Vladimir, telling him that their society was a collective and each person had strictly defined social roles, and that they live largely underground. The ET said that Olga's procedure "has to be done" and he apologized for the "medical suffering." He promised them an excursion as compensation. They placed him in a smaller ship and took him to see the Andromeda Nebula or galaxy. He also told Vladimir that they are interested in humans because of their emotions.

At one point, they tried to persuade Vladimir to procreate with one of their females. He refused at first until the ET changed its appearance into that of a beautiful woman. Now, however, Olga protested. The ETs seemed confused and asked her why. She had to explain to them about her feeling of jealously.

The ETs were surprised and asked them how they survived with emotions. They told him that there was currently a war going on in space, and many other things. At some point, Vladimir and Olga lost consciousness.

The next morning Olga immediately started talking about the strange alien dream she had. Vladimir was shocked as he recalled the same exact details as his wife. Both then became convinced that their experience was a reality and not a dream.

In February 2008, Vladimir met with researcher Yuriy Stephanov who regressed him. Vladimir recalled further details about the appearance of the craft and how it is able to become invisible by surrounding itself with a layer of plasma.

Most incredible, however, were the physiological effects which resulted from the encounter. Vladimir's hair, which was going gray, turned black again, and his physical powers of endurance increased.

Olga was cured of her chronic colitis, and also acquired a unique ability. By placing the palm of her hand against their forehead for two or three minutes, she could make a drunken person sober.[12]

In the following case, the witness had experienced frightening encounters for much of her life. But after being healed, she found that her attitude toward the ETs had profoundly changed.

CASE #267. ABDOMINAL HEALING.

In 2000, Teri Lynge of Florida underwent an eight-hour-long emergency surgical procedure to fix a life-threatening condition. While the surgery was successful, she was left with a constant ache in the stomach area which never went away. Eventually she just learned to ignore it.

Then in 2012, Lynge was sleeping in bed with her husband when she woke up to hear somebody calling her name. She rolled over, opened her eyes and saw a four-foot-tall "strange scaled extraterrestrial being" standing next to her bed.

She immediately focused on its large compelling eyes, which spoke to her telepathically, saying only two words: "Be still!"

She noticed that the figure held a "strange prong" in its scaly hand. Says Lynge, "The prong he held had two different extensions on it. It was similar to a 'Y' but yet somewhat different. The upper prong was curled tightly, like a biological stem seen in nature, but its color was slightly fleshy grey. It reminded me of a tentacle from an octopus, but just curled tightly. The other lower prong had a suction type head on it and it was very thin and long...it was hard to grasp what I was looking at. I had never seen or heard of anything like it."

At this point, the ET used the instrument to cure Lynge. "Both ends of this prong," says Lynge, "were inserted into me vaginally and I felt the curled prong unravel and wrap itself around the area in my lower abdomen. It felt warm and tingly. It was almost squeezing that area that hurt for so long. The other part of the wand attached itself to me and was firmly held in place with the suction head. I could see this as I looked down at the device coming upon me. I had an extremely strange feeling with all this happening. The next thing I remember, the device was pulled slowly out and the extraterrestrial was gone."

Lynge didn't see the ET leave; he just disappeared. She was still wide awake. She turned to her husband, who had slept through the entire ordeal. Lynge had experienced ET visitations before. Says Lynge, "It is certainly a violation to us who experience these things. But tonight was very different."

She didn't wake up her husband, who was skeptical of her encounters. Instead, she lay awake in bed until morning. When she finally got up, she got an incredible shock. Says Lynge, "I noticed while standing in the shower, my pain seemed gone! That aching feeling in the lower right abdomen area was not hurting me. I wondered how this could be? Had I been healed? I felt so odd I wasn't sure if I was accurate in my assessment or not."

She knew a couple of MUFON investigators and called them up for support. She even considered going to the hospital for an examination. She felt her abdomen where she had been sore for twelve years and there was no pain. And as the days passed, the pain never returned.

Says Lynge, "For some reason unknown to me, I had been healed! But why? I have always believed in miraculous healings, but this was unconventional! Aliens? Really? I now had this to deal with. I had to accept the fact that this healing had happened. It just went against everything I believed in. Because of this healing I have had to ask many more questions of the GOD I serve. I have had to rethink all I have come to know as truth and tradition. It has expanded my understanding to say the least!"

Lynge has served as the assistant state section director for Florida, MUFON.[13]

The fact that most people don't officially report their UFO experiences shows that there are undoubtedly many more healing cases waiting to be revealed. The following case was only reported because the witness felt ethically compelled to tell the truth about ETs.

CASE #283. ULCER.

"I thought it was important to report this event because it shows that ET can do miracles," writes Yolanda (pseudonym) of Woodbury, Minnesota.

On the evening of July 27, 2015, Yolanda was in agony from an ulcer. Unable to stand the pain any longer, she decided that in the morning she would go to the hospital emergency room.

That night, at 3:00 a.m., Yolanda was woken up by two "loud claps" coming from outside. She instantly became aware of a "mechanical presence" standing in the doorway. Lying on her stomach, and unable to see who it was, she tried to turn over, but found herself paralyzed.

"I saw a beam of light scan my body," Yolanda says. "The impression I received was: 'I'm just here to do a job.'" She not only saw the beam of light moving back and forth over her torso, she could feel an "extreme pressure."

Says Yolanda, "The pressure beam continued many times until I started to fear for my life."

At some point, Yolanda fell asleep. When she awoke the next morning, she instantly remembered the event, and was convinced that it was not a dream. It wasn't long before she had even more reason to believe in the reality of the visitation. "Within thirty hours of the event," says Yolanda, "my doctor performed an Upper GI procedure and found that my ulcers had been cured...ET healed me!"

Yolanda also recalled something else strange. On the night of the healing, she repeatedly heard what sounded like a ringing cellphone off in the distance. The only problem was, says Yolanda, "there were no other cell phones in my home that could make that noise."[14]

Not all cases are well-verified. Some are brief on details and have not been fully investigated and documented. But this does not reduce their veracity. In fact, though the details are sparse, these cases show once again that healings are likely more common than most people believe. The following three cases all come from the FREE survey and have yet to be fully investigated.

CASE #297. STOMACH PAIN.
A brief undated case comes from the FREE study and appears in the book, *Beyond UFOs*, edited by Rey Hernandez. A lady who was having regular contact with ETs woke up with severe stomach pain. She kneeled down in her bedroom and prayed for help. "A blue light appeared," says the witness, "and the pain went away."[15]

CASE #298. STOMACH ILLNESS.
Another undated case from the FREE study involves a lady who suffered from a "severe chronic unknown stomach condition." One evening she woke up to find herself apparently aboard a UFO. She was lying on a silver table while a "doctor" passed a "metal-looking cylinder" back and forth over her abdomen. Surprised, the witness tried to sit up. The ETs stepped back in shock, and quickly rendered her unconscious. The witness woke up to find herself being dropped back on to her bed. A voice told her, "Stay off your feet a couple of days and rest."
"They had apparently healed me," she says. "[They] had been operating on my mid to lower right abdomen. It left a scar which I found later." The witness no longer suffered from her chronic stomach condition.[16]

The alien anal probe is just one of many medical-type procedures that ETs perform upon humans. In the following case, also from the FREE survey, they did more than just probe, they healed.

173

CASE #299. HEMORRHOIDS.

An undated case involves a lady who had already experienced many UFO abductions by short gray ETs. At some point, she developed a severe case of hemorrhoids. During this time, she experienced an abduction. As the ETs examined her, she became terrified that they would touch her hemorrhoids and cause her pain. This didn't happen, and the witness eventually passed out and was returned to her home. "The next morning when I woke up," says the witness, "those monster hemorrhoids had vanished."[17]

The above healings of the digestive system show once again how advanced the aliens are. Their ability to cure such a wide variety of intestinal disorders betrays their superior knowledge of the human body. The majority of the healing cases in this chapter involve witnesses who feel that their encounters were positive. When ETs show up unannounced and instantly heal a person suffering from pain and disease, it's not surprising that the witness comes away with a feeling of gratitude.

Most impressive, however, is the sheer number of cases. As we shall see, there are many more encounters to explore that reveal the healing power of UFOs.

Chapter Twelve
Alien Eye Doctors

The eyes are among the most important organs of the human body. Although not essential for life, over ninety percent of all sensory information comes through the eyes. The eyes are often described as the window to the soul. Even the aliens are known for their large dark eyes which seem to see right through whoever they observe.

The list of known eye disorders is long and includes conditions both common and rare. Some of the more common conditions include near and far-sightedness, astigmatism, eyestrain, cataracts, sties, glaucoma, strabismus (crossed-eyes), conjunctivitis, dry eyes, color blindness, macular degeneration, detached retina and countless other disorders including full blindness.

Because of the sensitivity of eyes and their vulnerability to various problems, ophthalmologists recommend that each person should have their eyes examined every six months.

The field of eye medicine has made many recent strides. Many vision problems can be improved or cured through the use of corrective lenses or laser surgery. Cataract surgery can be performed on an outpatient basis. Doctors have made advances in treating glaucoma and macular degeneration. Even detached retina can be fixed using lasers or surgery.

Despite all the advances, perfect vision for everyone has not occurred. Up to fifty percent or more of the world population uses (or will use) corrective lenses.

With eighteen cases, only a very small portion of the population has experienced an ocular healing at the hands of ETs. And yet, the list of cases is long and growing, and for a specific part of the body, the eyes have received a lot of healing activity from ETs.

Some of the earliest cases of UFO healings involve the eyes, such as the following two, both which occurred during World War II.

CASE #006. BLINDNESS.

In April 1945 on the island of Okinawa in the Pacific Ocean, Howard Menger (a professional painter) was on one of the aircraft that saturated the Japanese-held island with bombs. After dropping hundreds of bombs and peppering the shoreline with machine-gun fire, the Americans took control of the island.

Still the Japanese continued to attack. Some had managed to survive the bombing by hiding in caves. These soldiers continued to attack in the style of guerrilla warfare. Also a nearby Japanese-held island shelled Okinawa constantly. Although it caused little real damage, it was one of these shells which proved disastrous for Menger.

One day as he patrolled the airstrip, another shell from the nearby island fell short of its target and landed on the airstrip. Menger heard it coming, so he fell to the ground and stayed low. After the explosion, he was relieved to have escaped injury. Then he felt something hit his eye. "As I got to my feet," Menger wrote, "I felt something stinging in my right eye. I put my hand to my eye and managed to pick something out with my fingers. It was a piece of shrapnel."

Menger rushed to the medical tent where he received treatment. Unfortunately, the eye became badly infected, and before long, Menger was totally blind in his right eye.

Unable to perform his duties, Menger remained in the medical tent under the care of the overworked doctors and nurses. Despite his treatment, his eye infection worsened and spread to his other eye. Soon Menger found himself totally blind in both eyes.

He was devastated and kept the news from his family back home. This wasn't the only secret Menger was keeping. Ever since he was a little boy, he had been repeatedly contacted by human-like aliens who claimed to be from various planets in our solar-system. Through the years, Menger had many typical contactee adventures. He was taken aboard a UFO and given a tour of the moon. He was given instructions about how to build an energy-free motor. He was told many predictions which later came true. He was able to take his friends to view the ETs' craft and was provided with further demonstrations to prove the existence of his alien friends. He was even allowed to photograph the UFOs, the aliens and his trip to the moon. Many of these photographs appear in the book he wrote about his experiences, *From Outer Space to You*. Like many contactees, Menger was also healed by the aliens.

"Something happened in that hospital tent that I have often wondered about," writes Menger. "Perhaps I can never be certain."

While in the hospital, Menger was visited by an unidentified, but very kind lady. Menger asked if she was a nurse, but the woman didn't reply and instead told him that he was the one she had come to see. Menger was struck by the fact that she seemed to know a lot about him. He had a sneaking suspicion that she was one of his extraterrestrial friends sent to help him. "She assured me my sight would be restored," says Menger.

Very gradually, Menger's sight returned and he was able to behold the lady who had helped him, an "attractive woman with wavy brown hair, dark eyes, and fine white teeth." She wore the normal Army nurse's uniform.

"Although I suspected she was one of the space people," says Menger, "she never made herself known directly. Near the time of my release she said that I would soon meet a very interesting person. I assumed it would be another contact."

Two weeks later, Menger had a strong impulse to drive to a remote area on the island. He did so and there he met a human-looking extraterrestrial. The ET told him that there would soon be a terrible bomb. Although the ET didn't mention Menger's recent healing, he alluded to why it had been done. The ET told Menger, "We have been spending a lot of time conditioning you and preparing you for your work to come. We are contacting people all over the world."[1]

Remarkably similar to Menger's case is what happened to Helge Lindross of Finland. Like Menger, he was blinded as the result of artillery in World War II. And then healed.

CASE #007. BLINDNESS.

On July 7, 1944, while fighting as a soldier in World War II, Helge Lindros of Lutto, Finland was struck in the face by splinters from an exploding shell. The splinters hit his eyes, causing total blindness. Lindros visited numerous ophthalmologists, but none could restore his vision.

One evening in autumn 1945, Lindros was visited in his home by three human-appearing men wearing white robes. They examined him with various lenses and multi-colored lights and told him that he had been selected to help other people and that they would heal his blindness, which they apparently did.

When they left, they walked through the wall and were gone. Lindros's vision returned shortly after the visit. He later claimed that his arm (which had been injured by a bullet) was also healed. Lindros says he enjoyed excellent health ever since. Later, he would have further encounters with the beings.[2]

In this next case, the witness began to suffer from a rare eye disease following a UFO encounter. What is not known is, did the encounter cause the illness, or did the ETs know of the illness and come because of it? Whatever the explanation, what happened to Marianne Shenefield is a good illustration of the ETs' interest human vision.

CASE #016. STARGARDT'S DISEASE.

In July 1952, eleven-year-old Marianne Cascio Shenefield of Agawam, Massachusetts, went outside to play. She was alone when a metallic object flew overhead. A few minutes later she noticed a figure with gray skin and large, almond-shaped eyes standing next to her. He wore a metallic-looking jumpsuit, a black belt, and a silver box with colored buttons on it. Before she knew it, Shenefield was abducted.

She remembered standing in front of a screen that showed her internal organs pulsing with life. She promptly vomited on the alien standing next to her. They put a tube to her mouth which seemed to give her oxygen. After examining her, they gave her a smooth, black stone with writing on it. She was then allowed to exit the craft.

Almost immediately after the encounter, Shenefield's vision began to deteriorate. Her eye doctor diagnosed her with the genetic disorder known as Stargardt's disease, which is a degeneration of the macula. The end result of the disease is the destruction of the central vision and portions of the peripheral vision.

Twenty years later in 1972, still suffering from Stargardt's disease, Shenefield heard strange beeping sounds outside her home. She went outside and to her surprise experienced another UFO abduction. Two years later, she began hearing the beeping sound in her ears. Then on March 15, 1974, for a brief interval of only ten minutes, Shenefield's eyesight suddenly and inexplicably returned. She called the doctor who told her that she must be hallucinating as her condition is irreversible.

Following the brief period of vision, her near-blindness returned, however she now began to have vivid psychic visions. She saw formulas, equations, genetic codes, colorful geometric shapes, numbers, letters and more. Her house also became plagued by poltergeist-like phenomena. When the doctor couldn't help, Shenefield went to a priest, who was also unable to help. Finally she found a paranormal investigator and began to come to terms with her condition.

Today, Shenefield's psychic sight is very well developed and in some ways she "sees" better than the average person. She says she can see auras and can tell by the aura whether or not the person is an abductee.[3]

One of the most striking features of alien entities is their eyes. Many witnesses remark upon their remarkable penetrating and hypnotizing qualities. It should come as no surprise that the ETs are proficient in eye healings. The following case is unique in that it's one of few cases in which the ETs inquired about a condition, and then proceeded to cure it.

CASE #042. MYOPIA.

One evening in early March 1968, Ricardo Castillo Trujillo, (a janitor from Valparaiso, Chile) was in an isolated section of the city when he saw a bright glowing object making an electric buzzing noise. The object landed and two figures in metallic uniforms emerged. They appeared light-skinned and spoke in a strange, echoing voice. He was unable to see their facial features. They asked Castillo about his myopic vision and told him that they could cure his condition, which they proceeded to do. "I didn't understand them too good," Castillo said, "but the fact is that I can see real good, and without glasses."

The beings told Castillo they would return for him. Castillo's story was told in the March 18, 1968 issue of La Nacion in Santiago, Chile.[4]

Today there are more than 300 reported UFO healing cases. Among the first to be publicly revealed was the following, which involved two incredible cures to a very credible witness.

CASE #045. MYOPIA, RHEUMATISM.

As reported by pioneering UFO researchers, Ralph and Judy Blum, on December 9, 1968, an unnamed Peruvian customs official saw a UFO outside his home. It was hovering at a high altitude and appeared to be disc-shaped. As he watched the object from his terrace, it emitted a long, thin beam of light. Before he could react, the customs official was struck on the face by the "violet rays that it emitted." While in the beam, the official was unable to move.

Before the encounter, the anonymous official suffered from severe myopia that caused him to wear thick glasses. However, after the encounter, he was able to see perfectly without glasses. Even more amazing, the man had suffered from rheumatism, but after being struck by the beam of light, his rheumatism was gone.[5]

180

Brazil has a rich history of UFO encounters, including many cases of healings. This next case, from Brazilian researcher, Mario Rangel, is interesting because it raises the dilemma of who is being healed and why. In this encounter, the recipient of the healing is a nine-year-old girl.

CASE #077. IMPROVED VISION.
In 1976, "Dirce" (a nine-year-old girl from Brazil) was performing poorly at her school. Her parents were mystified until one of Dirce's teachers discovered the culprit: Dirce's eyesight. It was so bad that Dirce was "almost blind." Her parents took their daughter to three different doctors. To treat her bad vision, the doctors recommended a special pair of eyeglasses, which they had to order from Japan. Before the eyeglasses arrived, something incredible happened.

It was around 7:00 p.m. one evening and Dirce went out to the backyard to feed the family's large dog. Without warning, a strange-looking, six-foot-tall being appeared. Dirce and the dog were unable to move. The being shone a light on Dirce. Following the incident, Dirce went back inside. Within a half-hour, Dirce's poor eyesight was cured.

Six years later, the case was investigated by Brazilian researcher, Mario Rangel, who later wrote about it in his book, *Sequestros Aliengenas*, *(Alien Abductions.)*[6]

UFO encounters can result in injuries, and they can also result in healings. There are a number of cases in this book, such as the following, in which people have been both injured and healed as a result of an encounter with ETs.

CASE #078. IMPROVED VISION, DEAFNESS.
In 1964, chicken and cattle farmer, Jose Benedito Bogeo (age 39) underwent elective nasal surgery to alleviate severe head pain. The surgery successfully stopped his headaches, however, it also resulted in total deafness, and a degradation of his vision, forcing him to wear thick glasses to see.

Bogeo married and had four young children. However, tragedy struck again in 1973 when his wife passed away, leaving him to care for his children by himself.

Then, around 1:00 a.m. on July 10, 1977, Bogeo was walking to his home in Pinheiro, Brazil, when a sixty-foot long, V-shaped craft appeared overhead and began to follow him down the road. The craft sent down a beam of orange light.

Bogeo, who carried a flashlight, turned it on and pointed it at the craft. Instantly, a powerful beam of light shot from the craft, striking Bogeo and knocking him unconscious.

When Bogeo awoke, he found himself on what appeared to be another planet. He was being held in a large room and observed by normal-looking people, except that they all looked extremely similar and were dressed identically in grey and brown clothes. When Bogeo left the room, he was surprised to see unusual transportation devices, including twenty disc-shaped objects landed on the ground. Bogeo was led into one of the crafts, at which point, he again lost consciousness.

When he awoke, he found himself alongside a highway, eight miles west of Sau Luis. He was more than seventy miles from where he had been first abducted.

Following the incident, Bogeo suffered from terrible pain in his lower back and right side, and for eight days, he had no appetite or energy, and used a cane to walk for nearly two months.

Before the incident, Bogeo needed strong eyeglasses to see clearly. "But it wasn't until I got home the next day," says Bogeo, "that I realized I lost them. Since then, I haven't needed to wear glasses anymore..."

Bogeo also reported a slight improvement with his hearing. Following the incident, he could hear loud noises, such as car horns, barking dogs, telephones ringing and people shouting. While the improvements appeared to be permanent, in the mid-1990s, Bogeo was in a severe car accident. He was knocked unconscious and hospitalized. When he woke up forty hours later, his eyesight had degraded, and once again, he was totally deaf.[7]

A third Brazilian case involves a healing that *almost* took place, but then there was a minor complication with the patient.

CASE #084. EYE INFECTION.

According to the *Centro Paraibano de Ufologia*, one evening in 1978, an anonymous gentleman from Jao Pessoa, Paraiba, Brazil woke up in bed to see two beings (not described) standing next to his bed. One held a crystal vase filled with blue liquid. The entity told the anonymous gentleman that they wanted to cure him of a festering eye problem. The witness, however, was terrified and reportedly refused treatment, at which point the humanoids walked through the wall and vanished. While a healing didn't actually take place, the ETs did make the offer.[8]

We have already examined several healings involving the Twiggs family. Here is another to add to the list.

CASE #148. STY.

In December 1989, Christopher, the son of Bert and Denise Twiggs of Hubbard, Oregon, was taken onboard a UFO along with his family. The reason for the visit? Christopher had developed a sty in his eye. Denise knew about the sty and planned to take Christopher to the doctor the following day. However, the Androme doctors beat her to it.

Christopher was sent to the alien examination room for treatment. Writes Denise, "After a trip to the medical room aboard ship, his eye was nearly healed the next day."

Both Denise and Bert had already received healings. This was Christopher's second healing. Earlier, he had been treated by the aliens for asthma.[9]

In the following two cases, it was the results of a dramatic eye healing that confirmed to the witnesses that they were having actual encounters. When confronted with indisputable medical evidence, witnesses and investigators alike are forced to face the fact that something is going on.

CASE #178. IMPROVED VISION.

Beth Collings of Virginia experienced alien abductions throughout her childhood. As an adult, she continued to be bothered by memories of abductions. In 1987, she met Anna Jamerson and began working at her horse farm. The two ladies didn't know it, but as children, they had both been abducted and brought together. When they met, they both felt like they knew each other. It wasn't until much later that they discovered their shared childhood abduction.

Meanwhile, Collings was still having additional encounters. In December 1992 she experienced a terrifying missing time abduction. She saw a "low flying aircraft," her car engine shut down and a bright light shone down. Collings remembered being "frozen to the spot." Her next memory was of racing home, realizing that she had lost an hour or more of time.

Almost immediately afterward, she noticed something strange. Prior to the experience, she suffered from poor vision. Afterward, her vision had changed for the better. "The first thing that I noticed from that first experience," says Collings, "was that my contact lenses appeared to be missing from my eyes, and I certainly had them in when I was driving."

Collings realized that her vision had improved dramatically. She eventually sought a UFO investigator and underwent hypnotic regression to recover her memories and discovered that she had a long history of encounters, some of which were extremely unpleasant, involving painful examinations and procedures. After one abduction, the aliens placed her outside her home on the ice, instead of back in her bed from where they had taken her, causing all the skin on the bottoms of her feet to be badly frostbitten. She is not happy with the ETs and calls them "little gray shits."[10]

CASE #179. IMPROVED VISION.

Anna Jamerson (owner of a horse farm in Virginia) was surprised by Beth's encounters, and even more surprised that her friend's eyesight had improved as a result of the latest experience. At the time, she had no idea that she herself had been abducted as a child and was soon to have another abduction. In fact, she would never have considered the possibility that she was also having experiences if not for one inexplicable fact: a miraculous cure almost identical to Beth's. "My eyes had improved dramatically," says Jamerson, "and I could think of no other rational explanation why my eyesight was improving unless I too was being abducted."

Anna underwent hypnotic regression and discovered that she had, in fact, been abducted on several occasions. During one abduction, the ETs chided Jamerson for her diet. "I have memories of the gray ones putting a patch on my chest (between the collarbones), and I watched, fascinated, as it was absorbed into my body. I remember being told that I must not eat fat because my fat-to-muscle ratio is out of balance." At the time, Jamerson was having trouble digesting fatty-foods, which caused her stomach pains. She had lost fifteen pounds as a result.[11]

Color blindness is a condition that effects about five to ten percent of the population. Men are diagnosed twice as often as women. In the following case, an abductee's color blindness was cured as the result of an alien eye operation.

CASE #169. COLOR BLINDNESS.
One case from the 1990s (date approx.) comes from respected UFO researcher, John Carpenter. The witness, Eddie, is a 21-year-old man from the midwestern United States. Carpenter was seeing Eddie regularly to conduct hypnotic regressions in order to investigate Eddie's many encounters. During one of Eddie's contacts, he was healed.

"During a physical examination by the beings," Carpenter writes, "Eddie's right eye was removed. He felt it pulled out and replaced. Afterward there was a redness, a physical soreness. He did not feel they were implanting anything behind his eye, only that they were 'fixing' him. The side benefit of this operation appears to be enhanced colors. The procedure was clearly for their purposes, not for Eddie's, but the partial accidental cure of his lifelong color blindness was a side-effect."

Carpenter further substantiated the healing by obtaining a statement from Eddie's eye doctor which said that Eddie suffered from "profound color blindness," and that after his experience, his vision "had improved up to green color blindness."[12]

We have already seen that ETs are proficient at healing injuries of all kinds. The following injury case could have been more properly categorized in part one of this book, but as it involves the eyes, it seemed more appropriate to include it here. The ideal UFO healing case would involve a credible witness, a trained observer, willing to allow their real name to be used, with a medically verified condition, who then had a healing, which was also medically verified. This next impressive case fulfills all those conditions.

CASE #233. TORN CORNEA.
Originally from Santiago, Cuba, Alberto Fernandez moved to Florida where he joined the army, then became a police officer and later, an agent for the Federal Drug Enforcement Administration. Throughout his life he experienced numerous UFO and entity sightings, with one particularly dramatic encounter with a gray alien.

In 2001, at age fifty-six, Fernandez suffered a fall, causing multiple fractures to the orbit of his right eye. Emergency room doctors treated the injury and recommended that Fernandez visit an ophthalmologist to assess his vision.

At the time, Fernandez and his wife were preparing for a long ocean cruise with their family, so he decided to forgo any further doctor visits and go on their vacation.

Although the swelling reduced, Fernandez's vision remained severely impaired. He went to visit the ship's doctor, who was shocked by the injury and wanted to evacuate Fernandez from the ship by helicopter.

Fernandez refused and they completed the cruise. Three weeks later, they returned to their home in Florida. Fernandez went to the eye doctor. The diagnosis was a torn cornea. The doctor treated the cornea, but told Fernandez that he would likely have a permanent loss of vision and develop glaucoma. His condition would necessitate regular treatment.

Five days later, Fernandez awoke to sense an alien entity in his room. The entity shone a bright green, laser-like light into the injured eye. The green light flashed multiple times, then stopped. The entity left.

The next morning, Fernandez was delighted to find that his vision was now perfect. There was no sign of any injury. Fernandez returned to the eye doctor for an examination. The doctor was shocked by the healing, and said that Fernandez's eye was now normal. Four years later, Fernandez would experience an equally dramatic healing of cancer.[13]

The following case provides a vivid description of what it's like to be healed by ETs, and to have further interactions with them. It's also a good example of someone who has come away from her experiences with a positive viewpoint toward ET encounters.

CASE #240. IMPROVED VISION.

In her online article, "My ET Eye Healing," contactee Alison Anton writes of a remarkable conscious contact with healing extraterrestrials. Early one morning in January 2005, Alison was woken around 4:30 a.m. to see images of mantis-like beings around her. Suddenly she felt a strong energy or force pulsing through her body. It didn't hurt, but felt strange and uncomfortable. The next thing she knew, she was looking at an orb about eighteen inches in front of her face. There was a light inside the orb. "The light," writes Alison, "was going right through my eyes and into my brain. They said to look at the light and not look away. 'Hold there.'...there was a lot of pressure in my eyes and a remarkable emotional response that made me nauseous."

They gave her the following message: "Make sure you look into the light every morning and every night." Alison woke up feeling like she had surgery, with a headache and a soreness in her eyes. However, she now believes she was healed. "I think this healing was to help me physically with my eyes, but also to help me with my clairvoyance."

Alison has had many other encounters. She writes, "I've had other ET experiences where I remember seeing the inside of my bloodstream, and even the insides of my organs and cells, magnified and projected in a way that I could see it for myself. The ET doctors would relay with me what they thought was happening...I'm pretty sure that I have implants inside my body that allow ETs, humans and human-hybrids to study my physical health, as well as how my body responds emotionally and energetically to stimulus...In any case, I don't mind...they seem to make themselves available to me too--to help me heal, grow, learn and to expand my mind."[14]

Night blindness, also called nyctalopia, has a number of causes, from poor diet, stress, eye diseases, old age and more. It involves the inability to see clearly in poor light conditions, particularly nighttime. In most cases, it's not serious, but can be an indication of an underlying condition. In the following case, ETs provided a treatment.

CASE #251. NIGHT BLINDNESS.
On the evening of January 10, 2008, an anonymous witness (who suffered from poor night vision) was driving westbound on Highway 160 out of Las Vegas, Nevada when he noticed two bright lights ahead of him. Although the sky was completely overcast and it was a very windy day, the witness assumed the lights were landing lights on an aircraft.

As he approached, more lights became visible, making it clear that the object was not a conventional aircraft. He drove directly underneath the object as it hovered low over the highway.

As he drove by, he pointed the UFO out to his wife, who showed no interest. The sighting itself was very brief, lasting only a few minutes. However, following the incident, the witness experienced a peculiar after-effect.

As he writes, "On the drive back to Tecopa I was astonished to find my night vision was restored. The halos I'd become used to seeing around oncoming headlights were gone and I could actually see the road ahead as the headlights passed. It lasted only a week or so, but *man*, that was a great thing. I don't know for sure that it was associated with whatever it was I saw in the sky, but I do know that my vision immediately after I saw the lights was a whole lot better than before."[15]

The above healing of night blindness may be the only one of its kind. This next case is also unique, and involves a very unusual alteration to the vision of the witness.

CASE #277. VISION ALTERED.

On October 4, 2014, a man was visiting his friend in Colorado Springs, Colorado. He smelled the odor of ozone and was puzzled as the sky was clear. He went outside around sunset, and after looking around for a while, was surprised to see a bright star-like light darting around in the sky at about 50,000 feet altitude. At one point it flashed bright, disappeared and reappeared in a different location. It repeatedly began to flash, disappear and reappear. The man called for his friends to come outside, but was able to persuade only one of them who came outside, looked at the object and said, "I don't know what it is."

The object stopped blinking, hovered and began to zigzag. The friend became frightened and ran back inside and refused to talk about it. The main witness stayed outside and watched as the object darted a few minutes longer, then began to move away. It was quickly intersected by a second object, both of which moved off into the distance. "The whole event seemed to take only about seven or eight minutes," says the witness, "but when they were gone, I went in and discovered nearly an hour had passed." He later found out that other people in Colorado Springs had also reported UFOs on the same night.

Weirder events were to follow. Says the witness, "For several weeks, a strange effect on my eyesight was very noticeable. Occasionally I could see for miles with almost binocular-like vision."[16]

The following recent case, published here for the first time, shows how some witnesses develop a benevolent relationship with ETs.

CASE #285. GLAUCOMA.

In 2013, Sonya (pseudonym) noticed her eyesight was worsening. She went to the eye doctor and was diagnosed with glaucoma. She was forty-six years old. The glaucoma caused her optic nerves to become thin, resulting in a deterioration of her field of vision.

Sonya was married, and both she and her husband had a history of UFO encounters. One evening in 2015, Sonya and her husband decided to go camping in the woods behind their home in rural western Maine. That night they kept hearing strange chittering noises in the forest.

They wondered if it might be related to the husband's contacts with ETs. He attempted to make a "mental connection" with the aliens and ask them to heal Sonya, who was dealing with chronic pain issues and glaucoma. Neither were sure if anything would happen. The aliens, however, were apparently listening.

"I slept on the ground inside a sleeping bag," explains Sonya. "In the middle of the night I awoke hearing what sounded like insect chatter above my head. This was like nothing else I've ever heard in my life. It was as if there were large insects that were talking to each one another. I know that sounds strange, but it's the best description I can come up with."

Sonya was lying face down. When she heard the strange chattering noise, she remained perfectly still. Without warning, she felt a strange vibrating energy strike her. "What I felt was a rotating force above the back of my head, ending in a zap in the center of the head, seemingly between the two hemispheres of the brain and in the general area of the optic nerve."

Afterward, Sonya noticed a dramatic improvement in her field of vision. She went to her eye doctor for tests. "My left optic nerve grew thicker, and I had the best visual field test in years, which astonished my ophthalmologist. After two years of a thinning optic nerve, it had grown thicker after the event!"

Sonya reports having ET visitations in her home, some of which involved healing events. Some of these were recalled as lucid dreams, or felt interdimensional. In one incident, Sonya reports the ETs were able to relieve her temporarily of chronic pain. "One time I was in bed," Sonya explains, "and I felt a slight vibration throughout my body. The pain goes away, and I realized I was getting another healing. It focused on my left hip area. When it was done, I felt as if a silky bedspread was being pulled out quickly from under me. When it went past my feet, I automatically sat up straight and there was a green alien."

The figure was bald, with large blue eyes and green skin. Sonya saw that her bedroom was gone and she now was in a small pinkish room. The ET stood in a low rounded doorway. Feeling no fear, Sonya told the ET, "You're cute."

"Then he did this funny quick walk to the side and returned with yellow eyes, which I didn't think were as nice."

Sonya reports other experiences. "They've done a lot of work on my brain, have worked doing some kind of energy healing throughout my body and have also focused on my knees, and my left breast and lymph nodes, which had a small suspicious spot that the doctors had been monitoring."

Sonya's encounters have been overwhelmingly positive. "It's been the most wonderful experience in my life. I've even told them that they've brought me a lot of joy...I'm seeking an on-going relationship with them to understand things better."[17]

We have already examined sixteen cases. That ET eye healings are actually taking place is difficult to deny. Another case came to light as a result of the FREE study.

CASE #304. DETACHED RETINA.

A woman who was having regular encounters with gray ETs asked them to heal her husband. The ETs took her husband onboard a craft and affected three healings--one of which was a detached retina.[18]

The above ET eye healing cases provide impressive proof of the validity of UFO healings. At least three of them come with before and after diagnoses by medical professionals. Those who are skeptical of UFO healings have to explain how the witnesses were cured of irreversible conditions such as color blindness, or how someone can experience a spontaneous healing of a devastating injury to their cornea, or be cured of glaucoma.

While the motives of the ETs remain a mystery, many of the witnesses feel blessed and consider the ETs their friends.

Chapter Thirteen
Alien Dentists

Few people enjoy going to the dentist, and yet we all know how important it is to keep our teeth healthy. Teeth are part of the integumentary system. Care of the teeth is a multi-billion-dollar industry. Dentists, orthodontists, oral surgeons, and other doctors spend many years studying how to diagnose and treat a long list of dental conditions.

The list of ET dental healings is surprisingly short, containing only about five cases. We've already examined a few cases of multiple healings, some of which involved teeth.

The following three cases, while few in number, provide some remarkable evidence of the reality of UFOs and extraterrestrials. This first case, from Argentina, remains one of the best-verified UFO healings on record.

CASE #058. NEW TEETH.
On December 30, 1972, nightwatchman Ventura Maceiras of Argentina saw a bright light hovering above his home. Inside the light, he could discern a metallic craft with portholes. And through the portholes, he saw humanoid figures. At this point, Maceiras was struck by a "brilliant flash of light" which shot out from underneath the craft.

In the weeks following the encounter, Maceiras suffered from symptoms typical of radiation sickness including hair-loss, headaches, nausea, diarrhea, eye irritation and "swollen red pustules" on his neck.

Doctors were baffled, but when Maceiras told them of his UFO encounter, they had no choice but to believe him. His symptoms simply could not be faked. Besides, there was more evidence to support his story. The tops of the Eucalyptus trees were scorched where the object had hovered. Maceiras' cat disappeared in front of his eyes when the beings came out of the craft. Forty-eight days later the cat reappeared with severe burns on its back. Finally, an abnormally large number of dead cat-fish were found in a small stream at the location of the sighting.

In fact, there was so much evidence that Maceiras' case attracted a lot of official attention. In less than a month, Maceiras was interviewed more than sixty times by many officials including doctors, police, government officials and UFO researchers.

Maceiras took weeks to recover from his injuries caused by the UFO. Then, less than two months after the encounter, came the final but most unbelievable symptom of all. Verified by numerous doctors, engineers, police officers and UFO investigators, Ventura Maceiras, although seventy-three years old, began to grow his third set of teeth.

UFO investigator Pedro Romaniuk was assigned to the case because of his credentials as a former commander with an international airline and technical investigator for the Argentine Air Force Aviation Accidents Investigation Board.

Romaniuk performed a follow-up visit to Maceiras, to check on his new growth of teeth. "Since approximately February 10," said Romaniuk, "Maceiras has observed that new teeth have been appearing in his upper left gum. At the time of my visit, I was able to confirm that two front teeth and two cheek teeth were coming through and were approximately two millimeters to three millimeters long."

In a later second encounter, Ventura Maceiras was approached by one of the beings who began to communicate telepathically. The being (described as short, with small facial features and fine hair) said his name was Arnoil and that he came from a planet called Prunio. He said the history of their civilization stretched back more than 14,000 years. Arnoil showed Maceiras a book which appeared to show surgical operations. They told him that cancer was a virus and could be cured.[1]

Journalist and UFO researcher, Bob Teets, (author of *West Virginia UFOs*) reports on the case of Daniel D., from Harrison County, West Virginia. It is one of a small number of cases in which a person asked for a healing and received it.

CASE #170. IMPACTED WISDOM TOOTH.

Daniel D. of Harrison County, West Virginia, says that he has had many contacts with "gray guys" and "tall green, lotus-looking figures." He believes the aliens are friendly. "They've never hurt me," he says. "That means a lot."

Daniel has other reasons to believe the ETs he's in contact with are friendly. One day, (early 1990s?) they healed him at his own request. "I think they've helped me in certain ways," he explains. "I've heard for years that I have to have my wisdom teeth out. One day they were bothering me really bad, and I was in no financial situation to get them fixed, no insurance. That night I was abducted."

During his abduction experience, Daniel telepathically asked the aliens if they would fix his teeth. They speedily obliged.

"I can remember," says Daniel, "it felt like they were stuffing things on my teeth where my wisdom teeth are. The next day they didn't bother me anymore and haven't bothered me since. This was a couple of months ago."[2]

A surprising number of people who have been healed are themselves doctors, including the following case, from the files of FREE, which again provides impressive evidence of the healing power of UFOs.

CASE #274. WISDOM TOOTH SURGERY.

In 2013, an anonymous physician from the United States had his right lower wisdom tooth surgically extracted at the office of an oral surgeon. After being sent home, he discovered that the hole left by his now absent tooth was continuing to bleed profusely. He called for advice and was told to apply pressure with gauze. He followed this advice, but the bleeding continued.

Feeling light-headed and clammy, he knew he should call for medical attention. Instead, he passed out in his bed.

He woke up to find himself being pulled out of his bed by a beam of light, and up into an apparent UFO. He was in a small circular room with a transparent floor, through which he saw many stars and a small distant Earth. With him in the room was a short, stout gray alien with large dark eyes.

The doctor passed out. When he woke up, he was back in his apartment. All traces of his wisdom tooth extraction were gone. There was no bleeding and he felt perfectly healthy.[3]

While dental healings are relatively rare, they once again betray the ETs' interest in and knowledge of the human body. We have not yet evolved a technology that can regrow human teeth. Apparently, the ETs can do this, and more. The ET healing technology appears to be incredibly advanced, able to cure minor problems such as tooth pain, or to completely regrow new teeth. As we continue our examination of the healing accounts, there appears to be no part of the human body that they have not studied and cured.

Chapter Fourteen
The Integumentary System

Of all the organ systems in the human body, the largest is known as the integumentary system. This includes primarily hair, skin, teeth and nails. Like all organ systems, it is vulnerable to a number of illnesses.

Extraterrestrials, as we shall see, have performed some of their most remarkable cures in this area. The following seven cases show the same patterns as the others. There are sightings, beams of light, onboard experiences, face-to-face encounters with large-eyed humanoids, operations and more. As one continues to objectively examine the ET cases, it becomes clear that healing is part of their agenda. How else can one explain the huge number of healings of virtually every part of the human body?

The following case is brief, but provides a good introduction to the healing of the integumentary system.

CASE #039. SKIN CONDITION.

At 7:40 p.m., February 21, 1967, Mrs. Wolfe (a nurse from Toledo, Ohio) was driving through town when she came upon a UFO described as an orange-yellow flattened sphere. The object hovered at treetop level and was sending down a wide beam of light. Mrs. Wolfe reports that the strange craft began to pace her car, at which point her speedometer and wristwatch both malfunctioned.

Following the incident, Wolfe told investigators that as a result of her close encounter with the UFO, her skin condition [not described] cleared up.[1]

This next case involves a young woman who experienced a close-up sighting with a group of eleven people. All of them were deeply affected by the encounter, including, in her case, a physical healing.

CASE #100. ECZEMA.

On the fourth of July weekend in 1982, Mattie (pseudonym), an aspiring actress from Los Angeles, California, joined a group of eleven friends on Catalina Island for a three-day-long annual campout at Blackjack Campgrounds located in the wilderness toward the center of the island.

On the evening of July 3, the group of eleven friends had just set up their tents when three hovering lights appeared. The witnesses, including Mattie, all gathered to watch. The three lights hovered for a while, then began to flash beams of light between each other. Mattie and some of the others became frightened and retreated toward the actual campsite. No sooner had she reached her tent when the three lights began to release four or five objects, which now began to fly around the campsite, sometimes approaching closely.

Suddenly there was a loud roar. Two military jets appeared overhead, chasing the UFOs away. The entire group was left traumatized and amazed. (see my book, *Undersea UFO Base*, for a full presentation of the incident.)

Shortly following the experience, Mattie quit her job in the entertainment industry, left her husband and became an alternative healer and astrologer. She also received an apparent healing. "It did blow open my psychic and spiritual doors," she said. "It changed my life...it sent me on a whole different path." Prior to the incident she suffered from severe eczema. Afterward, it cleared up and never returned.[2]

In most cases, moles are not dangerous, though some changes in moles may provide an indication of melanoma or skin cancer. Otherwise, they are simply growths of skin with a darker appearance. It is worth noting that in some cases, such as the following, ETs seem to take a particular interest in skin moles.

CASE #101. MOLE.

In August 1982, farmers Carl and Dagmar R. of northeast Iowa were in their home when they saw a strange light in the sky. In the days that followed, the couple found several circles of burned grass about thirty feet in diameter. One evening, Dagmar saw a figure with a strangely-shaped head and large eyes out in the field.

In October, Carl was outside when he saw the same strange light overhead. At 3:00 a.m. the next morning, he was awakened by his cattle bellowing. Looking out the window, he saw a landed disc-shaped object glowing with green light. He woke Dagmar in time to see three entities enter through the bedroom door.

The two were quickly taken inside the UFO. Both underwent a physical exam and had reproductive material removed. Dagmar also remembers her hair and fingernails being clipped. She was rubbed with a strange lotion. Shortly later, she was alarmed to detect the odor of burning flesh. To her surprise, the aliens were removing a mole under her left arm. A short time later, the young couple was returned to their home. The next morning, they remembered only parts of their experience, though their memory returned naturally after a few days.[3]

The following well-known case provides a good example of who is being healed and why. It is also a particularly well-verified case as the witness is highly credible, and his multiple health improvements have been verified by many witnesses.

CASE #125. INTEGUMENTARY SYSTEM.

Late in the evening of March 20, 1988, professor of Indian Studies at the University of North Dakota, John Salter, Jr., (born in 1934) and his son were driving near Richland Center, Wisconsin, when they both experienced a typical missing time UFO abduction.

Later under hypnosis the standard scenario of an alien physical examination was unveiled. Salter and his son were able to corroborate each other's testimony. They both recalled being

199

placed on a table, surrounded by gray-type ETs who injected their bodies with long needles.

Neither men felt any fear and likened the experience to a doctor's visit. Almost immediately after the encounter, both men--but especially John Jr.--experienced a large number of physiological changes.

Salter used to smoke a pound of pipe tobacco every week. Following the encounter, he slowly lost his desire to smoke and by May, he had stopped smoking completely.

Other changes were also immediately apparent. In fact, Salter reports that he had physiological improvements in more than eighteen areas.

Some of the more significant changes are "improved skin tone, circulation, eyesight, faster blood-clotting after cuts and scratches, and faster and thicker growth of toenails and hair."

Salter also reports other improvements. As he says, "...many facial wrinkles have disappeared and my skin is much healthier; some scars have disappeared and others are fading; my face has narrowed and my neck has slimmed (as has my entire body to some extent) and none of this has involved 'sagging.' My circulation has improved. Cuts clot immediately and heal very quickly; my energy level is way up; and I've had no colds or flu or any other illnesses since March 1988."

There were other changes. "My immunity is heightened... Some of my age spots have disappeared...Also, hair has developed all over my arms, legs, stomach and chest, which were almost hairless." Salter and those who know him have no doubt that these improvements are taking place, as the improvements are obvious. "After all these years," says Salter, "I have a five o'clock shadow."

Perhaps the most startling physiological effect was that following the experience, Salter grew two inches in height and his feet grew several sizes.

John Salter III also reports that his cuts heal at a very rapid rate.

In his seventies, in 2003, he was diagnosed with systemic lupus, which he says, he has successfully defeated. Writes Salter, "To come to the point directly: extremely comprehensive blood tests have indicated that I no longer have any signs of active SLE (systemic lupus) within me."

Throughout his eighties, Salter (who goes by the name: John Hunter Gray) continued his work as an award-winning social worker. He also lectured at UFO conventions across the country about his experience. He passed away in January 2019.[4]

This next remarkable case, from researcher Diane Tessman, betrays the ETs' interest not only in the health of humans, but in the health of plants.

CASE #144. WART.

On September 4, 1989, farmer Jan DeGroot of Amsterdam, Netherlands, returned to his home to find one of his greenhouses glowing with a strange light. He parked his car and approached the greenhouse and found a "large flat-topped disc" glowing with green light parked behind the greenhouse.

Suddenly Jan was approached by a human-looking man with dark hair and straight features, dressed in a dark-colored jumpsuit. The stranger told Jan that his tulips were being over-watered.

Jan's next memory is waking up the next morning with the feeling that his encounter was probably more extensive than he remembered. He instantly went to the greenhouse where he found a leak in his irrigation system, proving that the tulips were being over-watered.

He also received further evidence of his encounter. For many years Jan had lived with a very large wart on his neck. The ugly wart had been there for so long that Jan was accustomed to it. It wasn't until the day after the encounter that Jan made a remarkable discovery: all traces of his wart were gone. He attributes the healing to his encounter with the UFO.[5]

This next case is a vividly described account from respected researcher, Constance Clear M.A., M.S.W. Once again, it presents the enigma of a witness who experiences both injuries and healing as a result of an encounter.

CASE #213. MOLE.

"Andrew" was born in 1936. But it wasn't until 1996, at age sixty, that he began to investigate his UFO encounters. He had been suffering from depression, anxiety and terrifying nightmares. He contacted researcher, Constance Clear, and using hypnosis, looked into multiple bizarre incidents in his life, each displaying the markers associated with possible UFO experiences.

His first recalled encounter was in 1942, at age six, in San Antonio, Texas. A large group of gray beings entered his home and took him into a craft via a beam of light. Onboard, he saw many other children of different races being examined. Andrew was subjected to a long and sometimes painful examination, and was returned to his home.

This began a lifetime of abductions, each of which was shrouded in amnesia. Under hypnosis, he recalled many other onboard encounters, which almost always involved very uncomfortable and painful medical procedures.

The encounters were so unpleasant that Andrew became resistant and uncooperative during the events, which confused the ETs. They seemed not to understand his fear and anger, and told him that the procedures needed to be done.

On the morning of October 6, 1996, Andrew woke to find his knees hurting and a rash along the lower part of his body. Even stranger, a large mole on the left side of his head was missing.

Andrew scheduled a session with Constance Clear. Under hypnosis, he recalled that a gray being entered into his bedroom. The being took him through the wall and into a small domed room. Inside the room were additional grays and medical equipment.

Andrew became afraid he would never be returned, and one of the grays told him not to worry, that they would return him. The gray said that they had taken humans away from Earth before, and they had not survived.

They undressed Andrew and placed him next to one of the medical devices. It reminded Andrew of an "iron lung," but it turned out to be more akin to an X-ray machine, displaying the inner workings of his body on a screen. He was then placed before the second piece of equipment: a step-stair-like device with weird lights and a container of blue liquid. The ETs instructed him to watch the light and remain still.

Afterward he was dressed and returned home. "The next morning," writes Andrew, "I was combing my hair and I noticed that a mole that I'd had most of my life was gone. It was approximately one-fourth to three-eighths inches in diameter...located on the right side of my head...Later when I saw my barber, he noticed that my mole was gone. I told him I'd had it removed. I did this because I can't trust many people."

Following the incident, Andrew suffered from a headache, sore knees and a rash, and he had alternating bouts of constipation and diarrhea for about one month. Later, Andrew would experience another healing involving a kidney stone.[6]

While many cases of healings involve actual abductions, some cases, such as the following, seem to be caused by the mere presence of a UFO. It is also possible the witness experienced missing time, and is unaware of it. In either case, it appears that the witness was targeted.

CASE #224. MOLES, SPIDER VEINS.

On December 29, 1999, Natalie (pseudonym) was driving down 13th Street in Denver, Colorado on her way home when she saw a strange-looking object hovering very low in the sky ahead of her. It was rock-still, with two blue lights on either side, and a red light in the center. It couldn't be a plane, because the lights were too still. It must be a helicopter, she thought. Then she drove under it, and changed her mind.

"As I passed under the object, I saw a grayish-black, boomerang-shaped object. My mouth hung open, and I said aloud to myself, 'What in the #@*!% is that?'"

She wanted to slam on the brakes and jump out of her car, but seeing other vehicles behind her, she turned off at the next street, pulled over and got out. Only thirty seconds had passed, but the object was now gone. She pulled a U-turn and kept looking. She turned around a third time, but the object was nowhere to be found.

Convinced she had seen a genuine UFO, she reported her sighting to NUFORC, and to a MUFON investigator. Not long after the sighting, Natalie began to exhibit a number of remarkable medical symptoms. Says Natalie, "About two months after my encounter, all of the moles on my body began to fade, then completely disappear. To date, five moles have completely disappeared and nine more are in different states of fading. About five months after the event occurred, all of the hair on my arms and legs began to change to light blonde."

Normally Natalie had brown hair. She thought perhaps she was turning prematurely gray, but she's only twenty-nine years old. The hair changed color from the root upward, turning from brown, to reddish to blond over a period of about five days. The hair also became much finer.

Natalie had suffered from spider veins in her legs for several years. "About two months ago," she says, "my spider veins in my legs began to fade. Now one that I have had for about five years is completely gone, and another is fading rapidly."

Then came the "dreams." Says Natalie, "Since this has occurred, I have had 'dreams' almost nightly of entities who talk to me and claim to be an intelligent species from somewhere else. They keep trying to give me strange information I don't understand. I have woken up a few times and caught myself uttering some language that I have never heard before. But I have ruled out speaking in tongues because this 'language' seems to have structure and form."

Natalie has also noticed other changes. "Throughout the day I have feelings of hot and cold in different parts of my body. I get pulsating feelings on the bottom of my feet and up my legs and down my arms, and on the palms of my hands. Sometimes this pulsating becomes so intense, it is painful. I have also felt this heat/pulsating feeling right below my eyes, between my eyes, and in the front of my brain. I am very upset and confused as to what is going on with me."

Natalie is hoping to work with more investigators to deal with the after-effects of her encounter.[7]

So closes the chapter on the integumentary system. Once again, we are confronted with a continuing stream of healing cases. Excising a mole may not require ET technology, but the fact that there are multiple mole-removal cases betrays their interest in moles. It appears that in some of these cases, the bodies of the witnesses are being altered in ways that affect multiple organ systems and the entire body chemistry. The ETs' advanced understanding of the human body reveals not only their medical superiority, but our own ignorance. With ETs knowing more about the human body than we do ourselves, how can we even begin to explain or understand what they are doing? The fact is, however, healings are being reported, and the evidence is showing us that these cases are real.

Part Three
Healings of Serious Illnesses & Diseases

In part three, we begin our exploration of the more serious and chronic conditions that have plagued humanity for millennia. And as we shall see, the ETs have worked very hard to heal a wide variety of conditions. We shall explore healings of various vital organs, including the liver, the kidney, and the heart and lungs. We shall examine healings of infertility, arthritis, diabetes, muscular dystrophy, multiple sclerosis, polio, hypertension, tuberculosis, ...the list goes on. Cancer is, of course, included on this list, as is AIDS, and virtually all the other top ten killers of humans, including suicide.

While cures of minor conditions are impressive enough, the healings in this section are mostly chronic conditions, diseases that are beyond the ability of humans to cure, diseases that millions of people die of each year.

There are 122 cases of healings of serious and chronic illnesses. This doesn't include the cancer cases, of which there are forty. This means that fifty-two percent of the cases in which ETs have intervened to heal someone involved conditions that are serious, chronic or life-threatening.

This section not only provides convincing hard evidence of the veracity of UFOs and extraterrestrials, it reveals how truly advanced the ETs are, and what exactly their agenda is on this planet.

Chapter Fifteen
The Liver

The liver is a vital organ, meaning we can't live without it. It performs many essential biological processes, detoxifying wastes, synthesizing proteins, producing hormones, regulating glycogen, storing bile for digestion, storing vitamins and more. It is present only in vertebrates and is the largest glandular organ in the human body. This chapter covers five documented cases of liver healings of various types. The first case comes from a young girl in California, whose encounters were investigated by Edith Fiore Ph.D.

CASE #029. LIVER.
As an adult, abductee Linda X of California was healed aboard a UFO of a yeast infection. As a child, she had her first healing. Linda fell down and damaged her liver. This left the organ very weak and vulnerable to dangerous infections. As a child this caused her many health problems. Unknown to her at the time, (circa 1950s) Linda was being regularly treated by the extraterrestrials.

Under hypnosis she was surprised to find out that they had been caring and administering medicine to her for a long time. As she says, "…over the years they have been slowly refurbishing, just as if building, like building it up. The salve penetrates the whole body and generates new cells that will fight the infection and in turn will give new life in my body."[1]

This next case is perhaps the best-documented of the liver healings. It occurred to a UFO investigator whose illness was previously diagnosed by doctors. He continues to be active in the UFO field.

CASE #040. LIVER.

On December 7, 1967, Danish UFO investigator Hans Lauritzen and four friends were conducting an active field investigation of UFOs. Their research had led them to participate in routine sky watches in the hopes of observing a UFO close-up. Lauritzen had reason to believe that he might encounter a UFO in the near future.

One month earlier, Lauritzen had been contacted by a Swedish girl who told him that he was on the list of the Space People as one of the people to have a contact. However, sitting out in the field waiting for a UFO was particularly difficult for Lauritzen as he was suffering from an illness that made such work very tiring.

In February of 1966 while in Africa, Lauritzen had contacted severe liver hepatitis and had to retire and go on a pension. At the time of the UFO watch, Lauritzen was not only tired and weak, his liver was ten centimeters increased in size.

Just before ending the sky watch on December 7, the five men were surprised to see two "great, dim, yellow globes about a hundred yards away from them." Lauritzen immediately became hypnotically entranced, walked away from the group and had a telepathic communication with the UFO occupants. The conversation was about helping humanity. Lauritzen was told he had great power to help people.

After an hour, Lauritzen suddenly came out of his trance and heard his friends calling. He ran toward their voices and was surprised to find that he didn't even feel tired. As he says, "I ran and ran so fast that my four friends could not follow me. I had to wait for them. I realized that I had been cured of my hepatitis."

Lauritzen went straight to the doctor. Says Lauritzen, "I passed a medical examination, not mentioning my contact, of course, and to the surprise of the doctors, ten centimeters of my liver had disappeared so that it was now normal size. The blood test showed that it functioned now as any other healthy liver...before I had a sick liver. At one time it was as much as sixteen centimeters too large. Now I have a healthy liver. I am most thankful to the UFO for curing my otherwise chronic disease...I swear to God that I have told the truth as far as I can see it."[2]

One or two liver healing cases could be considered a coincidence. But there are many. This next encounter resulted in several different types of physical evidence, including a healing.

CASE #054. LIVER DISEASE.
At 1:00 a.m., March 5, 1971, Gilbert Camus (a radio technician) was driving to his shop located in Savigny, France. He was between the towns of Trenal and Condamine when he saw lights ahead of him on the road. Slowing down, he saw that the lights were attached to a metallic dome-shaped craft about fifty feet wide and twenty-five feet high. The craft had landed along the highway.

Camus was shocked to see three giant-sized, ant-like creatures crawling up the embankment. Alongside the object landed in the field, he saw about twenty additional figures, some standing up, others crawling around.

As he tried to drive past them, his car was struck by a blue beam of light and he lost control of the vehicle. The car slowed to about twelve MPH until it was suddenly released. Shaken, Camus continued on his journey.

When he arrived at his destination, he discovered several golden-yellow, rectangular-shaped marks below his waist. The marks quickly faded away. However, Camus also found weird marks on his undershirt. The paint on his car seemed to be affected and began to peel off. In an effort to understand what happened to him, Camus contacted investigators.

Examining the location of the encounter, investigators found a large imprint of crushed foliage where Camus had seen the craft land. It also appeared as if a large portion of dandelions had been picked from the field, where they also found large footprints, some measuring sixteen inches long.

Most amazing, however, was that Camus had been cured. Prior to the incident, Camus suffered from a liver ailment which gave him excruciating pain. Following the incident, his headaches stopped, and his liver ailment was apparently cured.[3]

The following brief case comes from researcher Brad Steiger. Because of his many years of research into UFOs, he has received reports from all over the worlds, including a liver healing from Finland.

CASE #171. ENLARGED LIVER.
A native of Finland suffered since birth from an abnormally enlarged liver. He had been told numerous times by doctors that his condition was chronic. Then, in the early 1990s, he was skiing down a mountain slope in a remote area when he was struck by a "white beam of light from an egg-shaped UFO." After the light left, the man realized he had missing time. He went to a doctor for an examination. It was then that he discovered the impossible; his liver was healed. As the report reads, "During this examination, the doctors found that his liver had been reduced to a normal size.[4]

In a small number of cases, people receive treatment for conditions they didn't even know they had. The following case is a good example, however, in this instance, the witness later received independent confirmation of the diagnosis that was given to her first by the ETs.

CASE #239. LIVER HEPATITIS.
In the early 2000s (date approx.), Dr. Alicia Flowers Ph.D. (also a UFO contactee) of Oakland, California, went through a three-year-period during which she experienced frequent abductions, some of which appeared to be for healing purposes. Says Flowers, "At times I received a treatment. Once a black box was placed at my feet and another placed at my head. A blue, lightning-like spark passed through my body. I was told I was receiving treatment for hepatitis--something I never knew I had. I

got myself tested and found there were indeed antibodies to hepatitis."[5]

As the above accounts show, liver cures are being reported by different people from across the world who have no knowledge of each other's accounts, and yet, their stories are remarkably consistent. Over and over again, people report sudden and total reversals of their illness after a close encounter with a UFO.

The conclusion is inescapable--UFOs are actively healing people, and have been doing so for a very long time. For those who believe that one or another of these cures are due to misdiagnosis, hoaxes, natural spontaneous healing or some other conventional explanation, there are always more cases to challenge their skepticism. To ignore evidence due to a prejudiced belief about how aliens should or would behave is wholly unscientific. The true scientist remains objective, examines the data and puts forth a hypothesis. And when it comes to UFO healing cases, the results speak for themselves.

Chapter Sixteen
The Kidneys

The human body contains two kidneys, glandular organs composed of tiny tubes lined with cells which separate water and waste products from the blood. Their main function is to secrete urine from the body. Like the liver, they are vital organs, without which the human body cannot survive.

The ETs appear to know all about the kidneys. As the nine cases below will show, ETs are able to cure a wide variety of kidney maladies. The cases date back to the 1960s, and have been occurring regularly ever since.

Most of the cases are verified by doctors who examined the patients before and after their encounters, and are unable to account for the spontaneous and seemingly miraculous healings.

Case #037. KIDNEY STONES.

In December 1965, Swedish construction worker and rock-blaster, Richard Hoglund, encountered a landed UFO and humanoid aliens near the town of Uddevalla. It was an icy cold morning, and Hoglund--feeling restless--decided to take a drive to nearby Grind Hult Lake. At the time Hoglund was sick from kidney stones and was scheduled to have surgery the following day. He had suffered from the condition for fifteen years.

Hoglund parked the car by the lake and began to walk along the ice-covered surface with his dog, Lizzi. He heard a strange whining sound above him, and looking up, saw a metallic craft descend and land next to him on the lake. Moments later, an opening appeared and four figures floated down from the craft and levitated a few inches above the ice. Looking more closely, Hoglund saw that the figures were human-looking, except that they were completely hairless, had smooth unblemished skin, large unusual eyes, perfect teeth, pointy ears and were wearing transparent plastic-like body suits that did little to hide their bodies. Each also wore a strange black bracelet with a yellow button on it. According to Hoglund, there was an older man, two boys and a girl.

Hoglund thought at first that they were foreigners, maybe Russians, until they approached him and he realized that they were not normal humans. They seemed very friendly and curious and began to communicate with him through gestures and sign-language. They were particularly interested in Hoglund's thick hair on his head.

Hoglund approached the ETs and tried to touch them, but each time, they backed away. As they tried to communicate, Hoglund indicated that he was experiencing pain in his kidney. The ET man returned to the craft and exited holding a microphone-like object about three inches in diameter. He moved behind Hoglund and pressed the instrument against Hoglund's back. Hoglund felt a strange "force" enter his body, at which point, his kidney pain disappeared.

Afterward, they talked a bit longer and then the ETs returned to their craft, which promptly departed the area.

The next day, Hoglund showed up for his surgery at Uddevalla hospital in Sweden. As is standard procedure, immediately prior to the operation, he was X-rayed. The X-rays showed no trace of the kidney stones, a fact confirmed by Hoglund's physicians, Dr. Hartman and his colleague, Dr. Karl Erik Svensson. Later Hoglund would experience another healing encounter during which he was healed of an apparent brain tumor.[1]

Removal of kidney stones is the most common kidney healing treatment performed by the ETs. Of the nine kidney cases, five involve this particular condition. The following case, like Hoglund's, is also verified by physicians and presents remarkable proof of the veracity of these types of cases. It's also one of several cases in which aliens entered into a human hospital room to affect the cure.

CASE #041. KIDNEY STONES.

In 1967, Ludwig F. Pallman was hospitalized in the Maison Francais Hospital of Lima, Peru. Ludwig was experiencing severe pains that were diagnosed as kidney problems. Several years earlier, in 1965, Ludwig was traveling through Europe. His career as an international health food processor and distributor made him, as he says, "a perpetual globe-trotter." While in India, he met a normal-looking gentleman named Satu Ra.

After several weeks of friendship, Satu Ra told Ludwig that he, Satu, was actually an extraterrestrial. Although initially skeptical of such an outrageous claim, Ludwig was soon given reason to believe. Satu actually invited Ludwig aboard a UFO. Ludwig, of course, accepted.

Like most contactees, he was told many things. And like many contactees, he later received a healing. He was in the wilderness in Lima, Peru when his kidney pain first appeared. He sought treatment and was happy to be in the Maison Francais Hospital, which was well-known for its expert doctors and modern equipment.

The doctors told Ludwig that he would have to undergo an operation to alleviate his kidney pain. Ludwig agreed as his fever was getting worse and the pain had him totally incapacitated.

While in the hospital, Ludwig awoke one night to find a visitor in his room. He recognized the person as Xiti, Satu Ra's sister, whom he met earlier aboard the UFO. Xiti wasted no time and immediately began treating Ludwig for his condition.

She began by passing her hands over his body. She then gave him a small pill to eat. Then, as quickly and mysteriously as she arrived, Xiti departed.

Within minutes after her administrations, Ludwig's condition made a complete reversal. He was instantly free of pain and his fever broke. As far as he could tell, Ludwig was completely healed. The doctors were called in, and were stunned. They realized that Ludwig was completely healthy, but could not explain why.

This case is well-verified by doctors, who knew that Ludwig should have been on the operating table. "All of this may be checked by any of my readers," writes Ludwig. "I became the miracle patient of the famous Maison Francais Hospital in Lima, Peru."

Ludwig had been scheduled for his operation that morning, so when the doctors examined him and found him perfectly healthy, they demanded he undergo a whole battery of tests. The tests verified the obvious, that Ludwig was perfectly healthy. As one doctor told him, "You're fit as a flea...this is really baffling. Yesterday you were a very sick man, and today you seem to be a different person."

Ludwig never had any more problems with his kidneys. He did have several more contacts with his alien friends and wrote a book about his experiences.[2]

The following encounter is one of the best-verified early abduction cases. It contains a surprising amount of physical evidence, not to mention outside witnesses who observed the UFO which abducted the witness and healed him.

CASE #066. KIDNEY STONES, TUBUCULAR SCAR.

On October 25, 1974, oil-field worker, Carl Higdon, of Rawlings, Wyoming was out hunting in the wilderness of the Medicine Bow National Forest. To his delight he saw five elk. He raised his gun, aimed it at a large buck, and fired. To his utter surprise, the bullet floated slowly out of his gun and dropped to the ground about fifty feet away.

At this point Higdon noticed that he had a visitor. He saw a six-foot-tall man with yellowish skin, no neck, no visible ears, small eyes, a slit-like mouth, straw-colored hair and two antennas coming out of his head. Like many aliens, the man was dressed in a one-piece jumpsuit with a large belt.

The stranger gave Higdon some pills and encouraged him to swallow one, which Higdon did. His next memory is being inside a strange craft, strapped to a seat. A helmet was placed over his head and strange images filled his mind. He saw futuristic cities and other bizarre structures.

Next, Higdon underwent a physical examination. He also saw three other normal-looking people aboard the UFO, as well as several animals, including the elk. Shortly later, Higdon was set back down. He radioed for help and blacked out.

Search parties were sent out. They found Higdon's truck mired in a field several miles from its original location. Also some members of the party saw unexplained lights hovering high in the sky. Higdon was finally found. Only under hypnosis was he able to recall what he saw aboard the UFO.

Prior to his encounter, Higdon suffered from a persistent and painful case of kidney stones. After the encounter, however, his problem with kidney stones was gone forever. He was completely healed.

Higdon also had a tubercular scar on his lung which disappeared. He attributes both healings to his encounter.[3]

Puerto Rico is a well-known UFO hotspot, producing a large number of close encounter cases, and consequently, many healing accounts. The following Puerto Rico case also provides a good description of the baffling alien technology that is often seen in healing cases.

CASE #083. KIDNEY DISEASE.
Around 10:00 p.m. on the evening of July 17, 1978, Carmela (pseudonym) and her family were preparing for sleep in their home in Cayey, Puerto Rico. Suddenly a bright light shone through the window. Carmela's husband went to check on their children, while Carmela stayed in the bedroom alone. Suddenly she saw two four-foot-tall figures at her doorway. They had large heads, huge dark slanted eyes, two tiny holes for a nose and a slit for a mouth. They wore tight-fitting silver suits.

One of the beings approached Carmela and touched her, causing her to relax. The being led her outside her home and into a hovering craft. Inside she saw a metallic hallway, and was led into

216

a stainless-steel-looking room where she was placed on a cot. A strange instrument with a screen dropped from the ceiling enabling Carmela to see all her organs inside her body. The humanoids pointed to the screen and then placed a strange box-like device with multi-colored lights on Carmela's head.

A taller human-looking being with dark hair, almond-eyes, and wearing a silver uniform came in. He proceeded to conduct a full medical examination, including taking samples, and talked extensively with the witness. The being told her that she had been cured of her kidney disease, and then gave her a dire warning about the future of humanity. She was then returned to her home.[4]

While the majority of healing cases seem to come from people with a history of UFO encounters, this is not always the case. In this next case, investigated by Virgilio Sanchez-Ocejo, the person who was healed had no prior contact with UFOs, but he was good friends with a UFO contactee.

CASE #093. KIDNEY STONES.
In August 1980, Hector Vasquez of San Juan, Puerto Rico was awakened at 2:00 a.m. by severe side pains that had previously been diagnosed as kidney stones. Hector knew that he would have to go to the hospital, so he sent one of his children to get his friend, David Delmundo, to drive him.

Delmundo is an ordained minister and also a contactee. After seeing many UFOs, he had a face-to-face encounter with a short almond-eyed, figure wearing a jumpsuit, who said he was from the Orion star cluster. Thus began a complicated series of contacts. Delmundo had received no healings of his own, so he had no reason to expect that his ET friends would assist his Earth friend. When he heard the news about the illness, he jumped up to drive Hector to the hospital.

On the way to the hospital, however, they had a close-up encounter with an "orange glowing luminous disc" which could be seen hovering above the road ahead of them. It then flew alongside the car, paralleling its course. Then it flew back in front of the car in a strange darting pattern. Vasquez was lying in the back seat, doubled up with pain, and when Delmundo said a UFO was hovering outside, Vasquez didn't believe him. Delmundo insisted Vasquez look, and to his surprise, Delmundo was right. By the way the object was moving, it was very clear to both men that the UFO was very interested in them.

Both of them wondered why the UFO was moving so strangely around the car. By the time they had made the twenty-minute drive to the hospital, they had their answer. Hector's crippling pain was completely gone.

Still fearing another attack of pain, Vasquez insisted upon a medical examination. The doctors checked him out and pronounced him in perfect health. His previously diagnosed kidney stone was nowhere to be found.

On the way home, the two men again saw the same object that had hovered around their car earlier. Hector Vasquez believed that he was healed of his kidney stone by the UFO. As of yet, he has had no recurrence.[5]

In the following case, the witness was not only healed, but was given information about the ETs' activities and their agenda on our planet. Once again, there is a human medical diagnosis showing that something strange occurred to the witness. This case also shows how witnesses can be spiritually transformed as a result of their encounters.

CASE #107. KIDNEY DISEASE.
From the case files of Canadian researcher, Chris Rutkowski, in early 1985, Veronica lived next door to a hydro station in the suburbs of Toronto, Ontario in Canada. One morning a few hours before sunrise, she saw a craft land in the back alley near her window.

Suddenly human-like figures appeared and took her out the window into a long, black limousine, which made a strange "whooshing" sound.

Next Veronica found herself apparently onboard the craft. The ETs said they were only going to examine her, but then proceeded to perform surgery to remove her eggs, Veronica believed.

At the time, Veronica suffered from a painful kidney problem that her doctor said required surgery to fix. The ETs apparently agreed and performed surgery on her kidney, putting in an implant to ease her pain.

The ETs showed her a room filled with tanks, each containing a human body at some stage of growth. They told her that it took them four days to grow a fetus to adult-size, but the body contained no "spirit." Veronica complained about the process, but the ETs told her that humans treat animals similarly. They lectured her about the way humans "spill or waste our seed, pollute our atmosphere and treat others with disrespect."

At some point during her experience, Veronica was looking at the human-like ETs, and realized that their human appearance was an illusion. Instead, she saw them as typical grays, with the large, bald head and large wrap-around eyes.

Following her experience, Veronica initially kept quiet about it. She went to her doctor who told her that there was a foreign body showing up in the ultrasound readings of her kidney. The object however, disappeared and was apparently flushed out through her urinary tract. As a result of her experiences, Veronica became a part-time minister and a vegetarian. She later went public with her account.[6]

Occurring the same year as the above account, the following Canadian case is brief, but it illustrates once again, the wide variety of ETs who are performing these healings. It's not just grays, mantids, Nordics and short humanoids. Instead we are confronted with a seemingly infinite variety of humanoids.

CASE #108. KIDNEY INFECTION.

One evening in the summer of 1985, a woman from Vancouver, British Columbia, Canada was suffering from pain due to a kidney infection. She decided to meditate to relieve her pain when a tall humanoid appeared suddenly in her room. Without warning, she found herself inside a circular room surrounded by

219

several seven-foot-tall humanoids with blue eyes. She lost consciousness and when she woke up, she was dismayed to find mysterious blood-stains on her bedsheets. Later, she discovered that her kidney problems had vanished.[7]

This next kidney healing case, from researcher Constance Clear, involves a witness who already received a healing involving the removal of a mole. This case also provides a wonderful description of alien technology, detailed enough that the human doctors involved in the case were not only impressed by the healing, but by the witness's description of the alien equipment used to affect the healing.

Case #214. KIDNEY STONES.

"Andrew" of San Antonio, Texas has experienced a lifetime of abductions, most involving unpleasant and sometimes painful medical examinations. In October 1996, he experienced a procedure in which a mole on his face was removed. A few months later, Andrew experienced a persistent pain in his side and went to the doctor. His doctor ordered a sonogram and confirmed the presence of a kidney stone. Andrew was scheduled for treatment.

On the evening of December 27, 1996, Andrew's kidney stone was bothering him so he placed a heating pad on his back and went to bed. Around 2:00 a.m., he woke up feeling burning pain on his side. Thinking he burned himself on the heating pad, he got up and applied some Aloe Vera.

He went back to bed. Suddenly, he found himself encased in a beam of light with a gray alien standing next to his bed. The ET explained that they had just taken him and were now returning him to his bedroom. The being said that they felt bad because they had accidentally scratched Andrew's body.

Andrew fell back asleep. When he woke up, he saw a large red welt on his side. One month later, on the evening of January 26, 1997, a gray appeared in Andrew's room and began to examine Andrew in his bed. The being looked at Andrew's side, and said that the previous procedure hadn't worked. There had been a malfunction, and they would have to take him back into their craft.

Next, Andrew found himself aboard the craft. Andrew was undressed. The gray applied a strange gel to his body, and a patch around his side where his kidney was, and then placed him in a plastic-like, floating bubble. Below his body was a strange piece of equipment. It was square, with a round dome on top and a telescopic-like laser. Andrew watched the gray turn on the machine. The dome filled with electric sparks, and a beam of light shot out from the telescope-part and shone on the patch on Andrew's side.

The being told Andrew that they've been working with his kidneys because they found something, but they don't know what it is. He said that they thought everything in their body served a purpose, and wanted to know the purpose of the stone in his kidney, and if it was part of his "filtering system." Andrew told the gray that the stone served no purpose. The alien was confused and asked him how he got the stone and would it harm him if they removed it. Andrew told them that the stone was not necessary and that it would hurt more if they *didn't* remove it.

The gray then attached a tube to the patch on Andrew's side and removed the stone. He warned Andrew that he would experience some pain for a while but that it would fade away, and that there would be no markings. He was then returned to his home.

Andrew woke with vague flashbacks of being inside a UFO and encased in a plastic, bubble-like container. His side also felt painful. He scheduled an appointment with Constance Clear, and under hypnosis, the above scenario emerged.

Andrew drew the medical device he had seen which had cured him of his kidney stone. Writes Clear, "At last Andrew had derived a benefit from one of his encounters. The kidney stone his doctor had previously confirmed with a sonogram was gone without a trace."

Following the event, Clear showed Andrew's drawing of the alien medical equipment to a radiologist. Writes Clear, "He was intrigued with the medical equipment. When he saw the box with the dome that the aliens used to remove the kidney stone, he said, 'That's *Litho Tripsy*.' He went on to explain that we have portable

221

and fixed units, which focus an ultra-sonic wave to shatter gallstones and kidney stones. He said we've had this technology for about ten years, and that the beam has to be very carefully aimed."[8]

One of the biggest mysteries surrounding UFO healings is who is getting healed and why? If ETs have the power to heal people, why do they allow so many people to die of conditions that they could easily cure? This question is not easily answered. In most cases it appears that the healings are on the aliens' terms and not our own. However, there are exceptions. There are a number of cases, such as the following, in which people have sent out powerful prayers asking for a healing, and then received one. It appears that the aliens are not only listening to our prayers, sometimes they answer them.

CASE #245. CHRONIC RENAL FAILURE.
It was July 2006, and Ms. E.A. Sabean (from Canada) was having a very bad year. Her father had just passed away, and now she was feeling very sick herself. She was exhausted and sad. Then her feet started to swell. As the weeks passed, her feet remained swollen, and the inflammation spread up her legs and her lower back. She felt nauseous, weak and had stopped eating, drinking and was unable to urinate. She went to the doctor and was diagnosed with hypertension and chronic renal failure. Her kidneys were failing, causing edema and toxins to spread throughout her body.

Her doctor gave her two options, dialysis or kidney transplant. Sabean was devastated. Neither option was good. The doctor said she had to be immediately hospitalized. By this point, Sabean also had a fever.

Still, she refused. She wanted to go home and pray first, which she did. She called up everyone in her family and asked them to pray for her. She emailed her friends, told her employer.

As she lay in bed that evening, she found herself surrounded by "brown creatures with hooded robes on."

Sabean was amazed at what happened next. "...[The] strange creatures massaged my kidneys all night, and by Saturday morning, my kidneys were working again."

Says Sabean, "Even before I felt totally safe that I was alone in my room, I had to go use the bathroom. This was a strange feeling since I had been unable to use the bathroom for days. I was amazed that my kidneys were apparently working again...When I went back to the hospital on Tuesday for another blood test, I was feeling much better...the tests showed that my kidneys were indeed working now and my doctor was amazed. When I asked him how this was possible when he [already] told me that it was impossible for kidney function to be restored, he just shook his head and said it was possibly a misdiagnosis on his part. I didn't tell him about the creatures. I didn't tell anybody for a long time...My sisters and friends were amazed at my recovery. And I simply told them that the angels came in the night and healed me. I left it at that. I didn't want to tell them the scary details, and at that time I was so frustrated if people didn't believe me."

While the beings cured her renal failure, Sabean still feels some sensitivity there. Nevertheless, she is thankful. "I decided these creatures must be angels or something. If not, then why--on a night that every person was praying for me--did they show up? They did not harm me. In fact, they healed me, apparently. They were obviously not of this dimension. And I heard them speak in a manner that was obviously not of this Earth...Regardless, I was left distressed and traumatized by the events of that night, although always thankful that my kidney function had been restored."

Sabean's UFO healing wasn't over yet. One year later, she had what appears to be a checkup. "I dreamed I was in this circular white room that was a strange type of medical examination room." She sat on a stool, while an unseen doctor held a tool against her kidneys. In front of her Sabean could see a full-color, three-dimensional, living model of her kidney, displayed on a table in front of her. "I was amazed at this technology...then I saw my liver...It was all black. The doctor told me this is what was happening to my liver from drinking diet coke, and I needed to quit drinking it because it was damaging my stomach and liver."[9]

The above nine cases provide incredible evidence of alien intervention. They have left a long trail of confused and amazed doctors, not to mention grateful men and women who, without the intervention by extraterrestrials, would have continued to suffer from their conditions, or be forced to undergo surgery by perhaps less proficient human doctors. Again we see cases in which aliens not only heal people, they dispense medical advice, warning people against the dangers of eating meat, or of drinking diet cola. Whatever the agenda of the ETs, it clearly involves maintaining the good health of humans.

Chapter Seventeen
The Heart

The single greatest cause of human deaths on our planet is heart disease. Nearly a million people die each year from some form of heart disease. Heart problems account for as many as one in four deaths.

This chapter presents fourteen cases of people who were healed of heart problems by extraterrestrials. As with the other healing cases, they come from across the world, stretch back decades and continue to the present day. Men, women and children are being cured of a wide variety of heart conditions. Once again, these healings show us how incredibly advanced the ETs are when it comes to medicine.

CASE #033. CONGENITAL HEART DEFECT.

This case comes from UFO researcher, "Leneesa," a member of UFOCCI, whose article, "Alien Healings," recounts several alien healing cases. Writes Leneesa, "A lady that lives in Los Angeles told about an experience she had when she was twelve years old (early 1960s?) She was born with a congenital heart defect. One side of her heart was huge and the other small. Her brother had died from the same condition. The doctors insisted she have open heart surgery to correct the condition.

"One night," continues Leneesa, "she had a dream that a man came to her and did something to her chest to the point [that] she felt like he was crushing her. The next morning, she woke up with such pain she was rushed to the hospital. When she was X-rayed, the heart was healed and totally normal."

The witness later visited a chiropractor. He took X-rays, which showed that she had surgery performed on her back. He pointed to a scar that was apparently associated with the operation and asked her when it had been performed. The witness, however, had never had back surgery.[1]

In the above case, the witness was cured as a child of a heart defect that had cost the life of her own brother. Thankfully, she was cured early. In the following case, however, the witness suffered from a congenital heart defect for most of his life. Then he had an encounter with ETs, who not only healed his heart, but transformed him in a number of ways.

CASE #043. CONGENITAL HEART DEFECT.
Victor Kostrykin became interested in UFOs in August of 1962 when he watched an unidentified glowing object zigzagging over the Blagoveschenka Prokhladnensky region of Kabardino-Balkaria in the Caucasus Mountain ranges in Russia. Following the sighting, he began to take groups of people out to see UFOs. Discouraged that they weren't taking the outings seriously, he went out on his own.

On the evening of July 7, 1968, he was hiking near the mountain village of Hushtosyrt by the Chegem Gorge, an area of high UFO activity, when he saw a bright object descend from the sky behind a nearby hill. He quickly ran to the area and saw a large disc. Near it stood a figure dressed in silvery overalls. It gestured for Kostrykin to enter the craft, which he did.

Inside, Kostrykin saw advanced computer-like equipment, and furniture that melded with the walls and floors. Other humanoid figures were aboard the craft, each of them so similar to each other that they looked like twins.

At one point during his long and complicated encounter, Kostrykin was approached by a figure wearing a remarkable pair of elbow-length black gloves. The figure thrust his gloved hand into Kostrykin's chest, through his shirt and skin and bones. Says Kostrykin, "I did not feel any pain or other sensations."

Then Kostrykin felt the hand reach his heart, and feeling a strange pain, he screamed. The figure withdrew his hand. Kostrykin experienced many other bizarre episodes and was

226

finally released from the object several miles from where he had been picked up. Before the encounter, he had suffered from a heart defect his entire life. Following the experience, his defect disappeared.

Kostrykin also reports a number of other changes. After the encounter, he kept hearing other people's thoughts. It became so pronounced that he could no longer ride the train to work. Other changes followed, including instances of telekinesis, precognition of disasters, and psychic healing.[2]

Yet another healing of a congenital heart defect comes from California-based researcher, Barbara Lamb. It may be the only recorded case in which the healing began *in utero*, before the witness was actually born! It's also unusual (but not unique) in that the witness received regular visits throughout his life to check-up on his condition and provide additional healing adjustments.

CASE #050. CONGENITAL HEART DEFECT.

A remarkable case of healing comes from a California abductee named "Harold." Throughout his life, Harold had dreams about aliens and experienced occasional episodes of missing time. It wasn't until his late forties that he connected all the weird events in his life and realized he was having ET experiences. He contacted researcher, Barbara Lamb and with the use of hypnosis, recalled a lifetime of contact, including a series of healings which apparently began prior to his birth, while still in the womb. Writes Lamb, "While his mother was asleep one night, she was visited by a gray male being who placed his hands on her abdomen, in the area of her womb where Harold was developing. The being said directly to him that his heart was defective, in that there was a hole in one chamber that would make it impossible for him to live after he was born. The being also indicated that he was placing an invisible, electromagnetic strip over the defect in Harold's heart in order that he would survive. The electromagnetic strip would be reinforced by him after Harold was born to keep his heart working properly."

Another one of these "reinforcement" procedures occurred when Harold was three years old. Under hypnosis, he recalled being placed on a table to be examined by an alien being named "Mazu," the same being who had originally helped him with his heart. "On this occasion," writes Lamb, "he [Mazu] placed his hands over the little boy's chest, apparently reinforcing the electromagnetic strip."

Under hypnosis, Harold learned that he had been abducted many times throughout the 1960s and 1970s, and that during each experience, Mazu would place his hands over Harold's chest to reinforce the energetic healing strip. Mazu instructed Harold in a wide variety of topics, including piloting their ships, meditation and telekinesis.

When he was forty-eight years old, Harold was instructed by Mazu to visit a heart surgeon and undergo surgery to repair the hole in his heart. Consciously unaware of the instruction, Harold nevertheless followed Mazu's guidance and underwent open heart surgery. Harold's wife, a registered nurse, observed the operation.

Writes Lamb, "She clearly observed the shock and confusion of the doctors upon viewing the silver-dollar-sized hole in his heart. They estimated it had been there for many years, but for some inexplicable reason, it leaked very little blood. At the time of the surgery, the entire medical staff was amazed that Harold was alive."[3]

The following incredible case involves a double healing-- both the husband and wife experienced a cure. Also interesting is that the ETs informed the witness that they were healing him because they "need" him in some way.

CASE #079. HEART DISEASE, FLU.
In 1977, Bernardo Vega of Ensenada, Puerto Rico was undergoing treatment for chronic cardiac problems at the local Hospital Oncologico De Ponce. On the evening of December 22, 1977, Vega was at his home caring for his wife, who was feeling ill and had been vomiting all night due to a flu-like illness.

Vega decided to go outside to the terrace and clean out the bowl his wife had been using. As he washed the bowl, he saw three bright lights approaching. He first thought they were fireflies until they grew close and he saw that they were large and bright. He fell to his knees and watched in fear as the lights descended onto the terrace right in front of him and transformed into three men.

They were "not ugly or pretty," said Vega. They were three feet tall, with short arms and legs and large hands. Their faces were large, with a big flat nose, thick lips and luminous eyes. They each wore blue divers' suits.

They began to speak at high-speed in an unknown language. Vega looked into their glowing eyes. The little men stared back, seeming to "penetrate" his mind.

One of the men turned to the other two and said, "He is sick, cure him."

At this point, one of the men approached Vega, placed his fingers on Vega's chest and said, "I am going to cure you." He moved his hand and Vega saw flashing lights. He felt nothing, but began to sweat profusely, "as if someone had emptied a bucket of water on me."

His wife called out, asking who he was speaking with at this hour of the night.

Vega replied that he would tell her later. The three men then held each other's hands, and told Vega, "We need you. Goodbye." The men transformed back into three orbs of light and flew away. Vega says that the entire event lasted about twenty-five minutes.

He told his wife and his mother. His mother (who was religious) thought it might have been a divine visitation.

Following the visitation, Vega visited his doctors who told him that he was inexplicably cured, that his heart was not only normal, but that it was functioning like that of a healthy fifteen-year-old boy.

Vega's wife also appears to have been affected by the encounter as she stopped vomiting and was no longer ill.[4]

As we have seen, people who are doing good work for humanity comprise a significant number of the recipients of the healing power of UFOs. ETs seem to be interested in helping people who help others. This pattern is particularly apparent with people who are themselves healers. Whether they are trained in modern medicine, traditional medicine, or spiritual and alternative methods of healing, ETs seem especially interested in healing doctors of all kinds. In some cases, such as the following, they specifically train people how to perform alternative healings.

CASE #109. HEART DISEASE.

In 1985, Marina Lukonina, a resident of Obninsk, in the Kaluga region of Russia, experienced an extensive encounter with seven-foot-tall aliens from the constellation of Libra. The ETs' ship landed outside of Obninsk, and Lukonina was invited onboard. They placed her in a deep armchair and transported her to their planet, which they called Sahra. They spoke to her telepathically, saying that they lived about 400 years. Upon arriving at Sahra, Lukonina met more giant ETs, some as tall as nine feet or more.

On Sahra, the ETs performed an "energetic" surgery to cure her of her heart disease. Not only did they cure her, they trained her to perform energetic healings on other people. They then returned Lukonina back to Earth, where Lukonina became deeply involved in non-traditional healing methods. She performed a number of "bloodless surgical procedures," telling her patients that the methods she used had been taught to her by her alien contacts.[5]

Among the rarest types of UFO healings are those that have outside witnesses. This has occurred in only a few cases. The following is a remarkable example of a healing that was observed by people around the patient. Like other cases of this type, it took place *inside* a human hospital.

CASE #139. HEART DISEASE.

On the evening of April 18, 1989, a woman terminally ill with heart disease was lying in her room at the Kirv Hospital in

Krasnoperekopsk, Crimea in Ukraine when a strong wind disturbed her room, a dazzling white light appeared, followed by a man dressed in white. The man's eyes radiated light. The patient asked the man where he was from and the man said, "the tenth dimension."

He told the patient that she would soon be able to walk. Then he disappeared. The following day, outside witnesses observed unexplained red and white lights moving slowly over the body of the patient. They then heard a loud voice telling her, "Get up and leave." The woman rose from her bed, apparently cured. The case was presented by Russian researcher, Sergei Bulantsev.[6]

Experts disagree on one's chances of being struck by lightning, with answers ranging from one person in 3000, up to 7000. Whatever the actual number, the chances of being struck by lightning is very slim. In fact, according to the Roper Poll, which found that one in fifty people show the markers associated with abductees (ie: missing time, close-up UFO sightings), you're more likely to be abducted by aliens than struck by lightning. In the following case, the witness was first struck by lightning, and then abducted by aliens.

CASE #142. HEART INJURY DUE TO LIGHTNING STRIKE.

On August 7, 1989, real-estate broker, Katharina W., of Portland, Oregon was injured by a nearby lightning strike while staying in Pensacola, Florida. She was struck by the bolt of lightning outside her home. Afterward, she stumbled inside, disoriented and afraid. She knew she had been injured by the strike, but decided to wait until morning in the hopes that her condition would improve.

That night, Katharina was taken aboard a UFO. She woke up to find herself lying on a table, suffering from excruciating chest pains. As Katharina watched from a dissociated state, gray-type aliens cut a square into her chest and attached a black mechanism with several extensions to the hole in her chest.

When the pain became particularly intense, the aliens telepathically told her, "We are repairing your heart. You will be okay now."

The next morning, Katharina woke up with a sore chest, but was otherwise healthy. As she says, "The first thing I did when I got out of bed was to look for a scar of a square cut into my chest. I found nothing. No blood on my sheets and no scar. My chest was sore throughout the day, but it was not as sore as I would have expected it to feel after such a radical operation. I believe this machine they had over my heart was realigning the electrochemical impulses in my heart because they had been altered by the lightning...somehow I believed the aliens were repairing the damage the high voltage of the lightning had done to my heart."

Katharina reports that she has undergone a large number of operations at the hands of aliens. As she says, "They have performed surgery on me many, many times!...It was shocking to remember the different times the aliens had performed surgery on me...What could the aliens be doing to me that would require my having surgery so often? It was not the first time I felt I may be a part of a huge experiment."[7]

Following the United States, the next biggest producer of UFO healing reports is Russia. UFO healing cases come from all across Russia. No matter what category of healing there is, Russia is almost always represented. The following case, from Germany-based researcher, Michael Hesemann, highlights a case in a specific area of Russia which has received a lot of healing attention from the ETs.

CASE #154. HEART ATTACK.

As researched by German investigator, Michael Hesemann, one evening (date not given: circa 1980s?), an anonymous factory worker from Georgia, Russia woke up with severe chest pains and shortness of breath. He had recently suffered two consecutive heart attacks, and he instantly recognized the symptoms of a third heart attack. Before he was able to take any action, he found himself surrounded by gray ETs. The aliens took a "ball of light" and put it inside the man's chest. He was then telepathically told that he should paint his experience.

The man then fell asleep. When he woke up the next morning, he felt no pain and was apparently healed. He immediately prepared to make a painting of the beings that healed him. Following the experience, he remained perfectly healthy and ran daily marathons in Gorky Park.

Hesemann says that he has investigated several healing accounts in this area of Russia. Unlike the United States, which abounds with frightening abduction accounts, Hesemann says that in Georgia, Russia, people are often eager to be taken onboard.[8]

The following case, from John Mack MD, involves a witness who has received multiple cures at the hands of his contacts. Previously he has reported a childhood healing of pneumonia. In this next instance, he was healed as an adult.

CASE #160. ARTERIAL SCLEROSIS.

Edward Carlos, a fine arts professor in Pennsylvania, has had many UFO encounters. In 1942, at age five, Carlos was healed of pneumonia by his ET contacts. Many years later, on April 15, 1990, Carlos was visiting the island of Iona between Scotland and Ireland when he saw an inexplicable beam of light coming down from the clouds. The beam struck Carlos and he experienced a missing time encounter. He had already had many encounters in the past, some of which he remembered consciously, and some which he did not. Unable to recall what happened on the April 15 experience, Carlos visited Mack and underwent hypnotic regression.

Under hypnosis, he recalled being examined by several entities, including a reptilian-like humanoid, small white-skinned humanoids, and insect-like robotic creatures. He experienced an anal probe, which was performed to determine his state of health. "They are clarifying that the inside of me is okay," said Carlos, "and they are operating on me...if there is anything not right, the process can be healing."

233

The ETs examined Carlos's various organ systems including his heart. They then used a laser-like light to apparently clear his arteries of blockages. "They can cause the change with their laser-like instruments," Carlos explains. "In my heart, I feel an extreme heat...I think it is healing something. Clearing arteries or something."

Carlos reports that his abductions--although they often involve healings (including a possible cancer cure)--have ironically left him with rashes, bumps and scars. Still he feels that his encounters are positive and transformative. "You are diseased and then you are healed," says Carlos. "With each healing, the emotional growth is established and connected in the human realm, and I can go and utilize that toward teaching others."[9]

For whatever reason, the Tbilisi, Georgia area of Russia has produced a disproportionally large number of UFO healing cases. The following is one of nearly a dozen cases from the same area.

CASE #190. HEART DISEASE.
According to researcher, Helga Morrow, many people in Tbilisi, Georgia (in Russia), have experienced contact with ETs. Morrow had the opportunity to view a rare Russian 1993 UFO documentary which presents many of the cases. Says Morrow, "After almost six hours of studying this film carefully, I feel it is the most outstanding firsthand information about extraterrestrials ever to be filmed anywhere in the world."

The film recounts several healings, including the following brief report: "The shaven stomach of a man shows a slight scar. He was permanently and painlessly cured of a heart condition."

Cures from this area have appeared earlier in this book, and as we shall see in a later chapter, it is the location of other dramatic cures by ETs.[10]

UFO healing cases sometimes occur in mysterious ways. As we have seen, the close approach of a UFO can affect a UFO healing. The same is true for the close approach of an alien being. In the following case, the witness experienced a UFO landing, followed by three confrontations with a strange alien entity outside his farm, resulting in a healing.

CASE #220. HEART DISEASE.

One day in the summer of 1998, Igor Nikolayevich Petukhov, a farmer from the Petrozavodsk region of Russia, was working in the fields when he heard a strange sound coming from an unexplained light above him. The UFO descended and landed behind his shed. Petukhov started to walk toward the shed. Suddenly a small humanoid dressed in a tight-fitting black uniform flew from the behind the shed and approached Petukhov. The farmer found himself unable to move. The ET hovered in front of him. Petukhov saw that it was short, with dark eyes, a tiny nose, and a slit-like mouth.

The figure said nothing, but began to fly up and down in front of him. At first afraid, Petukhov's fear vanished. The figure remained for about fifteen minutes then flew off.

The next day, Petukhov saw the same tiny man walking around in his garden. The being observed Petukhov, but said nothing.

The being returned again on the third day, this time hovering above the porch as though looking for Petukhov. As soon as the farmer saw the figure, it flew away, never to be seen again.

Following the three encounters, Petukhov, who suffered from chronic heart disease, experienced an improvement in his condition. The positive changes in his condition were also verified by his relatives and doctor.[11]

Like the United States and Russia, the country of Canada is also a prolific producer of UFO reports. The following case comes from Canadian researcher, Grant Cameron, and involves a multiple healing.

CASE #237. HEART MURMUR, INFERTILITY.

All her life, Mary X of Ontario, Canada suffered from a heart murmur, a condition which ran in her family. Later, as an adult, she learned that she suffered from infertility. Her doctors told her that she would never have children.

On January 7, 2003, Mary was traveling with a friend and a twelve-year-old child along a road in northern Ontario. The UFO experience began when the occupants of the car suddenly noticed that the highway around them was devoid of any other vehicles. Shortly later, they noticed UFOs pacing their car on both sides of the highway. They sped up to almost seventy MPH, but the objects continued to track them. The child was so frightened she climbed out of the backseat and sat between the two adults in the front seat.

The objects followed them for the next half-hour, at which point the UFOs fell back, turned on their lights and raced forward, buzzing the car at low altitude. The three of them rushed to their destination, finally leaving the UFO behind.

Later Mary had other encounters, at least one of which apparently healed her. Writes researcher Grant Cameron, "The woman who could not bear children just had her fifth child. The lifelong heart condition is a thing of the past.[12]

The following case, published here for the first time, involves a woman who has had a lifelong series of encounters with gray ETs, resulting in at least two healings.

CASE #263. HEART PROBLEMS.

Lynnette (pseudonym) had her first encounter at age three. It was 1957, and she was riding with her parents as they drove near LaGrange, Georgia when they encountered an egg-shaped UFO. This began a lifelong series of encounters with gray ETs, who often came to visit her in her home and take her into their craft. She experienced regular episodes of missing time, and began to discover multiple unexplained marks on her body. She had a number of unexplained pregnancies that first tested positive, then disappeared. All of these experiences were unwanted, unasked for, and created incredible havoc in her life.

Lynnette's experiences continued into adulthood. She married and had children. As they grew up, it became clear that they too were having encounters, a fact which caused her considerable distress. Around 2011 (date approx.,) Lynnette had an onboard experience unlike any she had ever had. She was fully conscious when gray ETs showed up in her bedroom and pulled her into a craft. She was placed prone on a table. One of the ETs then did something she couldn't believe. "He plunged his hand into my chest...like nothing was solid," Lynnette says. "It hurt. I could feel pain. I first thought he had something in his hands, but I don't know if he did or not. I couldn't see. I just saw the hand going in beyond the fingers, almost to the thumb. And I hurt, and I almost felt like I was burning. And he said, 'Your heart is physically and spiritually healed.'"

Lynnette wasn't aware of any problems with her heart. Afterward she suffered no ill effects.

This was not the first time Lynnette had experienced a healing. Earlier she had experienced a healing of a mass in her lung (described later.)

Despite the healing, the physical and emotional trauma she has already experienced at the hands of the gray ETs, and the fact that her children have become involved, have left her with a negative impression of her encounters. Although she is now in her sixties, her experiences continue to occur. She just wants them to finally stop.[13]

The following poignant case provides an example of how ETs not only performed a profound heart healing, but somehow warned the witness and inspired him to seek medical attention for a life-threatening condition he didn't even know he had.

CASE #270. HEART ATTACK.

In the middle of the night on June 9, 2013, Steven (pseudonym) of Manchester, New Jersey, suddenly woke up. This wasn't unusual, as he was a light sleeper and often woke up in the middle of the night. On this particular occasion, however, he was startled to see a tall, thin, glowing white humanoid. "With no sound, the being reached into my left chest area," Steven says. "I didn't feel any pain, pressure or discomfort. That lasted about five minutes. The being removed its hand from my left chest and stood there for about two minutes and then vanished."

Steven was baffled and amazed. He never saw a UFO, just the one humanoid. He felt physically fine, and wondered why the being had behaved the way it did. He had no chest pains, but "a strong intuitive urge" overwhelmed him; he had to visit a cardiologist. A few months following the experience, he finally went and got an EKG and stress test. The doctors told him that his health condition was dire and he was lucky to still be alive. He had arrived at the hospital just in time. They told him that he had been born with a bicuspid aorta valve; it should have been tricuspid. In addition, he was suffering from severe congestive heart failure. "So," says Steven, "I was rushed to the hospital to prep me for a triple bypass and a replacement aorta valve."

The doctors joked that Steven was getting a two-for-one operation, a bypass and a valve replacement. "My take and feelings on this incident," Steven says, "was the white, light being made temporary repairs for me to not have a heart attack or stroke ahead of time...It was a miracle...The white, light being made adjustments to give me the time and the strong intuition to get into a hospital to save my life."[14]

The above fourteen heart healings tell us many things about the ETs. The cases come from all over the world, from a wide variety of respected investigators. They reveal once again how incredibly advanced the ETs are. We are left with more amazed doctors, and more grateful people who owe their lives to extraterrestrial intervention.

Once again we see a wide variety of ETs reported, the presence of alien technology, and healings that are performed by mysterious and unknown methods.

With each additional healing case, we get another piece of the puzzle pointing toward the methods and motives behind these healings.

Chapter Eighteen
The Lungs

Of all the organ systems in the body, among the most vital are the lungs. They function to oxygenate our red blood cells and rid the body of carbon dioxide. Lungs appear in pairs in all vertebrate animals, in some fish and even in snails. They are large, spongy, air-filled organs that are prone to a wide variety of illnesses. Respiratory diseases are one of the top ten killers of human beings.

This chapter presents fifteen cases in which people were healed of respiratory problems by a wide variety of ETs. The following case is the third earliest documented UFO healing case on record.

CASE #003. PNEUMONIA.

In 1937, contactee Eduard Meier was only six years old when he contracted pneumonia. The family physician, Dr. Strebel, expected Meier would die. He told Meier's parents that nothing could be done and that they should prepare themselves for the death of their son.

That evening, Meier had his first extraterrestrial contact, with a human-looking ET named Sfath, who administered to Meier and cured him of his pneumonia. Meier had no memory of this incident and was told about it during a later contact. He asked his mother about it. To his surprise, she said it was true: as a baby he had nearly died of pneumonia, but had suddenly and inexplicably recovered. His mother remembered how they had spoken of his recovery as a "miracle."

As we have already seen, Meier was later cured of a rib injury following a motorcycle accident. Later in 1978, Meier also claims to have been healed on a third occasion, and this time, he had eyewitnesses.[1]

Another very early case also occurred to a child, Edward Carlos, who would later experience encounters throughout his life. We have already examined one case in which Carlos was cured of apparent arterial sclerosis. This next case is the second of three healings he has received from ETs.

CASE #004. PNEUMONIA.
From the case files of John Mack MD: In 1942, Edward Carlos (age five) of Philadelphia, Pennsylvania, developed a severe case of respiratory pneumonia. He had a high fever and was in a near coma. The illness was too much for Carlos to bear, and he had an out-of-body experience. Outside his body, he found himself surrounded by gray aliens.

His astral body was placed horizontally, and beams of lights were shone upon it. The lights, said Carlos, were "like laser beams coming into my body through the soles of my feet and the hands, and possibly through the whole body, expanding and changing color as the light grew to fit the whole body interior, thereby healing it."

The light was yellow in the middle and surrounded by concentric layers of red, blue and green. After the procedure was finished, Carlos was returned to his body. His fever broke and he came out of his coma.[2]

Behind the United States and Russia, England is the third largest producer of UFO healing accounts. The following case appeared in the second article ever published on the subject of UFO healings. The healing involves a man who was healed, apparently because of his advanced work in electronics.

CASE #038. HOLE IN LUNG.
On Easter weekend 1962, electronics specialist Fred White went fishing near Durhan, England. While fishing, he experienced a close-up sighting of a metallic craft with portholes. Through the

240

portholes, Fred could clearly see a human-looking person. After about five minutes, the UFO left.

Four years later, in September 1966, Fred was hospitalized because of severe chest pains and a collapsed lung. Fred had no idea what was wrong with him. To his dismay, X-rays revealed that he had a large hole in his lung.

During his stay in the hospital, Fred was visited by a man whom he thought at first was just another doctor. However, the doctor was strange. He had a peculiar accent, and when he entered the room, he immediately put his arm over Fred as if examining him. Fred noticed that the man wore "some kind of watch which glowed like no timepiece I had ever seen."

The two of them began discussing Fred's symptoms. The man also expressed some interest in Fred's work with electronics. After several minutes, the strange doctor left.

Fred reports that as soon as the stranger departed, he immediately felt better and could breathe without pain. The doctors gathered around and demanded more tests. X-rays were again taken. To the surprise of the doctors, no hole in his lung could be found and Fred was given a clean bill of health.

One astonished doctor told Fred, "Your lung is completely inflated. The hole you had in there is healed. We've never seen anything like it."

Fred White is convinced that the man who visited him in the hospital cured his illness. He also suspects that the man is the same person he saw inside the UFO while fishing four years earlier.[3]

This next vividly described case is one of four asthma cures appearing in this book. Asthma is an inflammatory disease of the airways of the lungs, causing difficulties in respiration. It's often chronic and while usually treatable, can be life-threatening. About 25 million people in the United States suffer from asthma, or about one in fourteen people. Around 4000 to 5000 people die of the condition each year. Despite the huge number of sufferers from the disease, only a few fortunate people have apparently been cured by ETs.

241

CASE #052. ASTHMA.

One evening in 1970, H.C. of Brooksville, Florida was inside his camper when he heard a whirring noise coming from outside. Exiting his camper, he was shocked to see a disc-shaped ship descend. Four legs extruded from beneath the craft, which landed nearby. Four short, masked, humanoids exited--three men and one woman. They spoke to H. C. in a high-pitched, singsong voice, but H.C. was unable to understand them. Through gestures, they invited him aboard their craft. Unafraid, H.C. followed them into the craft, which he said was sparsely furnished and reminded him of Army barracks. He was taken to the pilot's quarters, which had a few instruments covered with colored lights, but little else. H.C. remained on the craft for about ten minutes, after which the ETs told him it was no longer safe for him to stay onboard, and escorted him off. Once back outside, the craft made a loud whirring noise, flashed some colored lights and took off, disappearing upward. Following the incident, H.C. says that his asthma--from which he had suffered his entire life--disappeared completely and never returned.[4]

Swiss contactee, Eduard Meier has reported an earlier childhood cure of pneumonia. Years later, he was cured again. On this occasion, there were outside witnesses.

CASE #082. PNEUMONIA.

In July of 1978, Eduard Meier of Hinwil, Switzerland came down with a bad cold that developed into severe pneumonia. He became so weak, he could barely hold up a glass of water.

Around this time, Meier received telepathic instructions that there would be a contact. He was told to travel to a certain spot. Meier had his friends take him there. Evidently Meier's condition was life-threatening for the aliens boldly took Meier in full view of his friends. Several witnesses saw Meier disappear in front of their eyes in a "flash of blue light."

Meier was taken inside a craft where he underwent an operation. Human-looking aliens used "strange instruments" to

242

drain the pleural area of his chest of "a considerable amount of pus and liquid." His alien friends told him in no uncertain terms that if they had not intervened, he would surely have died. They told him that next time, he should not delay to see a human doctor.

A half-hour later, he exited the craft and joined his astonished friends. The change in Meier left his friends speechless. Before being taken aboard the craft, Meier was near death. His face had a "gray color" and his eyes had a "deep sunken appearance." Afterward, Meier's pneumonia was gone. He was "sprightly and smiling," and appeared to be "in perfect health."[5]

A surprising number of healing cases occur when a witness wakes up in their bedroom, looks out their window and sees a UFO. This is usually followed by a bedroom visitation, and/or an onboard UFO experience. Following the encounter, the witness discovers they are healed. This sequence of events occurs again and again, in case after case, coming from all over the world. This next case is a typical example of this pattern, except for the fact that it involves an unusual kind of witness: a famous celebrity.

CASE #113. LUNG DISEASE.

According to Italian researcher, Alfredo Lissoni, on December 27, 1986, a local celebrity from Milan, Italy (who insisted upon anonymity) was awakened by a strange impulse. Looking out his window, he was shocked to see a "spaceship." Suddenly an opening appeared, followed by an escalator-like device and finally several human-like figures--both men and women--wearing silver uniforms. Two of the figures, a man and woman, approached the celebrity and invited him aboard their craft. The celebrity declined the invitation. Nevertheless, he reports that following the encounter, a lung disease that he had suffered from prior to the encounter was now cured.[6]

A particularly compelling case of a lung healing comes from Jim Sparks, a home developer originally from North Carolina. Sparks has had abduction experiences for many years. We have already examined an encounter during which Sparks was cured of the flu. In this next encounter, Sparks reports a more unusual healing.

CASE #197. LUNGS CLEANSED OF CIGARETTE TAR.

Jim Sparks first realized he was having abduction experiences in 1988 while living in North Carolina. It started with vivid odd dreams in which he'd find himself paralyzed and being led out of his house by strange-looking creatures. Then one morning he woke up and found evidence that the dreams were real: there was a weird set of his footprints leading from outside the house, through a closed window, and into the living room. Furthermore, there were twigs and flowers from the back yard strewn inside.

Around this time, Sparks attempted to remember what was happening to him and discover if it was real or imaginary. To his shock, he began having fully conscious ET abduction experiences. Often he would be taken onboard and given various mental exercises to perform, or would be physically examined or given messages and much more.

In August of 1994, only a few days before he was scheduled to visit Budd Hopkins, Sparks was taken inside a UFO into what he calls the teaching room. In the center of the room was a table with a black cube-shaped box on it. Two gray aliens stood there. One said, "Look, a gift for you."

"A gift?" Sparks asked, trying to remain calm. "What do you want me to do with it?"

"Do with it what you will," the alien said.

The aliens stepped back.

Sparks tried to open the box for several moments before he finally slid the lid gently open.

"I noticed a foul odor rising," says Sparks. "In the box were about six or seven upright, long glass tubes. Each tube was about an inch to an inch and a half in diameter. In the bottom lay a thick, dark brown, sticky, smelly fluid, about two inches deep."

"What is this stuff?" Sparks asked.

"It's your gift," the alien replied. "We extracted it from your lungs."

"From my lungs? This trash was in my lungs?" At the time, Sparks smoked cigarettes. He was dumbfounded at the sight of the black goo, and didn't know what to say.

"Follow us," the alien said, and led him into another room where there was a strange mirror. In the reflection Sparks saw himself, but he appeared thin and frail and losing his hair.

"What's this all about?" he asked.

The ETs didn't answer. Sparks lost consciousness and woke up back in his home.

Later, Sparks visited Hopkins and agreed to be hypnotized to this event. Under hypnosis, Sparks recalled the same details as above, and something new. Before sending him home, the alien began to lecture Sparks. "The gist was that they wanted me to take more responsibility when I spoke of them and my interactions with them to other humans."[7]

Leading abduction researcher David Jacobs Ph.D. has authored several books on the subject. He has also uncovered several healing cases. Unfortunately, the details on the cases are sparse, such as the following two healings of pneumonia.

CASE #180. PNEUMONIA.

David Jacobs Ph.D., author of *Secret Life*, writes, "At least two abductees have reported that their cases of pneumonia were cured during their abductions."[8]

In their book, *Secret Vows*, Denise and Bert Twiggs revealed their many encounters with ETs, including a large number of healings. Each member of the family has received cures. In this next case, their daughter received a healing.

CASE #145. ASTHMA.

The Twiggs family of Hubbard, Oregon have received several cures, including of a C-section scar, a back injury, colitis, and a sty. The Twiggs' daughter, Stacey, suffers from severe asthma. On October 15, 1989, during the evening, Stacey's asthma was acting up. In the middle of the night, she was taken onboard the UFO and treated. The aliens explained that the asthma was caused mostly by pollution and that the only real cure would be clean air. They also gave her "some medicine to help her through her current attack."

In January of 1990, Stacey suffered another severe asthma attack. She was taken onboard and the alien doctor said that there was little that could be done, and that the attacks would get worse.

The next day, Stacey's lung capacity was reduced to a dangerous twenty percent. By the time Stacey made it to the hospital, one lung was in the process of collapsing. The human doctor confirmed what the alien doctors had already said. There was little that could be done, except to keep her on medication.

Still, the alien doctors did what they could. "The Androme doctors saw her each night," says Denise. "He was monitoring the Earth doctor's orders. He also added some of his own medication to her recovery."[9]

While it may seem incredible that people receive multiple cures at the hands of ETs, the cases speak for themselves. Spontaneous and miraculous cures are well-known among physicians, if not completely understood. While many people who have a sudden healing attribute it to ETs (such as the following), one has to wonder how many people have a UFO healing, and attribute it to something else. For this reason and others, UFO healings might be considerably more common than even UFO investigators believe.

CASE #158. LUNG DAMAGE.

Chuck Weiss (a driver from San Francisco, California) has reported multiple healings at the hands of gray aliens. At some point in his life (late 1980s?), Weiss fell into a depression and became addicted to crack cocaine. "It was the darkest time of my life," writes Weiss, "when I didn't care if I lived or died."

Weiss's health quickly declined, and he realized that if he continued, he would likely die from his addiction. Not wanting to leave his daughter without a father, he resolved to quit. It took him multiple attempts, but after six months of addiction, he finally quit for good. Says Weiss, "I slowly returned to the land of the living, but I had destroyed my lungs. I tired easily and it was difficult for me to breathe at times."

Then, after two years of suffering, the ETs once again stepped in to heal Weiss. "After two years of living with very little lung power, struggling for breath after even the slightest bit of physical activity, I suddenly became aware one day that I was able to breathe again deeply. I couldn't believe it. I had my lungs back!"

As with his other healings, the effect was instantaneous. Weiss can pinpoint the exact moment. "I first noticed it after I climbed the three flights of stairs to visit my mother one afternoon," writes Weiss. "Her apartment building didn't have an elevator, and each time I went to see her I would have to drag myself up the stairs, stopping at each landing for a few seconds to catch my breath. But one day I was amazed to find that I hadn't needed to stop for a rest and had made it to the top breathing normally all the way! I was dumbfounded and so very grateful to 'the powers that be.' I still am."

The healing wasn't perfect. He still suffered some numbness in his lower back. But his lungs were back to normal. Why had the ETs waited to heal him? "Over the years," Weiss writes, "the ETs have been very patient with me and my foolishness, but in this instance they were cautious as well. They waited two years before healing me to verify that I had resolved the issues that derailed my life, and that I was secure in my sobriety."

Of his cure, Weiss calls it "a wondrous spontaneous healing...for which I will be eternally grateful."[10]

This next case is a good example of a healing that occurs simply by being adjacent to a UFO. How exactly these healings take place remains unknown, but most researchers speculate that there is some type of energy involved. The following incident not only involves a UFO healing of asthma, but exhibits a rare phenomenon known as "angel hair," believed by researchers to be a byproduct of UFO engines.

CASE #174. ASTHMA.

On September 28, 1991, contactee Arve Gjovik and his friend sighted a UFO near Skogveien, Norway. The object was large, glowing, spherical, and emitted numerous "threads" which hung toward the ground. Following the incident, Arve's friend--who suffered from chronic asthma--discovered that his condition was miraculously cured.[11]

Some researchers have pointed out that even UFO abductions, as terrifying as they can be, might be similar to emergency ambulances treating people. Even here on this planet, people become nervous and afraid when visiting doctors. For example, few people actually enjoy getting shots or inoculations. And yet, we all know that these procedures are to benefit our health.

CASE #226. PNEUMONIA.

An undated account (circa 1990s?) comes from experiencer Joni Ferris. "In my contact experience, I was saved," writes Ferris. "I was in a hospital suffering from pneumonia for six weeks and NOTHING--absolute NO antibiotics were working on me. The specialists were trying Penicillin after Penicillin. Then one day I was 'taken up' through the ceiling and 'blacked out.' When I came back, I was in bed and my fever had broke and the pneumonia was gone."

Ferris felt compelled to report her encounter after reading a quote from researcher Jacques Vallee in which he described procedures done upon humans by the ETs as "sadistic." She disagreed with this characterization and writes, "I have heard case after case of people being hurt from abduction. So there is both good and bad. We don't know what the [ET] researchers are trying to accomplish. In other words, the work may appear to be 'sadistic' in the way an emergency medical team performing a life-saving operation--if not properly recognized and understood--could be considered sadistic."[12]

In this next case, a man was cured by being in the mere presence of a UFO. Most people who receive a UFO healing come away from the experience feeling that the ETs are benevolent. In the following case, the witness has had numerous encounters, some during which he felt a strong sense of love coming from the ETs.

CASE #254. CHEST INFECTION.

In 2008, Thomas X (pseudonym), a construction worker from the United States, suffered from a severe chest infection that left him weak and breathless. He had a long history of similar infections, but this was the worst he ever had. It was affecting his work performance, even causing him to vomit if he exerted himself.

On December 30, 2008, Thomas decided to take his dog out for a walk. His own behavior surprised him, as he had been planning to watch a television program that he had been looking forward to for weeks.

The dog immediately began to act strangely. Instead of running around sniffing and marking his territory, he stuck closely to Thomas, refusing to leave his side. Thomas also noticed that all the night sounds had disappeared and everything was weirdly quiet. Strangest of all, he couldn't see anybody else outside. Normally at that hour, several others would be in the park, but tonight it was empty.

For some reason, Thomas felt himself moving off the marked pathways, away from the park and into a local farmer's field--something he had never done before. "It would be unusual," said Thomas, "to walk this route even in the summer, let alone a freezing cold winter's evening."

As he walked through the field, he spotted two very bright lights low in the field. Thinking they were rabbit hunters holding flashlights, he walked over to talk to them. He was halfway across the field when he felt a sudden and intense fear, as did his dog. They turned and ran back to the edge of the field. Looking back, he observed "the most incredible light display," as the lights began to perform all kinds of maneuvers and gyrations. Occasionally a car would drive by, and one of the orbs would rise up and follow it, "as if it was playing or inspecting the car."

Finally realizing that he was seeing something very unusual, Thomas decided to run home and get his wife and kids so they could see the lights. "So I spun around and ran nearly half a mile back home without being even out of breath! Remember I could hardly breathe let alone walk before that, yet I ran home. I can't remember them taking me; all I remember is what I wrote. I had no missing time at this point. I don't know how they did it, but they fixed me."

Thomas reports numerous other encounters. During one, he says the ETs touched him and he felt a powerful feeling of love coming from them.[13]

The following two cases are both part of the FREE study headed by Rey Hernandez. While the cases are short on detail, they show once again that the ET agenda involves healing.

CASE #300. ASTHMA.

"I am asthmatic," writes the witness. "...I had been having a really hard time...When I woke up remembering they came that night, I was breathing perfectly...it was improved for quite a while after that."[14]

In the following case, the witness was not only healed, he was given stern medical advice from the ETs. The first part contains a scenario that is nearly identical to what Jim Sparks experienced. In case after case, ETs are acting more like doctors, nurses and social workers than the evil invaders they are sometimes portrayed to be.

CASE #301. LUNGS.

"I have been healed twice. Once when I was a smoker, they removed a bunch of black tar-like substance and showed it to me...the second time was an 'intervention.' I was drawn to smoking marijuana...The greys came and gave me a scolding like

250

nothing I ever had. They kept telling me, 'This is not the life we wanted for you.' They surely saved my life."[15]

It is one thing to have your doctor tell you to quit smoking. It's quite another to have your alien doctor dispensing this advice. And yet, this is exactly what is happening. Fifteen cases of lung healings show once again that ETs possess an advanced knowledge of human biology. We see the same patterns over and over again. Corroboration is the foundation of observational science. The pattern is clear. ETs are healing people. Motives aside, this fact becomes increasingly undeniable. ETs are healing people.

Chapter Nineteen
Arthritis and Chronic Fatigue Syndrome

According to the Arthritis Foundation, arthritis affects more than 50 million adults and 300,000 children in the United States. With 327 million people in the USA (as of 2018), that's about fifteen percent, a significant portion of the US population.

This chapter covers twenty-one cases of arthritis healings. Compared to 50 million, the number of twenty-one is insignificant, and most likely inaccurate. Due to the fact that most people do not report their encounter, it can be safely assumed that the below cases represent only a tiny sampling of the actual much larger number. Yet, as we shall see, enough cases have been documented to provide an accurate portrayal of what is occurring.

The earliest known arthritis cure appeared in the first article on UFO healings, by Gordon Creighton. The case has generated some controversy among researchers.

CASE #019. NEURITIS, LUMBAGO, IMPROVED VISION.

On July 30, 1954, Missouri farmer, Buck Nelson, was listening to the radio when it began to emit a high-pitched noise, and a strange foreign speech replaced the normal program. At the same time, his dog and pony outside began to act excitedly. He stepped outside and saw a flying disc about fifty feet in diameter flying overhead. He ran inside and got his camera. Returning outside, three discs were now in view. Nelson snapped a total of three pictures. The first showed the UFOs, while the last two came out blank.

Next, Nelson tried to communicate with the UFO using a flashlight. As he says, "The most extraordinary and frightening experience during this visit, however, came when I tried to signal with my flashlight to the disc that had come nearest to me. A bright beam of light, much hotter and brighter than the sun, was thrown onto me, jolting me with a current that threw me to the ground.

"Because I suffered from lumbago and neuritis, I was afraid to move and get up, and of getting another jolt. When I did get up, however, I was amazed to find the pains had gone. They haven't bothered me since."

Nelson also said that his eyesight had dramatically improved. Later that evening, the occupants of the saucers showed up, along with their dog. They looked like "normal-sized, big-boned muscular men." They spoke to him about the "Twelve Laws of God," which were nearly identical to the Ten Commandments as seen in the King James Bible. They also warned him about the misuse of nuclear power, saying, "We are here to see which way this world will use atomic power; for peace or war." Later the ETs returned and took Nelson, he says, on trips to the Moon, Mars and Venus.

Nelson published a booklet about his experience titled, "My Trip to Mars, the Moon and Venus," and became a minor celebrity throughout the Ozarks. At the time, numerous other contactees, such as George Adamski, Daniel Fry, Howard Menger and Truman Bethurum were also claiming similar friendly contacts with ETs.

Writes Creighton of the case, "I am perfectly aware that nowadays virtually nobody wants to put any credence in Buck Nelson's contactee story...nevertheless it is the policy of *Flying Saucer Review* to look most carefully and objectively at every claim that comes to us, no matter how preposterous it may at first sight appear. I suggest that, in view of all that we have heard and learned--if not about UFOs, at least about UFO reports--in the fifteen years since Buck Nelson told his story, you will be well advised to approach it with an open mind and be prepared to study every detail. For if Buck Nelson invented this affair, then it seems that many of the features of his account are nothing short of prophetic."[1]

One of the recurring features of UFO healing cases is that witnesses will visit their doctor and provide them with evidence of surgery on their bodies. And yet, the witnesses deny having gone to any hospital.

CASE #021. ARTHRITIS, NECK AND BACK.

Robert (pseudonym) grew up in Fort Erie, Ontario, Canada. "When I was a young boy," Robert writes, "I had what the doctors thought was a severe arthritis in my back. It hurt so much that I had trouble walking. I recall men, dressed in black, that used to take me out of my room at night while my parents slept. They would perform tests on me, and it was most always on my spinal cord. If I tried to scream out and wake my parents, the dark doctors would leave before my father could find a trace of them. I was then warned by these doctors that I should never speak of them, or else I could be in great danger. The treatments continued for a while, then finally just stopped. I've never had any problems with my back after that and have been able to carry on a regular life."

The visitations occurred around 1956. In 2001, Robert suffered an accident at work and had to have his neck X-rayed. The X-ray showed something very unusual. "It shows the vertebrae in my neck that has been fused, which shouldn't be that strange, except for the fact that I've never had any operations."

Robert also reports having strange "marks" on his back which have been there since he was a young boy.[2]

This next case, while only loosely tied to UFOs, appeared in Paula Johnson's article, which was the second to explore this phenomenon.

CASE #024. NUMBNESS, LEFT ARM AND FINGERS.

On September 27, 1959, in Coos Bay, Oregon, real-estate salesman, Leo Bartsch received a healing as the result of an apparent UFO encounter. Bartsch had been suffering from pain and numbness in his left arm. The condition persisted for three weeks and his doctor was unable to find any cause. "The trouble extended up my arm," said Bartsch. "It felt dead, as if blood did not want to enter it."

Then, in the middle of the night, Bartsch was woken up with a strange feeling of weightlessness and electricity. He had the distinct impression that "something out of the universe had just passed over…"

Immediately afterward, Bartsch discovered to his delight that all numbness was gone and he could move and control his fingers again. Bartsch believes he was cured by a UFO.[3]

The following case, while sparse on details, is important because it involves two witnesses, one of who was healed, and also additional physical evidence.

CASE #075. ARTHRITIS.

Around 8:00 p.m., September 8, 1976, two men were driving near Accopampa, Peru when they saw a sixty-foot-wide UFO land about 100 feet from their truck. The truck engine stalled as two men wearing shiny suits and carrying "lamps" emerged from the craft. One of the figures stepped forward and touched one of the witnesses. The witness felt a hot searing sensation and became unable to move. Following the encounter, he claimed "to be healed of his arthritis pain."

Investigators of the case also noted landing traces which were found at the site.[4]

While gray aliens are often portrayed as emotionless and uncaring, this is not always the case. In the following encounter, a police officer reports a benevolent, peaceful and physically healing interaction with gray ETs.

CASE #096. RHEUMATIC FEVER.

In 1980, Ivan Rivera Morales, a police officer from Puerto Rico, began to pray for a miracle. He lay in a hospital suffering from a severe case of rheumatic fever. He was in such severe pain that he was unable to move. The doctors were unable to help him and sent him home.

255

One evening, as he lay in bed, two golden spheres of light appeared and then transformed into four-foot-tall gray ETs. "Do not be afraid," they told him telepathically. Morales suddenly found himself inside a UFO which took off upward, then dived down into the ocean and into an undersea base. Morales described the base as dimly lit and freezing cold. As he was put on a metallic table, Morales saw other grays moving around. He was given a bitter-tasting drink. Samples of semen were taken and a strange mental-bonding took place, which Morales said imbued him with a great sense of peace. He remembers little else, and woke up in his bedroom three hours after he had been taken.

Following the encounter, Morales's rheumatism was markedly improved. While the cure wasn't complete, he no longer suffered from any pain or deformity caused by the disease.[5]

An inflammatory condition of the joints, bursitis has multiple causes, but is sometimes connected to autoimmune disorders like arthritis. In the following case, reported vicariously from a California abductee, the healing was affected using the most common method used by ETs to cure people--an instrument which emits a healing light.

CASE #136. BURSITIS.

California abductee, "Linda," who was healed of a yeast infection in 1988, also observed many other healings, including one of bursitis. While onboard the UFO, Linda saw a large, dark-haired man being examined by the aliens. They told her that the man suffered from a bursitis-like condition in which his left shoulder dislocates and becomes swollen. They tested the mobility of the man's arm by raising it. Finally, they cured his condition using an instrument with a "pulsating light."[6]

Another arthritis healing reported by Linda also involves an alien instrument which emits multi-colored lights. In this case, the ETs explained precisely how the instrument actually works to affect the healing.

CASE #137. HIP PAIN.

During her 1988 abduction, Linda saw a young boy being examined. The aliens told her that the boy suffered from chronic hip problems on his right side, and that the bones were deteriorating. He walked with a pronounced limp. Linda watched as the aliens placed a large L-shaped instrument over the boy. It emitted green, yellow, blue, pink and white light, which Linda was told would "promote new cell growth." After the operation, he got off the table, still limping but much improved.[7]

While contactees are often chosen to be healed, in a few scattered cases, people who are closely associated with a contactee receive the healing, such as the following case.

CASE #127. INFLAMMATION IN LEGS.

In May 1988, an anonymous professional male dancer was cured by a UFO of his illness. The event occurred at the Sebago Cabins Recreation Park in New York State.

The dancer joined about ten other people and contactee Sixto Paz Wells at a predetermined location in the wilderness. After doing a lengthy cleansing meditation, the group watched several star-like objects move in darting patterns. The objects responded to the mental commands of the group members by moving according to telepathic directions. At one point, strange flashes of light illuminated the group. "Another bolt of light hit our group that for some reason made me dizzy and nauseous," said Betty, one of the group members. "Other people in our group reported the same sensation. The queasy feelings left me after a few moments."

Wells told the group that they had received what the aliens call a "Xendra," which gives psychic and spiritual energy.

The anonymous dancer had come with his wife to the group. He was "very ill with his legs swollen and in pain." In the middle of the night both of them were awakened by a "brilliant white light that illuminated the room and soon went away."

The next morning, when the dancer woke up, he was surprised to find his pajama bottoms on the floor. He didn't remember taking them off. It was then that he realized his legs were "pain-free and not swollen anymore."

The dancer showed the other people in the group what happened, and several others also reported having contact in the middle of the night."[8]

While the healings of injury cases usually occur at the time of the injury, the healings of serious diseases typically occur after the witness has suffered from the condition for many years, such as the following case.

CASE #130. ARTHRITIS.

Ann DeSoto of Watsonville, California was driving with her boyfriend near their home one afternoon in December 1988 when their car was suddenly enveloped in fog. Shortly later, they saw a bright, orange globe of light hovering over a nearby field. Desoto had seen UFOs before and was very interested in them, so they turned the car and headed toward the light.

At that point, they experienced a period of missing time. Their next memory is walking into the boyfriend's house nearly five hours later. They both went inside and fell into a deep sleep.

The next morning, they found that the bedsheets had blood stains. DeSoto also had a strange-looking mark on her hip. Even more incredible is the healing that took place. As the report on her case says, "...the arthritis she carried for years in that hip, disappeared."[9]

In this next case, like the one above, the witness suffered from arthritis for many years before receiving a healing. However, in her case, there was a compelling need for the healing.

CASE #147. ARTHRITIS.

At 4:00 a.m., on December 15, 1989, Mae, a sixty-year-old waitress was heading home from her job at a truck-stop in Mississippi, when a bright light hovered over her car. Suddenly it was 6:00 a.m., and Mae found herself waking up with her car parked alongside the road. Vague memories of being in a strange

258

"doctor's examining room" filled her mind. She remembered several figures standing around her while a "doctor" stood next to her and "passed some kind of rod over her body again and again."

Mae was perplexed by her memories of the procedure, but she was shocked by the after-effects. She had suffered from severe arthritis for several years. Her condition had recently worsened to the point that she was about to retire, despite having no benefits. The arthritis was present in her wrist, knee and finger joints. After the missing time episode, Mae discovered that her arthritis was gone. She no longer felt any pain, allowing her to continue her employment.[10]

The following case from researcher, Virginia Aronson, involves a woman who has experienced multiple ET contacts, and multiple healings.

CASE #181. ARTHRITIS.
In 1992, Connie Isele of Sacramento, California, reported her second UFO-related healing experience. She awoke one morning to find three evenly-spaced bruises on her knee. Since the discovery, she also noticed that the arthritis that she carried in the knee completely disappeared. She has had no pain since.[11]

While most healings are on the ETs terms, and not our own, this is not always the case. In the following case, the witness asked for--and received--the exact healing he requested.

CASE #194. TENDONITIS.
California abductee, Chuck Weiss, says that he has received multiple healings at the hands of ETs. Shortly after being healed of a pulled muscle in his arm, he asked for--and received--a healing of tendonitis in his left middle finger. "I've evidently had a second spontaneous healing a couple of nights ago," he writes.

In April of 1994, he developed "a bad case of tendonitis" on his left middle finger. The pain persisted for two months with no sign of improvement. He eventually became "sick and tired" of the constant pain. Remembering his earlier healing, he decided to ask the ETs to heal his finger. He spoke out loud, asking and then demanding a healing, telling them, "You owe me!"

Apparently, says Weiss, the ETs heard his plea. "For the past two days I've had no pain in that finger and can use it as if nothing was ever wrong, although it now bends with a snap as if it's 'double-jointed.' It appears they had to shorten the tendon in that area. Those little guys can actually be useful!"[12]

A good example of who is healed and why comes from the following witness, a former Navy man who had a series of encounters, one of which resulted in a profound healing that changed his life.

CASE #195. TENDONITIS, ARTHRITIS.

William Shelhart worked first in the Navy, and then as a mailman for the U.S. Postal Service, where he was employed for many years. "I enjoyed my job," Shelhart says, "or I never would have put up with the pain that I received from it. If you can imagine jumping in and out of a mail truck five, six days a week, using my right foot to land on for almost twenty years, and slipping, tripping and twisting my ankle hundreds of times. So when I was offered early retirement in 1992, I jumped at the chance, as the pain was unbearable. Also my right wrist was in constant movement from reading and sorting mail, and [was] very painful."

Late on the evening of April 22, 1994, Shelhart was driving through New Mexico when he experienced a close-up sighting of a craft that hovered over his car, causing a period of missing time.

A few months later, he was back in his home in a remote and rural area of the Hawaiian Islands, when he had another strange encounter.

"I woke one morning and felt an itch on my right foot and discovered three puncture wounds in a perfect triangle. They were in the process of scabbing over. I sleep on a waterbed, so nothing could have scratched it."

Shelhart wasn't sure what to think about the strange marks. Then, a few weeks later it happened again. This time, he saw the

ETs coming. "I woke in the middle of the night with a bright light coming in the back window. It lasted about thirty to sixty seconds. I froze and could not get out of bed to look outside."

There was no way a light that bright could be out there. Shelhart wanted to investigate, but the next thing he knew, he was waking up the next morning. "My right wrist was itching. The same thing happened--three puncture wounds in a perfect triangle...I woke up and found those triangular pinpricks on my right hand."

Prior to the two incidents, Shelhart was suffering from chronic pain in his wrist and ankle, exactly where the marks had appeared. He had tried everything to relieve his pain. Following the encounters, things finally began to change.

"It wasn't until after my incident that things started to get better," says Shelhart. "I just know that I progressed and started to feel better. Since then I have been ninety percent cured. Only on occasion when the wet weather is extreme do I notice discomfort, but nothing like before. I am almost sixty-seven years old and I can hang off a twenty-foot ladder placing the weight on my right foot, and paint with my right hand, day after day. I don't care if people doubt my explanation. I know what I feel."

One year later, in 1995, Shelhart was visiting Sedona, Arizona with his wife, Rose, when they were both followed closely down the highway by a bright glowing light. Finally, it landed in the field next to them, causing a period of missing time. Years later, they both went under hypnosis and a friendly encounter with humanoids emerged. While William couldn't remember any details, Rose recalled they were both taken onboard, where they conversed with friendly ETs. Says Rose, "They said they are helping certain people here because they will help humanity. And something like, the more we help, the more they help us. But they can't interfere and just take over everything."[13]

An unusual case of an ET healing comes from a woman who was so transformed by what happened to her that she felt compelled to share it with the entire world. It is one of several cases in which people have been given highly specific medical advice by ETs, in this case a homeopathic cure. DISCLAIMER: Use at your own risk!

CASE #210. ARTHRITIS CURE.

In 1995, Lavinia Rittkiss was a healer based in Los Angeles, California, with a healing center for natural homeopathic cures. One evening, says Rittkiss, she was visited by ETs who offered her a cure for her arthritis.

Says Rittkiss: "Seven small creatures appeared out of the thin air, and they used their huge, glowing eyes to immobilize me. They appeared in the corner of my office and they seemed very loving and concerned. They told me they had a great affection and respect for humans and wanted to help us with this gift. I couldn't move or speak. I felt like I was dreaming. When I woke up, the spacemen were gone and the recipe was sitting on the desk in front of me...the aliens told me that it affects the electrical energy of the body, reversing the negative impulses that bring about diseases and unhealthy emotions."

The aliens wanted her to take the medicine and share the recipe with as many people as possible. After seeing the ingredients--many of which were well-known natural cures by themselves--Rittkiss decided to give the medicine a try. For one month she took one teaspoon per day.

Says Rittkiss, "I couldn't believe what it did for me. My arthritis is gone, my skin glows, even my teeth and hair are different. I feel like a teen-ager again."

In the interests of curing as many people as possible, Rittkiss is willing to share the formula with anyone.

"2 tsp. diced fresh garlic; 3 tbs. olive oil; 5 tbs. pure clover honey; 1 tbs. apple cider vinegar; ½ tsp. cayenne pepper; ¼ tsp. asafetida (optional); ¼ cup strong green tea, freshly made."

To make the syrup: "Sauté the garlic in oil for one minute, then add the other ingredients. Simmer and cook over low flame for five minutes, let cool. Strain into a glass jar, cover and refrigerate. Take one teaspoon per day."

Rittkiss says, "I have shared the recipe with hundreds of people and it has cured everything--acne, heart disease, depression and even cancer. The syrup is so wonderful...it's a miracle gift, a token of love from outer space."[14]

A particularly compelling and poignant account of a UFO healing of a young child comes from the country of Chile, whose government has been more forthcoming and truthful about UFO activity than most other countries.

CASE #221. RHEUMATISM.

On September 28, 1998, Asbel Ortega Flores of Puren, Chile was driving with her mother, Alicia, and her four-year-old son, Gabriel. They were returning to their home after traveling to Los Angeles, California, to visit doctors. Gabriel had been diagnosed with rheumatoid fever, which had severely damaged his heart. Gabriel's condition was so critical that his doctors said that crying or any slight agitation could cause a heart-attack and death.

Gabriel was asleep in the back seat of the car as they traveled between the cities of Angol and Los Sauces. They came around a curve in the road to see a large, round, glowing object with a grayish band around the center. The object was twenty feet in diameter, and hovered only a few hundred feet above the highway.

Flores, who had been traveling at around forty MPH, slowed the car down to observe the strange craft. At this point, both she and her mother noticed a strange sensation of heat inside their bodies. Neither felt any fear, only awe and wonder.

Suddenly Gabriel woke up. Says Flores, "He was very animated and chatty. Before that he had been very limp and unable to even raise his head."

Other cars began to approach from the opposite direction. Flores flashed her lights at them, trying to get them to look at the UFO, but none seemed to notice it. Flores did see an odd layer of "dark mist" where the UFO hovered motionlessly. After a total of about fifteen minutes, the object now moved to the right and disappeared over the treetops. Flores continued the drive to her home in Puren.

Later they returned to Los Angeles for more medical tests, confirming that Gabriel was no longer sick. "The doctor," says Flores, "was able to ascertain that my son was completely healthy. The doctor admitted to me that he couldn't find any explanation to the situation."

Investigators Ramon Nava Osorio and Raul Nunez conducted a full investigation, interviewing the family and even obtaining a statement from their doctor who said, in part, "...at that time, events occurred for which there is no known logical explanation."

The Flores family told them that since the encounter they have experienced several incredible "coincidences" which assisted them through difficult periods in their lives, and which they attribute to the UFO they had encountered.

"Is it possible that Gabriel's sudden healing had a direct connection with the incredible light that accompanied his mother's car that evening?" the investigators asked. "Although we are always reserved and expecting some other type of explanation, which we have not found up to this moment, we believe that it was the effect of this light that not only affected Gabriel, but his mother and grandmother as well, as both women felt themselves invaded by an intense feeling of heat from head to toe. This tells us that 'something' was going on at the time on that dark road..."

The investigators were able to locate many other reports of sightings along the same stretch of highway around the same time, including sightings, landings and car-chases. On October 21, 1968, less than one month following the Flores's encounter, an ambulance driver says that his ambulance was followed along the same stretch of road by a "brightly-lit UFO."

Write the investigators, "An experience such as this is uncanny, and certainly more than one reader will question its authenticity. They are in their right to do so. We can only say that as a policy, we never publish anything without having confirmed the original sources, and in this event, the protagonists themselves restated their experience, a fact that leads us to believe once more that we know very little about our surroundings, much less about ourselves, and leads us to think that on certain occasions, higher intelligences manifest on our earthly plane."[15]

The following account involves one healing, with the implication of several more, once again reinforcing the probability that this book represents only a small portion of the actual number of cases.

CASE #227. LEG PAIN.
This case comes from a young lady in the United Kingdom. One evening when she was nine years old (date not given, circa 1990s?), she woke up to find herself paralyzed in bed. "All of a sudden," she says, "this blue light shines through the bedroom window. I see my covers fall off to the floor as I get lifted through the window. I remember bits and pieces of being on a table in a room as other children are being examined too. There was a tall creature that looked like a praying mantis in a robe, over me, that put these needles in my legs. It didn't hurt, and it was talking to me telepathically about the procedure, 'helping me walk.' During that time, I had issues with my legs and had a difficult time walking. I black out and wake up on my bed, minus the covers that were now on the floor. I had three needle marks on each leg, where I remember the creature putting them. Ever since, I was able to walk a lot better and had no more problems."[16]

This short, uninvestigated case, while sparse on details, provides further evidence of UFO healings.

CASE #228. ARTHRITIS.
A member of the group UFO Contact Center International (UFOCCI) told the group that ETs cured her. For many years she suffered from acute arthritis in her shoulder. Writes Leneesa, "During a contact experience (circa 1990s?) a 'rod of light' was shoved through her shoulder. Since that day the arthritis in her shoulder has disappeared."[17]

A wonderfully sincere example of a benevolent encounter with healing ETs comes from Pennsylvania. The witness, an elderly woman, has no apparent history of UFO encounters, and has no idea why she was healed.

CASE #266. ARTHRITIS.

Born in 1949, today Joy Davies lives on the outskirts of the Allegheny National Forest in the small town of Warren, Pennsylvania. Davies is retired, but enjoys gardening, taking walks with her dog, Ben, and volunteering at the local Goodwill. In 2011, tragedy struck and Davies lost her husband, Jack, to a severe case of pneumonia.

Davies recovered from the loss of her husband, and went on with her life as best as she could. Things weren't always easy. Davies suffered from severe arthritis in her arms and hands and had to take pills daily. Even with the medication, she still wasn't able to be as active as she would've like.

On August 2, 2012, all this changed. On that evening--as she did most evenings--Davies took a walk with her dog, Ben, down the trail through the forest behind her house. She had walked only a few minutes when she came upon a group of figures. They were child-sized, but had very pale skin and no hair on their heads. They were smiling at her, and Davies heard a voice in her head telling her not to be afraid.

"I wasn't scared at all," said Davies. "They were very polite and I felt safe the whole time."

A large, white, peanut-shaped craft sat next to them, lighting the area around them with a soft blue glow. Suddenly Davies found herself inside the craft. "I don't remember entering the ship, but I knew I was inside because the walls were curved and the blue light was underneath me. Ben was next to me, and one of the aliens was scratching behind his ears, which he likes."

As she stood there, Davies saw a "tiny bright blue light, like a star, but about the size of a snowflake." The light appeared above her and floated slowly down. Davies was delighted, and laughing, she held out her hand to catch it. "The next thing I remember is standing on the path facing my house. One of the aliens was holding my hand. When he let go and turned back down the path, I don't know why I didn't turn to watch, but instead I just walked back to the house with Ben and made a cup of tea. I then went to bed, because somehow four hours had passed, and it was late."

Davies has no idea why she had this experience, but when she woke up the next morning, she had a wonderful surprise. All symptoms of her arthritis were gone and she was pain-free. She believes the aliens cured her of her arthritis. "Now I haven't got it at all and haven't taken a single pill since. I played tennis for the first time in several years...and [I] can knit again...now that the arthritis is gone."

One final side-effect was with her dog. "Ben seems more frisky too," she said.

Davies's case was investigated by Holly Thorne, a columnist for *The Morton Report*. Thorne interviewed Davies and then after some research, discovered that she wasn't the only person in the Warren area to report UFOs. "Prior to Joy's alleged encounter," writes Thorne, "four different people had reported strange lights in the area. Three sightings had been reported since April, and only a week before Davies had her experience, several witnesses reported military activity in the forest. Part of the forest was sealed off for three days, and when they left, some witnesses observed a military truck carrying something hidden beneath a large tarp. What it was remains unknown."[18]

The following case is perhaps unique in that it was initiated through a man who channels ETs. During the session, the witness asked for a healing. She never expected it to actually happen.

CASE #268. CHRONIC FATIGUE SYNDROME.

After a number of sightings of UFOs, paranormal activity in her home, and sometimes waking up with strange marks on her body, "Kay" (pseudonym) realized she was having her own experiences. Years later, in 1983, she saw an orb hovering over her infant son as he lay in bed.

In 2012, she began to research UFOs actively. During her research, she had the opportunity to speak with Paul Hamden, who claims to be able channel a being from Zeta Reticuli. Hamden came well-recommended so she agreed to see him. "I decided to request healing from a debilitating illness that had periodically ravaged my body for several years," Kay writes. "I knew that several experiencers with whom I had worked claimed to have been healed by ETs. Being a skeptical person, I had no expectation that I'd be healed."

Three nights following the session, Kay woke up to feel "excruciating pain and strong electrical tingling throughout my body." Alarmed at first and ready to dial 911, Kay remembered speaking with "Keek," the name of the Zeta Reticulan, and became calm. Perhaps, she thought, Keek was trying to make contact. The feeling eventually faded and Kathleen fell asleep.

The morning brought good news. "When I awakened, I felt like I was twenty-five again! I could feel none of the aches and pains that a person my age experiences on a daily basis. It has now been more than two years since I was healed. I haven't experienced one relapse, and I hope that it will continue. I documented the event by reporting it to several researchers and my physician. It left me with the opinion that this Zeta being is benevolent...I call it a miracle." In 2014 Kay wrote about her healing experience in an article called, "The UFO-PSI Connection in My Own Life."[19]

As we have seen, healings are a consistent feature of UFO encounters. Despite this, they are still rare, and there isn't a lot of publicity about them. Sometimes people who have a UFO encounter with a healing believe they are alone with the experience, and don't know where to turn for information. In the following case, an experiencer searched the internet for information about what was happening to her, and came upon my website.

CASE #286. CHRONIC FATIGUE, CHEMICAL SENSITIVITY.
"I am writing to you because I have just found you on a *Google* search on UFOs and healing...I am overwhelmed, just overwhelmed. I am pretty much just sitting here, almost

screaming and crying." So began an email I received from a woman (a resident of the Isle of Wight, in the U.K.), whom I shall give the pseudonym, Camilla. She was having an unusual experience involving an apparent alien entity that was healing her, and she had finally found some corroboration validating what was happening to her.

Camilla reports that her childhood was normal but that she was "a bit of a dreamy kid, a bit of a deep thinker, so I connected with the world in a way that was a bit 'magical.'" But she had no significant paranormal experiences or UFO encounters. As an adult, she suffered from depression, and then developed chronic fatigue syndrome. Her condition worsened when she developed another condition known as chemical sensitivity and electrical hypersensitivity. Chemicals of any kind made her sick. Nor could she stand to be around electronic machinery. In addition to making her feel ill, her mere presence would make electronic machines break down. The condition was so bad that by 2009, she was living as a virtual hermit. "I have a bad case of it," she wrote. "I have been ill for a very long time, very desperately ill."

Things became worse. In addition to her other symptoms, she began having trouble breathing. Her entire body began to fail her in multiple areas. "I was so sensitive, the air would literally cut me."

Unable to find relief through traditional methods, in early 2015 Camilla sought out a psychic healer. Unfortunately, her condition persisted. Then, two days later, her life changed forever. In the middle of the night, her room filled with white light. She sensed an invisible presence enter her body and possess her. "I was waking up unable to breathe, and the night it started, it was extremely serious. Looking back, I may have been dying that night. He came in like a wisp of energy and went into my tissues, extending very palpable filaments into the lungs."

She felt "a lot of heat" and her lungs felt as though they were being "intricately manipulated," as though the being was sewing up a rip in her lung.

This was just the beginning. Following this experience, the being began to visit her on a nightly basis. She could not only feel

269

its presence, but if she turned her head quickly enough, she sometimes saw its form, which appeared as a sparkly light. In the beginning, she felt as though the entity was trying to have intercourse with her. She was so concerned that she went to a clinic and obtained birth control. "I was afraid of getting pregnant by it," she said.

She told only the two people closest to her what was happening. "I was sure no one would believe me," she explained. She began taking photos and was surprised to see that a number of them showed anomalous lights around her body.

"At first it was harrowing," says Camilla.

Before long she began to communicate with the entity, and her relationship changed to one where she felt the being was actually there to heal her. "He talks to me, and he has a sense of humor."

By February 2015, the being was working with her "several hours a day and often through the night in multiple areas. My eyes, my stomach, my lymph nodes."

On one occasion, the entity patted her stomach. "Very bad," he said. "very bad, finished."

"I am certain I had cancer," she says. "And in a series of difficult operations, he has removed this from my stomach...I didn't know I needed so much done to my stomach."

Her encounters continued through 2017 and became increasingly benevolent. "A couple of times when I was absolutely terrified this year, he enveloped me in the most incredible feeling of a love which was timeless and immense, and I then experienced him to be a being of light, which was the first and only time that he was palpable in that way."

Camilla continued to see lights when the being approached, and sometimes caught them in photos. "It's not just any old light," she says. "The light is the thing that is healing me. It's like a precision instrument."

About one week before contacting me, Camilla had her first UFO sighting. It was a sunny afternoon with scattered clouds. "I was looking at the clouds," she said, and there was an object that was too low to be a satellite, and too slow by far to be a plane, but it was at the altitude of a plane. It was really odd and quite bright."

Camilla grabbed her camera and filmed the object. When she stopped the camera and set it down, the object disappeared. "I can't explain it," she says. "I am quite rational, and there are lots of things it could be, but it's not like anything I've seen before. It was too big to have just lost the angle of the sun to catch and completely disappear."

The good news is, Camilla has felt a steady improvement in her health condition. "Now it is more peaceful," she says. "This year I realize that it is a blessing...I have had multiple healings. I have it all documented...I'm sitting here almost normal on this computer today; it shouldn't be possible at all. Lots of other healings. It's all documented."

When her experiences began, Camilla began to search for answers. She discovered that the Isle of Wight where she lived is steeped in paranormal activity of all kinds. She now wonders if this might be a factor in her experiences. She also wonders if her ultra-sensitivity somehow attracted this being, or if the healer she sought had something to do with the entity that was visiting her. Camilla is still searching for answers. All she knows is that she has experienced healings from this entity, and that it is still with her. As she says, "He has yet to let me go."[20]

An analysis of the healing cases shows an underlying pattern of corroborating details. Despite this, each case is as unique as the individual who has them, and it seems that every case provides new insights into the UFO phenomenon. The following case has several rare details that are not often reported.

CASE #282. ARTHRITIS, DIABETES.

On the evening of July 23, 2015, "Rory" (pseudonym) sat in front of his computer in his home in Yonkers, New York, when he suddenly became unable to move. His dog, who sat next to him, also appeared to be paralyzed. Rory didn't see anyone, but he sensed a presence in the room. Suddenly, his electronics went haywire; his computer switched programs and began playing music, and the lights on his cellphone began blinking on and off.

Events went from strange to bizarre. Rory didn't hear anything, but he felt that the entities were telepathically questioning him, trying to judge and categorize him. "I just kept saying that I'm a good person, and deserving," Rory says.

Rory not only felt mentally linked to the unseen beings, but also to his dog, whose intellectual awareness seemed to be enhanced. "She was looking at me," Rory explains, "and I felt she was telling me to be calm and unafraid."

Rory wondered if one of the beings had taken over his dog and was communicating through her. At some point, Rory found himself naked and being anally probed. Then he was back in his computer chair, feeling as though one of the beings had taken over his body. The trance ended when Rory heard what sounded like a jet engine.

He ran outside but couldn't see anything due to a low cloud cover. "It was right above me, hovering loudly," he says. "It was no plane." He saw another person sitting in a car and asked him if he could hear the strange noise. The man said yes, but neither of them could see any object. Suddenly it became quiet, and Rory returned inside.

Following the experience, Rory's thoughts began to focus on profound and esoteric subjects. "I suddenly started thinking about the universe, creation, God, and seemed to have knowledge, or a better understanding of ideas I never thought about before, and a sense of how things came to be, and what we are in the universe."

Rory finally went to bed. Events, however, were still in progress. "The next day," Rory says, "my health was extraordinarily great. No aches or pains with my arthritis. My diabetes was like [it was] not there. My sugar wouldn't raise no matter what I ate, and this was for about a week, like I just got diabetes. My energy and strength were incredible."

Even his dog seemed altered, Rory said, as if she was more aware.

Three days following the event, Rory lay in bed with his dog when something very weird happened. "I felt a sudden dread, like something altered in the time-space dimension, and they left. My dog went back to being a dog with less awareness; that's the best way I can explain it. I realized for the past three days, she was more attentive and like a close friend. I know this is weird, but that's all I can say and remember."

Rory now believes that the unseen entities had been observing and interacting with him for the past three days. "These beings are dimensional travelers," he said, "and are in our time. [They] made me aware that death isn't the end, just different, and that we are made up of energy and control our environment...They were having fun with me, and were curious about my daily events."

Rory isn't sure if he was dealing with ETs or some kind of interdimensional beings, but ultimately, the experience was positive. "I'm not afraid or confused about these events. I feel comforted with the new awareness about life." He shared his experience with a friend, but when his friend expressed skepticism, he learned to keep quiet about what happened to him. A few months following the encounter, he reported it to MUFON.[21]

With each category of healings, the amount of evidence supporting these cases increases. Each category provides multiple cases, some of which are very well-documented by investigators and doctors. The continuing stream of cases is hard to explain away. Being able to heal arthritis with a beam of light may sound like *Star Trek*, but it appears to be a reality.

Cases like William Shelhart, Joy Davies and Asbel Flores seem to show a very benevolent side to the ETs. While the ETs' motives behind cures like these will likely remain a mystery, the people who received them remain healthy and thankful.

Chapter Twenty
Infertility

ETs, particularly the grays, express a strong interest in genetics and human reproduction. When a person is taken onboard a craft and examined, sperm and eggs are often taken. The missing fetus syndrome and the gray-human hybrid phenomenon are both well-known and widely reported. Many abductees have been told that the grays have problems with their own reproduction, and that this is the reason behind the hybrid agenda.

Because of the ETs' strong focus on reproduction, it should come as no surprise that there are some cases involving men and women who have been cured of this condition. What follows are five separate encounters involving cures of infertility.

CASE #059. INFERTILITY.

This case, investigated by Barbara Lamb, occurred to an anonymous female in Colorado in 1972. "There's another woman who's not a regular client, but I've had long conversations with her." Lamb says. "She had all kinds of reproductive problems. She was not able to conceive a baby, which she and her husband really wanted to do. They had all the testing, and she just wasn't able to get pregnant. They did that for a couple of years. Then he woke up one night to find that there was this large being having sex with his wife next to him in bed, right next to him in the same bed. He started to get up and they sort of zonked him out. And he couldn't move, but he still had his eyes open and he could see what was going on. There were two beings in the room and they were big, tall. And one of them was definitely on top of his wife having sex with her. And she looked like she was deeply asleep but also having a tremendous amount of pleasure. Now both of them forget that for probably about nineteen years. And then the husband who witnessed this started to remember. He did a regression about this and got the details of it. And then, of course, he told his wife, and she began to remember some of it too, and remember other encounters.

"To make a long story short, at a certain point, the extraterrestrials said to her in one of her experiences, 'Now you have given us two sons through this mating procedure. And now we will allow you to have two children.' So they did whatever they did, and cleared up her reproductive difficulties. And she was then able to conceive and bear two children, whom I met. They were teen-agers when I met them, and they are just fine. They're very human and normal."[1]

The following case, involving a police officer, is among the best-documented of UFO healings. The case involves a credible witness willing to use his real name, numerous outside witnesses to the UFO, and verification of a healing by Earth doctors, and the presence of a new baby!

CASE #095. INFERTILITY.
On November 28, 1980, police officer Alan Godfrey of the West Yorkshire Metropolitan Police Force in England was assigned to handle a peculiar situation. The station had received several calls about a herd of missing cows that had been seen in various locations.

Godfrey had been twice commended for investigative work involving murders, so this assignment seemed trivial. On the way to find the cows, he encountered a "large object blocking the road." At first he thought it was a double-decker bus, but on closer inspection he saw it was a metallic saucer-shaped object with colored lights hovering about five feet above the road.

He tried to radio the station, but his car's radio was dead. Godfrey had no police training for such an experience, but he quickly realized he was seeing a UFO as portrayed in science fiction movies. As he sat there sketching the object, Godfrey experienced a "jump in time." He found himself further ahead on the road, missing twenty minutes of time.

He rushed to the station and returned with several officers to the scene. Although it had been pouring rain all night, the area where the UFO had hovered was completely dry.

They found the cows in a fenced area where they appeared to have been deposited. There were no tracks in the area and the gate was locked at nights. "The only way they could have gotten there," said Godfrey, "is if something had gone plunk and dropped them there."

At first Godfrey was ridiculed by his fellow officers, but when other officers in neighboring counties reported similar experiences, the ridicule seemed to stop. Godfrey then received ridicule from another source, his superiors. They advised him to simply resign. When he refused, his police car was taken away and he was given a bicycle. Godfrey finally resigned.

Eventually he underwent hypnosis and recalled some of his experience aboard the UFO. Godfrey's wife, upon hearing his experience, made note of a peculiar event.

One year earlier, Godfrey was called to a local disturbance. As a result, he was severely beaten by three individuals. During the beating, Godfrey was kicked in the testicles, causing him to lose one testicle. He could no longer enjoy a normal sex life, and could not have children. "I was also told I would definitely be sterile for the rest of my life," says Godfrey. "I would not be able to father children."

One night a few weeks after the attack, Godfrey's wife was awakened by a strange sound over the house. She tried to wake up Godfrey, but inexplicably, he would not wake up. After a few minutes, the sound left. She never knew how to categorize the event until her husband mentioned his UFO encounter. Only then did she realize what happened. She believes a UFO was responsible for the sound.

That morning, something very unusual occurred. Godfrey seemed to be cured of his sexual disfunction. "The next morning," his wife said, "Alan and I made love for the first time since he was beaten up. And I then became pregnant."

Upon hearing of his wife's pregnancy, Godfrey became angry and assumed his wife was seeing another man. Then Godfrey went to his doctor. The doctor was stunned and said that Godfrey was miraculously and impossibly cured. "I don't know how it happened," the doctor told him. "Your condition has been completely reversed. The test shows you're fertile, back to normal."[2]

Pioneering UFO researcher Brad Steiger is among the most prolific of UFO investigators and writers. He has documented several healing cases, including the following.

CASE #155. INFERTILITY.

One day, Doriel of Chicago, Illinois saw a UFO (date not given, circa 1980s?) Shortly following the sighting, two mysterious beings appeared. They said their names were Leita and Gamal, and told Doriel that they wanted to "incarnate" through Doriel, that she was "one of them," and that she would be perfect for bearing a child.

Unfortunately, Doriel had already been diagnosed with infertility. Her doctor had told her in no uncertain terms that she would never get pregnant.

Doris was told by the aliens, however, that she would become pregnant in six months. Six months later, the aliens' prediction came true; Doriel became inexplicably pregnant. Nine months later she had a baby girl by natural childbirth. Because of the unusual conditions involving her baby's conception, she gave her the middle name of Leita.

Doriel believes that the ETs cured her of her infertility, and she has her daughter to prove it. "Physiologically speaking," Doriel says, "I had been told that I would be unable to ever become pregnant."[3]

The infertility cases have the unique feature of providing a healing that can be verified in a way that's impossible to fake: a baby. In all three of the above cases, the witnesses were cured of infertility and had a child as a result. This next case is no exception.

CASE #187. INFERTILITY.

As a young boy, Neal (pseudonym) suffered an unfortunate groin injury which left him infertile. He wasn't aware of his infertility until 1982, when he joined the Air Force. He was married, and he and his wife wanted to have kids. Over the next nine years, they tried to get pregnant, but never did. Finally, Neal visited an Air Force physician who revealed his condition. Neal recalled the childhood injury and asked if that might be the cause. The doctor agreed that it probably was.

Then, one evening in 1993, two years after leaving the Air Force he had a terrible nightmare that caused him to wake up in a cold sweat, in his Cambridge, Ohio home. He remembered nothing about the dream, however, he did notice a strange mark on his groin. It looked like a boil or perhaps a burn.

He didn't think too much of it until a couple of days later when he went outside to mow the grass and saw "three burn marks on the ground."

Each mark was two-feet wide, burned black, and situated in a perfect triangle about thirty feet apart. "One of the circles was in close proximity to one of our blue spruce pine trees," says Neal. "I thought that was peculiar, so I grabbed my flashlight and squirmed underneath the tree. On the trunk I found that the bark was burnt and a couple of small branches had been burned off. There was also some residue on the ground that resembled small chunks of yellow plastic."

It looked as if a thirty-foot-wide triangular object had landed in their field, burning the ground and the tree.

One month following this incident, Neal's wife missed her period. They took a home pregnancy test and discovered that she was, in fact, pregnant. Says Neal, "It's as though whoever put the burn marks on my privates, fixed whatever damage was there from childhood."

Neal's daughter was born in April 1994. As she grew up, she proved to be an exceptionally bright and sensitive child. She

278

earned straight A's in school, and also displayed "precognitive abilities."

In 2003, their daughter (nine-years-old) was sleeping with them in bed when she woke up in the middle of the night. Her parents were both asleep. She watched as the wall began to glow with a blue light and four alien-looking creatures walked in. They surrounded the bed and began working on Neal and his wife. The daughter was overcome with fear and hid underneath the blanket.

Says Neal, "You might think I'm totally wacko by now, but I swear on a stack of Bibles that this is the truth...I don't want my name published for obvious reasons."[4]

The following final case remains uninvestigated, but appears to be another case of infertility being healed.

CASE #302. INFERTILITY.

A brief undated case from the files of FREE: "It was twenty years ago that I was told that I could not have children...at my annual exam after my abduction experience, my doctor said she couldn't explain why, but I can now get pregnant."[5]

The above cases show that the ETs are concerned not only with their own fertility, but with ours. There are only five cases, a small number compared to other categories, but with enough evidence to prove that these cures have actually taken place.

The ETs' interest in the reproductive health of humans shows that there is little danger of humans going extinct anytime soon. The grays (and other races) have been collecting human reproductive material for a very long time. Even if humans should become extinct on Earth, the human race itself will continue elsewhere.

Chapter Twenty-One
Tumors and Cysts

The terms *tumors* and *cysts* are often confused and used interchangeably, but actually they are different entities. Generally speaking, cysts are usually the result of an infection or obstruction in a gland. They are usually benign, but can rupture and spill their contents, causing serious health risks. Tumors, however, are uncontrolled tissue growth. Tumors are more likely to be malignant, but can also be benign. They can appear anywhere in the body. Their causes are still not fully understood, but are believed to be mostly genetic in nature.

This chapter documents fourteen cases involving healings of cysts and tumors. The first case comes from Sweden, and involves Richard Hoglund, who experienced an earlier cure of kidney stones.

CASE #053. BRAIN TUMOR.

In August 1966, in the first of a series of contacts with human-looking ETs, Richard Hoglund was given a strange metal tray with alien hieroglyphic symbols etched into it. He was then instructed by the ETs to move to the Bahamas, which he did. More contacts followed, some of which were confirmed by Hoglund's wife. Hoglund claimed that the ETs were also in contact with officials from various governments.

Hoglund experienced his second cure in 1970, five years following his initial contact. On this occasion he was healed of a brain tumor. According to his wife, Gunvor: "He had a lot of headaches before, and took pills."

Hoglund told his wife that the ETs were going to come for a visit, and that she should not come home early from work. Gunvor, who was frightened by her husband's experiences, did as he said. "After that day," she says, "he never had any headache. They did something to him and he said he would not have survived otherwise. It was some form of tumor, which was removed. I looked at his head, but there was only a slight blemish. He was a bit pale and tired afterward and was told to rest a few days."

Swedish researcher Alve Holmquist later wrote a full-length book about the case. Hoglund believed he was contacted because of his strong psychic and telepathic abilities. In 1977, at age 64, seven years following his second ET healing, Hoglund died of a sudden heart attack.[1]

The following is a remarkable case involving the healing of a woman of a tumor. It is one of several cases in which a witness prayed for a healing and received one from an unexpected source: ETs.

CASE #089. THYROID TUMOR.
In 1979, Faina Maksimovna of Simferopol, Crimea (in Ukraine) was suffering from painful inflammation of her thyroid caused by an apparent tumor. Maksimovna was seriously ill and her doctors had scheduled her for surgery. But she was afraid of undergoing surgery and was worried that she might not survive. One evening shortly before her scheduled surgery, she prayed to God to save her, and fell asleep.

In the middle of the night, Maksimovna was woken by a bright light hovering right outside her balcony. She looked outside and saw a disc-shaped object covered with colored lights. Suddenly an opening in the disc appeared, a ladder came down, followed by three very tall human-looking figures dressed in shimmery silver suits.

Using telepathy, the beings spoke. "You will not be operated on," they said. "We will cure you without surgery."

One of them held a large bottle filled with red liquid. A thin hose was connected to the neck of the bottle. One of the beings placed the other end of the hose on Maksimovna's neck. She felt a little sting and fell asleep.

The next morning, Maksimovna's mother noticed a mark on her daughter's neck and woke her up. Maksimovna discovered that her swelling and pain were gone. She went to Kiev to visit her doctors, who were surprised and confused. Medical tests showed that her tumor had apparently dissolved.

Following the incident Maksimovna continued to enjoy excellent health. Writes researcher Alberto Rosales, "Apparently the mysterious guests not only cured Faina, but awarded her with very strong immunity. In 2004 she was eighty years of age and looked twenty years younger."[2]

From the files of Edith Fiore Ph.D., the following case provides a clear observation of the process involved when aliens cure people of tumors.

CASE #138. TUMOR.
The reported abductions and healings of California abductee, Linda, have been recounted elsewhere in this book. In 1988, Linda witnessed the healing of many other people. One of the healings she saw involved a man healed of his tumor.

The man with the tumor lay on a table. The aliens held a small circular item over the man's tumor, which quickly began to disappear. "They're pulsing it to shrink the tumor," Linda explains, "and I can almost see the tumor shrinking as they're working on it." After the tumor was gone, the man got off the table, and another patient came to be examined for health problems.[3]

Richard Rylka of New Jersey has received multiple cures at the hands of ETs. He has been healed of injuries, illnesses and diseases. In the following case, he was healed of a tumor. This time, he was able to prove the cure to outside witnesses.

CASE #140. TUMOR.
In the mid-1980s, Rylka developed a tumor on the right side of his forehead. He was told by doctors that the tumor was related to a leukemia-type condition from his childhood. He'd already had several benign tumors surgically removed from his

body, yet the tumors kept coming back. Rylka's alien friends advised him not to have more surgery. Unfortunately, the tumors kept reappearing, so Rylka was forced to have another operation.

Then, during his stay at a convention in Atlantic City, New Jersey, Rylka's alien friends, Koran and Nepos appeared and removed one particularly bothersome tumor, leaving no traces.

That seemed to solve the problem until years later, when a tumor appeared on Rylka's forehead. The tumor quickly became inches wide and showed no signs of healing. Friends and family began to express concern that it would affect his health.

By 1989, Rylka was also becoming concerned. Then on July 5, 1989, Rylka received a house visit by one of his ET friends. The ET told him that they were aware of his tumor and had been searching for a method to remove it.

The aliens took him aboard a UFO and told him that they were going to test a new healing device on him. They placed a small hand-held instrument that emitted a beam of light. Rylka was placed in an unconscious state and felt no physical sensation. When he awoke, the aliens told Rylka that the tumor was gone. He was instantly "beamed" back into his bedroom.

Rylka dashed to the mirror and saw that the aliens were right; his tumor had vanished. Nearly a hundred people had witnessed Rylka's tumor, so when it disappeared, it amazed a great number of people, all of whom verified the cure. Rylka states that many people seemed surprised, making comments like, "My God, they're not all bad, are they?"[4]

The disappearance of a tumor is difficult to explain. However, when a person is already having encounters with ETs, and then experiences the disappearance of a tumor, and can connect it to an actual encounter, then the explanation becomes clear.

CASE #156. CHEST TUMOR.

An anonymous man from East Kilbride, England, reports that--besides living in a haunted house--he has been abducted by gray aliens who claimed to be from the planet Venus, though on a

283

higher vibration of existence. During one occasion (circa 1980s?) the witness was alone in his home when an unseen entity grabbed his arms and pulled them up over his head. He was unable to move and lost consciousness. When he awoke, he felt a "terrific warm glow in the chest region." He was then overcome by a feeling of peacefulness.

The anonymous man had been previously diagnosed with a tumor in the chest cavity. Later, the man went to the doctor and discovered that his tumor had "mysteriously disappeared." He attributes the tumor's disappearance to the visitation at his home.[5]

Experiencers are sometimes at a loss when trying to explain to their doctors what has happened to them. In the following case, a woman experienced a missing cyst, and a missing pregnancy, leaving several medical professionals very confused.

CASE #177. CYST.

Alicia Hansen (pseudonym) has had numerous contacts with extraterrestrials. She has undergone hypnotic regression to recall her early encounters, but now experiences full conscious contact. Back in 1991, in Atlanta, Georgia, however, she had an experience which she didn't fully understand until years later. It involved the disappearance of a cyst.

"It was really weird," says Alicia, "because at the time I was pregnant. And I took a pregnancy test and it said positive. I didn't want to be pregnant and I was really upset. I went and I told my husband because we didn't have any money. I told him and I was crying. I said, 'Oh, my God! This is horrible!' And bla-bla-bla. And anyway, I got this cyst. So I was really worried about the cyst and being pregnant and all that."

"Don't worry," her husband said. "We'll work it out."

Says Alicia, "I was worried about getting health insurance and all that. I had already been diagnosed with the cyst by the doctors. I was having a lot of problems with it too. They did an MRI where they take a picture and look at the cyst. So they saw the cyst and I was going to go back and have surgery on it.

"So time went on. I don't know what happened, but I woke up feeling really uncomfortable. Then I went to go have another pregnancy test at the hospital."

"You're not pregnant," they told her.

"I already had a test," she said. "And I was pregnant."

"We're really sorry," they told her. "You're not pregnant."

Alicia was mystified. "I thought that was really weird. And I was gaining weight and everything. I knew I was pregnant. And I took a test and it said yes, a big T. So I thought that was strange. I thought, 'Okay, I have just somehow spontaneously aborted or something. I wasn't sure what happened.

"So I went back to the hospital to get another MRI done and make sure everything was okay. And the nurse said, 'Well, this is so strange,'--not the nurse but the person who reads the picture. They said, 'This is really weird because if we didn't know any better, we'd say that you never had a cyst. But what's going on here is there's fluid in your fallopian tubes. And the fluid--right where the cyst was--this fluid is not present when it ruptures. This is a fluid that is usually present after surgery. And that is when the fluid is there.'

"So it completely looked as if I had had surgery done, and I didn't. There was a pregnancy that had been taken, but I also had a cyst that was removed too."

Although Alicia doesn't consciously recall the surgery, under hypnotic regression, she not only recalled this incident, but many others she has had. She also received another cure of body injuries after an auto accident. Having had so many ET surgeries, she has become familiar with ET medical technology. "They use a lot of lights," she says. "They use a lot of lasers. And they use sounds too."[6]

While Budd Hopkins was for many years a leading abduction investigator, and he admitted that healings do take place, and that he's uncovered such cases, he never wrote about them in any of his books. As it turns out, the main witness from his book, *Intruders*, Debbie Jordan, experienced an ET healing herself, which she reveals in her book, *Abducted*.

CASE #185. UTERINE TUMOR.

On September 23, 1993, six days before she was due to have a hysterectomy, Debbie Jordan of Kokomo, Indiana, her fiancé, and two friends were watching TV when an unexplained flashing light drew them outside. Prior to this, Debbie had experienced several UFO abductions, which were frightening and unpleasant. They watched it for a few minutes, and also videotaped it. After about fifteen minutes it darted away.

Moments later, they saw a strange figure walking down the road toward them. At first she thought it was a deer, until it stopped, cocked its head and began to walk backward. "I estimated its height to be about four feet," says Debbie. "It was very thin and pale in color...its head was lightbulb-shaped and its neck and shoulders were very thin. Its legs and arms were quite long and thin too." The figure seemed to be almost translucent, or semi-materialized. It was too dark to see it clearly.

Realizing it wasn't a deer, Debbie screamed. At this point, the videotape stopped working and they experienced a period of missing time. The next thing they knew, they had forgotten about the figure, which was no longer there, and they began discussing a strange beeping sound emanating from the nearby barn. They saw another UFO dart by, and they all went inside. After reviewing the incident and videotape, Debbie estimates that she was missing almost twenty minutes of time.

Six days later, Debbie underwent surgery for a complete hysterectomy. She had previously been diagnosed with a large uterine tumor. The surgery was successful and Debbie began her recovery. Six weeks later, she went to the surgeon for a check-up. She asked the surgeon about the tumor.

"I was very surprised to hear him say that he found no tumor at all," says Debbie "but that I did have something called adenomatosis, cysts on both ovaries, scar tissue, adhesions and endometriosis. I definitely needed the hysterectomy, but had no tumor."

Had the ETs removed it? Debbie isn't sure. "No one will ever know," she says, "yet I can't help but think it might have had something to do with the sighting we had just before I went in for surgery. Under the circumstances, wouldn't you?"

When she discovered that she had to have a hysterectomy, Debbie called Budd Hopkins. "Budd didn't seem too surprised with what I told him," says Debbie. "He said I was probably one of the last remaining female abductees to still have all her female parts, that this happening to me was probably just a matter of time. He definitely felt that there was some connection between my current physical problems and the experiences I have had."

It was small comfort. Debbie underwent surgery and began her recovery, which turned out to go remarkably well. "As I write this in December 1993, it's been twelve weeks since my surgery and I still have no need for any estrogen supplements, even though I had a total hysterectomy. No symptoms of menopause whatsoever ...Something seems to be taking very good care of me for some reason."[7]

The following case, investigated by researcher Bill Hamilton, provides excellent proof in the form of before and after X-rays showing the mysterious disappearance of a tumor.

CASE #201. TUMOR IN BREAST.

Another family whose lives were changed by the UFO phenomenon are the Van Klausens (pseudonym) of Burbank, California. The case is well-known among southern California UFO investigators and is very well-verified. The Van Klausens have not only seen UFOs, they have received regular visitations starting in December 1986 and continuing through the 1990s. The main witnesses are Morgana Van Klausen and her son. The husband remained skeptical until he too experienced a visitation. Both Morgana and her son experienced regular visitations by a short gray-skinned, bald, large-eyed figure. Whenever it would visit, both would experience total paralysis. On a few occasions, Morgana was able to end the visitations by mounting a physical struggle against the paralysis. By breaking the paralysis, the bizarre figures would dematerialize. While skeptics may say that this sounds like sleep paralysis, the Van Klausen case also involves several close-up UFO sightings, missing time encounters, landing traces and medical proof of extraterrestrial intervention.

On December 4, 1994, Van Klausen went to the doctor and was diagnosed with a tumor in her breast. The chief investigator to the case, Bill Hamilton, says, "An X-ray found a peculiarity in the axillary segment of the right breast. This was followed by an ultrasonography over the same area. A small non-cystic mass measuring 1.6 x .6 cm was found in the problem area."

Surgery was scheduled for December 14 so that Van Klausen would have time to recover from a slight fever. On the day before the surgery, she was driving with her son when they observed a "white, triangular-shaped craft" hovering nearby. They watched it for a moment until it suddenly darted away. Her son became very excited and said, 'Mom, look! Wow, this is a good sign--they are protecting us. We are protected. You wait and see, you'll have no more problems."

That evening, Van Klausen was overcome by intense pain in the area of the non-cystic mass. She tried to get up out of bed, but was unable to move. She sensed strange figures in her room. At that point, she lost consciousness. She woke up the next morning and went straight to the doctor to have her surgery. That's when both she and her doctor got a huge surprise.

The doctor inserted a needle into the mass and took another X-ray. To everyone's shock, the new X-ray showed that there was no mass. Another ultrasound was ordered which confirmed that the mass had disappeared. Says Hamilton, "Both the radiologist and the surgeon confirmed that the previous diagnostic had revealed a solid mass and that solid masses don't just disappear."

Hamilton has obtained the medical records which confirm the disappearance of the mass. He speculates that the aliens may have been removing an implant, but as he says, "The explanation is only speculative." Whatever the case, Hamilton says that "Morgana reported that she felt an unusual sense of wellbeing after the mass was gone."[8]

While grays are responsible for most of the reported healings, mantids and Nordics comprise a significant number of cases. The following case, involving a human-looking ET comes from English researcher, Timothy Good.

CASE #215. CYST IN BREAST.

On March 27, 1977, the world's most deadly aviation accident occurred at Tenerife on the Canary Islands, during which 583 people were killed. Flight attendant, "Carmina," was one of the few miraculous survivors. As unusual as that experience was, Carmina was soon to find herself the recipient of an equally astonishing experience.

Twenty years later in March 1997, Carmina (now a clinical psychologist) worked as an insurance broker specializing in medical malpractice cases. She was working alone in her office in a tall building in downtown San Juan, Puerto Rico. The building was secure, so Carmina was startled by somebody knocking on her door.

It was a strange, smartly-dressed man, over six-feet tall with a tanned complexion and brown hair. He looked normal except for a few details: he had extraordinarily long fingers, he had no apparent body hair, and his eyes were extremely large and lilac-colored. Carmina was stunned by his appearance, and was also shocked when the man began to speak about her daughter, who was a TV reporter doing a special on UFOs. The man said that he had come to deliver a message: that Carmina should tell her daughter to continue her investigations, and that UFO researcher Jorge Martin (who Carmina's daughter was working with) was being observed by American intelligence officers. The man then revealed many true details about Carmina's life.

Carmina listened to the man as he spoke about other subjects. She then asked him about himself and his background. The man was evasive about his background, but as Carmina says, "It seemed to me he wasn't human, and he implied that he himself was an alien, collaborating with the U.S. government."

Finally the man finished speaking and walked from her office. She was baffled when he seemed to disappear. He didn't take the elevator, and the stairs were guarded by security personnel; everyone had to sign in and out. Her nameless visitor had somehow vanished.

Writes Timothy Good, who researched the strange case, "Whatever his origin and nature, Carmina's office visitor seems to have been a benefit to her. At the time of the encounter she had a large cyst on her left breast. Later X-rays showed no sign of it."[9]

While not very large, Puerto Rico is one of the top ten producers of UFO healings. This is likely due to the high levels of UFO activity reported there.

CASE #219. CYST.

On July 11, 1998, sometime after midnight, an anonymous woman was sleeping in her home in Puerto Rico when she heard a man's voice waking her up. The man grabbed her by the hand, and floated her up through the ceiling of her house and into a cloud-like object overhead. Inside, she found herself in a large silver room with windows on the side and benches all around. The man led her into a small room and told her to wait there. The room flashed hot and then cold. The man returned and took the witness from the small room into another room. Inside the new room she was put on a table. She saw three gray figures wearing white uniforms with a red star-like insignia. Another taller human-looking figure wore a metallic-blue suit which covered everything except his face. He told the witness that they were going to remove a cyst from her body, and promised her that they would not leave any scars. The witness fell unconscious and woke up later in bed. All signs of the cyst were gone.[10]

The following case of a healing of a brain tumor generated significant interest not only from MUFON, but also apparently from such companies as Lockheed, Martin and Boeing, proving that people within our government are paying close attention to the information being released about the ETs' ability to heal humans.

CASE #238. BRAIN TUMOR.

As investigated by MUFON Tennessee state section director, Kim Shaffer, on October 2, 2004, a country western singer by the name of "Sidney" was driving to his home in Bristol, Tennessee when he saw what appeared to be a fire in the trees near his home. He pulled over to investigate; immediately a 300-foot-long triangular craft with brilliant red-orange lights emerged from the trees and began to move toward him.

Sidney turned to run, but quickly realizing the futility of trying to flee from something so large, he remained in the spot and watched the object approach. It passed overhead about 100 feet above him, during which time he felt a tingling and burning sensation on his skin. He also heard a throbbing hum from the craft which seemed to permeate his entire body.

The witness returned home and went to sleep. When he awoke the next morning, he noticed some alarming symptoms including a nosebleed, a metallic taste in his mouth, and what appeared to be a sunburn on his back and face. Shortly later, he noticed that the watch he had worn during the encounter was fifteen minutes slower than all the other clocks: he had lost fifteen minutes of time.

More radiation-sickness-type symptoms followed. Sidney began to feel weak and nauseated, and then suffered abnormal hair loss. These symptoms were accompanied by nightmares. Also, following the initial encounter, Sidney was woken up on multiple occasions by bright beams of light entering his bedroom, and loud buzzing noises outside his home.

Shaffer, who investigated the case, says that Sidney is a devout Christian, with a strong moral code, and in her estimation, was telling the truth about his experience.

While most of Sidney's symptoms from the encounter have been negative, there was one very positive after-effect. Says Shaffer, "I might add that he was diagnosed with an inoperable brain tumor (very small--three millimeter) in the frontal lobe, just prior to the encounter...subsequent medical tests (MRI and ultrasound) revealed the tumor was gone--I think this was sometime in January 2005."

An interesting endnote to the case is that after Shaffer posted Sidney's case to the MUFON website, interest in the case came from some unexpected locations. Writes Shaffer, "I am shocked as well by the extreme interest shown by Lockheed, Martin, Boeing, and the U.S. government to the report on the website immediately after the encounter. As webmaster, I am able to see the domains which visit the site. There were hundreds of visits from the aforementioned domains, which have never visited before or since."[11]

This next case was reported anonymously to MUFON. It involves a man who, after being healed by gray aliens, said, "I see aliens as a grace from God himself."

CASE #288. PAIN FROM SPINAL SURGERY.

"I know for a fact aliens are real!" So writes "Ron" (pseudonym), a computer programmer from Mississippi who insists on anonymity. "I do not want my real name or identity spilled all over social media," Ron says, "because many do not know the truth yet, or fear the truth."

In 2009, Ron underwent surgery to remove a tumor located on his spinal cord. While the surgery was successful, Ron was left with chronic pain. Whenever he tried to walk, he felt "severe pain." He was also unable to sleep on his stomach as this position was too painful.

Four years earlier, in 2005, Ron experienced a missing time episode. In 2016, he decided to report it to MUFON. Only a few weeks after reporting this encounter, Ron had a second encounter.

That night his pain was very bad and before going to bed, he prayed to God to help relieve his spinal pain. Sometime in the middle of the night, he woke up feeling "strange vibrations" on his lower back area. He struggled to wake up and when he did, he saw two gray-type ETs standing by his bed table. Behind the two grays stood three additional figures who did not appear to be grays. They were about six or seven feet tall. Mostly his attention was drawn to the wall of his bedroom. The wall was now transparent and in its place was a bright light.

Ron realized he was lying on his stomach without feeling any pain, which puzzled him. He tried to get up but felt a strange force keeping him "strapped to my bed." At the same time, the vibrations on his lower back were going strong.

Ron craned his neck and seeing the aliens, he called out to them, "Help me!"

At that moment, "a light far brighter than any light I have ever seen before flashed, and I was blacked out!"

Ron woke up the next morning "in a very strange position, as if I went head-first into a pillow with my knees bearing some weight of my body, and a horrible pain in my neck from being in such an odd position."

The pain in his neck persisted for at least the next three days. In the weeks following the encounter, Ron noticed that his ability to recall his computer programming training (which had been decreasing), now suddenly increased.

The pain in his spine, which was mysteriously absent during his encounter, was still there. But not for long! Writes Ron, "About five months after this encounter, the sharp pains that occurred as soon as I stood up, or during sitting, started to decrease..."

The pain continued to lessen, and before long, Ron found he was able to walk without pain for periods of ten minutes or more.

Today Ron is deeply thankful to the ETs. He writes, "I see aliens as a grace from God Himself...I do not believe for one minute that all aliens are bad. Some may be deceptive, just as the human race is. However, from my encounter with them, I see some may mean well."[12]

This case, published here for the first time, involves Lynnette, whose heart healing appeared earlier. On that occasion, she was unaware the she suffered from any heart problems. On this occasion, however, her illness was medically documented, and she was in danger of losing a significant portion of her lungs. The ETs, however, were watching closely and ready to intervene. Lynette is one of several people in this book who were cured both of conditions they knew of, and others that they did not.

CASE #200. LUNG TUMOR.

Lynnette (pseudonym) has had encounters her entire life. In 2011 (at age 57), she experienced a dramatic and somewhat painful healing of her heart. (previously described).

In 1994, at age forty, she noticed an odd pain in her side. It worsened to the point where it hurt to hug somebody. She went to her doctor, who sent her to a specialist. The news was bad: she had a softball-sized tumor in her right lung.

Surgery was quickly scheduled. "They wanted to take out twenty-five percent of my lung," says Lynnette. "The day before surgery, the doctor came for some X-rays, and the thing was gone. It was gone. It had grown over a three or four-month period. They had no clue, and they were going to take out a quarter of my lung. But it was gone. There were X-rays and cat-scans of that thing. It was gone."

Her surgeon was baffled. "I don't know what the hell happened," he told her. "It's a spontaneous healing, I guess."

Lynnette, however, believes that the ETs are responsible. Despite having a heart and lung healing, Lynnette still feels that her encounters have been overall negative, largely due to the emotional trauma in her life. She also has concern for her children, who are also having encounters.[13]

The following case, though brief, is a good example of what sometimes happens when an experiencer visits a doctor after a UFO healing event.

CASE #303. BREAST TUMOR.

From the files of FREE, a woman was diagnosed with a "suspicious growth" in her breast. While meditating, she saw two "helpers" who had come to "help get rid of the growth." Apparently, it worked. Says the woman, "The next day I went for the mammogram and the nurse came to tell me the doctor wanted a second image...she said, 'He can't believe it. It's gone.'"[14]

The ETs' ability to heal is nothing short of miraculous. Tumors and cysts are removed with apparent ease. The fact that some of these healings are confirmed with before and after X-rays makes it impossible to deny their validity. When medical professionals see evidence of surgery having been performed on experiencers, they are shocked and traumatized as they are forced to accept the evidence before their own eyes.

The experiencers themselves are equally astonished. It's little surprise that many feel intense gratitude toward the ETs. Others, as we have seen, are more reticent. Unable to predict, control or prevent being visited by ETs, and suffering emotional, mental and sometimes physical trauma, ET contact is not always a healing event. And yet the physical healings are occurring. Reconciling the positive and negative aspects of UFO contact is a challenge faced by many experiencers.

Chapter Twenty-Two
Serious Illnesses and Chronic Diseases

The variety of conditions healed by ETs is astonishing. We have already examined more than 200 cases involving injuries and illnesses of many kinds. This next chapter presents thirty-nine cases of the most incredible kind. The healing of a cut, a headache or kidney stones is one thing; the healing of a life-threatening or incurable disease is another. With the addition of cases like these, it becomes unscientific to ignore them. When somebody has an encounter and comes away from it healed of a chronic condition, it's impossible to deny that cases like these are taking place. Faking a chronic disease is not impossible, but neither is it easy. Nor can one easily fake its disappearance.

These cases come from across the world. They occur to all kinds of people. They are reported by numerous high-profile UFO researchers. Many of them are verified by doctors. They have been occurring for about a hundred years, probably longer. And there are a lot of them.

CASE #002. TUBERCULOSIS.
In the mid-1930s, an anonymous gentleman, a famous broadcaster, reported that he contracted tuberculosis when he was thirteen years old. At that time there were no such things as vaccinations, inoculations or antibiotics. Diseases like tuberculosis could not be controlled. Says the broadcaster, "I got sicker and sicker, and the doctors thought I would die."

While on his deathbed, the gentleman had a "dream" in which he was taken aboard a spaceship and cured of his disease. "In the 'dream,'" he says, "a spaceship took me aboard and placed me on a table within a glass bubble...the creatures did medical procedures on me and I was made to understand that now I would be well and that for the rest of my life I would be healthier and stronger than normal humans. When the doctor saw me a few days after the dream, he found no trace of the tuberculosis."

Despite the miraculous cure, the gentleman was skeptical that he had really been onboard an actual UFO. In those days, stories of spacemen were very rare. It wouldn't be until the 1950s when such stories became more popular that the gentleman recognized what happened to him. Says the witness, "I began to hear other people recount incidents of being taken aboard alien craft, and their descriptions are much the same as mine, right down to the way the creatures looked."

Incidentally, the gentleman says that in the late 1980s, his car was hit by a train, totally destroying it. He was inside the car at the time, and didn't receive a scratch. It is his firm belief that the aliens saved his life. Reportedly, railroad investigators also believed that the accident should have been fatal.[1]

Some researchers maintain that UFO healings are being performed by the ETs for their own benefit. The healings, they speculate, are not being done out of kindness or altruism, but rather to maintain the health of their "lab" animals. Some cases appear to support this assertion. And as we have seen, many experiencers feel that they are treated with the respect of a lab rat.

And then there are cases such as the following, which occurred to an elderly woman with no apparent prior history of contact. Of what benefit is this healing to the ETs?

CASE #005. JAUNDICE.

In 1942, "Elsie," an elderly woman, lived in Halifax, England during the World War II black-out conditions. At that time, she was bedridden due to severe jaundice. One evening, she saw a large blue-colored sphere appear outside her window. Three figures appeared, each about five feet tall and dressed in silver suits with transparent helmets.

The three figures floated to the foot of her bed. Elsie says the room became supernaturally quiet. The beings came around the side of her bed and did something to her side. They then floated off through the wall and disappeared.

The blue glow was now gone, and Elsie felt elated. The next morning, much to the amazement of her family and doctors, the jaundice was gone. Elsie told them about her visitors, but they were disbelieving. Elsie, however, feels that it was a real experience, and she ascribed her unexplained healing to them.[2]

This next case involves an artist who, as a child, was healed of a very serious condition. In a later contact, the ETs told him that he had been healed because they "needed" him as a contact.

CASE #008. ANGIOMA.

In 1945, Ted X of Santa Clara, California, was about three years old when he experienced a fully conscious encounter with extraterrestrials. Says Ted, "I woke up from a nightmare and looked up and there was a person next to my bed." It was a strange figure, short, bald, with a large head and dark wrap-around eyes.

One and a half years earlier, Ted had been diagnosed with angioma, a medical condition involving a malformation of the blood vessels in his brain. As a result, he became paralyzed, lost his ability to speak and stopped growing. The doctors said he had only months to live.

Ted's condition deteriorated. He became emotionally unstable and suffered intermittent paralysis. His vision weakened until he had only double vision. He lost his ability to walk and was forced to crawl. By the time he was three years old, he could no longer talk or feed himself, and his body had stopped growing.

It was at this time that Ted had his encounter. Immediately, Ted's condition began to improve. Ted told his parents that "doctors had cut the top of my head off." He had other memories of figures that look like the *Pillsbury Doughboy* who would communicate with him telepathically.

Amazed by the change in his condition, Ted's parents placed him in a hospital in San Francisco where doctors performed exploratory surgery. To their amazement, Ted's condition had reversed itself and he was perfectly healthy. The surgeons said

298

that the tissue growth had not only stopped, but shrunk. They were unable to provide an explanation.

Ever since that time, Ted became "obsessed" with UFOs, spaceships, astronomy and aliens. The obsession remained with him throughout his life, and when he reached his mid-forties, he began to seriously question the source of this obsession. By this time, he was an accomplished artist and had drawn scores of highly detailed pen-and-ink drawings of various spacecraft. He finally sought out Edith Fiore Ph.D. to explore the extent of his experiences with UFOs.

Not surprisingly, Ted recalled a complex abduction at around age three. Under hypnosis, he recalled that the beings had large, bald heads, large eyes, and pale white-green skin. He also saw another type of being which looked "more like insects...kind of like a grasshopper."

Says Ted, "I'm in a room in some kind of craft. And the room is round and there's lights and dials along the walls...it's very clean, very smooth, and it domes. There's almost no furniture in it except for the panels of lights and this table that contours around the room."

At one point, Ted reports that he was probed by a metal pencil-like instrument. "When they turn the apparatus on, a beam of light comes out. It's very straight, and it's very thin. It's needle-like. It's very much like laser light. And it comes out and strikes my head, but it doesn't hurt...They take this probe and they touch different parts of my body...They press it up against the skin in different parts. This probe registers information on the dials that are on the wall."

Ted was next told that there were "enlarged tissues" in his head, and that he needed an operation. "They took an instrument and they cut open the top of the head, all the way around. And they were able to remove that part of the skull and look at the brain...they've taken a laser device and they've cut around the skull...they're taking an instrument, it's like a laser....to heal something. They probe around the brain, they touch all over and find the enlargement. And with the laser light, they're able to shrink it."

299

The light, said Ted, was the "thickness of a spiderweb," and seemed to be "almost like silk." After the beams were shone on his brain, another instrument was placed over his brain, and tan ash-like substance caused by the laser was removed. The top of his skull was placed back over his brain and another laser was shone on the wound, healing it. "And this time instead of cutting it," says Ted, "the cut was healed by the light. It mends the skull back together. The atoms go back together and there's no scar tissue. And when it's finished, there's no indication that the skull has been opened."

The ETs were fascinated with Ted, and told him telepathically, "We are here to help you." They told him that they were currently on a space-station distant from Earth. They told him that he was healed because he was needed as a contact, and that they would return for another contact when he was older.

At that point, he was "transported" back home. As he says, "I see these apparatuses coming down from the sides, and they're like laser instruments. They point these down at me, and there are four of them, and they beam energy down. And my body changes into a different kind of matter, into light particles. And I travel back to the place where I began, and at that point, I materialize. I'm inside of the house. I'm back in bed now. And I wake up, and this person is standing in front of me."

Ted was left only with the memory of the strange figure standing at his bedside and the feeling that doctors had cut off the top of his head.

Seven years later, in mid-1952, ten-year-old Ted had a second onboard UFO experience. Later, in his mid-forties, he recalled what occurred using regressive hypnosis. Says Ted, "I'm sitting in a chair in a room in a craft. It's run by a group of mechanical beings. Metal robots. They're checking my body. The room is filled with different kinds of instruments and dials and lights. I'm in a chair that's similar to a dentist's chair, with contoured arms on each side. There's another robot behind me. I'm being studied, but I don't know why."

Ted was unable to recall much more about the encounter other than the strange appearance of the robotic beings. Later in

300

1980, while in his mid-thirties, he experienced his third and latest encounter.

On this occasion, he was abducted from his apartment. Says Ted, "A beam of light came down through the apartment, surrounded me and changed me into a different molecular structure, and then it took me back into the small spaceship. And from there I was taken out...into space, away from Earth. And we came to this colony where all these different spaceships were. I was taken onboard a larger spaceship or space station. I'm in the chair. I'm being examined by the robots."

Ted recalled that several sensing devices were passed up and down his body. A blood sample was taken from his arm. He was then taken to another room and laid down. His next memory was waking up in his apartment. Since that incident, Ted has reported no further contacts.[3]

These next two cases both occurred to the same person. They are unique in that the witness is the only person on record who has received multiple healings as the result of a UFO encounter, not once, but twice!

CASE #011. CURVATURE OF SPINE, TOOTHACHE.

Born in 1947 in Ohio, "Donna" has experienced numerous UFO contacts throughout her life. After she was born, she had several health problems. Her parents had a different RH factor in their blood, and Donna's mother suffered from toxemia during her pregnancy. Consequently, Donna had to have a complete blood transfusion which resulted in mild brain damage, epilepsy, and poor vision in her left eye. She was also born with curvature of the spine, and PKU (phenylketonuria), a metabolic disorder.

Donna's first exposure to the healing power of UFOs occurred in 1950, between age three and four. Donna still remembers the event vividly. She had a toothache and her dad put her to bed early. She was alone in her room when her room filled with "shiny golden and silver light" and a being appeared. Even at that age, Donna was alarmed. The being moved toward her and then reached out and touched her right shoulder. "Whatever it was," said Donna, "it completely overcame any fear I had, because I accepted it."

As the light hit her, Donna had the sensation of "many fingers on my back, not five, but like twenty, thirty...it was like feelers." She felt as though a golden ball of light was lodged into the base of her brain. "It was all very pleasant," she says.

Immediately after the being touched her, Donna fell asleep. When she awoke the next morning, she felt a burning, excruciating pain. The mysterious pain bothered her intermittently for about three weeks. Her parents took her to get X-rays of her spine and were shocked. Donna no longer suffered from curvature of the spine. "It was completely cured," says Donna. Thankfully, her tooth pain also went away.

Donna believes this event may have also cured some of the nerve damage she suffered as a result of the blood transfusion she had when she was born. She's not sure, because it wasn't long before she had another dramatic healing event.[4]

CASE #018. EPILEPSY, VISION IMPROVEMENTS.

Around Independence Day 1953, Donna (then six years old) and several others witnessed a UFO that was flashing multicolored lights. When the lights flashed at Donna, the results were nothing less than phenomenal. "When the white light came on," says Donna, "I noticed a similar burning sensation that went from...the base of my spine and to the top of my head and centered in my throat. And after that my defective vision in my left eye was corrected, and I never had another epileptic seizure after that."

Donna believes the light also cured her brain damage. Following this event, her mental capacities also increased. "My intelligence went up after I was healed too," she says. She eventually took an IQ test and scored 150.

In 1957, at age ten, she saw another UFO. She also began having paranormal experiences. At age fifteen, her experiences slowed down dramatically. In 1975, while driving with her husband, she had yet another sighting. On this occasion, she felt the ETs were trying to contact her mentally.

Donna's encounters transformed her physically, mentally and spiritually. Says Donna, "When I'm in a certain set of circumstances, I can see auras, and I can go into a trance and receive messages telepathically."[5]

New Jersey contactee Richard Rylka has received numerous healings at the hands of his ET friends, including the healing of injuries from an auto accident, a crushed finger, a facial tumor, and an ear infection. Rylka also says that he was healed once of a very serious disease.

CASE #013. POLIO.

Sometime in the late 1940s or early 1950s, Rylka contracted polio in a public swimming pool in Newark, New Jersey. Unable to cure him, his family treated him with massage therapy. However, at night, Rylka was given medical treatment by the ETs who would come into his room and hold a "flat instrument" over his body. They would manipulate the instrument, which would flash brightly. After the treatments, Rylka's weakness and paralysis disappeared. He is convinced that the aliens cured him of his polio.[6]

Polio is a viral infection that can cause nerve damage leading to partial or total paralysis. Another case of a polio healing comes from a Canadian contactee. At the time, there was no vaccine for the disease. At least not from humans.

CASE #015. POLIO.

In the early 1950s, (date approximate) John Adams of Toronto, Canada was stricken with polio of the spine when he was just an infant. He spent three years in the Shriners Crippled Children's Hospital in Toronto. They treated him with gamma globulin (antibodies), but expected that Adams would die of the disease. However, to their surprise, the treatment seemed to work and he began a slow recovery.

Adams had always thought that human doctors were responsible for his miraculous recovery. It wasn't until many years

303

later that he began to realize he was having contact with ETs. He underwent hypnotic regression and discovered that he had been having contact his entire life. It was then that he discovered who was really responsible for the disappearance of his polio

Under hypnosis, Adams recalled "scenes of 'people' around me talking ('He has only six months to live') and exposing a part of my body, turning to me and asking, 'Do you want us to take out the black vein or the red one?'"

He believes that this is a memory of being cured of his condition by the aliens. Says Adams, "These, I am discerning, were contacts with other life forms." Adams now remembers more than seven separate contacts, and says that the visitations are still ongoing."[7]

In the 1920s, more than 100,000 people in the U.S. contracted diphtheria. At that time, a vaccine had just been developed. A long campaign has been fought to rid the world of the disease. But even as late as 2013, more than 3000 people worldwide died of the disease. This next case was originally revealed by David Jacobs Ph.D. in his book *Secret Life.* The main witness used the pseudonym Lynn Miller but has now released her real name, Alice Haggerty, in her audio-taped interviews.

CASE #035. DIPHTHERIA.

In 1962, Alice was struck with the sometimes fatal disease, diphtheria. Because of a religious background, she had not been vaccinated against the disease. For the same religious reasons, her parents refused to take her to the hospital. They did call in a doctor who said that Alice's condition was very serious, still Alice's parents refused to seek conventional treatment.

Over the next two weeks, her condition deteriorated. The doctor visited daily, and at the end of the two weeks, he told Alice's mother that he did not expect Alice to live through the night.

Alice, however, happened to be an abductee, and would eventually have several abductions throughout her life. On the evening in question, Alice was apparently abducted by friendly

304

aliens which she then described as "angels in white robes with silver belts." Alice remembers being transported inside a UFO where the aliens told her she would be cured. They waved a small "rod-like device" around her body, and then made her stand inside a "large blue cylinder" with a little window. The aliens watched as a bright light was emitted from the top of the machine until it was about eight inches from the top of Alice's head. The light then retracted and Alice was instructed to exit the cylinder.

According to Jacobs, the aliens "informed her in a matter-of-fact manner that she was now cured and 'cleansed.'" Alice then underwent more of the typical procedures that are often performed aboard UFOs. The next morning, Alice's mother found her playing on the floor as if everything was normal. Alice was ordered into bed by her mother and her doctor, but both admitted that the diphtheria was completely and totally gone.[8]

This next case involves the cure of an unknown condition. It is reported second-hand, but it presents additional confirmation that healings are a consistent feature of UFO encounters.

CASE #048. CHRONIC DISEASE.

In the late 1960s, "Mary" worked as a secretary for a corporation in Little Rock, Arkansas. At the time, she suffered from an incurable (but not life-threatening) disease. One evening Mary went with a friend to a restaurant. Afterward, they were driving home when they noticed a light blue Buick following them. It was unusual because Mary's friend lived in the "back roads."

They pulled into her friend's driveway and the Buick whizzed by them. Her friend made Mary promise to call when she arrived home. Mary agreed and left for her own home. About twenty minutes later, she arrived home without incident, and called her friend.

Her friend was furious and wanted to know why Mary hadn't called for more than two hours. Mary looked at the clock and saw that she was missing nearly two hours of time.

A few days later she went to the doctor. "She was completely shocked when the baffled doctor told her the disease no longer existed," says Mary's friend. "Mary left the office cured, but confused, with no explanation."

Years later, Mary began having memories and flashbacks of that night and now believes she may have been abducted and cured by aliens, and that inside the Buick that was following her were the Men in Black.[9]

The following is one of the best-verified cases of a UFO healing on record. The investigators of the case have obtained the medical records that prove the miraculous healing of a woman from Chagas disease. It's a serious disease that affects millions of people and kills up to 10,000 people annually. It's most prevalent in South America. There is no vaccine, but it can be treated with anti-parasitic medication.

CASE #061. CHAGAS DISEASE.

In the late 1960s, an eighteen-year-old housekeeper by the name of Bernadette from the small town of Goias, Brazil, contracted Chagas disease. Caused by bite of the Triatomine Beetle, Chagas disease causes fever, headaches, inflammation, severe damage to the heart muscle, and if left untreated, is often fatal. In fact, Bernadette's entire family died from the disease.

At the time, Bernadette worked as a housekeeper for General Paulo Uchoa, a three-star general in the Brazilian Army. By coincidence, Uchoa's father--Alfredo Uchoa--was a well-known Brazilian UFO researcher, often considered the father of Brazilian ufology. He was also a General in the Brazilian army, a physicist and the Education Director of the Brazilian Military Academy. Alfredo Uchoa had seen many UFOs throughout his life.

When a wave of sightings struck the Goias area, General Uchoa conducted live field investigations, trying to make contact with the UFO occupants. Dozens of people were involved in the fieldwork, and the group had many carefully documented sightings. At some point, Uchoa says he made mental contact with the ETs, and was able to take groups of people out to observe UFO displays.

It was during this time that their housekeeper, Bernadette's, condition worsened. The Uchoa family admitted her to the hospital where she spent four months in intensive care undergoing repetitive surgical treatments to remove the excess fluids in her heart.

Still, Bernadette's condition worsened and it soon became clear that the disease was going to kill her, as it had her family. One evening when Uchoa was performing live fieldwork, he telepathically asked the ETs for help with Bernadette, requesting that they "go beyond their usual visual displays by healing Bernadette and proving that their technology was indeed more advanced than ours."

According to Uchoa, the ETs agreed, and requested that Uchoa bring the sick girl to a certain location. Uchoa complied. He brought Bernadette and several other witnesses, all of whom observed the ETs heal her using a blue light.

Afterward, Bernadette was taken to the hospital for examination. The doctors were astonished to find that her heart now had no fluid in it, and appeared to be perfectly healthy. Bernadette's medical condition before and after the incident was fully documented. In fact, General Ochoa wrote several books about UFOs presenting his investigations of the Bernadette healing case and many other incidents. Forty-five years later, Bernadette is still healthy and married to a Papaya farmer in Varginha, Brazil. Researchers obtained her records, verifying the cure. Uchoa's granddaughter, Denise Uchoa Slater, has spoken extensively about the healing case and continues to keep her grandfather's UFO research available to the public.[10]

Hypertension, or high blood pressure, often presents no symptoms, but can lead to a variety of serious health problems. Thankfully, it is usually treatable with diet, lifestyle changes and various medications. However, for many people it remains a chronic and life-threatening condition. In the following instance, a woman experienced both an injury and a healing as the result of a single UFO encounter.

CASE #062. HYPERTENSION.

A dramatic case of physiological effects and healing as the result of a UFO encounter comes from Sao Paulo, Brazil. On May 27, 1973, Dona Geni Lisboa (age 57) was baking cakes early in the morning when she saw a glowing object approach her home. It circled around the garden and hovered above the wall about twenty feet away. The upper portion of the object was transparent, and she saw three short figures looking down at her. The object was emitting beams of light which converged on her, causing temporary paralysis, pain and dizziness. As the object moved away, Lisboa called out for her neighbor, who arrived too late to see the strange craft.

Lisboa's neighbor, however, saw that Lisboa's face was swollen and her eyes were bloodshot. Following the incident, Lisboa felt pain in her knees and other joints in her body. She then became worse and had to be rushed to the hospital for a prolapsed uterus, which surprised Lisboa as a previous gynecological exam six months earlier had pronounced her healthy.

Lisboa's eyesight became worse and she had to wear corrective lenses. There was, however, one apparent healing. Lisboa had suffered from high blood pressure and had to take medication. Following the incident, her hypertension disappeared. According to investigators Dr. Walter Buhler and Jose Wilson Ribeiro, who interviewed the witness, "a previous condition of hypertension seems to have made an improvement to the degree where she dropped all previous anti-hypertensive medication."[11]

The following case was researched by a large number of pioneering UFO investigators, and was one of the earliest publicized UFO healing cases in the United States.

CASE #063. UNDESCRIBED ILLNESS.

In October 1973, in the small town of Lehi, Utah, Pat Roach and three of her seven children experienced a simultaneous UFO abduction. All of them except the youngest experienced a period of missing time and only remembered the experience under hypnosis.

308

The case was investigated by several well-known UFO researchers including James Harder, Ph.D., Kevin Randle, and Coral and Jim Lorenzen. They performed hypnosis on the witnesses, and a typical abduction scenario was revealed.

The youngest child, Debbie "Dottie" Roach, retained full conscious memory of the event. Right after it occurred, Pat Roach assumed there had been a prowler. Debbie said, "They were spacemen...they didn't make me forget. They told me not to tell anyone except those in my family."

Debbie then gave a detailed description of the aliens, the ship, and what happened when they were all taken onboard. According to Debbie, they were all told to get on a machine. Debbie, who had been very ill all her life, was told by the aliens that she would be healed. "The one that stood in the corner asked my name," Debbie said, "And he said that I wouldn't be sick anymore."

According to researchers, "Pat had said that Debbie had been very sick before the aliens arrived and they had done something to or for her. The sickness was gone after the aliens left."[12]

Multiple sclerosis is a disease which attacks the nerves of the brain and spinal cord, resulting in muscle weakness, vision problems and more. The causes are not fully understood, nor is there any known cure. It's the most common auto-immune disorder of the central nervous system. In 2010, an estimated two million people worldwide suffered from the condition. While people can live for many decades with the disease, advanced cases can lead to death. In 2010, about 18,000 people died of the disease. In this next case, from researcher Wendelle Stevens, an Army officer was cured of the disease following a series of encounters which were viewed by his entire family.

CASE #087. MULTIPLE SCLEROSIS.
On August 30, 1979, retired Canadian Army officer, Jean Cyr, of St. Eustache, Quebec, and his family were drawn outside by a strange humming sound. Once outside, they saw a large, glowing

metallic disc rise from the fields behind their house, hover over their home and flash down beams of lights. They called the nearby Mirabel Control Tower and the Montreal International Airport who confirmed that they could see the UFO. The tower controller vectored in a plane, but the UFO winked out and came back when the plane left. Another attempt provoked the same response. Meanwhile, the neighbors of the Cyrs saw the object and called the police. Five hours later, the UFO left, leaving strange circular marks in the fields where it had apparently landed.

Mr. Cyr and his family were extensively interviewed by various UFO groups. Meanwhile, over the next few weeks, they began having more sightings. During one sighting, the UFO was again observed hovering low over the Cyr residence. Cyr was able to get an audio recording of the UFO. Many other people in the area also saw the UFO.

The Cyr case has many fascinating aspects, but important here is the apparent cure. Cyr suffered badly from multiple sclerosis, and had to go to the hospital for treatment every two weeks. Virtually paralyzed from the disease, he spent most of his time in a wheelchair.

However, following the series of encounters, Cyr noticed strange marks on his body that he couldn't explain. Nor could he explain something else: his multiple sclerosis was suddenly cured. Writes Wendelle Stevens, "...all symptoms of the disease have gone, and he hasn't had a stroke since."[13]

Muscular dystrophy is a genetic disorder and comes in many forms. It causes a progressive weakening of the skeletal muscles and can attack other organs. In severe or advanced cases, it can leave patients unable to walk. Millions of people suffer from the disease worldwide, mostly males. There are treatments, but there is no known cure.

CASE #090. MUSCULAR DYSTROPHY.

In 1979, Dean Anderson of Sturgeon Bay, Wisconsin experienced a voluntary visit aboard a UFO. Several of his friends also claim to have had contact with the same friendly aliens. Dean says that he has been aboard their craft many times. His alien friends look human, but say they are from Saturn or Jupiter.

While visiting aboard the UFO, Dean observed many things. Pertinent here is the healing he saw take place. According to Dean, during one contact in 1979, he saw a nine-year-old girl and her mother, both from Detroit, Michigan, aboard the UFO. He was told that the girl was suffering from muscular dystrophy.

Dean watched with fascination as the girl was placed on a table with a "glass shield" over her body. She was then "hooked up to an apparatus which caused the table to be suspended in mid-air; for twenty seconds everything glowed with a brilliant blue-white aura. The table settled, two short fellows came in, lifted the girl off the table, and she walked over to her mother--perfectly healed. I was amazed!"[14]

The full story of this next case is presented in the book, *Beyond UFOs*, published by the FREE foundation. It involves an artist and homeopathic healer from England, with a lifelong history of contact.

CASE #098. HIP DYSPLASIA.

"Ek Mau" was born in Canada in 1976, but soon moved to England. Ek Mau was a normal happy baby, however, as she began walking, she began to display symptoms of hip dysplasia. Her left leg would not work properly and kept becoming dislocated. It caused her great difficulties as she tried to walk. "I used to drag my leg," says Ek Mau. "I had to go upstairs sideways and pull my leg up with me, because my hip was born out of its socket."

Her parents took her to the doctors, but the doctors were unable to treat her condition. Strangely, not long after the visit to the doctors, her hip was miraculously healed. "It got better," says Ek Mau. "They took me back to the specialist and he said he'd never seen anything like it. So there I was with this miraculously healed leg at five years old. It only gave me problems when I walked long distances."

At the time (1981) Ek Mau had no idea what happened. But at age nineteen she had a profound encounter with Pleiadean

311

beings in her backyard in England. This was followed by a series of UFO sightings and humanoid encounters. She soon began experiencing onboard abductions. During many of these encounters, the beings performed various operations on her body.

In 2008, Ek Mau was surprised to see a praying mantis type ET carrying a screen which showed live images of the inside of her body. The mantis told her to "look away" as it performed an operation on her hip. Despite the ET's instructions, Ek Mau watched the operation. It appeared as though the ET was applying a bolt and screw-type device to her hip. The next thing she knew, it was morning. "I felt utter relief," says Ek Mau, "gratitude that these beings would come to see me. I was always grateful when they showed up."

Remembering her earlier hip problems, Ek Mau wonders if they were healing her again. In any event, her hip is still fine. "I've never had any problems with it," she says, "so I really feel very grateful to these beings."[15]

One of the leading killers in the United States and the world are strokes. According to the World Health Organization, fifteen million people suffer a stroke each year. One third fully recover, one third are left permanently disabled, and one third die. It is the leading cause of serious long-term disability in the United States. It most often occurs to the elderly, but can strike at any age. Immediate treatment can significantly reduce symptoms. Medication can lower risks, but there is no known cure. The ETs, however, seem to have found one.

CASE #099. STROKE.

In 1981, retired elementary school teacher, Marie X (pseudonym) of Willamette Valley, Oregon suffered a massive stroke which left her with highly impaired speech, and an inability to focus on even the simplest mental tasks. Her son, Douglas cared for her for ten years until 1991 when Marie's symptoms inexplicably disappeared.

At first, Douglas had no idea what happened to cause the miraculous healing, but he did notice a few strange details. First, both of Marie's pillow cases were so caked with blood that they had to be discarded. Second, the empty third bedroom had a very strong smell of ozone lingering in it.

Unable to explain the improvement in his mother or the other strange details, Douglas was mystified. When his mother next visited the doctor, he was also puzzled and asked Douglas how Marie had recovered so quickly and completely. Douglas was unable to explain it. The answer to the mystery came about six months later when Douglas had a dream in which he recalled everything that happened.

In his dream, he was watching the David Letterman show as he normally did each evening. Suddenly the hall light came on. Thinking his mother had woken up and was wandering around, he went to check on her. She was still sound asleep in bed, so he turned off the hall light and returned to watch TV.

Moments later, the light came on again. Douglas was about to get up when he saw something incredible. "Out of the third bedroom," says Douglas, "come a couple of creatures. They are overly lean and tall, of humanoid form, and they moved through the wooden door of Mom's bedroom without opening it. They come in and out of her bedroom for a period of what seems to be around two to three hours, but they always returned to the third bedroom as a kind of staging area."

They were dressed in floor length dark brown smocks and strange hats. They had egg-shaped black heads with no apparent features whatsoever. They glided across the floor as if floating, while carrying small gray-colored boxes. They paid no attention to Douglas.

That was the extent of his dream. Even though it was a dream, Douglas feels certain that it accurately portrayed the events of that strange night six months earlier. It certainly explained his mother's miraculous healing, and the accompanying physical evidence. Says Douglas, "My mother had six full years of stroke-free life after that before another massive stroke placed her in a nursing home." Years earlier, in 1981, Douglas was cured of Strep.[16]

One of the most unusual and well-verified healing cases on record occurred in Brazil, and involves the use of alien medicine. What makes this case unique is that samples of the alien medicine were saved for a chemical analysis, leading to some astonishing conclusions.

CASE #106. CEREBRAL ANEURYSM.

In 1984, Joao Vicente of Botucatu, Brazil, suffered a near-fatal cerebral aneurysm. He was rushed to the hospital and put on life support equipment. Unfortunately, the aneurysm was so severe that his brain was flooded with blood, destroying the nervous system. The pressure inside Joao's skull was so heavy that surgery was impossible. Doctors recommended removal of the life support equipment because "there was nothing that modern medicine could do for him."

One of Vicente's close friends was Joao Valerio, the hospital doorman, who also happened to be a UFO contactee. Valerio had been taken onboard alien craft on numerous occasions. He was given a tour of the solar system, predictions, physical artifacts, and was also permitted to take photographs of the UFOs and the aliens on their home planet.

Valerio was well-known for his contacts, so the doctors in the hospital asked Valerio if he would ask the aliens for some medicine. Valerio agreed and during his next contact, was given medicine by the ETs to give Vicente.

UFO investigator, Rodolfo R. Casellato was one of the principal investigators of the case. Writes Casellato: "Joao [Valerio] obtained from the ETs a substance that after a simple analysis showed a very low fusion point. It melts at body temperature...the instructions were that the substance was to be rubbed into the foot sole, and something would form on that place and the residue from the brain (hemorrhage) would come out there.

"And that is exactly what happened," writes Casellato, "and Joao Vicente started getting a little better. Sometime later, Joao Valerio brought another substance to be rubbed on the spinal column, and that is being done now...X-rays are showing now that a new nervous system is taking over the older one destroyed, new

314

arteries, and the damaged organs are being encapsulated by new tissue, all shown in the X-rays. The doctors call it a 'miracle.'...I saw Joao Vicente and he shook my hand and spoke some words and is getting better."

This cure is not only well-verified, but investigators managed to procure some of each batch of medicine for chemical analysis.

Neither substance was identifiable. The report on the first batch of medicine says, "The substance was in soft crystal form with the crystals about the size and color of raw sugar. The crystals had to be kept away from heat because they began to melt down at about 115 degrees Fahrenheit. When held in palms and rubbed together, they decomposed into a greasy substance that was then absorbed or evaporated away or both."

The final result of the testing was that the substance was "chemically unique."

The second substance was never analyzed due to lack of funds. The second substance, which was applied to Vicente's spinal column, was described as "a dark irregular granular material from very fine up to three millimeters across. It was not in true crystalline form, as it lacked regularity, but looked more like it had been crushed, more like small shards. These pieces were semi-transparent, and of a dark reddish-brown color like shattered garnet stones."

The full account of Valerio's contacts is told in Casellato's book, *UFO Abduction at Botucatu*, published by the UFO Photo Archives.[17]

The research of Brad Steiger has uncovered several instances of UFO healings. The following is one of his earlier cases.

CASE #115. PARALYSIS.

Another case of a UFO-affected healing took place sometime in 1986 to a gentleman from La Jolla, California. As reported to researcher Brad Steiger, the main witness, Richard T., was wheelchair-bound due an undescribed condition. While enjoying an evening alone on a nearby beach, Richard T. was shocked to see a 100-foot-long, torpedo-shaped UFO hovering above him. The next thing he knew, he was put into a kind of trance. He then felt himself lifted up into the craft still in his wheelchair.

Richard experienced no fear as he was examined by "smallish humanoids with large heads and enormously large slanted eyes." The next thing he knew, he found himself seated in the front seat of his van with his wheelchair tucked away in the back.

The most fantastic part of the whole experience, however, was the after-effect. According to Steiger, "Amazingly, over the next few weeks, his condition began to reverse itself--until he was finally able to walk again with the help of a cane."[18]

AIDS (autoimmune deficiency syndrome) is caused by the HIV virus and can be sexually transmitted or by direct contact with bodily fluids such as blood or seminal fluids. While there is no known cure, treatments have become increasingly effective, and many people have survived with the disease for decades. This next case is one of two known cases in which a person was cured of AIDS.

CASE #118. AIDS.
One evening in June of 1987, an anonymous thirty-year-old AIDs patient from the Drome region of France was driving along an isolated road when he came upon a round, glowing object hovering very close to the ground. The object emitted a bright beam of light and three short, human-like figures appeared. They were handsome-looking, with short dark hair and gray outfits. They spoke to the witness and invited him aboard their craft. The witness says that he was taken to a "space-station" which housed more craft like the one he had arrived in. The witness says that the ETs proceeded to cure him of his AIDS and then returned him back to Earth. The case was investigated by French researcher Denys Breysse of Project Becassine.[19]

This next case, from the files of MUFON, involves a man who was cured of what doctors told him was a permanent paralysis of his arm. It includes multiple eye witnesses, missing time, and a healing that has yet to be explained.

CASE #119. PARTIAL PARALYSIS.

On July 10, 1987, Reese (pseudonym) was in a severe car accident. He was rushed to the hospital, and learned that he had three compression fractures in the back of his neck, causing paralysis in his right arm. The doctors told him the paralysis was permanent. He would never move his right arm again. Seven days following the incident, he was sent to his home in Hollonville, Georgia to recover.

That evening, Reese was lying in bed next to his wife. Sometime in the middle of the night, he woke up to see three huge white lights in a triangular formation hovering outside, directly over the home of his brother, who lived next door. The lights were silent and reminded Reese of event lights. He woke up his wife and asked her, "Am I dreaming, or do you see those lights too?"

"I see them," she said, looking out the large picture window. They stared at the lights in shock.

"It was the most amazing thing I've ever seen in my life," Reese said. Strangely, the next thing Reese and his wife knew, they were waking up and it was the next morning. Reese turned to his wife and asked her if she remembered the lights. She did, but like Reese, neither of them recalled going to sleep.

They turned on the news and were amazed to discover that other people in their area had reported seeing UFOs. Reese called his brother who lived next door and told him about the incident, and how the UFO had hovered directly above his house. His brother didn't see anything, but said that the house had noticeably vibrated, but he had passed it off as a dream.

At some point in the days following the incident, the movement in Reese's arm mysteriously returned. "Three months later," says Reese, "I could move it and it has returned to 100 percent. Kinda makes me wonder if they did something to me."

After seeing a movie about UFO abductions, Reese realized that "it may have happened to me," and he felt compelled to report his encounter. Says Reese, "To this day that memory stands out in my mind like it happened yesterday."[20]

While the contactee era of the 1950s seems to have faded away, the truth is that these types of cases continue to occur all across the world. The following is a typical contactee account with friendly ETs who take the witness onboard their craft, and then to another planet.

CASE #121. ILLNESS (UNDESCRIBED).
In August 1987, 45-year-old "Viktor," of Simferopol, Crimea (in Ukraine) decided to take a hike near northern Mount Demerdzhi. While hiking, he became tired and found a glade to rest. He fell asleep and when he woke up, he discovered that it was now September. He had lost one month of time.

Thankfully, his memory of the missing month came back to him. He recalled being struck by a beam of light which pulled him aboard an extraterrestrial ship. He was taken to a mother ship and then to an alien base on another planet.

While on their planet, Viktor was given a very thorough medical and "bio-energy" examination. At the time, he was suffering from an undescribed chronic illness, for which his doctor had recommended surgery. Viktor says that during his examination, the ETs healed him of his illness and also implanted something behind his right ear. They told him that they had "changed the structure of his body, mind and nature."

Following the experience, he found that he was able to communicate telepathically with the ETs, and was given a lot information by them.[21]

This next case, from respected South African investigator, Cynthia Hind, is one of very few healing cases to come from Africa. Despite this, it matches other cases coming from all across the planet.

CASE #128. JAUNDICE.

On July 19, 1988, Diane and her daughter Phyllis (age 34) of Johannesburg, South Africa were driving to their home when a bright light descended over their car. They felt a presence in the car. Suddenly they saw a five-foot-tall woman with a tan complexion. The woman guided them into the craft, introduced herself as Meleelah and said she meant no harm. Diane and Phyllis found themselves completely trusting and allowed Meleelah to put them on a table for examination and tests.

There were several other people in the craft. Phyllis heard her mother gasp in pain during the examination and said, "you're not doing that to me."

"If there's trouble, we can't help you unless you allow," Meleelah replied.

At the time of the incident, Diane suffered from hemolytic jaundice. The being asked "What do your medical people call your condition?" Diane told the ETs about her jaundice, which she had since age twelve.

Writes Hind, "Since the abduction, her illness has apparently cleared up and she has never needed medical attention since she has been absolutely well. Prior to that, nobody had been able to find a cure for her condition."[22]

The stroke-healing cases are among the most astonishing of all UFO healing cases. In case after case, people whose ability to live a normal life after being ravaged by a stroke, are transformed after being visited by ETs and cured.

CASE #143. STROKE.

In the summer of 1989, Sergey K. of Kiev, Ukraine suffered a stroke which caused him to have problems speaking and also near-total paralysis in his left hand. He was in the hospital recovering, sitting by the window when he saw strange green lights approaching. The lights flickered, formed a semi-circle and approached right up to the window. Sergey suddenly felt mesmerized and unable to control his body. When the lights reached him, a figure in a tight-fitting white suit appeared--a tall man with long blond hair. The man waved his hand over Sergey several times, causing Sergey to become nauseous and hot. At this point, he lost consciousness.

When Sergey awoke, the green lights were ascending from the balcony outside the window and moving away. Sergey felt healthy and energetic following his encounter. He rose up and discovered that he could move his left hand freely. He felt almost totally recuperated from the stroke, amazing his wife.[23]

This next case comes from researcher, Virginia Aronson, and involves a witness who reports numerous cures at the hands of friendly grays.

CASE #151. SEVERE UTERINE CRAMPING.
Connie Isele of Sacramento, California had experienced a number of unusual events, but never attributed them to UFOs until 1989. Around that time, she began to be woken up by strange figures coming into her bedroom at night. Although she didn't realize it at first, she was encountering extraterrestrials. Says Isele, "The ETs are not too pretty to look at, though. One being I see frequently has a hideous head he hides behind a bright glow, and a long thin torso that moves like an insect's body. He reminds me of a praying mantis. This being seems to be an advisor or teacher, whereas the 'doctors' are short little beings. Being examined or operated on by a human doctor is not exactly fun, so being examined or operated on by nonhuman doctors with big bald heads and big black eyes can be even more uncomfortable. Yet I have no complaints...for example, in 1989, I received an ET 'health checkup' during which they injected me with a clear gel, similar to white grape jelly. I was informed that this was for my benefit, that this was for healing. There were also lights involved in the procedure."

Isele reports that when she awoke the next morning, the jelly-like substance still clung to her skin and had to be washed off in the shower. Isele is convinced that ETs cured her of severe uterine cramping, a problem she had been suffering from for several weeks prior to the experience. Following the visitation, all symptoms disappeared.[24]

According to the World Health Organization, about 800,000 people die by suicide each year. In the U.S., about 45,000 kill themselves annually, making it the tenth leading cause of death. Men are three times more likely than women to commit suicide. It is the third leading cause of death between people age fifteen to twenty-four. The seriousness of this problem has only begun to receive the attention it deserves. The following case provides a poignant example of ETs intervening to prevent suicide.

CASE #182. SUICIDAL DEPRESSION.
In 1992, John (pseudonym) was living in southern California and battling suicidal depression. On April 10 of that year, he made a fateful decision. "I drove to a location in the mountains to commit suicide."

Around noon, John found an isolated area outside of Lake Isabella. "When I got there, I got out of the vehicle and walked around it, looking around my surroundings to make sure nobody was watching...After about fifteen minutes of making peace with it and saying goodbye, I was now ready."

John held a 357 magnum, loaded, with the trigger pulled back and ready to fire. "I was no more than ten seconds from pulling the trigger," John writes. "I noticed something moving out of the corner of my eye."

John became upset because he thought people were watching. He turned his head and saw two figures. "Both stood facing me," writes John, "one motionless and the other one leaning...leaning just enough into my peripheral vision that I would see them. They were exactly like the small grays you see, like in the Roswell accident."

John could barely believe his eyes. "I saw them, twenty feet away from me. I even had a loaded gun and could've shot at them and probably hit them...[but] when I noticed that I was not alone, it simply voided the suicide, and I left, which I thank them for really."

As John drove away, he realized it was now 11:30 p.m., and there was a full moon. It was as if the moment the ETs appeared, darkness had already fallen. He had seen them only in the nighttime, which meant that there were about ten hours which he could not remember.

While the experience prevented him from committing suicide, it had other repercussions. "It took years for me to actually accept what I saw with my own eyes."

Now, however, John has accepted what he saw. "There is no doubt whatsoever, 100 percent absolutely positive beyond any doubt that I saw them, twenty feet away from me."[25]

We have already examined one case involving the cure of AIDS. The only other known case remains unverified and brief in details. If true, however, it shows once again the incredible ability of ETs to cure almost any disease.

CASE #183. AIDS.

At the 1992 UFO Abduction Conference at M.I.T., researcher Yvonne Smith revealed a case in which a man appears to have been healed of AIDs. "I have an HIV-positive abductee who now tests negative," she says.

I contacted Smith regarding the case and she graciously supplied further details. The gentleman had tested positive for the disease and then, after experiencing a few abductions, tested negative. Smith asked for medical records, but the gentleman moved to the eastern coast of the United States, and she lost contact with him. The last time she saw him, however, he appeared to be in good health. Also of note, there is one case in which information was given about the disease. Contactee, Richard Rylka was told that his alien friends were experimenting with introducing hydrogen peroxide into the body's system. Rylka has no idea how this is done, or what the effects might be.[26]

Another top ten killer of humans is the disease known as diabetes. A metabolic disorder, it can lead to a wide variety of serious health problems. Depending on type and severity, it can be treated with diet, exercise and medication. About 371 million people have the disease worldwide. According to the Center for Disease Control, it kills about 79,000 people annually in the United States. According to the World Health Organization, it kills about 1.5 million people each year worldwide.

CASE #191. DIABETES.

In Tbilisi, Georgia, Russia, a young girl told her family that she had been contacted by friendly aliens who cured her of her disease. According to her account, she was awakened by an extraterrestrial named Bonytari who took her aboard a craft. Onboard, she met another ET named Anuda who put a "respiratory-type of device" over her face. The aliens appeared human except their lips were very thin. They offered her a sweet drink, which she refused because of her diabetes. A third alien, Atari, told her that she was now cured. The girl was given some "mysterious stones" which she was told to place in a glass of water, and to drink the water "to assist in the cure."

Following the experience, the girl visited her doctor who gave her a blood test and told her that she no longer had diabetes.[27]

Most people who experience a UFO healing say it took place onboard a UFO, or perhaps in their bedroom. Some say they were cured while driving, or walking outside. A small portion are visited in their hospital rooms. In this next the witness was taken to a very unusual location.

CASE #208. HYPOGLYCEMIA.

Jill Wheeler, a stay-at-home mom, lives in a small town in Nebraska. It was shortly after her third child was born that she began to suffer from an unexplained tiredness. Soon it got so bad that she was actually passing out several times a day. She went to the doctors, who ran a battery of tests. They tested her for diabetes, her blood cell and hormone levels and more--nothing was wrong, they told her. Meanwhile her condition deteriorated. She carried food and juice with her wherever she went. Still, she kept passing out. She began to lose weight and within a few months, lost eighty pounds. Repeat visits to the doctors still brought no answers.

Researching on her own, she felt her symptoms most resembled a severe case of hypoglycemia. Her doctors insisted her blood-sugar levels were normal.

In 1995, Jill was walking through her living room when she suddenly found herself pulled mysteriously from her environment into a very strange place. Says Jill, "It was like inside a domed stadium, that kind of roof. It was all white, and it had backlighting in there. The walls were all lit up and light was coming down from the ceiling, but you couldn't see the light fixtures. It was just all lit up. And it was huge, just humungous. All throughout the whole place, as far as I could see from where I was sitting, were cubicles-- aisles and aisles of cubicles, like you'd find if you walked into a bank or a business."

The cubicles were blue and appeared to be ordinary. The floor itself was carpeted with a tough industrial-type carpet, common in many business offices. Jill continued to look around her and try to orient herself. As she says, "So I was sitting there and I began to notice what was in my immediate area. I was inside a cubicle and I was sitting on a long, steel table like you'd find in any doctor's office. I was wondering, *What the heck am I doing here? What is this?*

She saw many other people in the place, each of them in their own cubicle. Suddenly Jill saw a strange figure approaching her. She opened her mouth and screamed. "I thought that it was a human being, a very tall, very well-developed human being, until it got close enough for me to see its face. Then I knew it wasn't a human being. It had a cape on. It had on clothing that was tight. I can't remember the material; I just remember that I could definitely see its muscles through its clothing. It had a belt on. And as it got closer, I saw the face, and it was huge. Its forehead was way, *way* too high to have been a human being. And its hair was bright orange and sticking straight up about two inches. It was kind of like thin straw or wheat in texture. There was something about his chin too; it was way too big and way too broad. And

324

that's when I realized, something was really, really wrong. And at that point I knew that it just wasn't human."

The being stepped forward, and Jill automatically lay back on the table. The being then took off his cape and wrapped it tightly around her body. Suddenly, she was completely unable to move.

For the first time she noticed a tray with several strange instruments on it. The tall being also held what looked like a doctor's bag. The being looked Jill directly in the eyes and said, "Okay, it's your turn now, Jill." Jill felt a cold chill. As she says, "He didn't say it in a caring, kind, compassionate way. He didn't say it in a mean, cruel, evil way. He just said it like he was talking to a lab rat."

The nine-foot-tall figure then took two small, silver-colored, bell-shaped objects and placed them inside the cape on Jill's body. He placed one underneath her right side, below her ribcage, near the pancreas and liver. Next he lifted her up slightly, and slid the other bell-shaped object underneath her left side, near the kidney and adrenal glands.

Suddenly she felt a strange vibration or force coming from the bell-shaped objects and entering into her body. It felt like waves of energy were flowing into her body. This only made her more terrified and she screamed in abject fear. Although she wasn't religious, she thought about saying the Lord's Prayer, but she was too scared to even remember it.

Instead she lay there, screaming with a kind of visceral fear that felt almost physical. She could hear herself screaming, but was powerless to stop it.

Suddenly, she found herself standing in the middle of her living room. She was still terrified, but she was no longer screaming. She looked around her in shock: *she was back!* What had just happened? She felt her arms and legs. She was breathless and trembling, but otherwise all right. *Oh, no, the kids!* She ran into their bedrooms. They were all sound asleep.

For several moments, she couldn't wake them. Finally, she woke her husband and told him what happened. He had no idea what to tell her. He had no explanation, and neither did Jill.

325

The next few days passed quickly, and Jill was happy to put the strange experience behind her. The soreness in her side was slowly subsiding. Whatever had happened to her, it didn't appear to have left her permanently harmed. In fact, now that she thought about it, she was feeling better than she had in a long, long time. And looking back over the last few days, she had a sudden profound revelation: she hadn't gotten sick once!

Normally, she would become so tired that she'd nearly pass out after each meal. However, ever since the experience, she hadn't lost consciousness once.

After ten days, the soreness in her body had completely healed. Her weight had stabilized and all traces of her hypoglycemia-like illness were gone. She had been healed, but by what...*aliens*?

Her mind raced with hundreds of unanswerable questions. Says Jill, "At the end of that week, when I finally realized, 'What's going on here? I'm not getting sick anymore!' I connected it to what had happened that night. And at that point I began to wonder, who was that? And why me? Why would they come and heal me? Over the next month or so I began to lose a little bit of the fear and get a great curiosity. They hadn't hurt me. They had fixed me. I still did not feel any warm, fuzzy feelings toward them because that's not the impression they gave me. I was a lab rat; that's what I felt like was to them...I don't know what I am to them. Why would they come and heal me like that? I don't know. I really have no idea, and I would like to know why."

Jill would later have further encounters during which she was shown hybrid babies. The full account is told in my book, *Inside UFOs*.[28]

In this next case, the witness was not taken onboard a UFO, nor did he see any aliens. He did, however, have a close-up sighting that resulted in a profound healing both physically and emotionally. It's a good example of an encounter that at first seems to be a simple sighting, but turns out to have unforeseen consequences, in this case, positive.

326

CASE #217. SUICIDAL DEPRESSION, BODY PAINS.

As can be seen, UFO encounters are sometimes transformative experiences, leaving the witness profoundly changed in ways both spiritual and physical. Another such case took place in October 1997 to David Perez of West Covina, California. It was only a few weeks after the mass suicide in San Diego of forty-nine "Heaven's Gate" UFO cult members.

Perez stepped out of his apartment to smoke a cigarette when he observed an unidentified craft hovering a few hundred feet away. Says Perez, "It looked like a ship...All I saw at first were the lights all the way around it. I never saw lights like that around a helicopter or an airplane." As he watched, the object started to flash lights at him. Perez's cousin and girlfriend came outside and also observed the object, as did his neighbor. At one point, the object sent down a beam of light which apparently struck Perez. As he says, "This red bright light went on, and it seemed like it kind of penetrated my pupils, and my vision turned red. Everything that I saw was tinted red...that's when I got kind of scared. I thought it had screwed up my vision...I couldn't talk, and I couldn't move or anything. I don't know if it was the fear or what, but I just couldn't move anything."

A few minutes later, Perez had an argument with his girlfriend, got into his car and drove off. He reports that the object followed him from West Covina to Canoga Park, where it suddenly appeared again over his car. A strange feeling of comfort passed over him and he realized that the encounter was affecting him physically. Says Perez, "I was kind of stressed. I've always had problems with my back. I used to cough up blood once and a while. I was kind of sick. I had pains in my chest and on my side. Ever since that night, I haven't had any pain at all. And I was also suicidal. Ever since that night, I haven't been. I've been good. I've been feeling really good, really healthy."

Perez also started to experience premonitions and developed an interest in meditation and psychic development. He believes that the UFO is responsible for his spiritual awakening. As he says, "I kind of feel for some strange reason that they have something to do with God. Ever since then I've started talking about God."[29]

About 200 cases of leprosy are reported each year in the United States. It can cause severe nerve damage and lead to scarring of the skin, loss of limbs and other health problems. Medicinal treatments are highly effective. Back in the 1980s, there were about five million known cases worldwide. Today it is believed to be a few hundred thousand, mostly in less industrialized countries. In this next case, a woman was cured of the disease. It's the only documented ET healing of leprosy.

CASE #218. LEPROSY.
As investigated by well-known Russian researcher, Marina Popovich in her book, *UFOs over Planet Earth*, in 1997 Klara Doronina and R. Slavskiy (who was badly ill with leprosy) were vacationing on the east shore of Lake Baikal, Russia, when a UFO landed near them. Several human-appearing entities exited the craft and took Doronina and Slavskiy onboard. They reportedly took the two friends to a planet in the Pleaides, cured Slavskiy of his leprosy, and returned them home.[30]

The following case, published here for the first time, involves a man who was not only healed, but was spiritually transformed by his experience.

CASE #234. ENLARGED PROSTATE.
Dudley is a registered nurse, and a licensed chiropractor and massage therapist from the eastern United States. Says Dudley, "My niece claims she was abducted at the age of ten, and had a tissue sample removed from her thigh. You can see an indentation where some tissue is missing. She said her abductors wore blue uniforms with a little insignia on their chests, and that some possessed the stereotypical small body with big eyes, but that others looked quite human--so much so, in fact, that they were indistinguishable from normal human beings."

Dudley was amazed by his niece's revelation, particularly because he himself had been having strange experiences his entire life, some of which seemed paranormal, others which seemed UFO-related.

It was one night in 1998, shortly after he retired, that he had his first unambiguously UFO-related experience. Says Dudley, "I awoke to find myself bathed in a shaft of blue light that came down *through* the ceiling of my bedroom. Instead of converging toward the ceiling, the rays appeared to be parallel, which suggested that they either came down from a great height, or perhaps they were some type of laser beam."

Dudley sat up in amazement. Although the strange beam of light shone directly on him, he could feel no effects. After less than a minute, it suddenly blinked off, and the room was plunged into darkness. Dudley was completely mystified. As he says, "To this day I do not know the meaning of that experience."

The possibility that the event was connected to UFOs did not escape him. In fact, it was the only theory that seemed to explain what had happened. What other kind of beam of light could come through a solid ceiling?

A few years later, in June 2001, Dudley had another experience, this one involving an apparent healing. He had just retired to his own room. It was then that he had what he calls "by far one of the most remarkable experiences of my life."

Recently he had been having problems with his prostate, which caused him difficulties with urination. Although he was a nurse, he didn't think the situation was serious, and he just attributed it to an enlarged prostate, a common condition for men in their seventies.

That evening, he fell asleep as normal. But sometime in the middle of the night, he woke up to find that he was no longer in his bedroom. Instead, he was in a darkened room, lying on a table. He struggled to reach full consciousness, but found that he was paralyzed and unable to cry out.

Says Dudley, "I gradually attained the level of consciousness that I was permitted and found myself looking at a small flickering light--the only source of illumination in the room--

that was about a foot away from my face and attached to the edge of a table upon which I was lying. I was in the same semi-prone position in which an osteopath had placed me many years ago when adjusting my tailbone. It's called the Sim's Position.

"Slowly I became aware of what seemed to be a slender probe that had been pushed up inside me and was gently vibrating against my prostate. I wondered what in the world was going on. And then it dawned upon me that I was receiving--at the hands of aliens--some kind of radiation therapy, presumably for prostate cancer. I do have prostate problems, but didn't know that cancer was one of them.

"The session lasted about five or ten minutes. When it was over, I was, of course, tremendously grateful for this wonderful gift of grace, and repeatedly thanked the doctor who administered it to me. Because it was so dark, I could only barely see what he looked like. He was clothed in white. He was humanoid, but quite homely--almost misshapen--in appearance. He may have been hybrid--part alien and part human. I heard him quite distinctly convey the message, 'It was a small tumor.'

"I asked him his name," Dudley continues, "but perceived immediately that he was reluctant to give it. Nevertheless, he seemed to convey the word, 'June.' But then I thought, 'That can't be right. June is a woman's name.' Then I drifted off into unconsciousness."

When he awoke, Dudley instantly remembered what happened. Says Dudley, "I felt 'different'--as if, indeed something *had* been done to me."

Time proved his suspicions correct. His prostate problems began to subside. Over the next few weeks, they almost completely disappeared. While he still had some minor problems, his health was vastly improved from its former condition. He was, of course, astonished. The only conclusion that he could come to was that he--like his niece--had been abducted by aliens.

He remembered an episode on *Unsolved Mysteries* in which a Florida woman reported a similar experience of being healed. Further research convinced him that many people are being abducted by aliens.

Today, Dudley continues to enjoy his retirement. He has not had any other UFO-related experiences, but he would like to. His interactions with the phenomenon have all been benevolent, and coupled with his strong Christian faith, Dudley feels safe and protected.

As he says, "I find the whole subject of alien abductions to be a fascinating one, for there can be absolutely no question but that they not only occur, but as far as I am concerned, have occurred to me. I know that some people report having had terrible experiences at the hands of aliens. Personally, I am not too concerned about that type of experience happening to me. As a born-again Christian, it is my belief that no harm or evil can befall me except that which my Lord, in his infinite love and mercy, allows. Therefore, I expect not only good things from aliens, because they will definitely have to answer to the King of kings and Lord of lords (not to mention the universal law of karma-- sowing and reaping) for their treatment of me. I know it, and just as importantly, so do they."[31]

The following case involves a lady who not only received a cure from gray aliens for a life-threatening condition, they provided her with follow-up visits and medical advice.

CASE #232. BLOOD CLOT.

"Gloria" (pseudonym) was somewhat familiar with grays as she had encountered them in her dreams many times, and in a few cases, she had seen them face-to-face. In 2000 (date approx.) Gloria was taking an eleven-hour flight back to the USA. She stayed in her seat most of the flight and didn't drink enough fluids. For whatever reason, upon returning home, she developed a blood clot. "I knew it was a blood clot because my inner right calf was hard and felt crunchy to the touch," says Gloria. "...I freaked out, of course, but I had no insurance at the time. I just gave it to God because I did not have money to see a doctor."

It was then that the grays began to telepathically communicate with her. "They told me to drink massive amounts of fluids, wear tight stockings, move a lot. It was too late, I thought, because my whole right inner vein in my calf was solidified. I could feel it crunch when I pushed it."

After a month of this, one evening Gloria experienced heart pain. Then something happened. "I don't know what happened," Gloria says. "I felt better. I remembered during this time, I was sleeping and I felt my blankets being stripped from my body and being moved somewhere and that was it. I don't know what happened, but it felt good. I felt my leg afterward and the clot was gone and my heart was doing well."

Following the incident, Gloria experienced "frequent" visits by the grays. "I think they just wanted to make sure I was okay. I have no complaints. They did a better job than most doctors."

Five years later, the visits have pretty much stopped, though Gloria continues to enjoy good health. "I believe I am alive today because of my encounters with gray beings. I have insurance today and went to the doctor recently. Healthy as can be, he said. He did a complete physical and I am totally healthy. I have records to prove it...All I can say is, thank you God for the gray beings! I am on an extension of my life. Why they saved me is unknown to me. But I am eternally grateful for their existence on this Earth."

Prior to the incident, Gloria reports being frustrated and unhappy. She struggled with a bout of homelessness, and had little money. Following the incident, she feels that her life has purpose and meaning. "I thank God and the gray aliens for saving me and giving me hope," she says. "...I know the gray aliens are probably still observing me. I am hoping that they will continue to do good for others too. I feel blessed. God created all of his creations for a purpose."[32]

The following remarkable case involves a man who was healed, but failed to follow the ETs' medical advice, leading to disastrous consequences.

CASE #235. ATROPHIED LEGS.

On October 11-14, 2001, a large UFO wave struck the regions of Krasnodar, Stavropol, Rostov, Volgograd, Saratov and Samara in Russia. At that time, a businessman named "Oleg," was working on his cabin in a village in Nizhniy in Novgorod Province. Suddenly he received a call from the local security guards saying that a UFO was hovering over his home. Oleg looked outside and saw a large glowing object.

Moments later, several human-looking uniformed figures appeared in his home. The figures spoke telepathically, saying that they were there to solve certain technical problems, and that he should remain quiet and not interfere.

For three days the aliens remained in his home. They took over a room and used it to repair strange equipment which they would not let him see. After three days, they told him they were almost done and would soon be leaving.

Oleg said, "If you have great ability, can you help me, please? As you can see, I am an invalid. Can you cure my legs?"

Oleg suffered from a disease which had left his legs atrophied. The aliens said they would cure him, but he would have to run every day or his entire organism would "degrade." He would also have to keep the healing a secret.

Oleg agreed. The ETs proceeded to perform some type of "surgery." They then scanned him with a strange device and told him, "Now you do not only have normal legs, but very strong legs."

Oleg reports that he was healed and for several days was euphoric. But then he became afraid that the aliens might return and he reported his experience to UFO researchers. Word leaked out about his encounters, causing conflict with his neighbors.

Oleg reportedly became depressed, forgot to exercise, and again lost the ability to use his legs. As the ETs had warned him, Oleg's health began to fail. He died in January 2004, less than three years after his initial encounter.[33]

Another case involving the cure of muscular dystrophy involves one of the rarest methods used by ETs: medicine. And yet, the cure appears to have been effective.

CASE #309. MUSCULAR DYSTROPHY.

Morenci, Arizona has attracted a number of low-level UFO sightings, perhaps because of the copper mines and plants in the area. According to the UFOCCI, a man in Morenci experienced an onboard encounter with ETs in 2007 (date approx.) He told the ETs that he had a son suffering from muscular dystrophy and asked if they could heal him The ETs agreed and gave the witness five clear vials of liquid, and told the man to inject his son in the naval one time each day for five days and then his son would be cured. Reportedly the UFO researcher looking into the case was able to examine the vials and said that they appeared to be composed of plastic or crystal and that each one had a vial within a vial.[34]

A wonderfully sincere and vivid account of the healing of a serious medical condition comes from an outstanding witness who is working hard for the benefit of all humanity. The case is a perfect illustration of who is being healed, and why.

CASE #271. BLOOD CLOT.
Born in 1955, Reverend Michael J. Carter had his first encounter with ETs on December 28, 1989. He was thirty-four years old and living with his girlfriend in an apartment in Manhattan, New York. He woke to see a gray alien next to his bed. The being was "chalk-white, had a pear-shaped head, had a tight-fitting jumpsuit that looked like aluminum foil, had the wrap-around eyes, a spindly-looking gentleman."

The encounter terrified Carter. He became even more concerned when the bedroom encounters continued. Realizing he was having ET encounters, he sought help and went under regressive hypnosis with Dr. Jean Mundy. Carter was able to recall being taken onboard a ship. He found himself in a round room with no corners and indirect lighting. The temperature was cool, and reminded Carter of "being in a doctor's office almost, when you go for an exam."

Thankfully, his experiences slowed down and stopped.

Then in 2013, while living in Asheville, North Carolina, his right leg became suddenly painful and swollen. Over three days his condition worsened. Carter went to the hospital and was diagnosed with a severe blood clot in his right leg.

The doctor prescribed a months-long treatment using blood-thinning medication, and ordered Carter to return weekly for close observation.

Carter's leg was swollen to twice its normal size. On the evening of July 4, 2013, he lay on his back in bed unable to sleep. Suddenly a human-looking figure appeared at the foot of his bed. "He was very big and muscular," says Carter. "[He wore] one of those cowls that monks wore back in Renaissance times. He had long blond hair, shoulder length, and [he was] pale...I was just stunned. And he put out his hand--I think it was his right...and this blue light came out of his palm, energy or whatever it was, and it hit me. And I saw it hit me, but I didn't feel anything. And then he just dissolved."

Carter was amazed. The figure was seven feet tall, wore a gray robe and glowed with a white aura. The entire experience lasted only seconds. Afterward, he grabbed his bedside journal and wrote down what happened.

The next morning, he was excited to tell his family what happened. "I put my legs down on the floor to get out of bed," says Carter. "And I looked, and my legs were the same size...the right was the same size as the left. And not only was it the same size, but the veins in my leg looked like they had changed position, like they had been re-routed or something, that's the best way I can put it."

A few days later, Carter returned to his doctor for a routine check-up. The doctor was shocked and asked him, "How did this happen? You were just here."

Carter declined to tell the doctor about the bedroom visitation and said, "Just be happy for me."

Two weeks later, while meditating, Carter saw the same figure again, and another--a woman. Both figures were strong, muscular-looking with long blond hair. Carter feels that they were checking up on him, and letting him know that they were around him.

Carter feels that his experiences have given him a strong boost in his intuitive and healing abilities and accelerated his spiritual growth. He is now the author of several books about UFOs and religion. He's a speaker, a healer and a human-rights activist. He was recognized by President Clinton for his efforts in community outreach and anti-racism.[35]

While a UFO healing is undeniably a positive thing, many witnesses are understandably upset by the experience. Having your body operated upon by alien beings, without warning or having given permission makes experiencers realize just how vulnerable they are to alien intrusion. In the following case, a medical professional received a profound healing. Unfortunately, the cure was temporary and ended up causing severe trauma in the witness's life.

CASE #280. GALLBLADDER.

Marla [pseudonym] and her family had seen UFOs many times outside their home in Marysville, Washington. In January 2015, Marla had gone to bed when she heard someone banging around in the kitchen. She assumed her oldest daughter was cooking and thought nothing of it. But as she lay back down, events became very strange. "Suddenly," she says, "I heard a loud, high-pitch ring. It was disorienting. My bedroom door opened [and] and I saw three beings walk into my room. I couldn't make out what they looked like. Light bathed behind them, so they looked dark [and it was] hard to make out the detail."

The figures were short, stout, with large heads and a short neck. "As soon as I saw them, I sat up and tried to speak. They walked to the foot of my bed. And then one touched my foot and *bam*, I was out like a light."

Marla woke up the next morning to one of the most shocking sights of her life. Marla worked in the medical field and was familiar with surgery and surgical procedures. At the time of her visitation, she was suffering kidney disease and gallstones. She was due to have surgery to remove the gallbladder in one week. "The next day, the very moment I woke up, I exhaled what tasted like gas," Marla explains. "It was a familiar feeling and tasted like I had just woken up from surgery and had been put to sleep with an anesthesia. I was groggy, so I tried to sit up in bed and felt a sharp pain in my abdominal area. I looked under my shirt and I indeed

336

had an incision. This was like no incision I had seen before. First, it was very straight as an arrow, and was very clean. The skin looked void of blood at the incision. Second, no bedodine or other substances were used to prep a patient's skin to prevent infections...third, it was glued together, no stiches or staples. Not only did it not have any dried blood or cautery marks, but most of all, the odd thing was: it could be pulled apart and still no blood. And when you let go, it sealed right back together until you pulled it apart again."

Marla freaked out. She opened the incision two inches deep, but became frightened and closed it back up again. She showed it to her family, who were equally baffled and alarmed. At the time of the incident, everyone had been in bed, though a few of them had also heard the banging in the kitchen. They inspected the kitchen, but nothing had been disturbed.

Marla told nobody but her family what happened. "As someone who worked in nursing and surgery for years, I knew I couldn't talk to my doctor about it without being labeled crazy."

The surprises were still coming. Says Marla, "A few days after this happened, the incision rapidly healed, far faster than any I have had before. Most of the time my incisions took well over a month to heal due to my bad kidney disease."

One week before the incident, Marla was scheduled to have another pre-surgery ultrasound and exam for her gallbladder-removal surgery. By this time, the mysterious incision on her abdomen was gone. She went to the doctors to get her ultrasound. "When they did the ultrasound, the stone that was as large as my gallbladder was completely gone. This stone I had was far too large for me to pass, and it had to be removed along with my gallbladder. But when I got the ultrasound, the stone was gone, yet my gallbladder remained. This baffled the doctors. A gallstone surgery has to include removing the gallbladder. Yet mine was intact, sans stone."

Marla has no idea why this happened to her, and unfortunately, the ultimate results were not good. One year following the incident, she had a new, larger gallstone and had to have it surgically removed. While she believes the aliens healed her, it was only temporary. "This event changed my life, in a bad way," Marla says. "Even though I am thankful to whoever helped heal my body from a bad stone, it scares me that I have no idea who it was, or why they took me to do such a thing... This has made me fear who could remove me from my home, perform a surgery on me, and put me back without anyone else being the wiser. Also, to not know who did this to me, our own government, or some non-human, has made it quite hard on me. I want answers yet have no way to ever find out who did this."

Marla began to suffer from anxieties, and was afraid to reach out for support from the medical community for fear of being labeled deluded. Luckily her family was very supportive.

Then, a few months later, in the summer of 2015, it happened again. On this occasion, Marla woke up to find a clean, precise surgical scar across her sternum area. As before, it healed very rapidly. "I still have both scars," Marla says. "I need answers. But most of all, I want people to know that life is not exactly what we think it is when someone else can remove you from your home, and you have no memory of what happened, no power to stop it. It's scary, yet I know people need to know it does happen."

Marla finally reached out to MUFON to report her experience. "I am willing to provide medical records and proof of my gallstone being there, and disappearing. I also would do a polygraph to prove I am being honest."[36]

The following three cases, each from the FREE study, are undated, not fully investigated, and sparse on detail. Yet each provide more evidence of the ETs' healing agenda on our planet.

CASE #304. HYPERTENSION, DETACHED RETINA, LEG PROBLEM.
A lady who was experiencing regular encounters asked the ETs to heal her husband, who was suffering from severe hypertension. The ETs abducted her husband and examined him using computer-like equipment. Following the encounter, her husband's high blood pressure was cured and remained normal. Now age 73, he has the blood pressure of a young man. The ETs

also used the opportunity to heal him of a detached retina, and a crooked leg.[37]

CASE #305. APPENDICITIS.
"One of my sisters was ill...she would get sick and in pain. Later we found out that her appendix was removed, but she never had surgery to remove her appendix."[38]

CASE #306. SUICIDAL DEPRESSION.
"I believe the contact experience was healing me. I had been seeing a psychologist about suicidal thoughts...but after contact, I didn't have suicidal thoughts anymore."[39]

How many UFO healing cases need to be listed before these types of cases are taken more seriously? An objective review of the data from the above cases alone should be enough to convince even the most die-hard skeptic of their validity. If people are truly being cured of strokes, diabetes, muscular dystrophy, tuberculosis, multiple sclerosis, AIDS, polio, diphtheria and so much more--and this is what the evidence is showing us--then the importance of these cases cannot be overstated. If we could learn to understand and apply the methods used by the ETs, it could lead to a revolution in the medical field, saving untold millions of people from a wide variety of health problems, including death.

Chapter Twenty-Three
Cancer Cures

This next chapter focuses solely on cases of people who have been cured of cancer as the result of a UFO encounter. Of all the reported disease cures, with forty cases, cancer is by far the most common. A wide variety of cancer cures are reported, involving numerous organ systems.

No matter what the condition, each healing provides compelling medical evidence pointing toward the veracity of a case. The cancer cases, unlike other healings however, seem to provide far more evidence. As with serious and chronic illnesses, the healings of cancer cannot be faked. When a person is taken from the edge of death to a miraculous recovery, and can point to the reason for it, what other conclusion is there?

The huge number of cases, the excellent credibility of many of the witnesses, the before and after diagnoses provided by doctors, the multiple eyewitnesses--all of these add up to build a convincing case for the truth of these cases. If these people aren't being healed by aliens, then what exactly is happening here?

Many close encounter reports come with little or no evidence whatsoever. Many people experience profound onboard experiences, and have no way to prove it to anyone. The healing cases provide this proof, and of all the healing cases, the cancer healings are among the best evidence that UFO healings are a real phenomenon, one that is likely affecting far more people than the few hundred portrayed in this book.

The first cancer healing we shall examine appeared in the first article ever written on this subject. It is one of very few cases involving entities that are non-humanoid.

CASE #012. CANCER.

In July 1951, Fred Reagan of Atlanta, Georgia, was piloting a Piper Cub when he collided with a glowing unidentified flying object. Reagan was badly injured. His plane was also severely damaged and began to tumble downward. Reagan, however, felt himself being sucked upward by a strange force. He found himself inside the UFO surrounded by three-foot-tall shiny figures with the appearance of "huge stalks of metallic asparagus."

The beings spoke to him in English, and apologized for colliding with his craft. Onboard the craft they gave him a medical examination and told him that he had cancer. They then proceeded to perform an operation to remove the cancer "as a slight reparation of the loss that we have caused you."

Reagan lost consciousness. When he awoke, he was unhurt, lying in a farmer's field next to his destroyed plane.

The case ends one year later with the following press release: "Fred Reagan, who made headlines last year when he had been a visitor aboard a flying saucer, died today in the State Asylum for the Insane. Cause of death was determined to be degeneration of the brain tissue due to extreme atomic radiation. Authorities are unable to offer an explanation."

Gordon Creighton published this report in the 1969 issue of *Flying Saucer Review* in the first article about UFO healings. The report was first uncovered by FSR editor, Derek Dempster in 1956, but was not published at that time.

Creighton believes the fantastic nature of the report prevented its initial publication. He tried to verify the report however, as he says, "...despite years of trying, I have failed to find anyone who can or will throw any light upon the story for me, or authenticate it...It may be untrue. But I do not think that it is. It contains far too many elements which, in this summer of 1969, seem to me to possess the ring of truth, but which very understandably may not have seemed to possess it in 1951."

In his article, Creighton wrote that he withheld details of the story--details which have never been revealed. Today the case remains controversial. Other investigators have also been unsuccessful in verifying the case or even the identity of Fred

Reagan. A few have gone on record with their belief that the case is fictitious. Creighton, despite his own misgivings, wrote, "We have heard too much since 1951 to be able simply to dismiss it out of hand."[1]

One of the most profound and earliest-reported healing cases on record occurred in 1957 in Brazil. Only a few cases exist in which any outside witnesses observed the healing of the patient firsthand. In this case there were many witnesses. The case remains a classic and its authenticity has never been disputed.

CASE #022. STOMACH CANCER.

This case was first revealed by Brazilian journalist Joao Martins and UFO investigator Olavo T. Fontes, who was the official medical investigator of UFOs for the Brazilian government.

According to the report, the family was very wealthy, and the father was a powerful and influential figure in society. The man's young daughter was suffering from stomach cancer and doctors expected she would die. The daughter's disease progressed quickly. She was suffering intensely on the night a UFO visited the family.

What follows is the firsthand testimony of Anazia Maria, who was the family's maid and an eyewitness to the event. It appeared originally in *UFO Abduction at Mirasol*, published by Wendelle C. Stevens of the UFO Photo Archives. It was this letter which first brought the case to the attention of UFO researchers.

"Dear Sr. Martins: I have read your articles and desire to compliment you on them. I believe in the existence of the flying discs because I personally witnessed the incident here related. I don't know if you will believe me, but I assure you that what I am going to tell you is the truth. I am poor but honest. I will not mention the whole names involved, but I am sure you will understand.

"My name is Anazia Maria. I am 37-years-old and actually live in Rio De Janeiro. I have worked in the home of Sr. X since December 1957. You must excuse me for not mentioning his name for he is a wealthy and influential man of this city. The daughter of my employer suffered from cancer of the stomach. She suffered considerably, and I was employed to serve as a sort of governess, and to assist the Senorita Lais, the daughter with cancer.

"She had been given many and diverse treatments to control the cancer, but the doctors had said there was no hope. In August of 1957 my employer sent the whole family to a small farm near Petropolis, hoping his daughter would improve in the better climate. But the days passed with no improvement. Lais could no longer eat and her suffering was horrible and became worse every day. She was given constant injections of morphine to control the pain.

"I remember the night of 25 October very well. We expected her to die as the pains of Senorita Lais were terrible. The injections seemed to have no effect. Her father was singing a verse when suddenly a strong bright light came on to one side and shone directly on the house. We were all in the room of Senorita Lais whose window was situated exactly on the side of the house from which the light came. The only light inside was a small lamp at the head of the bed.

"'Look,' cried Julinho, a brother of the dying girl, as he ran to the window and saw a disc-shaped machine there in the light. It was not very big, and I am not learned enough to be able to say what its diameters might be or its height. I know that it was not very big. The upper part was enveloped in a luminescence of a yellowish-reddish color.

"Suddenly, a port automatically opened in the object and two small beings emerged. They came toward the house while a third one remained in the port of the disc. I noticed on the interior (of the disc) through the port I could see a green light like can be seen in 'night clubs.'

"The 'humans' came into the house. They were short, about 1.20 meters tall, smaller than a younger son of my employer who was ten years old. They had large heads on top of their shoulders, reddish ears, small slanted eyes (like Chinese) but their skin was a vivid green!

"They had something on their hands that I thought were gloves. Their suits were white and seemed to be thick--the chest, the sides and the cuffs shined brightly. I do not know how to explain. They came up to the side of Senorita Lais, who moaned in pain, eyes wide open, and not understanding anything that was going on around her. Nobody moved or spoke in the terrible tension. I was there in the room with Sr. X and his wife, Sr. Julinho and his wife, and Otavinho, the younger son of my employer.

"Those 'humans' looked at me silently and stood at the side of the bed, placing the instruments they carried on the top of the milky coverlet. They made a gesture toward my employer and one of them placed his hand on the forehead of Sr. X and 'discussed' the case of Senorita Lais with a bluish light that showed all of her interior. We saw all there was inside the belly of the girl. With another instrument that emitted a noise, 'he' pointed it in the direction of the stomach of Lais and we could see the cancer. The operation lasted about a half hour. Then Senorita Lais went to sleep and 'they' left. But before leaving the house, they communicated with Sr. X telepathically that he would have to give her medicine during one month. Then 'they' gave him a sphere made of stainless-steel-like metal which contained some thirty small white pills. She was to be given one per day and she would be cured.

"Lais later returned to her doctor, who verified that her cancer had been cured.

"I have left that house, but I promised to absolutely guard the secret of this case. Therefore I have told you, but I must guard the true identity.

"If you mention this case in your articles it is of no consequence because I have withheld the names of the people involved in this. But I assure you everything I have said is real.

"Lais was condemned to die of cancer of the stomach and in spite of this she was saved by an instrument that looked like a flashlight, that emitted rays that 'dissolved' the cancer, and she survived. They saved Senorita Lais and the same night returned to their flying machine and were gone."

This case is significant for many reasons. First, it was one of the first reported UFO healing cases ever released to the public and therefore could not have been influenced by earlier reports.

Second, the incident was witnessed by many people. Third, a patient who was diagnosed with terminal cancer survived as a direct result of the UFO encounter. Another interesting aspect of this case is the physical evidence obtained. There are at least a dozen other cases on record in which people were given medicine by aliens. In a few cases, samples of the medicine were saved for analysis. Probably the most important aspect of this case is the obvious sincerity of the letter. It is a complex encounter, and stands as one of the pioneering cases of UFO healings.[2]

Coral and Jim Lorenzen, the founders of the Aerial Phenomena Research Organization (APRO) were among the first researchers to recognize the validity of onboard UFO experiences. Not surprisingly, they also uncovered some healing cases.

CASE #057. STOMACH CANCER.
From the files of APRO comes a healing which occurred on November 6, 1972, in the Dominican Republic. According to the report on the case, "During an evangelist church service in Paya...a UFO passed over the house where the service was being held and lit up everything inside, causing everyone to panic. A strange-looking being entered the building, took the pastor by the hand, and reportedly healed a woman of stomach cancer. During the healing, the woman reported a sensation of cold from the alien's touch."[3]

Many people who suffer cancer go through a variety of treatments searching for one that will be more effective. Some of these people experience a UFO encounter while undergoing Earth treatments in addition to their own homeopathic methods. It's difficult to say where the healing is coming from in cases like these, but the likelihood that the encounter was a factor cannot be discounted.

CASE #064. THROAT CANCER.
In 1973, 49-year-old factory worker, Denise B. of Marseille, France, was suffering from a worsening case of throat cancer. She

received regular treatments of chemotherapy. Unfortunately, it did little to halt the disease, so she slowly discontinued the treatments.

Meanwhile, the cancer got worse. Denise had become partially paralyzed and had no reflex actions left.

By 1974, she had stopped all treatments. She still visited the hospital every month. On August 15, 1974, her doctors stated that her cancer was worse and she must return to the hospital on September 15.

On the evening of September 14, Denise was taking a walk with her dog. The dog disappeared into some bushes, and Denise followed, dragging her feet because she could barely walk.

Suddenly Denise was overcome by a feeling of "having her insides all mixed up." Shortly later, she felt strangely tired, and her flashlight stopped working. She then felt something grip her neck. She noticed that her whole body was engulfed in a beam of light coming from above. She was unable to move and felt the beam lift her into the air.

Her next memory is of seeing another light near the ground. Then the light disappeared and Denise returned to the road. She noticed that she could walk fine and her legs no longer hurt. She recovered her dog and returned home, thoroughly frightened.

The next day she went to the hospital. According to the report on the case, "...the medical assistant examined her: no more cancer! This was confirmed by another doctor and she was told she could go home."

Denise told one of the mystified doctors that it must have been the goat milk she drank that cured her.

Today Denise is elderly, healthy and free of cancer. Although she is not religious, she does believe her experience was unusual. As she says, "If only this miracle could lead to a cure for cancer."[4]

In the following cancer healing encounter, we have another well-verified event, with numerous eyewitnesses, landing traces, doctor reports and a firsthand account of extraordinary detail.

CASE #068. PANCREATIC CANCER.

Helene Charbonneau claims to have received multiple cures from ETs and perhaps other sources. Her first miraculous healing took place when she was only nine years old. At the time, she suffered from tuberculosis of the spine and could only walk with the aid of braces. She went to visit and pray at a Catholic Shrine in Quebec, Canada. While there, she felt something like a bolt of electricity strike her, vibrating her body from head to toe. She leaped from her seat and knew instantly that she had been healed.

While the healing seemed to be a result of visiting a sacred shrine, Charbonneau would later be the recipient of at least two additional healings at the hands of ETs.

In May of 1974, Helene was diagnosed with cancer of her hip-bone. Doctors quickly had the cancer surgically removed. A short time later, a cancerous growth was discovered on her pancreas. The doctors again operated on her and removed most of the cancerous material. Unfortunately, there were unforeseen complications. As Helene says, "They were not able to remove all of it, so they just closed me up."

A year later, the cancer had spread to Helene's bowels. She went through chemotherapy and lost almost fifty pounds. The treatment did not stop the spread of the cancer, and doctors told her in no uncertain terms that she would die soon, and that she should see her family before it was too late. "I looked like a walking corpse," Helene said. It was May 1975, and the doctors told her she had one month left, maybe two.

Helene was so weakened by the disease that she was barely able to walk. One evening she was too tired to even eat and just went to bed. At 1:00 a.m., she woke up to hear her name being called. "Helene," said the voice, "get into your car and meet us on the way to Lunde. We'll meet you there."

Lunde was a small town about seventeen miles away. Helene was unable to resist the impulse to get in her car and go. "I was seven miles out of town when I saw a large white globe in the sky," says Helene.

As though hypnotized, she drove her car to the location and walked up to the object which was beginning to descend. The object floated to the ground and two small creatures in tight-fitting metallic suits exited the craft. They had small ears, nose and mouth, but their eyes were large and "loving."

Helene was quickly taken onboard. Inside she smelled ozone and a metallic smell. "Do not be afraid," they told her. "We are here to help you."

Although she was frightened, Helene felt that the aliens were friendly. "We are not going to hurt you, we are here to help you. Would you disrobe and lay on this table?"

Helene felt as if she had no will of her own. She lay down on the table, which looked like Plexiglas with a bluish glow inside it.

Helene asked why they were helping her and they replied, "We may need you later on, and besides, we were asked."

Next Helene was examined with a small reddish instrument shaped like "an upside-down mushroom." The aliens passed it over her body several times, and told her that she had cancer in her left breast, liver, right kidney, pancreas and spleen.

They then began a long and sometimes painful cure. First an instrument shaped like a "metallic tray with a handle on either side of it" was passed over her body at least ten times. Each time the instrument went over a cancerous area, Helene felt intense heat and excruciating pain. She was able to withstand the tortuous operation only because the Earth doctors had already done much worse.

After the tray-like instrument, the aliens pulled out a foot-long tube filled with a "purplish-colored fog." They took this tube and injected a fluid into Helene's abdomen. A short time later they injected her with another tube and extracted several ounces of dark-colored blood. Helene was then given several more injections on her abdomen, sides and back. Then more strange instruments were passed over her entire body.

Afterward she was told she could get dressed. The aliens showed her a map and explained that they were from a solar system beyond Orion. They told her to take no medication, and that her cancer was completely cured.

Helene exited the craft, drove quickly home and went straight to bed. The next morning, she was still very weak and appeared to be suffering as badly as ever. She told her son about the experience. He was skeptical until they drove to the location and found a large depression in the earth where Helene remembered the UFO had landed.

That afternoon she began vomiting foul-smelling "black stuff." She was rushed to the hospital where doctors gathered Helene's family and told them she was about to die.

For two days Helene was violently ill and lapsed in and out of consciousness. Doctors offered numerous medications, but Helene, following the orders of the aliens, refused them all.

By the third day, Helene began to recover. Tests were taken and revealed that all traces of the cancer were gone. As she says, "It was just like I had never been sick."

Two weeks later, Helene's skin color returned to normal and the doctors had to admit that she was miraculously cured. Her cancer diagnosis and subsequent cure are verified by doctors and by her medical records. Following the event, Helene remained perfectly healthy and began to manage her own business. She says that when the time is right, she will go public with her experiences.

The fact that she has experienced this second healing at the hands of ETs raises interesting questions about her first healing. UFO researcher, "Leneesa," writes of the Charbonneau case: "Who can really say who the perpetrator was?"

In 1985, as an adult, Charbonneau suffered a car accident, breaking some vertebrae in her back. Doctors inserted metal rods to help her heal. Unfortunately, a bone-chip resting on her spine aggravated her condition, and doctors were unable to help. Four years following the accident, in 1989, Charbonneau had a visitation by extraterrestrials who removed the bone chip and healed her.[5]

Another well-verified case of a cancer healing comes from a city councilwoman from Florida, Lynne Plaskett, who--long before UFO healings were being talked about--bravely went public with her own personal account. She even appeared on the television program *Sightings,* which televised her case to a national audience.

CASE #072. CANCER.

In 1975, Lynne Plaskett of New Smyrna Beach, Florida was dismayed to be diagnosed with T-cell lymphoma, a malignant cancer. Despite treatment, her cancer worsened. The doctors told her that her case was fatal, and that she had about three months to live. Then one evening something strange happened. She was lying in bed, but was still awake.

Says Plaskett, "I felt myself lifting straight off the bed, it must have been about nineteen inches. Then I saw a silvery disc-shaped object, about eight inches across. It was hovering beside me. It had tiny windows like portholes, and it made three sweeps over my body, as if carefully examining me. I wasn't afraid, just a little surprised. I felt warm and relaxed."

Moments later, the object disappeared, the fog dissipated and the buzzing sound became silent. Plaskett felt herself lowered to her bed. "I fell into a wonderful sleep," she says, "and I knew I was going to be all right. I wasn't going to die. Within days, tests showed my cancer was disappearing and now I'm in total remission."

The cancer immediately reversed and within four months, all traces of it were gone. Plaskett is convinced that a UFO cured her. "It sounds fantastic, but it wasn't from God or this Earth; I'm convinced that I was cured by some kind of alien."

Interestingly, Plaskett was a city councilwoman, though after revealing he encounter, she was not re-elected.[6]

Like the other healings, the cancer cures come from all over the world. The following, from Bogota, Columbia involves a healing done by Nordic ETs.

CAS1E #073. CANCER.

In 1975, engineer Juan Osorio was working near Bogota, Columbia when he saw a huge, glowing, disc-shaped craft overhead. Suddenly he found himself being taken onboard via a platform made of light. Inside the UFO was a group of tall human-looking men and women wearing shiny silver clothing. Juan felt peace and tranquility as he was taken to another room. Researcher

Alberto Rosales writes, "There he was bathed in a soothing red light that appeared to purify him. Later he was asked to remove his clothing and was told to put on a uniform similar to theirs. He was taken into another room, and there a luminous orange-colored rectangle enveloped him. A blue-violet haze encased his head, apparently going through some therapeutic process. Soon after his release by the extraterrestrials, he was diagnosed totally free of cancer, a disease he had suffered from for some time now."[7]

Researcher Christopher O'Brien, author of *The Mysterious Valley*, uncovered the following case during his research into UFO activity in Colorado.

CASE #085. OVARIAN CANCER.

Barbara Benara (pseudonym) was very sick. She had just been diagnosed with ovarian cancer and was preparing to be treated for the disease. Only one week after diagnosis, however, she had a visitation with strange beings she calls "the little brothers." All her life, Benara was visited by mysterious entities who only came at night to her home in the San Luis Valley, Colorado. The visits started around age seven. She always knew when they came as she would have a bloody nose afterward. She was frightened by the visits, but was always reassured and comforted by one of the beings who told her not to be afraid.

While the visitations continued, they were always at night, and she had only vague memories. That all changed in 1978 after her cancer diagnosis. She felt restless one evening, and was having trouble sleeping. Suddenly she woke up to find herself lying on a soft table in a white circular room. She was paralyzed, but strangely calm.

"You need our help," a voice said.

"Can I see you?" she asked.

The beings moved around to the front of the table. "There were four of them," said Benara, "all identical. They were three to four feet tall, ivory white, and had large almond-shaped eyes."

A fifth taller being appeared and stared into Benara's eyes, telling her not to be afraid. It was the same being from her childhood. Benara next found herself immersed in an L-shaped tank. A long arm-like device came out and inserted itself inside her. "It wasn't painful," said Benara, "but it didn't feel comfortable. I had to relax and trust the voice that kept telling me not to be afraid.

The next thing she knew, it was morning. She was exhausted. Four days later, she went to her doctor and asked for more tests. To the shock of both herself and her doctor, she now appeared to be cancer free. "They cured me of cancer," says Benara.

It wasn't her last encounter. Five years later, on November 25, 1992, Benara (now age forty) felt suddenly compelled to drive seven miles away from her home. She was confused and couldn't understand what had taken over her. It was now 8:30 p.m., and she realized that she had left her children unattended. The next thing she knew, the inside of her truck was freezing cold, it was now 10:30 p.m., and she was suffering from a nosebleed. She knew instantly what had happened. "I don't remember anything during almost two hours in my truck," she says, "but I know it was the little brothers."[8]

One feature of the cancer cases that's different from the others is the onboard experience. While many healings do not involve an onboard experience, most of the cancer cases do. And those that don't usually involve face-to-face contact with entities, possible missing time, or an extremely close interactive encounter with a UFO.

CASE #088. BONE CANCER.
Early one evening in the summer of 1979, "Myriam" and her mother were driving along Highway 2 in Bayamon, Puerto Rico when a weird darkness descended upon their car, obscuring everything from view. They heard a loud humming noise and felt confused and entranced. The car seemed to float and then became filled with light.

The next thing they knew, they were arriving at Arecibo with no idea how they got there. It was two and a half hours later than they remembered. Years later, Myriam underwent regressive hypnosis. She recalled seeing her mother being pulled up through the roof of the car and into the object. A beam of light then struck Myriam and pulled her up through the roof. She looked back and observed her automobile floating at a tremendous height very close to the object.

Once inside, Myriam saw a tall humanoid figure with pale gray skin, a large head, dark eyes and a soft, friendly smile. "Come with me," he said telepathically. "Don't be afraid." They told Myriam that her mother was being cared for and they then took Myriam through the craft, which had curved corridors of a beautiful pearly-silver color. She was taken to an examination room where there were many three-and-a-half-foot, gray-skinned beings. Myriam was told that she was there so that they could help her.

They examined her, pressing fine, long metallic rods on or in her body, and said that they were giving her "an energy reinforcement so as to improve the condition of her organism." They then put clamp-like instruments on her legs which caused a powerful heat energy to rise up through her body. Next to her, the little gray beings were busy manipulating computer-like machines with lots of little lights.

The tall gray being told Myriam that she had bone cancer, and that they were curing her of the condition. They told Myriam that they were also curing her mother.

He put an instrument on her forehead and explained that it would deepen her psychic intuition. Myriam saw other human-looking beings aboard the craft. At one point, Myriam felt love and goodness emanating from the being. He warned her of upcoming Earth changes. Looking outside, she saw trees, and the being explained to her that they had temporarily landed in the high Swiss Alps.

After conversing with the ET, Myriam found herself back in their car. Myriam's mother, Sonia, also underwent hypnosis and recalled being sucked up into the craft, where she was taken into a room and examined by a small gray humanoid. She also saw other types of beings, including human-looking beings.[9]

353

In the following case, a man and his wife experienced a missing time encounter that resulted in a profound healing. Under hypnosis, the whole story emerged, and the witnesses--despite the healing--were not happy with what they recalled. It's one of many cases in which the grays' bedside manner could use significant improvement.

CASE #094. SKIN CANCER.

Fifteen minutes before midnight on November 19, 1980, "Michael," an art teacher and his wife, "Mary," were driving home from Denver to Longmont, Colorado when they heard a loud swishing sound. At that moment, a bright beam of blue light locked onto their car. The car headlights dimmed, the radio failed, and the car suddenly levitated into the sky.

The next thing they knew, they were back on the highway, only it was now five minutes before 1:00 a.m.; they had lost one hour and ten minutes of time.

When they got home, Michael, who had several large melanomas on his legs, found that they were greatly reduced in size and coloration.

Mary, (who was two months pregnant) found an inexplicable rectangular mark on her abdomen. A few months later, she contracted streptococcal pneumonia. The doctors were concerned about the health of her baby, who ended up being born two months early, but otherwise healthy and normal.

In an effort to discover what happened during the missing time episode, Michael elected to undergo regressive hypnosis, though his wife, due to her illness, postponed any sessions.

Under hypnosis, Michael recalled that after being struck by the blue beam of light, the car was drawn up into a domed craft. Once inside, he smelled an electrical odor. Meanwhile, a gray-skinned being with a bald head, narrow chin, and wearing a shiny, gold uniform appeared and led them both into a brightly lit area. The being separated Michael from his wife. Michael was undressed, laid out on a table and physically examined by a "floating light."

354

Michael's memories were pulled from his mind, and the beings told him that there are multiple dimensions co-existing with our own. The beings, who communicated via telepathy, returned Michael and Mary to their car, placed the car back on the road, moving at fifty-five MPH, and returned them to full conscious awareness.

The investigation, which was being conducted by the J. Allen Hynek Center for UFO Studies, (CUFOS), was halted when Michael began to experience psychological conflicts about the event.

The case was also investigated by Linda Moulton Howe and Richard Sigismond. Michael told them that he disliked the aliens who abducted them. Mary agreed and said that they had examined her body in a way that left her enraged. She felt as though she had been violated or raped.[10]

The following case is a poignant account of a child being healed of cancer. Many of the cases in this book involve the healing of very young children.

CASE #110. CANCER.

In March 22, 1986, a poor couple was caring for their six-year-old, cancer-stricken daughter in their home in a rural area outside Teocaltiche, Mexico. On that evening, the couple suddenly found themselves unable to move as a seven-foot-tall humanoid wearing a shiny jumpsuit entered their tiny hut. The figure held out his hand and emitted a green-blue light from his palm. He then picked up the daughter and gently placed her on the kitchen table. For the next two hours, the being spoke to the girl in an unknown language. He then placed two glowing metal tubes on either side of her head, next to her temples. Five minutes later, he removed the instruments. The daughter jumped off the table. She no longer showed any signs of illness. The being then exited their hut and entered a black, bullet-shaped object which was landed next to the house. The case was investigated by researcher, Lillian Crowner Desguin.[11]

355

The main witness in the following case, reported anonymously to NUFORC, leaves no doubt how he feels about his encounter with "three cloaked beings" who saved the life of his young daughter.

CASE #114. BRAIN TUMOR.

Jacob (pseudonym) is a medical professional from Jay, Florida. In 1986, his daughter was very sick from an inoperable, malignant brain tumor. "We were visited late one night by three cloaked beings," writes Jacob. "I awoke to find them standing at the foot of our bed. They were communicating with one another, but making no sounds to me. I thought at first I was still asleep. I could see my daughter lying next to me. When I reached out to touch her, I realized I could not move. All that I was able to move was my eyes. Then they came to the side of our bed, and a peace came to me. The one that was directly to my right shoulder leaned over me to touch my daughter, and all went quiet.

"The next day," continues Jacob, "my daughter had a massive nosebleed. The clot that came from her nose was so large that it gagged her when we were removing it. A few months later, I took her for a new CT scan; it was one of many past scans. When we arrived at the doctor's office a few days later, he said the brain tumor was gone. He said it looked as though someone had lasered it out."

Jacob isn't sure why his daughter was cured, but he knows how he feels about it. "She is now cancer free. Why? We may never know the truth. But one thing is for sure: she is still alive, and now twenty-seven years old. The moral to my story is not one of horror and probes, but one of truth and goodness. If not for those beings' visit, I would be placing fresh flowers on a grave instead of hugging and kissing my most wonderful gift. Thank you, who or whatever you were."[12]

In the following case, the witness was undergoing an examination by ETs when they explained to her that her birth control device had damaged her body. They then said they would heal her. Like many people who experience a lifetime of contact,

356

she has had both positive and negative experiences. Her case reveals the ETs' intense interest in human reproduction.

CASE #120. CERVICAL CANCER, INFECTION.

Kate was only four years old when she first recalled being visited by ETs at her Michigan farmhouse where she lived with her family. As time went on, she experienced several visitations. At first she thought the experiences were interesting and pleasant, but as she grew older, she grew afraid. As an adult, she found herself constantly changing her place of residence, always hoping that a move would stop the alien encounters from happening. No matter where she moved, however, they always returned.

In July 1987, Kate decided to attend a retreat on an Indian reservation near Reno, Nevada. On the first night of the retreat, she woke up at 1:30 a.m. to go to the bathroom. The only bathroom was an outhouse. As Kate returned to her room, she sensed a familiar presence. Somehow she knew instantly that it was the ETs. She sensed that they were coming for her, and that they wanted her to go with them. Suddenly afraid, Kate didn't want to go. However, as in previous experiences, she was unable to resist and found herself walking to the opposite shore of the lake near the reservation and down the side of a mountain. Says Kate, "It was like something was drawing me."

According to researcher Marcia Jedd (who investigated the case), Kate was led to a spacecraft. Her next memory was of looking out a large window in the craft through which she saw rocks floating in space, a "distinct blue dot" and another bright white dot. Kate realized she was seeing the Earth and the sun, and that the rocks were asteroids.

Her next memory was of being examined and healed by the ETs. Says Kate, "They looked inside my uterus and saw damage from a birth control device. They told me they were repairing the damage and to expect bleeding."

Kate says that years earlier, the birth control device caused an infection which nearly killed her. Although they healed her, the ETs then took steps to make sure that Kate would forget the encounter. They told her that after they let her go, she would see an owl, at which point she would forget the entire experience.

They then let her go. It was now about 4:15 a.m. As Kate walked back to her campsite, she saw an owl. She found that she was too tired to even think about what happened, and just went to sleep. All memories of the experience were gone upon awakening.

About eighteen months later, Kate's health began to suffer. She was experiencing uterine bleeding and had to undergo a dilation and curettage procedure. She was put under general anesthesia, and the doctors began the operation.

During the middle of the procedure, Kate did something the doctors had never seen before: she woke up from the anesthesia.

Kate says that as she lay there on the surgical table surrounded by doctors and instruments, the memories of her abduction near Reno flooded back in detail. Before then, she had no idea that an abduction event had occurred.

Since then, Kate has had many other encounters. During one, she believes the ETs cured her of her recently-diagnosed cervical cancer. Kate still has mixed feelings about her encounters, but feels that the beings are a "protective force." She says that numerous members of her family are also having experiences, including her three-year-old niece and both her parents.[13]

Edward Carlos has reported a cure of pneumonia and one of arterial sclerosis. He also believes that his encounters may have been at least partially responsible for his recovery from cancer.

CASE #124. CANCER.

In the mid-1980s, Edward Carlos of Pennsylvania discovered a mark on his lower body that was later diagnosed as cancerous. Carlos immediately had an operation and the cancer went into remission. Carlos, however, attributes the remission not only to the operation, but to the energies he experienced through gardening, water-color painting and to the "energies transmitted to him by the abduction process."[14]

This next case has not been widely reported, but is typical of the cancer cure cases. Once again, we have an onboard encounter involving a painful operation. Despite the unpleasantness of the encounter, the cure appears to have been effective, and is proven by doctor records obtained by the witness.

CASE #152. COLON CANCER.

Licea Davidson of Los Angeles, California has been having UFO contacts since early childhood. Then in 1989, she was diagnosed with terminal cancer. Doctors were unable to operate because the disease had metastasized throughout her colon. She was given three months to live.

She then experienced an abduction, during which ETs placed her on a table in a small rounded room and gave her an extensive operation to cure her cancer. Says Davidson, "I was abducted. They told me I had cancer. They said, 'Relax.' And they did a cure. It was excruciating."

Davidson was then returned to her home. She made an appointment with her doctor, and was not surprised to discover that all traces of her cancer were gone. She has recovered her medical records and reports that her cure has been verified by a major medical university. She also states that she fears the United States Government (who has harassed her extensively) more than she does the aliens.[15]

While the number of cancer cures caused by UFOs is impressive, likely there are many more that go unreported, simply because people are afraid of ridicule. In some cases, such as the following, it's not fear of ridicule that keeps people silent, but governmental threats.

CASE #159. CANCER.

An anonymous Hungarian woman told UFO researcher Wendelle C. Stevens that she was a contactee. Stevens says that the woman told him that she had been taken onboard UFOs on four separate occasions in the 1980s (date approximate.) While onboard, she claims to have met friendly aliens who cured her of

359

cancer. She refused to go public with her experiences after being warned by the Hungarian government to remain silent.[16]

A small number of healing cases presented in this book come from Linda, a California abductee whose case was researched by Edith Fiore Ph.D. While onboard a UFO, Linda had the opportunity to observe almost a dozen instances of healings. In the following case, she experienced her own healing. Like several of the other cancer cures, it involved a painful operation.

CASE #133. STOMACH CANCER.

Linda and Sherri of northern California are sisters who have shared amazingly positive onboard UFO experiences throughout the 1980s. While neither of them had any conscious memory of this, Linda sought help from psychiatrist Edith Fiore Ph.D. to deal with depression. Fiore placed her under hypnosis and a complex contact scenario emerged.

Linda recalled being inside a strange room and lying on a table. She next recalled that strange beings were operating upon her. "They're opening me up here, my stomach. I don't understand what they're doing. There's no blood. They just open me up. It looks real dark inside. They're suctioning something up...kind of cleaning me, inside...they're cleaning this black junk out of my stomach region. They said I had cancer! They were trying to help me."

The cancerous material was quickly removed from Linda's abdominal area. The stomach was then closed up, leaving no scar.

Linda next recalled that the beings placed various instruments on her body. "It's like glass, little round pieces of glass...they're round and smooth and they had little lights on them. And they placed them all over my body."

Then they passed another instrument over her body, causing intense pain.

She was then quickly deposited back into her bedroom.

On another occasion, in the late 1980s, Linda was given a cure for an apparent cancerous tumor in her left breast. She was again put on a "long table, like in a doctor's office."

The aliens then took a "metal tube with a light on the end" and held it over Linda's left breast. Some form of energy was emitted by the object which pulsated and glowed. The tube was then removed and Linda was told to get off the table to make room for another patient.

Linda describes the aliens as, "very, very small, very small heads, kind of pointed...They've got big eyes."

She recalled undergoing several other strange procedures. The beings communicated with her, warning about upcoming Earth changes and teaching her alternative healing methods. They implored her to meditate daily, exercise and eat correctly. "They're telling us we have to learn these things, it's for our survival. The world will come to an end if we don't learn these things..."

The aliens told her, "You should understand that we mean no harm. We are here to change the world...to keep it from disaster. Which is imminent, if people keep living the way they do...There will be changes so powerful that only the strong will survive. We are here to give knowledge and understanding to the world of light and the world of children of God."

Linda recalled many other remarkably positive events. She saw several members of her family onboard. She recalled seeing many other people healed of various ailments including bursitis, intestinal worms, tumors and more. Linda remembers her sister, Sherri, received surgery for an unidentified illness. Afterward, Sherri jokingly asked the aliens if they could also do breast enlargements.

Linda also recalled how the beings return her to her home. "They put us in smaller vehicles. They're full of light. There's lots of lights going...there's a driver. They take off. We're going over some trees. Aha...I'm home. I'm back in bed."[17]

This next report comes from southern California-based UFO researcher Sean Atlanti, and recounts a remarkable healing by Nordic-type ETs which took place in late December 1989 in Queens, New York. Most of the cancer cures involve extensive operations with the use of multiple alien instruments. This is one of few cases which was apparently affected in the witness's home.

CASE #149. HODGKIN'S DISEASE.

From the files of Sean Atlanti: "Eddie Sosa, who had been suffering from Hodgkin's Disease, suddenly woke up in the middle of the night completely unable to move. Five tall human-like figures then materialized in the room. These were described as blond-haired with blue eyes and wearing white robes. They smiled at the witness and then proceeded to insert several needle-like instruments into his lower abdomen area. The witness finally woke up the next morning feeling very good. The next day he visited his doctor and was told that the cancer had somehow gone into total remission."[18]

There are a few cases on record in which UFO researchers have themselves been healed by ETs. The healing of Hans Lauritzen is one of them. This next case is another.

CASE #157. BRAIN TUMOR.

Willie Durand Urbina is a prominent UFO researcher from Puerto Rico and a frequent contributor to *Inexplicata* (a leading UFO publication established in 1998.) Urbina had been writing about UFOs since at least the early 1990s. When asked how he first became interested in the paranormal, Urbina revealed a remarkable story of healing which may have been partly caused by ET guidance. "I was a few hours from undergoing surgery for a brain tumor which was causing me constant headaches," says Urbina. "In those anguished moments I was visited by a 'spirit guide' who engaged me in a dialogue regarding the operation. It told me to pray to heal myself from this condition. During prayer, I underwent a paranormal experience within myself--I felt that something broke away from my body and my temperature was raised above forty degrees. I managed to see myself free of the condition, although I was completely drained of energy. A CAT scan would later show that there was no trace of the tumor. Following this experience, I had two experiences with UFOs."[19]

This next case of a cancer healing again involves a missing time abduction, though details of the onboard segment were not revealed. It's a good example of how Earth doctors are forced to confront evidence that flies in the face of medical science.

CASE #172. STOMACH CANCER.

Former contributing editor to *UFO Universe* and columnist for *Fate* magazine, UFO researcher Antonio Huneeus writes, "Perhaps one of the most interesting cases not only in Peru, but in my files from anywhere in the world, involves a truck driver who was allegedly cured of a malignant stomach cancer following a close encounter with a UFO that emitted a powerful beam of light."

The case occurred in the early 1990s (date approx.) and was originally researched by Peruvian ufologist, Anton Ponce de Leon. The truck driver was driving one evening when he suffered two consecutive flat tires outside the city of Santa Rosa. He called in for help.

During this time, the truck driver was suffering the intense pain of stomach cancer. His doctors had been urging him to have an operation, but he remained hesitant. However, while waiting in pain for help to arrive, the truck driver decided he would go ahead with the operation.

While waiting, the sky became illuminated by a bright object. He exited the truck and looked up. To his surprise, he was engulfed in a bright beam of light. He then experienced a period of missing time.

Shortly later, the UFO left and help arrived. When the truck driver returned home, he discovered he was no longer suffering any stomach pains. He decided to see the doctors again. "...He still had doubts and asked for a new analysis and X-rays," writes Ponce de Leon. "To the doctor's surprise--he still doesn't know what happened--the stomach cancer had disappeared and so, naturally, he was bothered by the entire situation and was unable to give his patient any definite answers. Mr. X remained with his secret and the doctor continued to be upset because he never did find out what really happened. I investigated this case firsthand, and I know it's a very important one."[20]

In the following case, investigated by Ann Druffel, a woman was healed of breast cancer by bluish-skinned entities. Despite her healing, the witness is not happy with the aliens.

CASE #201. BREAST CANCER.

One night in early 1995, Jean Moncrief of Los Angeles, California, was awoken out of a sound sleep by three bluish-looking entities who came into her bedroom through the closet wall. The visits continued semi-regularly, and Moncrief became increasingly concerned. She had recently been diagnosed with a lump in her breast, and not having medical insurance, she was reluctant to go to the doctor for surgery. Around this time, she had another experience with the entities, only on this occasion she recalls being taken away to some other location. Her recall was limited only to "being floated back to the bedroom." However, the next morning, the lump in her breast was gone. The only evidence left behind was a perfectly circular mark of lighter skin where the lump had been. Despite her healing, Moncrief still feels violated. As she says, "The things don't give a damn about humans."[21]

As we have seen, it's not unusual for a person to report multiple healings. The following case involves a man who claims to have been healed by ETs on at least four separate occasions.

CASE #211. SKIN CANCER.

Chuck Weiss, a driver from San Francisco, California, had already been thrice healed by gray ETs. In 1994, he was healed of a strained muscle. A few months later, he was healed of tendonitis. He also experienced a lung healing. One year later, Weiss had a fourth healing.

In 1995, what looked like a precancerous node appeared on the left side of Weiss's nose. Over a period of a few days, the node flared up to three times its normal size. As a professional driver, Weiss knew that the left side of his face was particularly vulnerable to skin cancer. Now, it appeared that the node was becoming cancerous.

"I procrastinated and didn't call my doctor," says Weiss. "After about a week, I woke up to find that it had shrunk back to its original size. It bled slightly when I touched it that morning, and I later found a bloody spot on my bath towel."

Although Weiss had no specific memory of being healed, he has no other explanation for the sudden disappearance of the node. It wasn't long before he received further confirmation.

"Six months after that," says Weiss, "I noticed that another precancerous node that I had had on my nose for years had suddenly grown in size. A few days later I woke up to find that it had been dealt with in the night in the same manner as the previous one."

Again, Weiss credits his cure to gray ETs. He now believes the ETs were continually monitoring his condition. Ten years later, he received powerful evidence of this.

"In May of 2006," writes Weiss, "another node that had developed on my left cheek was removed completely, before it showed any signs of becoming inflamed like the others. I guess they caught on to the fact that I don't like going to doctors, and because of my stubbornness, decided that they would have to take care of the problem themselves."[22]

The following brief account doesn't reveal many details, but provides another hint that UFO healings are likely more widespread than is being publicly reported.

CASE #212. UTERINE CANCER.

In 1995, researcher Richard Boylan Ph.D. confirmed the case of a woman who was cured not only of a yeast infection, but of cancer. In a letter, he wrote that the woman experienced another encounter during which she "was cured of a cancerous growth on her uterus, which, when later examined by the surgeon, could find no trace of the previously diagnosed cancer." Unfortunately, he has not divulged any further details on the case.[23]

While the Twiggs family has reported many healings, they also have friends around them who have also had encounters. In this case, one of their friends observed Bert Twiggs being healed.

CASE #229. LUNG CANCER.

Elizabeth is one of many friends who Bert and Denise Twiggs have seen aboard the Androme mothership. On one occasion, (circa 1990s) Elizabeth witnessed Bert being cured of cancer he didn't even know he had. Elizabeth clearly remembered that the aliens diagnosed Bert with lung cancer. They promptly performed surgery and removed the cancer from the lung in which it had appeared.[24]

If true, the following case may provide irrefutable photographic proof an ET healing that took place in an Italian hospital. Unfortunately, whoever has the proof has yet to come forward.

CASE #236. CANCER.

As reported by researcher, Wendelle Stevens, around 2002-2003, a man in Italy was cured of cancer while in a hospital. The healing may have gone unnoticed except for the fact that it was allegedly recorded on video and observed on the monitor in the nurses' station. The tape reportedly shows three humanoid figures wearing light blue iridescent suits like "fish scales." The figures glowed light from their arms and legs, and carried an instrument in their hands. The tape shows them enter the room, and pass the instrument up and down the man's body, at which point, he was "completely healed."[25]

An incredible and well-verified case comes from, *Beyond UFOs*, edited by Rey Hernandez, which presents the results of a years-long in-depth survey of experiencers from FREE. This case was chosen among many for a full investigation, and joins the ranks of well-verified healings. Researched by Dr. Joseph Burkes MD, it provides outstanding evidence of a UFO healing.

CASE #242. LUNG CANCER.

In 2005, retired Federal Drug Enforcement agent, Alberto Fernandez of Miami, Florida was diagnosed with lung cancer. Earlier Fernandez had battled and recovered from prostate cancer. A later follow-up visit revealed a baseball-sized mass in his lungs. It was so severe that his doctor ordered immediate surgery.

Fernandez had experienced UFO contact throughout his life, and had earlier experienced a healing from a torn cornea. He had no reason, however, to expect a second healing.

Fernandez was admitted to the local hospital. Accompanied by his wife, Fernandez was being readied for more X-rays when something very strange happened. As he lay on the exam table, his entire body started vibrating with unusual energy.

"They're here! They're here!" he shouted to his wife. Mrs. Fernandez saw that the curtain around her husband's bed was moving in a strange sine-wave pattern. She rushed to her husband and observed his body shaking violently.

Seconds later, the shaking stopped. "They cured me!" Fernandez told his wife.

The X-ray technician returned, completed the X-rays, and gave them to the specialist who was going to treat Fernandez. The specialist reviewed the X-rays and became angry. The X-rays showed that Fernandez's lungs were perfectly healthy. There was no sign of any tumor. The specialist accused Fernandez, and his original doctor of wasting his time.

Fernandez's original doctor who had diagnosed the cancerous mass reviewed the new X-rays and verified the disappearance of the mass.[26]

The following case has elements of both a near-death experience and a UFO abduction. It may be both. In either case, it provided a healing at the time when the health of the witness was on a rapid decline.

CASE #243. PANCREATIC CANCER.

On April 18, 2006, "E.R." (age 50), suddenly experienced intense back pain while in her home in Argentina. Four days later, with her pain worsening, she went to the doctor. The doctor found that her liver, kidney, bladder, pancreas and left lung were badly inflamed. Tests confirmed the diagnosis of pancreatic cancer, along with severe cardiopathy with arterial lesions and persistent hypertension. E.R. began her medical treatment.

Unfortunately, E.R.'s condition declined. She became so weak she was confined to her bed. One day, feeling very ill, she found herself floating toward a white light. She was about to be absorbed into the light when she felt something grab her and tell her that this was not the time.

E.R. became fully lucid and was surprised to find herself lying on a soft, oval-shaped platform. A metallic, silver object above her shone down an intense light.

Five beings stood around the table. They were tall, thin, with long arms and blue skin. They each had tall a forehead, small features and slanted eyes. No clothing was visible.

The five beings began to debate the critical state of E.R.'s health. The beings said that "there was no other alternative than to go in..."

At this point, four of the beings held her arms and legs, while one seemed to push its hands and arms into the left side of her body, just below her ribs. She felt intense pain and the sensation that some sort of material was "torn out and dragged" from her body. The material was given to the other beings to handle, and E.R.'s pain was replaced by a sensation of growing relief.

"From this moment you will put aside all medications," the beings told her. "From this moment on, you will be a different person."

The next thing E.R. knew, she was back in her bed at home. After forty-eight hours, her pain was gone and she was strong enough to get out of bed. She went to the doctor who verified that her condition was improved. In the days that followed, E.R.'s condition continued to improve and eventually stabilize. While her health still has room for improvement, she has not taken any medication since the incident.[27]

Researcher Ardy Sixkiller Clarke has uncovered a number of profound cases involving medical healings as the result of a UFO encounter. The following case provides compelling evidence that ETs are healing people from altruistic motives and that they are taking active measure to ensure the health and wellbeing of human beings across the planet.

CASE #246. LUNG CANCER.

Around 2006 (date approx.,) Salvador, a Mayan farmer from the small village of Uxmal, lay bedridden in his home, dying of lung cancer. He was being cared for by his wife, Carla, and her sisters. Salvador had been sent home from the hospital to die. Twice the priest had been called, but each time, Salvador rallied.

One evening, the residents of the village were startled to see a V-shaped craft with red lights hover over the village, shining down bright beams of light. After a few moments, it turned and left. Later that evening the UFOs came back, this time targeting Salvador.

The entire family woke to find the object hovering directly over their home, shining down red lights. Salvador lay in his hammock too weak to move. The UFO left.

Then later that night, Salvador was woken by a bright light illuminating the room. Says Salvador, "Five balls of light circled my hammock. They slowly went up and down my body. One centered over my head and stayed there. It was warm and felt good. The others centered on my chest, which became very warm. Suddenly I could breathe."

Salvador sat up, at which point, the balls darted out the door. He jumped up to follow them into the backyard. Says Salvador, "Five men came out of the balls of light. They stopped and looked at me. I saw a beam of light come from the tree above and they disappeared into the light. I watched as the V-shaped machine moved upward. Red lights outlined it. It climbed into the sky and was gone."

Ardy Sixkiller Clarke spoke with the witnesses firsthand. Salvador told her, "I knew I was healed...for the first time in years,

I could breathe easily...The doctors said there was no sign of cancer. They did not understand."[28]

As we have seen, some of the reports of UFO healings come not from the recipients of the healing, but from outside observers, or second-hand accounts. These types of accounts hint at the possibility that UFO healings are more widespread than has been publicly documented.

CASE #293. CANCER.
An undated case (prior to 2006) comes from abductee Daved E. Rubian who tells the story of another female abductee. Says Rubian, "There have been many healings done by some ETs-- one experience comes from a woman whom I have known for many years and admire very much, who had ovarian cancer and was preparing for surgery. She remembered being taken from her bed and awoke on a table that had been indented for her form. She then witnessed the ETs doing corrective surgery on her. She even remembers the instruments that were used. I have found that there are benign ETs and those that are not so benign, just as there are good and bad in all people. It appears to me that there are many more benign ones."[29]

While many missing time cases are reported only by the witnesses themselves, in some cases, such as the following, outside witnesses are looking for the people who have gone missing, and they're not where they are supposed to be. This corroboration from outside witnesses brings an added level of credibility. If the witnesses are not being taken onboard a UFO, then where are they?

CASE #248. CANCER.
In the spring of 2007, an anonymous woman from the Gyanja area of Azerbaijan ventured into a field near her home and disappeared. When she failed to return, her relatives called the police and instituted a search, but were unable to find her. After three days, the woman mysteriously reappeared. She was

confused and at first couldn't remember what happened. After a period of time, however, she began to have some recall of her missing time. She remembered lying down on a shiny table surrounded by humanoid figures, which she couldn't see clearly as the room was so bright. She was unable to recall anything else.

Prior to the experience, she was suffering from a rare form of cancer. She had been treated by doctors in Russia and Germany. In autumn of 2007, she visited her doctors and found that she was now totally cancer free. The woman is unable to remember how the cure was done.[30]

How does it feel to be cured of cancer by grays? This next case provides an excellent description. It also illustrates the dilemma many experiencers face when being healed. Why were they healed? Was it for the ETs' benefit, or their own?

CASE #249. CANCER.

Starting in 2005, Maria M. Rivera and her family (all devout Christians) were repeatedly visited by gray ETs in their home in Aguada, northwest Puerto Rico. The first encounter occurred on November 10, 2005 when Rivera and her daughter saw a huge silver disc with portholes move over the house and apparently descend into the rainforest behind their home.

A few months later, on April 28, 2006, Rivera was in the backyard when her dog became paralyzed and a gray emerged from the forest and began to communicate with her telepathically. The entire family then experienced a period of missing time.

Following this encounter, the visitations occurred every couple of months or so, usually involving the grays outside or inside their home.

After a half-dozen or more visitations, Rivera experienced a full-blown abduction. On November 3, 2007, she woke up to find her bed surrounding by grays. She was rendered unconscious, but woke up shortly later to find herself in a strange room lying on a steel table, still surrounded by the grays. She was unable to move as the ETs placed a round, metallic, suction-cup-like instrument on her abdomen. Says Rivera, "It felt as if my flesh was being

371

stretched and my inside was being sucked out like a powerful vacuum. I was in excruciating pain when they did that, but I was unable to scream or move."

During this time, Rivera was suffering from ovarian cancer, which had spread throughout her body. She had undergone operations in New York City to have malignancies removed from her intestines and her breasts. But the cancer kept returning. Currently she was suffering from constant stomach pains and had traces of blood in her stool and urine. Her doctors tested her, informed her that the cancer had spread again, and said that she needed another operation.

Says Rivera, "After the encounter with those creatures on April 28, 2006, I returned to New York, several tests were performed, and no cancer was detected. The pain and bleeding had stopped. I truly feel that those creatures cured me."

Despite her cure, Rivera is not quite ready to embrace the grays. "They could be benevolent and compassionate creatures, but I'm afraid of them. They do not have my permission to do with my body whatever they please. Although I believe they had cured me, I am not their guinea pig...I think it is fair to say that those beings have tagged, branded and are actively tracking abductees like myself. They're quite awful creatures and have no regard for humanity and animals living on Earth. To them, we're just a science project. I could be wrong, but I think the creatures cured my cancer because they need a healthy specimen for their experiments."

Rivera says that during the operation in which she was healed, she managed to communicate briefly with the ETs, calling them "Martians." They informed her that they don't like to be called Martians and prefer to be called "creatures."[31]

This next complex case comes from the files of MUFON and contains many unusual elements, including a dramatic healing of cancer. In this case, the healing appears to be a spontaneous side-effect of a series of encounters. How the actual healing took place remains unknown.

CASE #256. LUNG CANCER.

In 1988, Scott (pseudonym) moved with his parents, siblings and extended family from Puerto Rico to the United States, settling in Towson, Maryland. It wasn't long after they moved that they observed bright blue lights illuminate the entire backyard, despite the presence of tall leafy trees. The lights appeared regularly, but remained elusive. The sightings happened repeatedly, year after year, yet nobody else beyond their property seemed to see a thing. A few times they called the police, who denied any knowledge of the lights and agreed to investigate. The police found nothing unusual.

The sightings continued. Scott's aunt, who slept in another room, often with the window opened, said she saw strange beams of light that had the ability to bend around corners. In 1994, Scott's older brother announced that he was joining the army. He told Scott that he had seen strange entities in the house and he joined the army just to get away from all the strange activity. He refused to tell Scott exactly what he saw.

Meanwhile, they noticed that many of the trees on their property were mysteriously dying. When more trees died, they wondered if the UFOs might be causing it.

One evening in the summer of 2008, Scott was visiting his friend, Steve's house located 150 miles southeast, in Ocean City along the coast. In the middle of the night, Scott woke up in a panic to hear an odd thrumming-clunking sound. As soon as he woke up, the sound faded, but Scott was left with the conviction that there was more to the event than he could remember, and that he may have even been abducted.

Several weeks later, Scott was back in his home in Towson when it happened again; a loud thrumming noise coming from outside woke him up. The dogs were barking furiously. He got up and checked outside, but the sound was gone and the dogs stopped barking.

The next morning, he had "a feeling" that he should call his friend Steve, which he did. Scott asked him if he saw any UFOs last night. "As a matter of fact, I did," Steve replied, and proceeded to tell Scott how he had woken up to see a bright light flooding his room.

Steven's dad, who had observed the light seeping out from the crack of Steve's door said, "Shut that thing off!"

"It's coming from outside," Steve told his dad. While Steve went to look out the window to examine the lights, his father went to the bathroom. Looking out the window, Steve not only saw the light, he could feel heat radiating from it. Feeling pain in his eyes, he stepped back and looked away. Then he decided to get dressed and check it out.

"It's just a helicopter," his father said. "Go back to bed."

"No, there's no helicopter noise. I'm going outside and check it out."

The moment Steve stepped out the door, the light winked out and everything was normal. However, the next morning, Steve found that one of his trees, which was healthy the day before, was now dried up and dead. Another tree nearby was still alive, but badly damaged.

After discussing the incident, Steve and Scott spoke with another friend, "Al," who also lived in Towson. Al told them that on that evening, he saw a metallic structured craft emitting blue lights. It hovered right outside his window. At that moment, he heard a metallic clanging noise on the concrete patio, and the object went away. The next morning, he found an eight-inch octagonal piece of metal with strange symbols carved on it. Al is convinced it came from the object. It has not been tested, but appears to be stainless steel.

Often when Scott would visit his friend Steve, he would bypass the front door and knock on the window to sneak into the house. One evening, Steve heard a knock on the window. Expecting it to be Scott, he was shocked to see a "creature with huge black eyes standing close to his glass door, staring at him."

It was one week after this, that something even stranger happened. Steve's father was a heavy cigarette smoker, and had been recently diagnosed with lung cancer. He was undergoing treatment and having regular check-ups. However, when he went for his latest check-up, the doctor found that the cancer was gone. Says Scott, "He had been cured of his lung cancer!"

Steve and Scott can't prove it, but they suspect the UFOs might be responsible. "They probably helped cure him," says Scott. "I really believe that these particular visitors are harmless, and are definitely friendly."

With the coincidence of all three friends experiencing something on the same night, the constant UFO sightings, the entity sighting and the strange piece of metal, and finally the healing, Scott is convinced that they have been targeted by the UFO entities. "Very bizarre stuff," he says.[32]

This next case enjoyed brief attention in the German media. Reporters obtained interviews from both the witness and her doctor, revealing many details to support the veracity of a remarkable healing of leukemia.

CASE #253. LEUKEMIA.

It was the best and worst day of Greta Brandt's life. "I found out that I was pregnant and had leukemia on the same day in December [2008]," said Brandt. A resident of Berlin, Germany, Brandt was only thirty-three years when she received the shocking news. Ultimately, it was more than she could handle, and Brandt found herself contemplating suicide. "In fact," says Brandt, "I had just about made up my mind to take my own life when two men with long pointed noses and ears approached me as I was getting into my car. When I turned toward them, they looked at me with piercing black eyes and motioned me to follow. I wanted to resist, but couldn't."

Despite her attempts to get away, Brandt found herself following the men to a vacant lot miles from her home where she saw a saucer-shaped object the size of a school bus and pulsating a blue light. The strange men took her aboard the craft, into a dark round room and strapped her down on a table. "One of them pulled a large instrument and light down from the ceiling and pointed it in my face. I didn't feel any pain, but the men were so frightening, I must have passed out."

When she awoke, Brandt found herself sitting in her back yard. Five hours had passed. The only visible evidence was a small needle mark on her right temple.

The biggest shock was yet to come. Brandt was not only still pregnant, but all signs of the leukemia were gone. "They saved my life and the life of my child," says Brandt. "My own doctors said we were doomed, and there was nothing they could do for us. But those strange men knew exactly what to do. They used all sorts of strange lights and instruments to cure me of the killer leukemia."

Reporters interested in Brandt's case contacted her obstetrician, Dr. Frans Wenderoth. He confirmed the leukemia diagnosis and the fact that she no longer suffers from the disease, but he refused to discuss Brandt's actual UFO encounter. All he would say is "that something miraculous must have happened to have given her this cure."

Brandt is overjoyed and says, "Whoever or whatever these men were, I want to thank them with all my heart."[33]

As we have seen, a significant portion of the reported healing cases occur in hospitals. As incredible as this may sound, UFO researchers have long known that encounters can occur anywhere, including very urban areas. Furthermore, since hospitals are full of sick people, and ETs appear to have an agenda to actively heal people, it makes perfect sense that some encounters would take place inside a hospital. Of all the hospital-ET encounters in this book, this next one is one of the most incredible. The story was first revealed by medical personnel who witnessed the remarkable events that allegedly took place in a Spanish hospital.

CASE #257. LEUKEMIA, CANCER.

According to UFO researchers, Jon Von Allon and Willie DeNard, in February 2009, a fantastic UFO contact took place at the Pyrenees Children's Hospital in Andorra, Spain. They interviewed fourteen doctors and staff members who told them that extraterrestrials appeared in the cancer ward of the hospital, where they performed cures on four children who were terminal and about to die.

The ETs were seen by all who were present, and described as about four and a half feet tall, with large heads, large almond-shaped eyes and brownish skin.

Nurse Lupe Montoya was working in the pediatric oncology ward when the first visit occurred. "I was filling out reports when I looked up and saw two little creatures as they moved toward me along the corridor," she said. "At first I thought that two of the boys were out of their beds, so I got up to bring them back to their rooms. But when I approached, I saw that they were not human...[and] did not look like something that is on this planet. I was scared because it seemed so strange. But at the same time I felt a feeling...I was sensing kindness, love and intelligence in those strange eyes."

Montoya watched as two beings walked into the room of seven-year-old Juan Lopez who was at the end stages of leukemia and expected to die within the week. She called for the security guards and called over Dr. Tomas Ruiz, who was treating another patient.

Says Ruiz, "When we entered the room of the small Juan, it was bathed in a shining golden light. The aliens were standing next to his bed. There seemed to be a mystic bond between them and the boy. One of the beings touched the front of Juan gently with his long finger and he was immediately surrounded in an aura of light."

The two beings exited the room and left the hospital as mysteriously as they arrived. Dr. Ruiz immediately performed X-rays and blood tests on seven-year-old, Juan. To their amazement, the boy was "completely free of cancer, healed!"

This remarkable event turned out to be just the beginning. Over the next month, the ETs returned on three separate occasions. Each time they chose a young child who was on the verge of dying from cancer and healed them. Nine-year-old Maria Munoz, eight-year-old Anita Pena, and nine-year-old Hector Gomez each received a miraculous cure.

"There is a pattern in these visits," Dr. Ruiz told investigators. "They always occur at 1:00 [a.m.], and the ETs always come in pairs and always heal with a touch to the forehead."

According to UFO researcher Diego Garcia, the Pyrenees have been a hot spot for UFO activity for many years.[34]

In the following unusual case, it was a strange photograph that led some investigators to wonder if a miraculous healing that a young girl had just experienced might have a different explanation than angelic visitation. It is one of few experiences involving photographic evidence.

CASE #269. LEUKEMIA.

In February 2007, "Erin," a young girl from Kirkland, Ohio, was diagnosed with childhood leukemia. When her condition worsened, Erin underwent a bone marrow transplant in an attempt to cure her of the disease, and was about to undergo a second, when something very strange happened. It was May 2013 and Erin's father was looking over some recent photos of their young daughter. In one of the photos, a tall red glowing being could be seen behind her. It was not visible when the photo was taken. At the time, Erin's father thought it might be a sign that Mother Mary was watching over them. The photo caught the attention of UFO researchers who thought it might be extraterrestrial. Others are skeptical of the photo. Erin's father says, "I know she's not alone; I know we are not alone, and people who don't want to believe it, that's okay. Whatever happened, you know something powerful and special was there with us. I definitely have my moments when I'm falling apart and I'm terrified, and I literally grab my phone and stare at that picture."

Erin underwent the second bone marrow transplant, and others after that. While her healing cannot be proved to be caused by ETs, the photo remains intriguing evidence of possible healing intervention.[35]

As we have seen, a small number of healings have occurred after the witnesses pray for a healing. In the following case, the witness had no reason to believe that her prayer would be heard. With no prior UFO history, she wasn't even praying to ETs. However, it was the grays who answered.

CASE #259. BREAST CANCER.

In her book, *Aliens Across America*, Megan Moxon tells the story of "Michelle," an active housewife and parent of three pre-teen-age boys. In the summer of 2010, Michelle developed a soreness in her right breast. When it continued for a full month, she went to the doctor for a check-up. She was referred to a specialist who ordered testing. The results were not good: Michelle had a cancerous lump in her right breast.

She told her husband and they lay together in bed praying and crying. Michelle was amazed at what happened next. "When I finally fell asleep, I remember being surrounded by a very bright light and three small alien-looking creatures...the room seemed fog-like...their heads were huge compared to their bodies."

Upon awakening, Michelle felt like it had been a "very real" experience, and not a dream. She went to see the specialist the next day. "When she went to do another screening of my breast that day, she saw that the tumor was no longer there," says Michelle. "I couldn't believe my ears...Had I really been abducted by aliens and cured?"

The doctor said that they do sometimes run across spontaneous healings or that the body heals itself. Says Michelle, "I believe God sent these extraterrestrials to save me. I know it sounds crazy, but in so many ways I feel like I got a second chance at life. It reminded me that each day was a gift and to this day, I continue to live my days to the fullest."[36]

As we have seen, many of the cancer cases are very well documented. The following case provides further compelling evidence that ETs are curing people of cancer. The witness, Lauren Kurth, is a strong proponent that ET encounters can be benevolent.

CASE #279. MELANOMA.

Lauren Kurth of New Zealand has documented her own experience with a miraculous healing of melanoma. In 2014, she was diagnosed with the disease, but declined conventional medical treatment. Instead she used herbs and other natural healing methods. Slowly her melanoma decreased, but after five months, the wound on her back still had not healed.

Then she read an article about cases in which people had been healed of various illness and diseases as a result of UFO contact. She recalled her own experience, and wondered if she might appeal to the aliens to heal her. She and her son both prayed for a healing encounter. That evening, it happened. Says Lauren, "I got this amazing energy come over my body...I knew I was going to have a contact experience...I went straight to sleep and I went straight into a UFO...It was a beautiful mother-of-pearl room. It was all round...I was on a table that didn't really have legs, it just came out of the wall. I had this beautiful pink light come over me. I did feel something on my back, and then I had no memory."

The next morning, Lauren's body was zinging with energy. Even her family members could feel it. She felt certain that she had gotten the requested healing, and it turned out she was right; her healing suddenly accelerated. "My back healed in two and a half weeks more than it had in five and a half months. All my blood results went back to normal. My brain function...all went back to normal, which I consider a miracle healing."

Currently, Lauren works doing alternative healings using sounds and tones, speaks publicly about her experiences, and holds public sky-watches and UFO stake-outs. More often than not, says Lauren, they will have some sort of sighting. She says that on a few occasions, people have reported physical healings.[37]

This next incredible case might be unique in that it could be the only case in which a person has actually filmed their own UFO healing as it was taking place. The case is among the best-verified, providing further proof in the form of before and after reports from doctors, not to mention many other forms of evidence. The full account appears in the book, *Beyond UFOs*.

CASE #281. CANCER.

Born in 1964 in Winnipeg, Canada, Jim Schaefer's first UFO sighting occurred when he was three years old. As he grew up, he had a steady stream of unexplained experiences. He suffered severe nosebleeds and nightmares about monsters visiting his room. He began seeing UFOs. Twice while a teen-ager, he woke up to find his eyes burned as though he had looked at an arc-welder.

His strange experiences continued through adulthood, and included many sightings of strange orbs around his home. In 2012, at age forty-eight, the experiences increased, and he began to wake up with strange marks on his body, including unexplained bruises, scars, scoop-marks, painful incisions and puncture wounds. In 2014, Schaefer woke up to severe foot-pain. He went to the doctor who said that his foot was fractured.

In January 2015, Schaefer began to suffer from a sore throat. His glands started to swell up, and blood-tests showed that his white blood-cell count had skyrocketed. More tests were performed. The news was very bad. "I found out that I had a tumor in my lymph nodes in my neck. They sent me to CancerCare in Manitoba. They did a biopsy on it."

The tumor was malignant and pressure from the growth was causing pain and necrosis. Surgery was scheduled for March 13, 2015.

Two weeks later, the tumor had increased significantly in size and was now projecting out the side of Schaefer's neck. On February 28, 2015 (two weeks before the scheduled surgery,) Schaefer lay down in bed. He grabbed his cellphone and turned on the video to see if he could record any orbs. "I just pushed record on my camera," says Schaefer, "and as soon as I did, I saw this bright orb drop down...as it hit the floor, it turned blue and started coming toward me. It turned down on itself and then it dove into my stomach."

Schaefer was shocked by the event and felt like the orb had appeared purposefully so he could film it. He put his phone down and eventually fell asleep.

The next morning, he looked in the mirror and received a huge shock. The tumor was gone. "I look in the mirror," says Schaefer, "and my tumor--that was wrapped around the base of my neck, and protruding from my neck, and bone-hard--was completely gone. There was nothing there. The whole thing was dissolved and gone. It was absolutely shocking."

Two weeks later, Schaefer showed up for his surgery. His doctors were baffled. Says Schaefer, "My doctors at CancerCare Manitoba said it was extraordinary...they couldn't believe this had happened."

The surgeons went ahead with the surgery to remove necrotic tissue. No sign of cancer was found. Schaefer has no idea why he was healed, but he's certain it was done by the ETs. "There's no doubt about it for me."

Unfortunately, in 2017 he was diagnosed with prostate cancer. As of yet, the ETs have not healed him of this condition. His encounters continue.[38]

As much as a skeptic might like to deny the veracity of a UFO healing case, there is always another to take its place. The sheer number of accounts can be overwhelming. This next account comes from a second-hand source, but reveals some interesting details and shows again that UFO healings are not as rare as one might think.

CASE #307. CANCER.

Carol X. has been a lifelong experiencer, but has never had any healings performed by the ETs. Of these types of cases, she writes, "I know of many who claim similar experiences. In all cases they were healed of their infirmities after being returned from the alien ships. The only direct participatory experience I know of is that of my neighbor. He was diagnosed with a cancerous growth in his intestines, inoperable because of significant entanglement with blood vessels."

According to Carol, her neighbor witnessed a UFO from his backyard. During the sighting, he felt tingling and warmth, and felt as though the UFO occupants were communing with him. "I do not know if he was taken up," says Carol, "but I do know he was healed. The growth that was cancerous became benign, and he is utterly convinced that the aliens affected this healing. I told the story here (on an online UFO forum) some time back, and some pooh-poohed it, while others suggested the growth had been misdiagnosed originally. Everyone is of course entitled to their own opinion, but I am certain he was healed, and I am convinced that he's not the only one." Interestingly, the neighbor calls the ETs "angels."[39]

In this next case, we see a pattern that is apparent in several of the healing cases. Often a healing takes place *immediately prior* to the scheduled surgery. This "wait to the last minute" pattern turns up in enough cases to raise the question, why do the aliens procrastinate some healings until the last possible moment?

CASE #308. CANCER.
Contactee "Gary" of Texas (a soldier in the military) says that he was diagnosed with cancer and was actually on his way into surgery when the "visitors" showed up and cured him. They told him that cancer was parasitic in nature. His full story was revealed in an interview with Anne Strieber on the radio show, *Unknown Country.*[40]

The above cases complete the catalogue of known cancer cures at the hands of ETs. With more than forty cases, there's little doubt that these cases are real. There are simply too many of them, occurring for too many years, coming from a wide variety of people from all over the world. Any explanations involving hoaxes, hallucinations, or misperceptions are simply not tenable. The evidence speaks for itself.

While the above cases provide considerable evidence that aliens have the ability to cure cancer, there is further evidence.

Many people have been told by the ETs how to cure cancer. Gary X (above) was told that cancer was parasitic in nature. Ventura Maceiras, who grew new teeth following an encounter, was told that cancer was actually a virus. There are many other people who were not healed by the ETs, but were instead given information on the causes of cancer and its treatment.

An Alien Cure for Cancer?

This happened to Kathleen Compardo of Pennsylvania in 1950. She was lying on her bed when two transparent figures appeared at her bedside. The figures were about three feet tall and told Kathleen that they were friendly aliens who wanted to help Earthlings, but were afraid of their war-like ways. They said that they were "far advanced in the fields of science and could cure cancer with a simple machine." Unfortunately, they did not elaborate.[41]

Some ETs have been more forthcoming. Contactee Cynthia Appleton of West Midlands, England, (who witnessed an ET heal himself of burns) was given much knowledge of a technical nature by her contacts. They also gave her a report on the "nature of cancer" and told her that one effective method of treatment involved "shocks to the body organ most in use at the time, creating a sort of frequency change in the vibrational rate of the particles inside the atom."[42]

In August of 1956, Orlando Jorge Ferraudi of Buenos Aires was fishing along the coast when he experienced a visitation by human-looking ETs who took him aboard their ship and into an underwater base. Ferraudi's contact was complex and involved several discussions with the ETs about various subjects including religion, death, nuclear energy, science and medicine. The ETs told Ferraudi that he would lose his memory of the event, but that it would return to him later. They then returned him to the location where he had been picked up.

As predicted, Ferraudi forgot the encounter, and assumed he had fallen asleep. Two weeks later, he spontaneously recalled the entire event, including information from the ETs on the causes of cancer, and also, how to construct a machine that will cure the disease. Ferraudi prepared a manuscript which he titled, "Cancer: its origin and development."

Writes Ferraudi, "The origin of this disease lies in the altered function of the ductless glands, which due to their bioelectrical balance having been upset, drain into the blood incomplete humors that lead to the irrational forming of the cells. This phenomenon leads to the immediate consequence of these humors circulating throughout the whole body, since blood is a vehicle, thus incomplete humors look for the weakest organs where they can exert their influence within a favorable field."

Investigators of the case were impressed by Ferraudi's medical knowledge, as is researcher Timothy Good, who writes, "In July 1975, years after Orlando Ferraudi outlined his theory, Nobel Prize-winner (1937) Dr. Albert Szent-Gyorgyi came out with his 'electromagnetic theory' of cancer, which was expressed in a very similar way to that of Ferraudi--despite the fact that the abductee had only the most rudimentary knowledge of medicine."[43]

Another case involving alien advice on how to cure cancer comes from a well-known California abduction case originally investigated by Ann Druffel and D. Scott Rogo.

In the mid-1950s, Sarah Shaw experienced several abductions from her home in Tujunga Canyon, California. After the encounters, she developed an obsessive interest in medicine, and began going to medical school.

Years after the abductions, she underwent hypnosis to recover her lost memories. She recalled that during one of the encounters in 1953, she was given directions on how to cure cancer. The gray-type ETs told her that cancer was basically a problem of "rotting." She was told that the cure was not for herself, but that in the future, she would meet a certain doctor whom she would recognize. She was instructed to give the cure to this doctor.

The aliens told Sara that cancer could be cured by swabbing vinegar directly on cancerous growths.

A few years later, Sara was very surprised and excited to recognize the doctor to whom she was supposed to give the cure. Coincidentally, her friend and fellow abductee, Jan Whitley, was suffering from breast cancer at the time, and it was her doctor whom Sara recognized as the right man. She was even more surprised when the doctor showed interest in her story and promised to try the cure on some of his patients who were looking for alternative methods of healing.

According to the doctor who performed the UFO-prescribed cure, he said that, "...he had repeatedly applied vinegar to some skin cancers by using a swabbing technique and had indeed procured some success with this method." The doctor did indicate, however, that his patients were also undergoing numerous other treatments to cure the cancer, and that the improvement may have been attributed to another treatment.

Nevertheless, the results were intriguing. Further study by the investigators of this case revealed that according to folklore, vinegar is believed to be a cure for many other ailments. Also curious is that some cancerous tumors may actually secrete acetic acid, the scientific name for vinegar. The doctor originally told Sara that acetic acid couldn't possibly cure cancer as vinegar is already found around cancerous tissues, and that the cancers may actually secrete the substance. Sara pointed out that the presence of vinegar around tumors could just as well mean that the body was producing the vinegar in an attempt to fight the cancer.

In an interview, the doctor also admitted that he had another patient who had the same revelation as Sara. This man also told the doctor that aliens had told him that vinegar is an effective cure against cancer. The doctor knew that cancers thrive in an alkaline medium, and since vinegar was acidic, it also seemed worth trying.

Thankfully there has been some research in this area. The investigators of the case brought it to the attention of a physician who specializes in cancer immunology. He told them that vinegar alone has failed to cure cancer. However, he says that a chemical closely related to acetic acid, but much more potent "is currently being used with significant results."[44]

Then there's the case of abductee, Bret Oldham. During one of his abductions, a tall gray said, "On your planet you have a disease of cancer. Would you like to know the cure to this disease?"

"Of course, I would," Oldham replied.

Suddenly a screen appeared beside the gray, showing a long, mathematical equation.

"What is this?" Oldham asked.

"This is the formula for the cure to cancer," the gray replied. "You may take this back with you when you leave."

Oldham asked for something to write the formula down.

"No," the gray replied. "You must remember it."

Oldham became agitated and then angry as the gray told him that it was time for him to go. Two small grays appeared and escorted him from the room. Needless to say, Oldham was unable to reproduce the equation, and if the ETs had a cure for cancer, it remains with them. Oldham does report that he had what appeared to be a cancerous mole which disappeared, presumably because the ETs removed it.[45]

The cancer healing cases are the most numerous of any specific disease. Most of the accounts provide a wealth of detail. Most come with before and after diagnoses from doctors. And while the ETs have not provided a cancer cure that can be used by everyone, they have shown that even advanced cases can be cured.

Part Four
Beyond UFO Healings

With 309 cases in which people have been cured as the result of a UFO encounter, we can safely conclude that such cases do happen, that they are widespread, and will continue to occur. However, the healing power of UFOs is not limited to specific healing events. UFOs are having a positive influence in many other ways. In part four of this book, we explore cases in which people have received "health upgrades." In these cases, people are not healed of a specific illness, but instead feel that they have become smarter, stronger and healthier as a result of their encounters.

UFO healings are not limited to humans. We shall also examine cases in which animals received healings, and even plants!

Beyond the healing cases is another extraordinary phenomenon: the connection between UFOs and psychic healing. Proving that healing is a primary ET agenda is the fact that many people are transformed by their encounters and become themselves, healers. As we shall see, ETs not only heal people, they teach people to heal themselves.

We shall explore many "miraculous" healings from other sources than UFOs. Native American healings, cures from religious figures and shrines, lightning cures, healings from near-death experiences, astral travel, past-life therapy and more--healings, we shall see, come from many sources.

Finally, we shall examine and analyze all the evidence. We will try to make sense of all these myriad healing cases, draw what conclusions we can, and see what this means for the future of humanity.

Chapter Twenty-Four
Health Upgrades

One category of UFO healing that is often overlooked involves a general upgrading of the health of the witness. In case after case, experiencers report unusually rapid healing of injuries and illnesses. In these cases, the gifts of good health were somehow enhanced as a result of an encounter. The witnesses aren't necessarily cured of a specific illness or condition during an encounter. Because of this, these cases are not included in the list of total accounts. The healing itself comes afterward due to physiological changes the witness sustained at the time of the original encounter. The witnesses often claim that their encounter made them healthier than they were before. Not only healthier, some claim, but faster, smarter, stronger and more. Some, including the following, were told that ETs are working on increasing human longevity.

Health Upgrades

Author and college professor Dr. Darrell D. Davisson believes that aliens may be maintaining our health without our knowledge. In his book, *Holographic Worlds*, Davisson recounts a series of telepathic conversations with an apparent extraterrestrial. Channeled through his keyboard, Davisson makes no claims as to the authenticity of his material and is more interested in the message coming from the alleged ET, who he calls "X." The material covers many aspects of human civilization, and at one point, broaches the subject of health.

"X" told Davisson that they have abducted millions of people without their knowledge (including Davisson) in order to make "genetic upgrades." Says X, "We changed your DNA so you would live longer."[1]

Bicyclist Upgraded

Upgrades in health to people who are otherwise healthy is a recurring theme. In 2009 (approx.,) a group of five Mexican bicycle racers had an experience with a UFO that left one of their team members--Rodrigo--profoundly changed.

It was late at night when the five men--all from the same village--were about two miles from home, bicycling against rain and high winds. Up ahead of them on the road, they came upon bright lights. They first thought that there had been a highway accident, but as they got closer, they realized the lights were much too bright. Rodrigo told his teammates to stay back while he investigated. Rodrigo's friends watched him disappear into the light.

Thirty minutes later, Rodrigo still hadn't returned. Together his friends went to investigate. They approached the light and saw that it was a "some sort of a craft." They called out to Rodrigo and tossed a stone at the craft. After a few moments, the light dimmed and a door opened in the craft.

Says Pablo, one of the bicyclists, "A stairway descended. That's when we saw them. There were eleven of them, eleven humans. They all came out of the UFO. Rodrigo was the second to appear. I ran toward him and pulled him out of the light. But the others just stood there with nowhere to go. The UFO suddenly moved upward. Within seconds, it was gone. All around us was darkness."

The four remaining bicyclists started a campfire and herded the confused people from the UFO off the highway. None of the eleven abductees knew each other. Says Rodrigo, "One man was from Mexico City, there were three from Merida, one from Valladolid, two from Vera Cruz, and I can't remember the others. But they were from all around Mexico."

None of the eleven people--including Rodrigo--remembered anything about what happened. To this day, Rodrigo doesn't even remember seeing the UFO.

But Rodrigo did report one dramatic change. "I don't know what they did to me," he says, "but after that, I was the fastest bicyclist in Mexico. Maybe they did something to make me faster."

Ardy Sixkiller Clarke, who interviewed the witnesses, writes, "I often think of Rodrigo's belief that the UFO had given him supernatural powers and made him a more powerful rider. Though it was hard for me to wrap my mind around such an incident, I suppose stranger things have happened."[2]

Longevity Increased?

On May 9, 1974, seven people were driving home along Highway 57 near Mount Vernon, Indiana when they encountered a large object hovering at a very low altitude. Suddenly the object approached their vehicle, hovered right over it and sent down a blast of heat. All the witnesses except one passed out.

The remaining witness felt himself drawn upward and found himself being examined by five-foot-tall beings with light skin, huge almond-shaped eyes, and a small lower jaw. They called the witness by his name, and exhibited great strength as they handled him.

Following the abduction, the man believes that his aging process was slowed down as a result of the encounter.[3]

A Healing Experience

UFO forums on the world wide web provide a platform for experiencers to share their own encounters and learn about others. In one of these forums, "Greyman," reached out to share his own encounters. "All my life I have believed that UFOs exist and have had two and possibly many more encounters," he writes. "My last one happened about a month ago while I was in bed. I saw myself and others being healed by UFO beings. At first I was scared, but later on I realized that it was a healing experience."

This realization came following the encounter when the witness discovered several physiological improvements. "My eyesight is better," he writes, "my shoulders are stronger and healthier...my knees were swollen bad and the tendons and muscles in the knee area were tight and stiff. My knees are slowly becoming better, and I believe they will be stronger than they were before. I have also noticed a big increase in my psychic abilities."[4]

Health Maintenance

While researcher John Mack MD has uncovered several cases of UFO healings, he has also uncovered instances in which people weren't healed, but were given treatments to maintain their good health. One woman he interviewed, "Isabel," is a good example.

Writes Mack, "Experiencers often report that the examination-like procedures they have undergone represent some sort of health-monitoring and maintenance program on the part of the aliens...Isabel has the impression that the beings 'really need to take her physical body to maintain her health as a breeder ('for tune-ups'.)' As part of this process, they give her a bitter liquid to drink and 'put in' her what she calls a 'vaccine.'...The drink, she believes, is 'just like medicine' or 'a super-vitamin.'"

Isabel speculates that the aliens need to keep her healthy so that the hybrid babies she carries and nurses for them will also be healthy. Regarding this type of health maintenance, Mack writes, "Whether this is for our benefit, or to keep our organs healthy so that the beings might use them for their own purposes later, as some experiencers have suggested is one of the questions that seems to depend, in part, upon how we choose to interpret the phenomenon...Isabel attributes her excellent health and apparent immunity to colds and other illnesses to the alien health-monitoring program. As 'a loving parent would talk to a child,' the beings warn her about smoking and other dangers to her health. They even instruct her about what to eat or not to eat, and where to go, whom to meet or avoid, and where to find things she has lost."[5]

Alien Check-ups

Jim Sparks (a NC-based house developer) has had many contact experiences and at least two apparent healings, one of the flu, and another during which the ETs removed black tar from his lungs.

Sparks reports that the ETs have often examined him and monitored his health. Beyond this, they have also advised him to adjust his diet.

"Some of these alien medical exams unfortunately include anal probes," writes Sparks. "Yuck! A subject I do not enjoy talking about, writing about, or experiencing. Of course, not everything I write about is comfortable to relive, and in this case I feel it is necessary...I found myself face down on an examination table, in tremendous pain. They had inserted a deep anal probe into me, and I could feel it churning about in my guts. I felt so miserable that I cried out, 'What the hell are you doing to me?'"

"An examination of your system," the alien replied.

"The pain is awful! You're hurting me!"

"Then I blacked out," continues Spark. "When I regained consciousness, I found myself face up on the table, sore inside, but not in pain. Two aliens were present, and it appeared they were just finishing up their procedure."

"It is necessary that you stop eating animals," one of them said, communicating telepathically. "Your system is overloaded with trash. Intelligence dictates that you do not have to kill to survive."

Sparks was surprised by their use of their word: *trash.* After the experience, he found himself in a dilemma. Prior to the encounter, he had been "a true carnivore," eating rare steak, hamburgers, meatloaf, pot roasts, pork ribs, roast pork and more. "It would take an Act of Congress for Jim to stop eating meat," his friends told him.

Or an act of aliens, as it turned out. Following the experience, Sparks quit eating red meat, limiting himself to fish and fowl. Precisely thirty days following his alien colonoscopy, the aliens returned and began to conduct another one. "They were poking and prodding me," Sparks said, "And I hated it."

"Damn it!" he shouted. "Why are you doing this again? I stopped eating meat!"

"We know," they said. "We had to make sure it was helping you, and it is."

Again, Sparks was sore afterward, but years later, his diet still remains largely vegetarian "I have met many fellow abductees," says Spark. "The bulk of them are vegetarians. I find that odd, don't you?"[6]

Reptilian Health Upgrade

Ever since he was a child, Darrell (pseudonym) experienced weird lights and apparitions in his home in Ohio. "Around age eighteen," says Darrell, "it started turning into physical abductions at night, and randomly seeing craft periodically. This carried on all throughout my life until the age of thirty-two. At the age of thirty-two, it turned into something completely different."

It happened suddenly in the beginning of 2016. Darrell began to see orbs of light around him, and sensed an undefinable energy. "It's an energy that I do not completely understand," he says. "It's part of me and incomparable to anything I've ever seen. It changes color and can move through solid objects. It reacts intelligently. The energy is inside me and outside of me at the same time. It never leaves me or stops existing. The energy regenerates my body and mind. It heals me, and can heal others."

Darrell's transformation took place over a period of months, during which he became changed by the energy. "At one point during the transformation," he says, "there was an etheric injection in my arm. I felt a spark jump, and it shocked me. Now my eyes glow different, and I feel like I have more energy and soul than I did before. There's a lot of energy work going on with my chakras while lying in bed at night."

During Darrell's transformation, ETs began to communicate with him and he learned the causes for his lifelong history of unusual events. "The race of aliens I'm in contact with are the Reptilians," says Darrell. Using holographic images to communicate, the Reptilians told him that they evolved from velociraptors, and that there is a "some kind of war" going on within their society. They said that Darrell was a Reptilian-Human hybrid. There were many hybrids, they said, but most weren't evolved enough mentally, physically or spiritually, or they were brainwashed by religion and fearful of Reptilians, and that many had been killed.

"As of now," says Darrell, "there's only a handful of awakened, empowered hybrids. So, there it is. I'm in direct contact with Reptilians. They exist, and we've formed a bond. They're really good to me. They guide, protect and upgrade me. I wouldn't be alive without them. They've saved my life multiple times. I trust them more than I do most humans."

Darrell says he now has the ability to recognize the Reptilians who walk in disguise among the human population. "I can always tell when it's one of them," says Darrell, "because the women are always perfect, with a glow to them, and stars in their eyes."

The Reptilians, says Darrell, mingle among the population for days or months at a time. They are extremely powerful mentally and technologically, and live largely undetected on our planet. "I stand by this, firmly. I've spent almost thirty-three years of my life spinning in their web."[7]

Reptilian Medical Advice

Late in the evening of November 12, 2008, "Lisa" (pseudonym), a resident of New York State, prepared for bed. It had been a good day at work, and she had no reason expect anything unusual. However, no sooner did she climb into bed when she felt as if she had been struck by a mysterious whirlwind.

She found herself standing alongside a highway, with a house to her right and a tree in front of her. Despite the darkness, the area around her was bathed in light. She looked up and saw a bright glowing object with blue, red and yellow lights hovering silently overhead. Her heart pounded in shock.

Looking to the right, she saw a male figure, a hybrid Reptilian being. He looked half human, half lizard. Speaking telepathically, he said, "Someone wants to meet you."

Lisa found herself walking with the hybrid toward a red van. Above them, the UFO followed. Inside the van was another hybrid. The first reptilian said, "This is Jayson."

The being looked at Lisa and said, "If you love nature so much, why are you destroying it?"

The next thing Lisa remembers, she was back in bed and the experience was over.

A few months later, in 2009, Lisa was preparing for bed when she felt a strong telepathic link-up. She knew instantly it was Jayson. "Where are you?" she asked.

"In a craft, nearby," he replied, and told her that he came back to finish what he had tried to tell her earlier, but was unable to do so because of her fear of him.

Jayson proceeded to provide Sarah with about a dozen spiritual aphorisms. He said that his race loves God, and that she should love God with all the might of her soul. God is evolution, he told her, and that He creates all things, and there is no such thing as sin. He said that humans are the descendants of another ET race, and that Jayson's race is envious because humans are more numerous than his race. He said over-harvesting of our crops is destroying them and depleting our planet. He told her that although his race comes in peace, others may not. He also claimed that his race contacted the Jewish people in ancient Egypt, and taught them. Finally, he had advice about caring for the human body, including the importance of bowel movements and that "All disease is created in the mind, thought of in the mind [and] the cure is in the mind."

"This was the last I heard of him," says Lisa. "After our last encounter, I woke up one evening to a large, luminescent orb overlooking my bed. It was a little bigger than a basketball. It hovered, a bright light, then in an instant, it shot left, out of the window. It was closed."[8]

Alien Health Advice

In case after case, the ETs seem to show concern about human health. Cindy, a California-based abductee whose encounters were researched by Barbara Lamb, has had contact with multiple types of ETs who have given her much information. They told her that the planet is moving into a higher dimensional vibration and that there would be many future natural disasters.

At some point, they said, large numbers of people would be removed from the planet for their own safety. They told her that the human race was genetically engineered, and that they are interested in our ability to experience emotions. They also gave her medical advice. Writes Lamb, "Regarding human health, the ETs said that certain memories could promote disease, but deep muscle therapy could release those memories and thus prevent loss of health."[9]

Upgraded!

Martin (pseudonym) has a form of autism called Asperger's Syndrome. He grew up in South Dakota and as a result of his condition, was given heavy cocktails of prescription drugs. By age sixteen, he was still under five feet tall, suffering from depression, and in a drug haze. Believing the drugs were stunting his growth, he decided to go cold turkey, and he took himself off the Ritalin, the Paxil, the Abilify and the Zoloft. That year, he grew to six feet two inches in height, and gained 120 pounds. His Asperger symptoms and depression became much more manageable and "hardly noticeable."

There were other beneficial effects. "My creative levels jumped through the roof. I was suddenly able to draw, paint, work with ceramic. I could look at patterns and discern things that nobody else could see was there. My intelligence level jumped from near genius to well above."

What happened to cause this sudden boost? Martin wonders if it was more than just getting off prescription drugs. The reason was, Martin thinks, a secret that he's kept from almost everyone. "I have had close encounters of the fourth kind, for many years, several times a year...For nearly as long as I can remember--the first instance being at the age of four--I will have a visit from what I refer to as a gentleman, three to five times a year, every three months or so, sometimes with an extra one thrown in. I wake up in the middle of the night in a panic for no apparent reason, very similar to what some might call night terrors--instantly, fully awake, terrified, panicking, unable to move...The only thing I can control are my eyes and my breathing. And near me, maybe two or three feet away, is a small gray."

Martin describes the "gentleman" in familiar terms: "Small, smooth grey skin, almond-shaped, jet-black eyes, tiny nostrils, thin-lipped mouthed, usually hairless. They scare the daylight out of me."

He has no memories of being poked, prodded, anally probed or implanted. The figure just stands there and observes him. "He is older, I can tell that much, how, I'm not sure. He doesn't do much. He observes me, passes a hand over me now and then, but he never touches. He doesn't poke or prod or anything of the sort. He simply observes. And occasionally he will wave a hand about in the air, almost as though touching a computer screen...My waking state goes from petrification to irritation. There is no threat except for the fact that I am restricted."

Martin has tried to send the being thoughts. When he does, the being "usually stops and stares, cocks his head to the side and makes another note." Martin isn't sure if the being understands him, but occasionally, Martin picks up "images" and "snippets" of the alien's thoughts and emotions. He believes the ET has no desire for world domination, and is merely curious.

"...I personally think that they may have injected nothing more than a few cells into my body that they take readings, and they can read when they are in close proximity to me. It would certainly explain why they run their hands through the air above me, reading something magnetic perhaps."

When they first appeared at age four, there were multiple grays. After that, it was always just one. It would appear once or twice a year. However, at age sixteen, when he took himself off the prescription drugs, the visitations increased to three, four or five times a year. Usually, the gray would remain for a half hour, maybe an hour. Now, when it arrived, it stayed for three or four hours at a time.

It was then that Martin began to notice that there were some very unusual things about him physiologically. First, he has two unexplained scars on his abdomen, which have been there as long as he can remember. Even more strange, however, is his unusually hardy physical constitution. "I have never broken a bone in a serious way, even though I have been in a serious accident-- my knuckles a few times in a fight [and] my knee cap in what should have been a fatal ninety-MPH accident while not wearing a seatbelt. My wounds heal at a rate about twice as fast as predicted by professionals...I hardly ever get sick. Family members around me will be sick for three weeks at a time, while I will be sick for two to three days with the same symptoms."

Are the ETs responsible for what he calls his "medical oddities?" Martin believes they might be. "I'm convinced there's a connection between the increase in visits and length and my unusual physiology, that for some reason or another, they took an interest in keeping me alive for observation."

Martin isn't sure why he was chosen to be studied by extraterrestrials, but he has his theories. "Perhaps they are interested in autistic individuals; perhaps Asperger's individuals specifically. I've always been a little off, a little different...I just wish they'd talk to me instead of restraining me. I hope one day that my curiosity to converse with them will overpower the fear I have while they are in my presence..."

On February 25, 2015, Martin's wish came true. He was dozing in bed when he became fully awake, suddenly consumed with a petrifying fear of an approaching presence. His bedroom door opened, and in walked a gray-type ET unlike any he had seen before. "He was tall," Martin explains, "above eight feet. He had to stoop to avoid hitting the ceiling with his head. His body was thin, very thin...his face was comparable to the beings which I have seen before, but it was ancient beyond anything I can describe-- withered and hard, but with an emotion I can only describe as softness in the corner of his massive, black eyes."

A long telepathic conversation followed. The being said his name was Prou (pronounced Prow), and that he was pleased to meet Martin. Says Martin, "I, in a moment of incredulity, extended my hand and he shook it with his. It felt strange, wooden in texture, but warm and soft. It enveloped my entire hand, and he held it for a moment before telling me it brought him joy to experience friendship with someone he had studied closely for so many years."

Strange images filled Martin's mind. "Flashes of colors, scenes from distant worlds I can't describe in any way other than fantastical, soaring skyscrapers, flashes of movement, bizarre creatures with too many eyes and limbs that moved like fluid, glass domes and red and gold skies over green oceans."

Further conversations followed. "He apologized for the many years of fright and assured me there was no reason to be afraid. He told me there was a purpose behind their visits, and the visits of millions of other people around the world have, but are completely unaware of."

What is the purpose of their visits? According to Martin, "They harvest memories. They observe our world, our culture and our society through our eyes...In harvesting this information, they have been able to greatly advance their own culture. His explanation was that humanity and humans as individuals are vastly more creative than their own. They are a logical people, and as such, have limitations. Humans, he said, are basically insane, and as a result, think so far out of the box that we end up inventing things far beyond our time. And we are so diverse that we devote massive amounts of time to thousands of projects...They seek out unique individuals, those with genius intellect, the mentally unstable but still functional, the creative thinkers, and they observe their minds for the spark of motivation. They take our mundane, day-to-day ideas and they create each and every one of them. If you are one of their subjects, every crappy daydream invention you've come up with, they have made it, utilized it, improved it, tested it, and incorporated it into their lives."

The being told Martin that he was surprised that Martin was able to consciously recall the visitations, and that the vast majority of people they visit have no memory of it, not because of them, but because of the human mind's tendency to repress memories. "The ETs have no hand in making us forget," says Martin. "Our mind does not want to remember, so it does not. My accurate memories of visits and contemplation of them makes me very unique in their books, it would seem."

He told Martin many other things, that the human race is unique in how it has technologically progressed so quickly, that many other races fear our aggression, which is delaying the progress of our society, that their civilization is nearly 20,000 years old and that we may be related to their ancestors, that they implant humans with a biological-type implant which records all the information they need from us and much more.

Says Martin, "That's my crazy tale. Think of it what you will."[10]

Rapid Healing

A common comment among those who have contact is that they heal more rapidly than the average human. The following case is a good example. One dusky summer evening around 1969, nine-year-old Ruben (pseudonym) of Stephensville, Texas went outside to take out the garbage. He walked through the backyard toward the fence where the trash-can stood when he saw a ten-foot-wide circle of light shining on the ground. "I looked up," he said, "and all I could see was the light. It was bright, but it didn't hurt my eyes. It lasted about fifteen-twenty seconds, not long."

The light was bluish, and betrayed no visible structure. After it switched off, Ruben emptied the can and returned inside.

Ruben didn't think much of it, and fearing that people would call him "loony," he told nobody. In the months following the incident, Ruben noticed something strange. They had a lawn of St. Augustine grass which would die out each winter. However, that winter, exactly where the circle of light had shone on the ground, the grass grew green and lush. It was annoying because Ruben was forced to mow the spot on a weekly basis.

Many years later, he got married and told his wife about the incident. She said that she believed him. Then, in 2008, the small town of Stephensville was hit by a sizeable UFO wave which garnered international media attention. Ruben's wife urged him to report his sighting officially, which Ruben did. Says Ruben, "She also thinks now that because of the incident, I heal faster than just about anybody I know."[11]

Cleansing

According to researcher, Fabio Picasso, In March of 1969, engineer Alberto Zecua had his second encounter with ETs. His first encounter had occurred one year earlier in Tulancingo, Mexico. He and others were out camping when they came upon a craft hovering just above the ground. They saw three tall human-looking figures with fine features and exotic eyes. The beings collected plants and took off in their craft.

Now, in March of 1969, Zecua was woken up in his home in Mexico City to see the same figures he had seen a year earlier. They wore strange metal bracelets and had glowing boxes strapped around their waists. Using telepathy, they told him not to be afraid, that they were there to help him. They used a box-like instrument to levitate Zecua above his bed. The beings surrounded his bed and Zecua became numb and heard a humming sound. He floated back down and smelled a strong odor similar to menthol. The beings told him that they had performed "an internal cleansing" of his body, and then vanished.[12]

Area 51 Employees Upgraded?

In 2004, *Fate* magazine conducted an experiment in which they asked their readers to psychically view Area 51 in Nevada and see what they could find out about the inner workings of the base. The results were surprising; the respondents' reports (all women) agreed on many details. They reported seeing research into UFOs and reverse engineering, experiments with genetics, research into germ warfare, gray-type ETs working along with humans and more. Important here is that several of the respondents reported that employees of the base had their health boosted by the ETs.

Carol Gourlay of Lansing, Michigan felt that the employees had been genetically enhanced. Kathleen Nelson of Island Pond, Vermont sensed that some of the higher-level employees of the base had been genetically altered and enhanced using alien technology. Theresa Benken of Carson City, Nevada saw that innocent citizens were being abducted and taken to the base for medical and hybridization experiments. She says that some of the employees of the base who work in close cooperation with the aliens have been given alien technology to help them live a longer life. Says Benken, "They have been mated with robotic parts that perform vital functions, until these people are nearly immortal." She says that there have been many hybridization and genetic experiments to make people adaptable to other planets.[13]

As can be seen, these witnesses aren't reporting healings of specific illnesses; instead they feel that they have been made stronger, faster, smarter, better able to heal from injuries and illnesses, and even live longer--all due to a UFO encounter. These types of cases show that ETs are not only healing people, they are practicing preventative medicine and are closely monitoring humans and maintaining their health in ways we are only beginning to understand.

Chapter Twenty-Five
Even the Animals

In two previous cases in this book, witnesses who were healed also reported that their dogs were healed. One witness, Joy Davies, who suffered from arthritis reported that her dog was also more active. And another gentleman whose condition of diabetes and arthritis was improved, also reported a corresponding enhancement in his dog.

The two above cases are unusual, but they are not unique. There is now a small but growing number of cases in which animals have received UFO healings.

CASE #026. ROOSTERS.

One summer afternoon in 1959, in Pleasanton, Texas, thirteen-year-old Susan Nevarez Morton went to attend a cockfight with her sister, her brother-in-law and their family. The entire group drove to a secret location and joined a huge crowd of people on wooden bleachers. In the center of the crowd, two roosters began to fight a battle which Susan knew would be to the death.

The two roosters were fiercely fighting when suddenly the attention of the crowd was caught by a large, glowing object which was hovering over the area. Without warning the object emitted two beams of light. Nevarez described the object as "an enormous red globe with two shafts of white light inching down toward us."

Everyone watched in amazement as the beams targeted the two roosters, who were now lying on the ground, nearly dead from their injuries. Then something amazing happened. "Their small broken bodies glowed eerily for a few seconds," said Nevarez.

"Then slowly, they both got up on their little chicken feet and began strutting around with robust enthusiasm."

The crowd became extremely agitated, until, after a few moments, the beams of light retracted inside the object, which now changed from red to orange and streaked away at high speed. The two roosters showed no trace of their former injuries, but the cockfight was cancelled.[1]

Roosters are not the only animals being healed. In the below encounter, a man claims that his horse was healed.

CASE #033. HORSE.

On November 12, 1960, Ivor Sercombe who owned a farm near Devizes in England, heard a voice in his head telling him to check his horse, Daffodil.

Daffodil was suffering from an illness in her hooves. Sercombe went outside to his stables. Inside, he saw a golden glow. Standing beside Daffodil was a six-foot figure wearing a sports jacket.

The figure spoke telepathically, saying that he was a vet and would cure the horse. He held up a machine which looked semi-solid, semi-transparent. It reminded Sercombe of a dental X-ray device; it had a central column with two arms projecting on either side, at the end of which were metallic spheres. The being moved the instrument along the mare's forelegs, focusing on the hooves. Sercombe saw blue-purple sparks and felt a powerful electric force. The treatment continued for fifteen minutes, at which point the strange visitor gradually disappeared. Sercombe was about to check on his horse when he heard a voice say, "Leave the horse alone, there is nothing you can do."

Sercombe returned into his home. His horse reportedly experienced a full recovery.[2]

When it comes to animal healings, roosters and horses are the exception. All the other cases involve dogs. About 90 million dogs live as pets in the United States. Despite this, there are only a few reported healings.

CASE #056. DOG.

Throughout his life, Danny Enderson of Mt. Kiera, New South Wales, Australia had many strange and unusual experiences. One evening in 1971 while lying in bed, a whirling red light appeared in his bedroom and he found himself being pulled upward into a large room with flashing lights and strange instrument panels. A seven-foot-tall humanoid in a green suit instructed Enderson to sit in a weird chair.

The humanoid placed his hand over Enderson's eyes, causing pain. "Before long though," said Enderson, "the pain gave way to a beautiful peaceful feeling and I knew I never wanted to leave that place. A moment later I was back in bed."

Back at home, Enderson discovered his sense of hearing and touch were now both ultra-sensitive. His face was red and swollen and two hieroglyphic-like marks appeared on his chest.

Following this, Enderson experienced repeated visits with insectoid beings, Bigfoot-like beings and more.

One afternoon, Enderson was watering the plants in his garden when he saw a mantis-type creature exit Sam's dog-shed, and disappear behind it. Sam was Enderson's pet dog. He was old and crippled with arthritis, and would yelp with pain if anybody petted him. Enderson was planning on having old Sam put to sleep.

Enderson rushed into the shed to check on Sam. The dog was not only fine, he was healed. "His coat was suddenly glossy and his eyes were brighter than they'd been for years. From that day, the arthritis never troubled Sam." There was no sign of the mantis being. Enderson feels humbled to be connected to these beings who he says are "full of love and peace."[3]

Of all the animal healings, this next case is the perhaps the most compelling. There are multiple witnesses and medical records verifying the medical condition before and after the healing. One of the witnesses was so transformed by the incident that he has now become a prominent figure on the frontlines of UFO research.

CASE #264. DOG.

For most of his life, Reinerio Hernandez J.D., M.C.P., (an estate tax attorney from Miami, Florida) considered himself a "material rationalist." He did not believe in UFOs or the paranormal and scoffed at those who did. In 2012, Hernandez had an experience which caused a complete transformation in his world view.

On March 3, 2012, Nena (his fifteen-year-old Jack Russell Terrier) became paralyzed. She had previously been "very ill" because of severe arthritis and a heart condition. They immediately called their veterinarian who informed them that Nena had likely suffered a cerebral hemorrhage. Devastated, Hernandez and his wife made plans to euthanize Nina the next morning.

That evening, Hernandez's wife (who was Catholic) prayed earnestly for "angels" to help Nena.

The next morning, at 6:00 a.m., on March 4, 2012, Hernandez's wife carried Nena downstairs to the living room. Without warning, a "small, silver-covered translucent metallic object" appeared, hovering in the corner of the room. Realizing her prayers had been answered, she fell to her knees and prayed. She screamed for Rey to come downstairs. When he didn't, she ran upstairs and pulled him out of bed and downstairs to the living room.

Hernandez was shocked to see what appeared to be a "plasma energy being." The next thing he knew, forty-five minutes had passed. Says Hernandez, "I woke up forty-five minutes later, where I found my wife celebrating in our living room, and Nena running around like she was a young puppy...Before this miraculous medical healing, Nena was not able to either run or jump because of her severe arthritis and her heart condition. Now she was running around the house in joy celebrating her new lease on life."

Hernandez's wife was overjoyed and told her husband that the angels cured Nena. "This experience felt like an atom bomb blew up in my brain," says Hernandez, "and I was in total shock and confusion. My wife did not know that she had 'disappeared' for forty-five minutes...She also did not see the Energy Being, because she was 'taken' before this Plasma Energy Being appeared. It was a state of total chaos and celebration for the miraculous healing of our beloved Nena by what my wife perceived to be "Angelic Intervention."

Hernandez was shocked, and immediately began to research what happened to them. He soon discovered that their experience sounded very much like a UFO encounter. Following the experience, both Hernandez and his wife experienced several close-up UFO sightings and other paranormal encounters. In this space of a few months, Hernandez became completely transformed. His life had taken a left turn and he became inspired to research UFOs and the paranormal. One year later, he became the co-founder of the Dr. Edgar Mitchell Foundation for Research into Extraterrestrial and Extraordinary Experiences (FREE), bringing together leading researchers in the field to study the topics of extraterrestrials, the paranormal and consciousness with a scientific approach. The FREE organization began distributing a worldwide survey to experiencers, collecting firsthand accounts of unexplained experiences. FREE quickly became an influential force in the UFO field. The landmark book, *Beyond UFOs*, (co-edited by Hernandez) was published in 2018. It's the first of a series, and reveals the results of the FREE survey, showing that UFOs and the paranormal are inextricably connected and that the key commonality appears to be the phenomenon of consciousness. While their dog, Nena, died only a few months after the encounter, Hernandez and his wife would never be the same.[4]

Another case of a dog-healing comes from a woman in Arizona. Like a few of the above cases, the witness has had multiple ET encounters.

CASE #287. DOG.

An animal control officer from Arizona, Jujuolui Kuita, has had encounters her entire life, beginning at least around age five when tall grays visited her in her bedroom in Indiana, apparently implanting her. Her encounters continued, including in the dream and astral states. She also had a number of very strange UFO sightings. After many years of benevolent contacts with lots of communication of knowledge, Juju considers the ETs her family.

In the mid-2000s, she got a dog, Katrina. Juju adored Katrina, and felt almost as though they were soul-mates. She became closer to Katrina than any other pet she'd ever had.

In 2016, Katrina developed valley fever, a systemic fungal infection that can cause fever, nausea, lung problems, joint pain, inflammation, and more--and in some cases, it can be fatal.

At the time, Juju knew that Katrina wasn't feeling well, but she didn't know why.

One evening around March 2016, Juju found herself apparently onboard a UFO. "It looked like the inside of a football," she says. "The floor came up and met the ceiling that came down. It was not real sharp, but there was a curve in the wall."

The room was dimly lit. She felt no sensation of movement. There was a floor-lamp-like device in the corner. Two men stood in the room, one was white-skinned, stocky, with blond hair and appeared Caucasian. The other was darker skinned with dark, curly, short hair, and looked almost Italian. Both wore full-length white robes. But what really caught Juju's attention was that the Caucasian-looking man was hunched over her dog, who had her legs up in the air and appeared to be unconscious. Her first thought was that the man was hurting Katrina. Anger swept over her and she took instant action.

"I saw that he had my dog," says Juju. "She was on her back, and she was kind of whimpering. She seemed scared. And I thought this guy was hurting her. So I grabbed what looked like a floor-lamp. I grabbed this thing and I was going toward him."

Juju had played softball and was ready to knock the guy over when the Italian-looking man stepped in front of her. "Hold on," he said, peacefully and calmly. "Please just wait three seconds."

Only then did Juju fully realize what was happening. She was on a craft. These were not humans, but ETs. She realized instantly, she could trust them.

409

She looked down at her dog and was amazed at what she saw. "This guy was bringing his hand out of her chest, and she wasn't whimpering anymore. But it was like his fingers extended, and were elongated, and went actually through her body, and he was bringing them back out. And he did this really gently."

The man deferentially bowed his head at Juju and allowed her to see Katrina.

"And I looked down," says Juju, "and Katrina gets up. She just looks at me. I kneel down to pet her and be next to her, and that was it--it ended."

Juju woke up back in her home. She checked on Katrina, who seemed to be fine. However, as the days passed, Katrina still seemed unwell. She decided to take her to the veterinarian, who diagnosed Katrina with valley fever.

Katrina loved to dig around in the dirt and it appeared that she had become infected by fungus. Despite treatment, Katrina's health declined and one year later, she passed away.

Juju believes that the ETs did heal Katrina, keeping her alive during a difficult and important time in Juju's life. "I think what they were trying to do was help her," says Juju, "because they were so loving and benevolent to me, toward me and her. I truly believe they were helping her."

Following Katrina's passing, Juju was contacted by her ET friends who told her that Katrina was actually of ET heritage, as Juju herself was. Finally it made sense why Juju always felt a special closeness to her.

Juju suspects she may have had her own healings and benevolent intervention. Once as a child she fell down and heard a voice telling her to raise her arms. She obeyed and was shocked to find that the fall hadn't hurt her at all. On another occasion, as an adult, she experienced a sudden degradation of her vision. She went to the eye doctor who said it was normal and gave her glasses. A month or two later, her vision suddenly improved back to normal. On a third occasion, she had a contact during which she perceived that the ETs were working on her kidneys. As a child she had some kidney problems. Unfortunately, she couldn't be sure about any of these incidents.

The incident with Katrina, however, left a lasting impression. She continues to have experiences with the ETs. "I've had the most beautiful, healing, loving lessons from them that help me in my Reiki, how to channel energy."[5]

While the healings of animals are rare in comparison to the number of human healings, these cases show us that ETs are doing healings beyond just the motive of "maintaining human health." If their care extends to animals and humans, it strengthens the possibility that their agenda is at least partly altruistic.

And if healings of humans and animals aren't enough, how about plants?

Extraterrestrial Gardeners

In my book, *Not from Here: Volume Two*, I present a collection of cases in which ETs have intervened to improve the health or accelerate the growth rate of a wide variety of plants.

One case (documented by Diane Tessman) occurred in October 1990 to a forestry worker who was employed to care for the forest preserve in County Tiperrary in Ireland. While out in the field, the worker saw a UFO appear to land. Shortly later he was visited by a human-looking man with long hair who said that the poplar trees in the forest were very sick, and then proceeded to give explanations on how to cure various tree diseases.

Another case from Tessman's files occurred in June 1991 to "Ita" of Belfast, Ireland. One evening a UFO hovered over her garden, sending down a powerful beam of light. The next morning, Ita went outside and discovered that her plants had acquired about three weeks of growth over night, astonishing both herself, and her neighbors, whose gardens remained normal.

Jacques Vallee reports on a case which occurred in April 1976 in Redding, California, in which Jean Kirk saw an object hover over an area behind her home. In the months that followed, the weeds where the UFO hovered surpassed all the others in size. Normally the weed growth reached about three or four feet. One year after the incident, Kirk measured the weeds at an amazing eight feet. Some of the grass reached a height of five feet and was

411

very dense. The accelerated growth continued for one more year before returning to normal.

In 1967, the James family of Colorado was growing a carrot by the window in their trailer. One evening a UFO hovered overhead, sending down a powerful beam of light. The next morning, the carrot, which had just started to sprout before the incident, was completely transformed. "Something drastic and truly puzzling had happened to it," said Jerry James, "for the carrot did not resemble a carrot any longer. It had spread out, as if having grown for weeks in a tempered professional hot house. Roots were everywhere, running outside the dish and reaching almost to the floor."[6]

These cases, and others like them, indicate that ETs show an interest in the biology of not only humans, but also animals, and even plants. And with their ability to apparently accelerate the growth rate of plants, they show once again their superior understanding of life on our planet.

Chapter Twenty-Six
Friends in High Places

In some cases, ETs provide help in more ways than just a physical healing. Many people believe they have been helped, rescued or saved from tragedy by ETs. This help comes in a surprising variety of forms. In case after case, ETs have literally rescued people from various types of potentially tragic events. What follows are twelve cases in which people were rescued from hazardous and life-threatening situations by ETs.

The first case, from Ardy Sixkiller Clarke, is a good example of how ETs extend help to people in unexpected ways.

Protected from the Storm

On the east coast of the Yucatan Peninsula is a small Mayan village outside Tulum. In 2004, the village was being battered by hurricane force winds and rain. A resident of the village, Geraldo, and his family were worried about the village being flooded and like many others, were preparing to evacuate. At this point, a brilliant light appeared and the rain stopped. "Overhead, just at treetop level," says Geraldo, "there was a UFO. It was round, and it lit up the whole village. The rain stopped. The wind stopped. The UFO was like an umbrella. It was protecting us. For several hours the UFO stayed over our village. When the wind and rains lessened, it moved on."

Geraldo says that everyone in the village saw the craft and a few reported abductions. Geraldo asked the Mayan Elders what they believed the explanation was. "They said the Sky Gods came back to protect us," says Geraldo. "They said our village survived because it was a reminder of the injustice visited upon the Maya people by the Mexican government."[1]

One of the leading killers in the United States are automobile accidents. There are several cases in which ETs have healed people of injuries caused by auto accidents *after they occurred*. There are also cases in which ETs have had the foresight to prevent accidents.

UFO Prevents Automobile Accident

"In 1977/1978," writes the anonymous witness, "I was living in Forest Hill, Texas...I was about twenty-one years old and had BS'd my way into a job in which I had no skills. One skill I needed was typing so I had immediately enrolled in a night typing course which was in Fort Worth, Texas. I was traveling home on I-20 east. There was not much traffic that time of night. In fact, I do not remember any traffic at all, which now seems rather strange to me. All of a sudden, there was a huge light--the brightest light I have ever seen before or since...I slowed down to see what it was, but could only see the light. I then realized what the light was showing me. There was a mattress in the lane ahead of me that I would never have seen, which would have caused me to have an accident.

"I pulled to the side of the road," the witness says, "forgetting about the mattress, and rolled down the window. My first thought was that it was a helicopter, but there was absolutely no sound. When I say no sound, I mean no sound--as in any normal sounds of night or traffic, much less a helicopter sound. I wasn't scared. As a matter of fact, I felt a feeling of peace like I have never felt. All of a sudden, the light was gone."

The witness went home and called nearby Carswell AFB, who denied any knowledge of unknown aircraft, but still seemed interested and questioned the witness about the sighting.

The witness finally reported the sighting to MUFON, after viewing a television program about UFOs. The witness writes, "What I experienced back then was the most awesome and peaceful event that anyone could experience. I do not know what it was, but I do know that it was real, very real. Whatever or whoever it was saved me from what could have been a horrible accident. It could not have been something from this Earth."[2]

One of the most common types of helpful ET intervention is saving people from auto accidents. This second case is a very unusual account in which a woman was saved by MIB-like figures.

MIB Prevent Car Accident

An incredible case of helpful ETs occurred in the spring of 1980 to a lady who was driving outside of Cave Junction, Oregon. "I somehow got off on a logging road which was winding along a steep mountain," the lady explains. "After a while, I noticed that the road was narrowing and I was afraid to follow it any further. I decided to try and turn my car around and drive back to Cave Junction, which was about thirty minutes away. As I was backing up the car, it went off of the road--the rear end was off the road and the car was tottering. I slowly got out and was trying to figure out how to get my dogs out, which were in the kennel in the back of the car. If I tried to reach them, the car could tumble down the cliff.

"While I was trying to decide what to do, a big car pulled up and four, tall Oriental men, with a strange skin tone (too orange) got out of the car. In spite of the 100-plus degree heat of the day, they were all wearing black trench coats. I said, 'Hello.'

"They did not reply. Without a word, they went to the front of my car and picked it up, and sat it back on the road, facing the direction back to home. I do not think that even twice that number of humans could have lifted my car from the front end only and placed it back on the road.

"I do not remember how I got past their car, or they passed mine, as they were headed up the firebreak road, as I was originally as well. The after-thought of the encounter left me really scared, and as soon as I was back in town, I rented a hotel room and slept for a couple of days...Those weird men on the mountain saved our lives, but they still scared me."[3]

Another case of helpful ETs comes from Lillian Richter. In her book, *Visitors Behind Our Stars*, Richter reveals a lifetime of UFO and ET encounters.

UFO Saves Lady from Car Accident

In 2001, Lillian Richter lived in southern California. One weekend, she went to visit her mother, who lived out in the desert area. Richter spent some time with her mother. It was almost a three-hour drive back home, and already almost 4:00 p.m., so she began the return journey. She had been driving for about fifteen minutes and was cruising along the highway at about seventy MPH when her red engine-warning lights began to blink on and off. There were no other cars around her as she began to apply the brake to slow down and pull over.

To her shock, the car began to accelerate instead, first up to eighty MPH, and then ninety. At the same time, water began to pour out from under her hood, which was banging up and down as though it was being hit by the engine.

"I continued to apply pressure on the brakes...but instead the car started to accelerate again. Now I was moving at a speed of 100 miles per hour. By now, I was starting to panic."

Richter tried slamming the brakes down. They had no effect. When she looked at her speedometer, it read 130 miles per hour. At the same time, she realized that the steering wheel had become locked. Certain that an accident was imminent, she began to pray. Immediately the car decelerated to fifteen MPH and pulled off the road by itself and turned off. "It was like someone else had control of my vehicle," Richter says.

Shocked, she saw that the movement under the hood had stopped. She put the gear-shift into park and tried to start the ignition. The car was now totally dead. The lights, the horn, the engine--nothing worked. The engine had been tuned up two weeks earlier with no problems.

There were still no other cars on the road, so she tried to use her cellphone. Strangely, the cellphone was also dead. Repeated efforts to get the car or phone to work failed.

She sat there wondering what had happened to her car and phone, and what she could do to fix her situation. Movement through the sunroof overhead caught her eyes. She peered upward and couldn't believe her eyes; a huge black craft was hovering mere feet above her car. It flashed a bright white light, temporarily blinding her. When her vision returned, the craft was gone.

She tried her phone and car again, but both remained inoperable. Suddenly, she saw that the black craft was back. It hovered about 300 feet away and ten feet above the ground, featureless and silent, manta-ray in shape, and about the size of a house. It had red and white lights on the bottom and a greenish-glow in the back. She saw what may have been a porthole or window, but couldn't be sure.

She shouted at the craft, blaming it for stranding her. She grabbed her camera. The craft moved forward as though posing, but as she tried to take a picture, the camera malfunctioned. It was a new camera, only two weeks old.

Richter tried to start the car again when she heard a voice say, "Do not start your car."

She felt strangely calm. She tried her cellphone again, but it was still dead. She decided she would get out of her car to take a closer look at the strange craft.

"Do not try to get out of your car," the same voice said again, as though somebody was right next to her.

"I have to go home," Richter said. "I am afraid to stay here. I need to get back on the highway before it gets dark."

The craft didn't respond and Richter had no choice but to sit there and look at it. A few moments later, the voice said, "You can go now."

She tried the ignition again and to her amazement, the car engine started normally, and all the dash lights and instruments were working. It was now 5:00 p.m. She had been pulled over for about thirty minutes.

As she drove off, she was surprised to see the craft was now pacing her car. She sped up and so did the craft. She slowed down and it slowed down too. It approached to within 150 feet, still cruising only about ten feet above the ground. "It was so amazing to see this up close," says Richter. "I was never afraid of this craft at all. For some reason I felt secure. It gave me a nice sense that I couldn't put my finger on, but I knew I was safe."

It paced her car for another fifteen minutes. She sent it a mental thank you, and the craft bobbed up and down, then went straight up at super high speeds, becoming a tiny black dot before disappearing from view.

The craft had delayed her journey, but now she could get on the freeway and get home quickly. But as she got on the freeway, she saw that the traffic was badly congested. Suddenly it stopped completely, and looking ahead of her on the road, she saw firetrucks and ambulances with their lights blinking, blocking the roadway completely. There was a very bad accident involving at least five cars.

She and other drivers exited their vehicles to wait for the rescue crews to clean-up the accident. She spoke with the other drivers and learned that the accident had occurred only fifteen minutes earlier.

"I stood there stunned," says Richter. "All of a sudden it hit me that I would have been in this accident if I hadn't been pulled over. I realized that it could not have been coincidental that the black craft held me back...this black craft had pulled me over for that reason, and saved my life."

Richter saw that some of the cars in the accidents were SUVs, and one was the same make, model and color as her own. "It convinced me right then and there that the craft had done this remarkably kind act and saved my life."[4]

It may seem strange that ETs would prevent car accidents. Strange or not, many people are making this claim. The following case is a good example and involves a rare type of encounter that investigators call a "car lift" case.

UFO Rescues Stranded Motorists

In the fall of 1959, three friends (all teen-agers) left their homes in Hollywood, California and ended up in Goldfield, south of Tonopah, Nevada. One of the witnesses, fourteen-year-old Bradley (not his real name) had also brought along his girlfriend.

Bradley writes that they had pulled off the highway and their pickup became stuck in the sand. Attempts to extricate themselves only ended up burying the truck more deeply, until it was buried up to its hubcaps. The teen-agers spent the next few hours trying to dig themselves out, but the sand was too deep. They decided that one of them would have to walk out in the morning and they resigned themselves to spending the night in the desert.

The four of them sat in the truck star-gazing and talking when the conversation eventually turned to flying saucers. Bradley's girlfriend said, "Let's see if we can contact a saucer to help us."

Only half-serious and not expecting anything to happen, Bradley and his girlfriend "started trying to telepathically contact a saucer."

Writes Bradley, "Not long afterward we all saw a light approaching. I don't know the direction it came from. It looked just like a bright star, except it was moving toward us. It got much brighter as it drew overhead...At that moment we felt the truck move. It rose straight up in the air about a foot or two off the ground, floated to the middle of the road, and gently set down. Then the light moved back in the direction it came from and blinked out."

At the time, Bradley recalls that they all screamed in fear and left the area. However, forty years later he was able to contact his former girlfriend. Writes Bradley, "The first thing she said was, 'What do you remember about that night?' We agreed on all the details except I remembered screaming and she remembered laughing."

While the case does admittedly have fantastic features, the witnesses have sought no publicity and insisted upon remaining anonymous. Nor did they report the sighting until many years later.[5]

Help from ETs comes in many forms. In most cases, intervention comes only in extreme need, to save a person from devastating loss. The following example may be unique in that the purpose for the intervention was to secure the financial wellbeing of an abductee.

ET Employment Agency?

In his book, *Abducted by Aliens*, Chuck Weiss describes his lifelong contact with gray ETs, including numerous healings. While he has had many interactions with the grays, one particular incident stands out above the others.

At the time, Weiss had been unemployed for a prolonged period. One evening, he had one of his alien "dreams." Writes Weiss, "I was given a sheet of paper by my supervising Gray and told to look at it very carefully."

As usual, Weiss felt complete deference to the gray and believed that his cooperation with the ET was extremely important. He studied the paper carefully. It showed columns of letters grouped together, along with slashes. "It didn't make any sense to me," says Weiss, "and that's where the dream ended."

A few months later, Weiss's employment agency sent him to a company that specialized in copying and dubbing radio and television commercials. Weiss was given the job of reviewer. His duties were to review work orders to make sure they were coded correctly.

"After a round of introductions in my new office, I was shown the paperwork that I was expected to proofread. My jaw dropped to the floor when I saw a column of station call letters running down the left side of the paper...It was exactly what I had been shown months earlier by my supervising Gray!"

Weiss was shocked. Had the grays set up this job opportunity for him? Writes Weiss, "It was suddenly obvious to me that it had been determined long before I went to work there that I would find employment at that particular company and in that particular office of the company. I was blown away. Aside from a couple of spontaneous healings that I couldn't be sure weren't to just keep their rat running the maze, this was my first real indication that, for whatever reason, I was somehow special to them. I had never heard before of the ETs going out of their way to find a job for an experiencer, nor have I since. After five months of working at the company as a temp, I was made a permanent hire with vacations and full benefits."[6]

Of all the UFO-rescue cases, this next example is perhaps the most dramatic, and involves people who were lost at sea.

Rescued Castaways

In the first week of June 1994, an event occurred which--up to that time--was unparalleled in the history of sea-lore. Each year, scores of boats sail in a massive regatta from New Zealand to Tonga. The event attracts sailors from across the world, and this year was no different. Dozens of boats were strung out across the South Pacific Ocean. Some were professional sailors; others were families with little sailing experience. It was an annual event that was supposed to be fun. However, this year, disaster was going to strike.

With little warning, the pathway of the race was hit by a storm bomb--a Force 12 storm. In a matter of hours, weather turned from gusty, to nasty, to life-threatening. One minute, scores of people were enjoying a nice day of sailing; the next minute, they were fighting for their lives.

More than a dozen boats fell into the path of the rogue storm. Each attempted at first to battle the ever-increasing wind and waves. The wind worsened quickly, reaching speeds in excess of 100 knots. And with the wind came waves, reaching at first fifty feet high, then seventy, and finally an incredible 100 feet in height!

One by one, the boats began to capsize, roll, become de-masted, and swamped. Suddenly the Royal New Zealand Navy, the Royal New Zealand Air Force and several other private and commercial boats found themselves embroiled in the single largest South Pacific rescue operation in human history. Dozens of unfortunate people found themselves fighting for their lives in a Force 12 storm.

The rescuers quickly surveyed the situation and began to rescue those who were in the worst distress. Those who were severely injured or about to sink were put first on the list. Those who felt they might be able to hang on a few hours longer were forced to continue the constant battles against the screaming wind and terrifying 100-foot waves.

The rescuers performed their work quickly and smoothly. One by one, they plucked the helpless survivors from the sea. They knew they had to work quickly before the sea claimed any victims.

As they expected, they ran into problems. One problem was locating the boats in the mountainous seas. Because so many boats had their EPIRB radio-beacons activated, the signals had become crossed, making it impossible for the rescuers to pinpoint the position of many of the survivors.

Rescuing the survivors was all but impossible if they couldn't be found. Although the rescuers and survivors were in radio contact, the survivors were not able to give an exact position because of the cloudy skies, mountainous seas and the fact that all their energy was being spent on trying to stay alive. It was extremely frustrating for both the rescuers and the survivors to be so close, and yet not be able to make physical contact.

One of the boats struggling to survive was called the Ramtha. The crew consisted of two members, Bill and Robyn Forbes of Australia. Both of them had battled the storm for more than a day. They were badly bruised and completely exhausted. It was only after their sails became stripped and their steering mechanism broke that they decided to radio for help. They were both terrified and knew that they could capsize at any moment. They had to find some way to make their position known and get off their boat. Yet all they could do was pray and continue their struggle for survival. The rescuers assured them that they were on their way, if only the couple could hang on a little longer.

As they clung to their bunks inside the small cabin, the couple's attention was drawn to a bright light hovering low in the sky above their boat. At first they thought it was a flare, but there was a strange quality about it. "Something had changed," writes Tony Ferrington (who authored a book about the storm.) "Something was different. At first Robyn had trouble identifying it. Then she realized they were bathed in light. She moved out of the shelter and stared in awe at a green orb that hovered to port, illuminating the angry world about them. She couldn't believe her eyes.

"It was impossible to pinpoint the exact source of the light. It was unlike anything she'd experienced before, certainly completely different from the lightning that had shattered the darkness earlier in the evening."

"Bill, come look at this," said Robyn.

"What the hell is it?" he asked.

Neither knew the answer. They watched the globe of light as it hovered in place a mere twenty feet above their mast. It was obvious to both of them that it was neither lightning nor St. Elmo's Fire because the light lasted so long and was so bright. Furthermore, it began changing colors, turning from white to orange, then green to white and back to orange.

Bill Forbes was also a pilot and knew that this light was definitely unusual. "I've never seen anything like it," he says. "It's massive. Maybe it's a fireball. It's not lightning. It's just hovering."

Meanwhile, unknown to them, the rescuers--the crew of the commercial vessel Monowai--were a mere twelve miles away, but still unable to locate the Ramtha. Then suddenly, they saw the light. They too thought at first it was a flare. This caused some obvious confusion. Aboard the Monowai, they argued over the possibility of the light being a flare, but the unusual nature of the light caused them to rule out this theory. Nevertheless, the captain ordered that a radio message be sent asking if any nearby boats had launched a flare.

Back aboard the Ramtha, Bill and Robyn Forbes heard the message and immediately radioed the Monowai, saying they had seen the strange light. The rescuers asked if they had launched a flare. They denied it, but said that the light was hovering directly over their boat. The rescuers confirmed the sighting and location of the strange light and recorded the event in the Monowai's official logbook.

Rescue was impossible until morning, and there were still other vessels in worse distress than the Ramtha. Luck, however, was with the Forbes, and because the Monowai was so close and now knew the exact location of the Ramtha, it was decided that they would be rescued first.

At dawn, the crew of the Monowai executed a quick and efficient rescue, saving the Forbes from what could have been an awful ending. The Forbes had begun their voyage in hopes of reaching spiritual enlightenment In fact, the name of their boat, the Ramtha, comes from a popular channeler who coincidentally, claims to be an extraterrestrial from the Pleiades. It seems clear that a UFO was integral to the Forbes' rescue.

Afterward no mention was made of the UFO and its role in the rescue operation. But it was apparent to everyone, however, that something strange had just happened. Although nobody wanted to admit it, it was apparent that a UFO had appeared and accurately pinpointed the exact location of the stricken Ramtha, effectively saving the crew.

Why would extraterrestrials concern themselves with the rescue of two people in a sinking boat? Why these two people and not others. Around this time--several miles away--another boat sank, and a young couple lost their lives. Their bodies were never found, nor was any trace of their boat. The only evidence left behind was their empty life raft found skidding over the waves.

But as it turns out, there was another boat in the same storm that also had an unusual experience. The boat was called the Heart Light, crewed by Diviana Wheeler, her husband and two children. They were all only amateur sailors when they suddenly found themselves caught in the massive storm, sailing a very small boat in 100-foot waves.

Diviana, however, was a UFO contactee. She has had ET contacts and psychic premonitions her whole life. In fact, before they left on their journey, she had a clear premonition that she and her family would soon have one of the most terrifying experiences of her life. In her premonition, she clearly foresaw that their lives might be in jeopardy and that they would travel "to the edge of peril." She confided to her husband, who told her not to worry. They had just recently experienced a severe storm, and he thought that perhaps her premonition had referred to that. He knew better than to simply ignore her visions; they had proved far too accurate in the past. However, he was extremely eager to continue the trip. The weather was perfect. There was no logical reason not to go, except for the premonition. After much discussion, they finally decided to continue their journey and be cautious.

A few days out from New Zealand, they noted the worsening wind, and checked back at weather stations. There were no reports of any storm. However, it was obvious the wind was blowing harder and the waves were getting higher. And then, almost instantly, a huge wind swept over their boat and a series of forty-foot waves began battering the hull. The storm had struck with lightning speed, and now they knew that Diviana's premonition had come true.

As the storm worsened, Diviana suddenly felt the presence of her alien visitors. They repeated to her the same message over and over: "The Kingdom of Heaven is near at hand."

The storm became worse, until those aboard the Heart Light knew that they were in peril for their lives. By now they had turned on their EPIRB radio-beacon and had asked to be rescued. However, they now discovered that there were many others in worse distress and that they were going to have to wait.

Shortly later, the boat was knocked down by the waves, turning the cabin into chaos and sending the crew flying into the walls. It was to be the first of many near-capsizes.

Diviana felt the presence of her alien visitors very strongly and began to receive personal messages for each member of the family. Diviana shared the messages with each of them. "I have been told we are going into a vortex, that is where we are being taken. The boat is going to go to her spot and your job is to keep her moving." Diviana told them how they each had to stay awake and just steer the boat by instinct. She told everyone exactly where to stand and what to do in the event of capsize. She didn't tell them that she had meditated earlier and saw in a precognitive vision, the Heart Light sinking beneath the surface of the sea. She knew it was only a matter of time before their boat actually sunk.

The waves continued to batter the Heart Light until, suddenly, inevitably, like nearly every boat in the path of the storm, the Heart Light was broached by a wave. Although they didn't capsize, the engines were flooded, the steering mechanism

425

jammed and the hull had a huge crack in it. Almost immediately they began to take on water.

The Wheelers were lucky--a commercial fishing vessel was only thirty miles away and was able to easily locate their position. They had been forced to wait a long time for rescue, but managed to hold on. By now the storm was beginning to blow itself out. However, the Wheelers were still delighted to see the rescue boat. By the time the boat had pulled alongside the Heart Light, they were all exhausted to the point of unconsciousness. But they were alive, thanks in part to Diviana's ET friends. They abandoned their boat, taking with them only a few belongings.

Almost immediately, the Heart Light settled lower in the water. In less than a few hours after they abandoned the Heart Light, the Wheelers stood aboard the deck of the rescue ship and watched their boat sink to the bottom of the sea. They knew that if the rescue ship had come only three hours later, they would be following the Heart Light to wherever it landed.

Incidentally, the Heart Light's original name was the Pleiades Child. The fact that another boat was named the Ramtha may seem to stretch the possibility of coincidence to the limit. And yet, that is not the end of the story.

The Wheelers had no idea that a UFO had been seen nearby and was involved in the rescue operations. Neither did any of the rescuers or other survivors know about Diviana's connection with UFOs. It all comes together to form one of the strangest events in UFO history. Aliens rescue stranded sailors. It sounds like science-fiction, and yet, the event is extremely well-verified.

The whole ordeal ends on an even stranger note. About one week after the storm, after everybody had been rescued and all traces of the storm were gone, another private vessel was sailing through the area when they spotted a strange light hovering above the surface of the sea. They radioed to the New Zealand Air Force who sent out a plane to the location of the mysterious light.

To their surprise, they found the wreck of the Ramtha. The UFO had again pinpointed the exact location of the boat. It just so happened that the owners of the Ramtha, Bill and Robyn Forbes, had lost everything they possessed when they abandoned their boat. However, because the "strange green ball of light" had guided rescuers to their boat again, the Forbes were reunited with the Ramtha and regained possession of their craft. It appears to have been one last gesture of goodwill on the part of the UFO.[7]

In this next case, ETs didn't prevent a vehicle accident, but they provided help on the scene, rescuing the witness from what would've been a very hazardous situation.

"They Fixed My Motorcycle"

One evening in the early 1960s, real-estate agent "Sherri Jamison" was driving her motorcycle along an isolated road through the Watchung Mountains of rural New Jersey, when she lost control of her motorcycle and crashed.

It was the middle of the night and nobody was around to help her. While she was okay, her motorcycle had been damaged and the kick-starter was so bent, that the engine could not be turned on.

Moments after the accident occurred, Sherry was shocked to see two strange figures approach her. "They were like grays, but they were not grays."

The figures were tall, with large dark eyes, white skin and bald heads, but otherwise looked almost human. They wore beige-gray body suits.

Says Sherry, "There were two of them. They looked at me and silently picked up the motorcycle, took the [kick]bar and straightened it...I nodded and kicked it...and off I went."

Sherry reports that the ET used his hands to straighten out the crumpled metal. No words were spoken, nor messages received. Sherry felt some fear at first, but realized they were trying to help her. "I wish now I could have not been so worried or disturbed," says Sherry, "that I could have paid more attention. But they weren't threatening...It was very strange."[8]

As we have seen, most cases of benevolent ET intervention occur only in life-threatening occasions. But for every rule, there are exceptions. We have already examined one case in which an abductee's employment was secured. In this next case, ETs again secured a person's financial wellbeing, though in a different way.

Aliens Lead Man to Gold

Late one evening in July 1939, gold prospector Joao Lucindo was camping in an isolated area near Serra Do Gordo, Brazil when he was woken up by a loud whistling sound. Lucindo grabbed a lantern and a rifle and went to investigate. He found a light in the forest where he saw two tall humanoid figures almost six feet in height, each wearing metallic body-suits.

The men told Lucindo to look up. When he did, he saw a large metallic disc-shaped object. Suddenly the two men grabbed him and all of them went up into the craft. Inside, Lucindo was examined and told that his experience would benefit his family.

The night after being released, Lucindo had a strange dream during which the humanoids he had seen told him precisely where to dig for gold in the mountains. He eventually went to prospect where the humanoids had instructed. At this location, he found a rich vein of gold, which improved his family fortunes.

Lucindo died in 1970, shortly after sharing his experience with Brazilian UFO researcher, Jackson Luiz Camargo.[9]

While encounters with reptilians are often described as unpleasant, as we have seen, there are cases during which reptilians have healed people. In the following case, a person was saved from certain death by a reptilian.

Reptilian Saves Man from Drowning

In January of 1977, twenty-year-old Jose Alvarez was hiking in the high basin area of Amazonia, east of Lima, Peru. He was seeking a water source when he fell into a marsh and became trapped. "In spite of my efforts," he said, "I could not get out of it and I had lost all hopes to survive when, suddenly, four small beings appeared...They were less than one meter tall, the body covered with green scales, and their hands had three fingers with claws...Uttering growls and gesticulating, they held branches to me that allowed me to pull myself back on firm ground."

Once freed from the swamp by the strange creatures, Alvarez fainted. When he woke up, the beings were gone.[10]

The above account may sound unusual, but in fact, this next case is nearly identical, only it occurred many thousands of miles away. In this case, the witness was not only healed, but as with many people who have had healings, he feels that his intelligence was increased.

ET Saves Boy from Drowning

A similar account is that of a young boy from outside Cidra, Puerta Rico. He lived on a six-acre farm with his mother and siblings. At age six, he was hunting for flowers and fell into a marsh near his home. The witness reports that he was up to his neck in mud and was sure that he "was not going to make it." He lost consciousness.

When he woke up, he was lying in the grass alongside the pond. A small figure wearing reflective clothing stood next to him. Shortly after the boy woke up, the figure disappeared in a flash of light. Following the incident, the boy says he was taken from his room about twice a week. He never remembered where he went, but feels that the ETs increased his IQ. His teachers were amazed at his progress, and he graduated first in his class of more than 400 students.[11]

A third example of a person saved from drowning comes from a woman who's had contact most of her life. This life-saving incident occurred when she was only four-years-old, and was to be the first of many incidents of contact.

ET Saves Woman from Drowning

Rose Shelhart has had UFO experiences her whole life. Her husband, William Shelhart is featured in this book, having experienced a healing of his tendonitis and arthritis. While Rose hasn't been healed, she does recall a miraculous incident that occurred in the mid-1930s in Rotenburg, Germany. She was only four years old and was playing in the woods behind her home when she fell into the river. "I was playing with some children's dishes," says Rose, "and all I remember was, I'm drowning, I don't know which way is up or down. Then somebody pulled me out and didn't say a word. And when I looked around to see who it was, they had disappeared."

It wasn't until years later, after many UFO encounters, that Rose discovered who had rescued her. While undergoing hypnotic regression to recall a recent missing time encounter, Rose was instead brought back to the childhood incident where she had nearly drowned and learned that her rescuers were the ETs that had been visiting her throughout her life.[12]

This next example of benevolent ET intervention is among the most unusual, and shows that help can come when you least expect it, from the most unexpected of sources.

UFO Prevents Rape

One evening in August 1986, Carolyn (pseudonym) found herself in a dangerous situation. She was at the Waweep Campground near Page, walking along the shore of Lake Powell, Arizona. She was alone when, without warning, a bald-headed man attacked and tried to rape her. He forcefully threw Carolyn down so that she was half-in and half-out of the lake. Then he climbed on top of her and pinned her to the ground. Looking up, Carolyn saw a pair of what she first thought were shooting stars. One disappeared, but the other suddenly dropped down and "seemed to land at the end of the lake."

Carolyn assumed at first that it must be an airplane, but then suddenly it moved toward them. At the same time, the winds began to pick up. The "plane" now took on the appearance of a "big ball of fog." It approached closer and the wind became so strong it was lifting up small stones which struck both of them.

At this point, Carolyn's attacker stood up and looked at the object. He became frightened and ran away, yelling to Carolyn, "We better get out of here!"

Says Carolyn, "I looked at him and the ball of fog and decided I would rather go with the ball of fog. So I started walking out into the water toward the ball of fog. Then it just vanished. The water and wind calmed down and it was quiet again. I did not know what to make of this. I have not heard of many reports like this, but it seemed like it made a special trip down from the sky just to rescue me from this man."

Carolyn reported her account to NUFORC in the hopes of finding more information about her experience."[13]

These types of UFO rescue cases are not well-known, even within the UFO community. And yet, as can be seen, many different types of rescues have occurred. Once again, we are left with the question, why are ETs saving people? What does this say about their relationship to us, and their agenda on our planet? Could it be that some aliens are altruistic?

Chapter Twenty-Seven
Experiencers and Psychic Healing

Medical healings are now a recognized symptom of an encounter with a UFO. Another lesser known symptom is that many experiencers are themselves psychic healers, often as a result of their contacts with ETs.

Among the first to remark on this was Gordon Creighton, who wrote the first article about the healing power of UFOs. Creighton also studied psychic healing and even underwent it himself. He was impressed by the similarity of how cuts have been healed in both UFO accounts and during psychic healings. "The body is laid open paranormally," writes Creighton, "as if the operator were opening the magnetic body, unzipping it, so to speak. There is almost no blood. A few passes--still never touching the flesh--then he zips it up again."

Creighton speculates that psychic healing accounts and UFO healing accounts appear to share remarkable connections. Writes Creighton, "It's an intriguing coincidence that in both Brazil and the Philippines, all of these healers began to develop their powers around 1947 and 1948--after the modern wave of sightings began."[1]

John Mack MD has also noticed a connection between UFO encounters and the ability to perform healings. Writes Mack, "Many abductees seem to gain healing powers themselves. Although abductees may continue to resent the abduction experiences and fear their reoccurrence, at the same time many, in one way or another, come to feel that they are participating in a life-creating or life-changing process that has deep importance and value...In addition, many abductees...appear to undergo profound personal growth and transformation. Each appears to come out of his or her experiences concerned about the fate of the Earth and the continuation of human and other life-forms."[2]

A case from Brazil is that of Vera Lucia. One night in 1956, Lucia was in her home in Valencia, Rio De Janeiro. Suddenly a man carrying a flashlight approached her home. She experienced missing time. Later under hypnosis, she recalled seeing a man and woman with Asian features and dark olive skin float into her room. They both wore tight silver suits and carried luminous wands. They appeared to be testing Lucia's body. When they stopped, there was a flash of blue light and the figures were gone. Following the incident, Lucia learned she had the power of healing, a power which never left her.[3]

UFO-inspired healers are turning up across the world. On January 7, 1970, two men (Aarno Heinonen and Esso Viljo) were skiing near Imjarvi, Finland when they saw a bright light approach. A round, ten-foot-wide, metallic object hovered about twelve feet above the ground. The object emitted a beam of light and the men saw a three-foot-tall being wearing green coveralls and boots, and a conical helmet. Its skin was pale and it had a hooked nose. A mist descended over the area, there was a flash, sparks and a flame and the craft departed. Both men suffered negative physiological effects from the encounter, including numbness, vomiting and more. Viljo refused to discuss the experience, however, Heinonen says he obtained special abilities as a result of the encounter, and afterward, became a clairvoyant and healer until his death in the 1990s.[4]

Case after case can be marched out. Consider Antonio Alves Ferreira of San Luis, Maranhao, Brazil, who claims to have had numerous contacts with humanoids with dark skin, Asian eyes, pointed ears, thick eyebrows, large heads and fine black hair. Beginning on January 4, 1975, Ferreira claims to have taken eleven trips to the ETs' planet. He had many unusual experiences. During one visit he was made by them to swallow a small whitish pill. Afterward, his bio-electric field became charged and sometimes when he touched metal objects, they would bend and break. During this period, he was "able to affect medical cures in people..." Interestingly, despite his healing abilities, Ferriera himself was unable to walk without crutches, a condition the ETs never cured.[5]

Still another case is that of Joyce Bowles of Winchester, Hampshire, England. Bowles, a British Rail powder room attendant was abducted on three separate occasions in 1976 and 1977. The case follows the standard patterns of abductions, including some paranormal effects. Bowles has a history of psychic experiences and is well-known in her neighborhood for her ability to cure animals.[6]

As presented earlier in this book, several cases of UFO healings have occurred in Tbilisi, Russia. There are also a few cases there in which witnesses have become psychic healers. One lady became a healer after an entity entered her body, giving her the ability to see where a person's illness is manifesting, and then guiding her to administer a psychic cure. Another Tbilisi case is that of Professor Bochereshoni, a mental health doctor. While working in the hospital, the doctor was visited by aliens who assisted him in diagnosing and curing patients with mental illnesses. According to the report, the aliens also provided written formulas to cure a variety of illnesses.[7]

Another person who claims to have a dual alien-human identity and resultant healing powers is Francisco Ramon Jimenez of Torrente, Valencia in Spain. In 1978, when he was eleven years old, Jimenez experienced a contact with ETs who said they were from Ganymede. Jimenez claims that the contacts continued. "Since then," says Jimenez, "I heal with the hands, and without drugs...when I sleep, my body remains on Earth and I go to the planet Ganymede...they have explained to me how to cure people...given me energy."

While in school, Jimenez reportedly exhibited an advanced knowledge of medicine and psychology. When he began to see the insides of people's bodies, he started to perform hands-on-healings, treating people with blindness, paralysis, cancer and more.

Jimenez says that he "charges the batteries" each night with the ETs, and returns to Earth by day to perform healings. "I cannot even cure myself of a simple cold," Jimenez said. "All the energy I have I must use for others."[8]

In 1981, New York psychic healer Jane Allyson told listeners at a conference in New York City that she received her healing power as the result of a close encounter with a UFO on the roof of her Manhattan apartment building.[9]

Jane Allyson is not alone. No discussion of UFOs and psychic healing would be complete without mention of Adrian Dvir. Born in 1958, Dvir became a computer engineer specializing in military computer systems. In 1992, while living in Israel, he began to exhibit mediumistic abilities and soon found himself channeling apparent ETs. Dvir found himself not only in communication with ETs, he became a healer. After a number of successful healings, Dvir began to train others and open up new clinics. People visiting the clinics report a wide variety of healings including of cancer, liver cirrhosis, back pain, headaches, diabetes, immune-deficiencies, and more. In his book, *Healing Entities and Aliens*, Dvir describes his experiences. The healings are reminiscent of Edgar Cayce, providing diagnoses and explanations for illnesses and conditions that traditional medicine was unable to cure. The alien treatments are done in clinics, while Dvir and other mediums channel the ETs. Some patients feel odd sensations of heat, cold, tingling and itching. A few report seeing images of ETs or receiving messages.

Dvir caused a media sensation across Israel and the world, and despite his sudden death in 2004, his influence is still being felt today. Dozens of alien healing clinics across the world use Dvir's model to conduct channeled cures.[10]

Judy Carroll of Brisbane, Australia is making waves in the UFO community with her claims of being a human-gray alien hybrid. Carroll has had UFO experiences her entire life, including missing time abductions, which she describes in her book, *Human by Day, Zeta by Night*. Her early encounters were shrouded in fear and amnesia. However, starting in 1983 when she was thirty years old, she began having fully conscious experiences of being taken onboard a craft. Once onboard, Carroll found herself to be in gray alien form. Her job involved working in a "clinic" where she would assist in the healing of humans. She was trained by an alien teacher named Maris who instructed her in meditation and healing techniques.

Carroll was also healed herself. She suffered from a tightness in her throat. Maris was able to cure her, she says. "I remember him massaging my neck and putting his long fingers in my mouth and down my throat, where I said I was tight."

Today, Carroll works as a healer both on Earth, and aboard the UFOs. Her UFO abductions occur at least once a month. She says the gray aliens' single greatest agenda is the healing of human kind.[11]

Southern California abductee, Linda, and her sister, Sherri, have reported multiple healings. Linda says that the aliens have taught her and her family how to perform psychic healings.

Linda recalls being taken to a room inside a UFO that contained more than sixty people. There was a large crystal in the center of the room that emitted a strange type of energy. The group was told by the aliens that they were being taught. Linda felt a strange electricity flowing through her body and out her hands. "I'm being told I can learn to heal, myself," Linda says. "It's okay to use this power."[12]

Budd Hopkins has also run across these types of cases. Michael Bershad (whose account appeared in Hopkins' book, *Missing Time*, under the pseudonym Steve Kilburn) reports that his back was physically opened by the ETs who then proceeded to activate certain nerves as if they were testing his nervous system. Afterward, they closed up his back, leaving no scars. Ever since the abduction, Bershad has suffered from unexplained back pain. He does not feel that the ETs were friendly, and after subsequent abductions, he began to explore various techniques to keep the ETs away.

In 1993, Bershad spoke at the Los Angeles, California chapter of MUFON. One attendee asked if there were any positive effects caused by his experiences with the ETs. Bershad said that as a result of his abductions, he has become a psychic healer. He was able to provide examples of this ability, stating that he was able to cure two ladies of cancer. The cures were performed over the phone.[13]

Another case of someone who became a healer as a result of a UFO abduction is Mr. Cao, of Beijing. One December evening, Cao experienced an abduction. Afterward he healed a Chinese girl from Qinhuangdao, Hebei Province using "alien energy." Zhang Jingping, the director of the department of the World Chinese UFO Association investigated Cao's claims in 2000. He had Cao placed under regressive hypnosis, and also gave him a lie detector test, which he passed. Using the information retrieved, Jingping was able to locate the girl who had been healed. He called the case the most reliable of all the cases he investigated.[14]

John Mack MD writes that a number of his clients have exhibited healing abilities as a result of their alien encounters. Scott of Massachusetts is one of several examples. Writes Mack, "Scott himself, in addition to his increasing curiosity about the spiritual dimensions of the phenomenon, has begun to meet with an acupuncturist, and more recently, with a shamanic healer. He is also increasingly challenging the traditional model."

Scott himself says of some therapists, "I feel I could heal, I could help them more than they could help me..."[15]

Another of Mack's clients, Paul of New Hampshire, has experienced many UFO encounters and has become increasingly interested in alternative healing methods. Paul says he was given volumes of ideas concerning "healing technologies." He has also become a healer himself. Writes Mack, "Those who know him outside of the therapeutic setting, such as Pam, Julia and other abductees, all testify to his extraordinary intuitive and healing abilities."[16]

UFO researcher Don Worley investigated the encounters of a woman named "Ann." Ann was told by her contacts to move to Colorado to be safe from upcoming Earth changes. Ann reports the ability to talk to spirits and give psychic readings; and she says that her bio-electric field constantly affects machines.

"Ann also possesses wonderful healing powers," writes Don Worley. "Her ability to do this came about accidentally when her husband stepped on a nail and drove it all the way through his foot. By using visualization and without ever touching his foot, she used her mind to get his foot very hot and tingly at the wound, and she was able to stop the pain. The next day the hole in his foot healed and was even gone."

Regarding her ability to heal, Ann says, "I have never practiced Reiki, nor have I ever attempted to learn how. I just knew how. I can run my hands over someone and feel the pain as well as visualize it. I am very adept at sending away pain, sickness, injury and even depression. I have done remote healing the last several years with some success."

At first, Ann found herself exhausted and ill after performing a healing. She eventually learned to release the negative energies and draw new energies from the atmosphere around her. "I bet the whole process looks crazy or silly," she says, "but it does work."[17]

There is no shortage of cases like this. In 1994, southern California abductee Kim Carlsberg appeared with several abductees on the short-lived television program, *The Other Side*. Carlsberg, who has experienced several terrifying abductions, spoke for herself as well as the entire panel when she said that many of the experiencers she knew, including herself have done psychic healings. As he said, "All of us on this panel are hands-on healers."

Researcher Barbara Lamb reports that abductees are "often" trained in various "healing techniques." Many of her clients have come away from their experiences with the belief that they have the ability to heal themselves and others.

Writes Lamb, "There is a woman I've been working with, and she is doing Reiki healing. She's been doing that for three or four years now and is very serious about that and really does effectively run energy. And some of her experiences with extraterrestrials involve her being taught healings, and with all that being very enhanced. And her son, who is now about six years old...starting at age three...was talking about going on these trips with his space friends at night and riding around in the craft, and the things that they'd have him drink, and the strange baths that they'd have him get into, and all this stuff he'd never heard anywhere before. She knew he hadn't encountered anything like that in the media or anybody that knew anything. And he and his little cousin, a little girl who is two years younger than he is, have been trained by the extraterrestrials in doing physical healing. And there was one time when the mother, my client, was preparing lunch for him and his little cousin who was visiting for the day. And she cut her hand very badly with a paring knife. And it was bleeding, hurting and stinging...And it looked like she might have to take herself to the emergency room. She was, of course, concerned.

"And these two kids hopped off their lunch counter stools there in the kitchen and said, 'Oh, we'll heal it. We'll do our space Reiki on you.' And so they went into these movement which she said looked very akin to Tai Chi type of movements. Maybe they were Chi Gong movements for all we know. But anyway, they just healed this cut. She said within a half a minute, the pain really reduced and the blood stopped and it started to congeal and heal up. And I saw her probably about three days later, and it was just barely a little line on her hand that I could see had been this big, open, bleeding cut. She could feel the heat coming toward her from them.

"Another woman that I work with...does body work, massage work. And she's only done that for a few years too. She used to work for a corporation and do stuff that was really different. And in some of our regressions we realized that she is learning a lot of energy healing work from the extraterrestrials when she's onboard the craft...she still does some of the energy work with them, learning a lot about human energy fields."

"Erica" is one of Lamb's clients. Writes Lamb, "Because of her encounters with extraterrestrials, Erica has developed an increasing amount of psychic ability and healing powers, which she uses frequently in her life."

Another of Lamb's clients, "Marcia" had repeated contacts with a gray-type ET who gave her very specific training with healing. "This particular being," Lamb writes, "seemed to be very concerned about the Earth children who suffered from autism, and she trained Marcia how to treat them. Marcia credited her contacts with this particular being for inspiring the dedication she developed to the care of autistic children. She avidly pursued reading books about the subject, and she spent time volunteering at a center for autistic children. With great success, she promoted the unusual methods of treatment that she had learned from her ET encounters."

Another of Lamb's clients, "Simon," has been having contacts with gentle mantis-type beings most of his life. He has also received training in healing. Writes Lamb, "They communicated to Simon that they had been aware of him for a long time, and they were training him in healing skills in order that he might assist huge groups of humans in the future after large-scale disasters would occur on the Earth."

Yet another of Lamb's clients, "Katherine," also reports being trained in energetic healing techniques. "In one regression," writes Lamb, "Katherine described finding herself in a small round craft, standing at a table similar to a massage table and surrounded by several Zeta beings. They were performing some kind of healing work on an abducted human male who was lying unconscious on the table. Katherine recalled them meticulously instructing her on techniques for working on the energy system of the man, as well as techniques for healers to intermingle their own energy and surrounding energy in the atmosphere with the energy of the man in need of healing. Although prior to her regressions, Katherine had been unaware of the training she had received from the Zetas, in her waking life she had been actively involved in learning some methods of energy healing. Eventually Katherine left her corporate management job and established a successful practice in energy healing work."

A final example from Lamb's research is the case of "Sara," who was given the ability to heal by an apparent reptilian being. She was taken onto a craft and told to sit in what looked like a barber's chair. Writes Lamb, "A male being, standing behind her, pressed her temples with his hands. This action radiated an energy or vibration into her head that became increasingly uncomfortable. He conveyed to her that he was transmitting energy to her that she would be able to use in her healing work on

440

Earth. She had already been doing healing work for a few years and was very interested in learning new methods. He also told her that her ability to receive telepathic messages and to do channeling would increase."[18]

In my own research, I often hear similar stories. Pat Brown, whose story appeared in my book, *Extraterrestrial Visitations*, is a good example. After experiencing a series of terrifying encounters with grays, she overcame her fear and her encounters became profoundly spiritual. She quit her job as a telephone operator and became a healing massage therapist. She says that sometimes while doing healing work, she sees blue light come from her hands, and in her mind's eye, she can see images of gray ETs working with her to help channel the energy.[19]

Another case is Alicia Hansen, whose two healing accounts (car accident and cyst) appear in this book. In 1995, Hansen cured someone of a fractured toe using the technique of laying on of hands. The patient and doctor were both suitably impressed.

I later had the opportunity to receive an energy healing from her. With my permission, she placed her hands on the soles of my feet and closed her eyes. Strong pulses of energy flowed instantly up my legs. It was a unique and new sensation to me, unmistakable, and somewhat similar to a light electrical shock. She did this for a few moments and then stopped, asking me if I could feel it. I sure could!

On another occasion, I went to a healing session with Mattie, whose account of an eczema healing also appears in this book. No sooner did she begin doing energy work over my body when I saw pastel flashes of color around her hands, followed by an incredible sense of relaxation and calm.

Many other cases could easily be listed. There are enough accounts like the above to fill an entire book. One more case should suffice. Virginia Aronson, whose book *Celestial Healings* recounts many cases, also had the opportunity to experience a healing from an experiencer who channels ET. Diagnosed with cancer and facing a daunting series of medical treatments, Aronson began to investigate alternative avenues of healing. She found David Miller, an Arizona-based healer, and scheduled a session.

Feeling like it had a profoundly positive effect, Aronson cancelled her upcoming surgery to remove her cancerous thyroid. Years later, she's happy and healthy, a fact she attributes at least in part to her UFO healing.[20]

The pattern is clear. In many cases, experiencers come away from their encounters with the ability to heal. It has been reported consistently and often enough to be a predictable effect.

Still, there is more research to be done. Why are aliens teaching people to heal? How effective are these cures?

According to a study by Thomas Bullard of 270 abduction cases, the single most common experience is being physically examined. Second to that, however, is being given messages. This is a pattern I have also seen in my own research.

The messages usually fall into three main categories. One is being given warnings of upcoming disasters or Earth changes. Secondly, there are messages given about alternative energy sources. Third, and most important here, are messages about spirituality and alternative healing.

While it's easy to speculate about UFOs, facts are facts, and actions speak louder than words. The ETs' interest in the health of the human body cannot be denied. Also, it is evident that ETs are interested in teaching people to heal themselves.

Hopefully, cases like these will become the focus of future research so that we can benefit from this knowledge in a more practical way.

Chapter Twenty-Eight
Other Miraculous Healings

Before we can begin to understand and analyze UFO healing cases, it's necessary to understand other forms of miraculous cures. Not all cures are coming from ETs. Miraculous cures have been reported from many sources other than UFOs. People have reported cures from shamans and medicine men and medicine women of indigenous cultures. Other cures have been made by religious figures, angels or at sacred/holy sites. There are countless numbers of accounts involving psychic healers. Near-death experiencers and astral travelers also report cures. Seemingly miraculous cures have also been reported as a result of past-life regression therapy. There are incredible natural cures resulting from lightning strikes. As can be seen, healing comes from a wide variety of sources. By examining these different types of healings, we can arrive at a better understanding of how miraculous healings occur, and their relationship to UFO healings.

Native American Healings

Cures by Native Americans have been well-documented. Some of these include healings performed by world-famous medicine man, Rolling Thunder, a spiritual leader and official spokesman for the Shoshone and Cherokee tribes. He has gained a reputation for performing cures of a wide variety of diseases and injuries.

One well-documented example occurred in April 1971 at the Menninger Foundation in Council Grove, Kansas. Rolling Thunder was there to give a speech when a young man became gravely injured. His leg had been gashed and the wound became badly infected. Medical doctors who were at the scene recommended that the man be rushed immediately to the hospital.

Rolling Thunder volunteered to perform a healing ritual. The man was unable to walk and was in considerable pain. Rolling Thunder began the ritual by lighting his peace pipe and handing it to the patient. A piece of raw meat was placed in a basin to capture the negative energies associated with the injury. After counseling the patient and determining that the healing was justified, he began a "wailing chant" and then sucked at the wound. He turned and vomited into the basin. This procedure was repeated, after which Rolling Thunder placed his hands over the wound and made repeated passes with a sacred feather.

Afterward, the doctors rushed forward to examine the wound. To their shock, the color of the flesh was normal, the swelling had decreased, and the injured man said that he no longer felt any pain. The infection was gone. Minutes later, the man was back on his feet, playing ping-pong.

Rolling Thunder has performed healings regularly for many years. Some other well-documented cases include the partial healing of a polio-related condition, and another of tumorous growths in the throat of a singer.[1]

Another well-known shaman-healer was the Apache Scout, Stalking Wolf, the teacher of Tom Brown Jr., who runs the largest wilderness school in the United States. Says Brown, "Grandfather was a tremendous healer...He had tremendous command of the uses of the plant people, using herbs to cure illnesses that doctors and modern medicine had given up on...His ability to help cure people overcome all illnesses bordered on the miraculous."

Brown describes one event involving a lady stricken with cancer. It had metastasized throughout her body. She was in a coma and expected to die within hours when she met with Stalking Wolf. Tom Brown Jr. watched the healing as it took place. "I saw Grandfather's body begin to vibrate slightly, almost imperceptibly. In the dim room, I could see his hands, as if they glowed, and I had to shake my head to make sure I wasn't seeing things. At that moment, like a dull flash, the old woman's body glowed also, as if illuminated from within, then her body fell back into the original shadow."

Immediately the color returned to the lady's face and she awoke from her coma. Stalking Wolf told the amazed onlookers, "She will walk within the hour but have no recollection of what has taken place. She will be restored to her full health within seven suns."

How had the cure taken place, Brown asked. Stalking Wolf told him that it was the "life force" and "the spirit which moves through all things."

They visited the woman a few days later and found her in perfect health. "All traces of illness and coma were gone," says Brown.[2]

Another well-known shaman healer was Evelyn Eaton, who was taught by a Paiute medicine man. One dramatic healing involved her neighbor's cat who had been hit by a car. The cat's back was broken and the cat was totally paralyzed. The vet had been called to put the animal to sleep. Eaton wasn't aware that the cat was injured when she passed her hand softly over the cat's back and squeezed its tail. The cat jumped up, perfectly healed. The owner was amazed. Since then, Eaton became a well-known psychic healer until her death in 1983.[3]

Another common source of healings comes from religious figures of all kinds. Angels, saints, religious shrines, holy springs...all have produced healings.

Healings from Religious Figures, Angels and Sacred Sites

Miraculous healings come from a wide variety of sources. J.Z. Knight, who channels Ramtha, believes she was cured of cancer while in church. The minister was praying for her recovery when "there was a sudden flash of blue light from the top of the tent. The flash became an electrical flash, almost like lightning and just as bright. The blue lightning streak went vertically down, straight through my body." Afterward, Knight was diagnosed as free of cancer. She later performed miraculous cures on her own children.[4]

Consider the healings which have taken place at a spring in Lourdes, France. In 1858, a young girl named Bernadette experienced a vision of the Virgin Mary near her home in Lourdes. In the years that followed, the area was visited by thousands of people seeking a healing from the spring which appeared there. UFO researcher, Jacques Vallee noticed the many parallels between religious visitations and UFO events, and made a study of the healings which have occurred at Lourdes. One involves a man cured of a severe leg injury after drinking the water from the Lourdes spring. Another was allegedly cured of blindness. Vallee notes that the healings are "not limited" to illnesses that could be considered psychosomatic, but "extend to such improbable cures as tumors and broken bones."

One such Lourdes healing occurred in 1875 to Pierre de Rudder of Belgium. Rudder suffered a compound fracture to his leg, which became infected. Doctors recommended amputation. Rudder refused and begged to go to Lourdes. Before being taken there, Dr. Van Hoestenberghe examined Rudder's leg and said, "There was no sign of healing...the lower part of the leg could be moved in all directions. The heel could be lifted in such a way as to fold the leg in the middle. It could be twisted with the heel in front and the toes in back, all these movements being restricted only by the soft tissues."

At the Lourdes spring, Rudder was overcome by a "strange feeling." His leg was suddenly healed. His wife promptly fainted and Rudder was rushed to a nearby home to be examined. "Not only was the wound closed, but the leg had become completely normal again." Rudder's doctor examined his leg, broke into tears and said, "You are completely cured, de Rudder. Your leg is like that of a newborn baby."

De Rudder became a near celebrity and continued to enjoy excellent health until his death by pneumonia in 1898.[5]

Another similar event is the "Miracle of Fatima" which occurred in Portugal in 1917. One of the most widely-viewed "miracles" in history, thousands of people witnessed a bright light, described by some as metallic, hovering overhead. It began when three children were given messages from the Virgin Mary, who told them that there would be a display on a certain date. This prediction attracted thousands of witnesses, all of whom saw a glowing disc moving through the clouds. Some people also reported miraculous healings. One witness said, "My mother who had a large tumor in one of her eyes for many years, was cured. The doctors who had attended her said they could not explain such a cure."[6]

Modern cases of religious healings continue to occur. In 1987, sixty years following his death, Italian physician, Dr. Giuseppte Moscati (b1881-d1927) was granted sainthood by Pope John Paul II. One of the reasons was because Dr. Moscati was appearing as an apparition and curing terminally ill people of their conditions. A blacksmith dying of leukemia said Dr. Moscati appeared to him and said, "You are well." The blacksmith went immediately to his doctor to discover that his leukemia was gone. In a second case, a man with Addison's disease was sent home by his physicians to die. The man prayed to a portrait of Dr. Moscati and had a dream that the man was operating on him. The next morning, he went back to the hospital where his doctors confirmed that he was cured. In a third case, a young man was dying of meningitis. His mother prayed at Moscati's tomb in Italy. When she returned to the hospital, her son had miraculously recovered. In all three of these cases, the cures were verified by doctors who testified before the Vatican commission on the canonization of saints.[7]

Many other examples could be listed. Jesus himself reportedly performed countless healings of a wide variety of conditions including blindness, lameness, leprosy and more.

Of course, healings are not limited to religious figures. Cases of so called "angelic" healings are not hard to find. After fracturing her spine, Lee Kirk was facing a long difficult path to recovery. Instead she experienced an instantaneous cure after being struck by beams of light from what she perceived to be God. Her self-published book, *I Was Healed by the Light*, presents her experience in detail.

Or take the case of Ralph Walker, an avid tennis player who was diagnosed with a malignancy in his right arm. Doctors recommended an immediate operation and told him to give up any expectations of playing tennis in the future.

Walker's mother prayed for a healing. The night before the operation, Walker was awoken by a man "wearing a white scrub suit with a stethoscope around his neck, carrying blood pressure equipment."

Walker assumed the man was a normal doctor. The man told Walker that he would be all right and would be able to play tennis again. He stared into Walker's eyes and Walker found himself overcome with a feeling of "warmth that seemed to permeate both arms and legs and then his whole body."

The next morning, he mentioned the visit to his doctors, thinking they had arranged it. His doctors denied any visitation and said it must have been a dream. Walker denied this and said the man was "like any doctor. Dressed in white. I sure didn't dream him."

At the hospital, more X-rays were taken, showing that the cancer was gone. His doctor told him, "I have to say that nothing like this has ever happened in my twenty-three years of practice...I mean, Mr. Walker, that these new X-rays show absolutely no trace of any cancer...there is no need for an operation." Ralph now believes he was visited by an angel. Could it have been an alien?[8]

Angels or aliens is not a question easily answered. Consider this case: On January 30, 1985, Steve, a security guard from, Liverpool, England, saw seven glowing figures hovering over Brownlow Hill. He flashed his light, and they swooped toward him. Afraid at first, he saw they were beautiful glowing "angels" and he tearfully thanked them for saving his mother from an ordeal which occurred one month earlier.

Following this incident, a second incident occurred in which a woman crashed her car along the highway nearby. Immediately following the accident, the woman was trapped in the wreckage, then she passed out. Unknown to her, outside witnesses saw "glowing figures" approach and remove her from the vehicle. The paramedics in the ambulance found the woman thirty yards from her vehicle. The woman had no memory of the glowing figures, but said that as she recovered in the hospital, two women approached her and said that they had saved her so that she could continue her "good work." The woman joined a church group and devoted her life to charity work.[9]

One pattern that becomes clear with miraculous healings is that they seem to come from interdimensional sources, from saints, angelic figures and other denizens of the so-called heavenly realms. Even the Native American healings talk of the Spirit Which Moves Through All Things. Another source of healing are near-death and out-of-body experiences, again showing that physical healing seems to come from non-physical sources.

Healings by NDEs and OBEs

Kenneth Ring's book, *The Omega Project*, studies the similarities between near-death experiences and UFO encounters. One of his cases involves what appears to be a miraculous healing.

In 1977, daycare center operator Beryl Hendricks of New York State discovered a tumor in her breast. Doctors promptly removed it. To Hendricks' relief, the tumor was benign.

One year later, Hendricks was shocked to discover another tumor the size of a golf-ball in her breast. She resolved to call her doctor the next day. She went downstairs, joined her husband on the couch and fell unconscious. Her husband was unable to feel a pulse.

Meanwhile, Hendricks found herself apparently out of her body, aboard what seemed to be a spacecraft. "The next thing I remember," Hendricks says, "I was looking out of a round window and seeing the blackest blackness with tiny white sparkles…" She turned around and suddenly realized she had been placed on "some kind of operating table," which was surrounded by several "tall thin figures." A bright light was shining down upon her. The figures spoke telepathically, "Look and see--it is gone." The ETs told Hendricks to "follow her husband," evidently because of recent marital difficulties.

Hendricks then found herself racing back to her body which lay unmoving on the couch. She woke up and began vomiting. Two hours had passed. Almost immediately, Hendricks made the astonishing discovery that "the lump was gone--totally."

Was Hendricks healed as the result of a near-death experience or a UFO? "When you read it," says Kenneth Ring, "please decide into which of our two categories it should be placed."[10]

An equally astonishing case was published in *Beyond UFOs*, edited by Rey Hernandez. In 1980, a motorcycle driver had a bad accident, injuring his body very badly. He felt himself pulled from his body by a magnetic force, into a tunnel of white light. A wise old man appeared, and told him if he went through the tunnel, he could not return, and if he returned, his body was so damaged, medical technology could not fix it. The old man told the motorcycle driver that if he agreed to work for the betterment of humanity, they would heal him. The driver agreed. When he regained consciousness, he was in a hospital bed. His only injury was now a badly broken leg.

Leading NDE researcher, Dr. Melvin Morse MD has documented several cases of NDE-healings. After being diagnosed with cancer of the thyroid gland, "Kathy" underwent treatment. The treatment failed to halt the spread of the cancer and her doctors told her that her case was terminal. She developed pneumonia and was admitted to the hospital, where her condition worsened. She had a cardiac arrest and a near-death experience. She went out of her body and met a "being of light" who filled her with light and told her to return. Upon awakening, she began an immediate recovery from pneumonia. A few weeks later, all traces of her cancer were gone. Writes Morse, "...I find it hard to believe that the NDE did not have a direct influence on the cancer."

Morse presents the case of "Loretta," who as a child, suffered from a case of scarlet fever. Her condition worsened and her doctor and family feared for her survival. Loretta had an NDE and found herself flying out of her body, through a tunnel, and into a wise, loving light. She returned to her body, and to everyone's amazement, began a speedy recovery. Loretta was convinced that the NDE led to her rapid healing.

Then there is the case of "Janet" who had a cancerous lesion on her nose. Two days before her surgery, Janet was woken from sleep to see a "large sphere of light floating about five feet in front of me." The sphere spoke, saying, "You aren't afraid, are you?" Janet became filled with peace. Suddenly the light darted inside her filling her with a powerful feeling of unconditional love and a huge burst of white light. After the experience, Janet's cancer disappeared.[11]

Many other cases could be listed. I interviewed a lady who was in the hospital suffering from uterine cancer. She had a powerful near-death experience involving a journey through a tunnel of light and a trip to a heavenly realm. Upon her return, all traces of her cancer were gone.

Advanced out-of-body travelers report a wide variety of healings, some of chronic or allegedly incurable conditions. There are a surprisingly large number of cases of out-of-body healings on record.

Albert Taylor, an engineer by profession, became interested in OBEs after reading Shirley' MacLaine's book, *Out on a Limb.* After trying the exercises, he found himself to be pretty good at it. This was especially fortunate when he was diagnosed with a major illness.

Writes Taylor, "In early 1992, I was diagnosed with the debilitating disease of multiple sclerosis, better known as MS. After suffering two devastating attacks, I was hospitalized with severe vision and equilibrium problems. My diagnosis was not good. My doctor explained that my physical health would probably degrade over the next few years. Shortly after receiving this less than welcome news, I began to have consciously controlled OBEs. I knew at that time that I had very little to lose by trying this method of healing. Well to make a long story short, be it coincidence or not, I can gratefully state that I have absolutely *no* outward symptoms or physical manifestations of this otherwise crippling disease."[12]

Some astral-travelers have been cured of relatively minor conditions. Terrill Wilson worked alternately as a construction worker and a Mississippi riverboat crewman. In his mid-thirties, he began meditating and having OBEs. About one year after his first OBE, he became ill with the flu. As he says, "I woke up in the middle of the night with a fever and a very sore throat."

As he lay there, Wilson recalled that other astral projectors had been able to heal themselves of illness by simply going out-of-body. Little did he know, he was about to experience the awesome healing power of OBEs.

Writes Wilson, "Curiously wondering if something like this could happen to me, I mustered all the will power within me to try to leave my body. I began thinking of myself as a bodiless unit of awareness moving further and further out the top of my head into blackness, trying to let go of all mental ties to the physical body and physical world. Being sick made it especially difficult to hold this thought pattern, and to keep from forgetting, I had to mentally remind myself over and over what I was trying to do. Finally, maybe forty-five minutes or an hour later, I drifted into sleep.

"I was able to leave my body three times that night, for short intervals that I spent in an Earth-like world with several other people present. I made the acquaintance and talked for a while on two occasions with a fellow who was about my age, but twice I lost control and returned to my body instantly. Each time I returned, unable to tell how sick my physical body was or whether any miraculous healing had taken place, I exited again to the inner world. One time a very noticeable tingling sensation at a spot about two inches from the center of my head caught my attention, and I contemplated on it for a while."

Wilson continued to go out of his body a third time. When he returned to his body, he discovered that he had been healed. "Lo and behold, my fever, nausea, sore throat and head congestion, even my tiredness, were completely gone. Upon waking the next morning, the only trace of sickness in me was a slight sniffle...Similar Soul Travel healings have happened to me a number of times since then, but at the time I looked upon this unexplained healing as something of a miracle."

Another time, Wilson was healed of an eye infection. "A contact lens problem had caused a slight infection in one of my eyes, and it was sore that night at bedtime. I fell asleep and became conscious of being out of my body in an inner life-like world. I consciously moved out of my body a second time later that night, and upon awaking to go to work I noticed that my sore eye was completely healed. Such infections usually required at least a couple of days to heal, but this one was cleared up overnight."

Out-of-body healings seem to be affected by powerful currents of astral energies. Writes Wilson, "One night I was feeling somewhat sick, I woke to find a current of energy flowing through my physical body, funneling into the top of my head and exiting out my feet. It felt something like electricity and the increasing intensity of this current woke me up mentally, although my physical body remained asleep. It rushed through me like a powerful flood of water, seemingly cleansing my physical body. As this was happening, I knew instinctively that this current flowing through me had a potential strength far beyond what I was now receiving, far beyond anything I could even imagine. As the seconds passed, this energy current flowing through me slowly began to subside, and within five seconds or so had faded away altogether. I went back to sleep feeling much better physically, and upon awaking an hour or so later for work, my earlier signs of sickness were completely gone."[13]

Paul Twitchell is probably best known for heading the school of *Eckenkar*, a spiritually-based philosophy which promotes out-of-body travel. Twitchell learned how to travel out-of-body from his father and sister. Says Twitchell, "It was these elementary lessons that saved my life when I was five years old."

At age five, Twitchell had a cold which developed into a severe case of pleurisy. When Twitchell's condition steadily worsened, his sister Kay-Dee recalled that their father said that healings could be performed from the astral state. She assumed a lotus position and after meditating deeply was able to leave her body. She then went over to her sick brother Paul and pulled his astral body out of his physical body. At first, Twitchell thought he had died. His sister, however, explained that he was having an out-of-body experience and to "think of good health, of recovery, of goodness and strength."

Says Twitchell, "The next thing I remember is that I was awakening to find the family and our doctor standing by my bedside. The doc was saying something about a miraculous recovery,"[14]

Robert Bruce began projecting at around age four and is today, a leading researcher and out-of-body explorer. In the late 1990s, Bruce noticed an unexplained pain in his hip which he believed was linked to a "psychic attack."

When his condition worsened, Bruce sought help out-of-body. He traveled into the astral realms where he contacted an advanced spirit guide. Says Bruce, "Twenty or so feet in front of me sat a being, in appearance a small, thin old priest well into his eighties. He was wearing a full-length white cotton robe with a plain rope belt tied at the waist."

Bruce approached the man and they began to discuss Bruce's problems. Writes Bruce, "At one point, as the priest began talking about my right hip, he moved his hands and beckoned me toward him. I felt myself gripped in a powerful force. I was rolled onto my side and drawn to lie horizontally in front of the priest, facing him, floating just off the floor, suddenly finding myself naked. The priest moved his small hands over my body and finally laid them on my hip. My hip joint moved and felt like it was being turned inside out. This did not hurt but felt rather uncomfortable.

"The priest moved his hands slowly back and forth and a murky-dark roughly shoebox-shaped object, shot through with dull-reddish and orange lumps and grisly black lines floated out of my hip. He pulled this away from my skin slightly and showed me angry red and black cords extending sticky strings into my hip, groin and upper thigh."

The priest explained that the cause of the condition was actually a curse. He laid his hands over the area and "a brilliant-white light then spouted from his hands and bored deep inside me, all around and through the strange thing on my hip. I felt nerves twanging and pricking and then a tickling, almost erotic feeling flooded through my groin as the thing brightened suddenly and then faded. It changed visibly, filling with sparkling-white motes of light, then dissolved back in my body."

454

Bruce reports that the procedure greatly improved his health. As he says, "It felt like a great weight had been lifted off me and my hip felt tender and a little numb...I awoke the next morning greatly refreshed, with no cramps or pain at all and my hip felt a whole lot better."[15]

Marilynn Hughes began having out-of-body experiences following the birth of her first child. She soon discovered that she had very strong natural abilities for extensive astral travel. After several years, Hughes had many very advanced experiences, including out-of-body healings.

After being diagnosed with an ovarian cyst, Hughes turned to astral travel to remedy the situation. After exiting her body, she found herself taken to a healing dimension. Writes Hughes, "My being lay in mid-air as six entities, some of whom were my guides, stood around me, three on each side. Observing the colors and vibrational patterns of my being, they determined what medical problems I was experiencing and the reasons for the manifestation of an ovarian cyst. My husband wanted another child and we were trying to have one, but deep down inside, I was not ready for another child. Perhaps I would never be ready for another one...The entities raised their hands as beams of white light shone down from them, healing my auric disturbance causing the cyst. Immense warmth was felt, as the healing ensued.

"When they were finished, one of my guides explained that my other problem, which was later diagnosed as asthma, could not be healed yet, as I did not understand the reason for the manifestation. Some soul-searching would be in order. I returned to my body, and as expected, my cyst had disappeared."

On a later occasion, Hughes was able to take steps to cure her asthma condition. Writes Hughes, "Entering into the vibratory state, I left my body. Suddenly seeing from another vantage point, my etheric body was displayed before my eyes. An obvious energy disturbance could be seen in my chest area, a discoloration. Resembling thermal photography, my consciousness was displayed as a white light with a red color emanating from the area of disease. Realizing the need to deal with my lung condition more thoroughly, I worked on refining the energy. As I brought my energy pattern back to balance, I knew I would need to work on understanding my disease, and the creation of it."

Probably the most amazing of Hughes' healing experiences occurred after she broke her finger in a car door. Writes Hughes, "When I opened the door, my finger came out bent to the right and then to the left, obviously broken in two places. It was numb and I could not move it...Calming myself, I put my hand over the finger and I began to ask the spiritual guides to help me. For five minutes I sat, and I felt a warmth going over my hand. When I looked again, the finger was completely straight. I could move it, but the pain was minimal. All that remained was a little bit of swelling."

That evening, Hughes had an OBE during which further healing occurred. "I was taken to a healing zone. In a blue-green room resembling a doctor's office, I lay down waiting for assistance. A spirit came in and without a word laid two bluish-green glimmering stones on my finger and left the room...When I returned to my body, the swelling was completely gone, and all that remained was a tiny scab where the skin had broken. Miracles *can* happen!"[16]

Rosalind McKnight is the mother of eight children, a teacher, a social worker and a prominent paranormal researcher. She was one of the original out-of-body explorers working closely with Robert Monroe, a leader of the out-of-body movement. While working at The Monroe Institute (TMI), she had thousands of OBEs.

One day in the early 1980s, McKnight suffered a severe attack of bleeding hemorrhoids. When she arrived at TMI to perform OBE research, she was given an OBE healing. McKnight narrates what happened during her session.

"They are trying to help me. I feel there is someone there, but all I see are two discs and a light. I was put on one of the discs and I began spinning around. I'm still lying on the disc. The light is shining over my body, and is getting brighter. I think the light is coming from the other disc, which is up over me. It's as if I am between two energy discs."

McKnight was astonished by the astral "technology" used to heal her. As she says, "The Invisibles then started to work with heat and color. They sent colors through me from my head to my toes, as if I were a tube. Then they concentrated on the dark areas of my body, where the pain was, beaming in purple energy. The purple changed to blue, with an occasional flash of red. Finally they put me back into the purple light and spun me on the disc again."

Afterward, McKnight was instructed to return for a further healing. On the next occasion, she was again placed on the spinning disc. Writes McKnight, "A light beam centered down on the dark area of my body that needed the healing. Some sort of energy rods were then inserted across my abdomen one by one. After that they worked with the violet and blue energies again. Another beam came from the back of me, through my spine and up through the rods."

The Invisible Helpers told McKnight that they would continue to send her healing energies throughout the next week to clean out the dark areas of her physical and emotional bodies.

McKnight reports that the healing was highly effective. "After this second session, I felt wonderful. And the next day the hemorrhoids were completely gone."

On several occasions, McKnight was given lessons on energy and breathing to help remove blockages that cause disease. She was also given information to help others. Writes McKnight, "They also focused on Bob's health problems and questions on a number of occasions. Bob would think a question, and my helpers would often answer it without knowing he had a question, or what it was. And they offered Bob much health advice when he openly asked for it. On one occasion they did a diagnosis and a healing for my mother living in Dayton, Ohio."

McKnight describes the above healing: "My invisible Friends are checking on my mother now and doing a diagnosis. They say there is something wrong with the gall bladder, and there is also some kind of poison in her kidneys. They are beaming energy rays into her. Now I'm going to try to do some healing on her myself. I am stepping into her energy body. I want to feel and experience the problem. I can feel the energy beams that are being directed into her body."[17]

Bruce Moen has written a half-dozen books that detail his many highly advanced travels to distant areas of the astral planes. Moen, an engineer by profession, began having out-of-body experiences as a young man. In 1991, he attended the Monroe Institute Lifeline Program and became a highly proficient astral traveler.

Moen spends much of his astral time doing various types of social work, often rescuing lost souls who do not know they have died. He has also had some remarkable healing experiences.

In the mid-1980s, Moen began to feel pain in his abdominal area. It steadily worsened until he was forced to seek medical attention. He was given a long series of medical tests, and numerous doctors were unable to diagnose his condition. Finally, he was given exploratory abdominal surgery to locate the problem.

Then came the grim diagnosis: *sarcoidosis* of the liver, gallbladder and lymph system. Affecting only one person out of 900,000, sarcoidosis has no known cause and no known cure. It manifests as an uncontrolled inflammation of the liver. Eighty percent of patients recover in two years. The remaining twenty percent are chronic or degenerative. Most in this category die from the disease. Unfortunately, Moen found himself in this latter category, and after five years of suffering, his condition was getting steadily worse.

Then in 1991, he attended the Monroe Institute and began having regular controlled OBEs. Many of his forays involved exploring his past-lives. Like other projectors, Moen discovered that his current illness was actually connected to a past life. While out-of-body, Moen discovered a past life involving a young soldier named Joshua. During a battle, Joshua was pierced in the abdomen by a large spear. He died slowly and in intense pain. When Moen encountered him while out-of-body, Joshua was still under the impression that he was alive, and had been writhing in pain ever since he died several hundred years ago!

Moen took Joshua off the lower astral plane and transported him to a higher level where he could be treated and

458

healed by spirit guides. This simple act of uncovering the trauma of his past-life apparently caused a rapid healing of his sarcoidosis.

Writes Moen, "The memory of that wound and infection were expressing through my physical body. I had carried into this lifetime the memory of that infection from a part of myself left dying long ago. I had carried that memory into my present physical body...By retrieving parts of myself, bringing them back into memory and expressing them, I had the opportunity to heal myself. This healing could be physical, mental or spiritual depending on what each part of myself that I retrieved needed...I had absolutely no doubt my sarcoidosis was already beginning to heal. I could feel the swirling movement of energy throughout my liver and the right side of my chest."

Moen's recovery was not instantaneous. He began to feel increasingly better, but still had problems with his lungs. He then uncovered another past life in which he and his family were killed in a house-fire. The guilt of being unable to rescue his family combined with the memory of the pain of breathing in smoke and hot air had also been carried into this lifetime. By exploring the experience and releasing the guilt, his recovery became complete.

Since these events, Moen has been sent on other healing missions, including helping several people overcome deep mental depression. In each case, he projected to the patient and found him/her surrounded in a sticky black tar-like substance generated by negative emotion and thought. The only way to remove it was to strongly visualize the patient free of the sticky black stuff and "see it not there." Moen died in 2017 at age seventy.[18]

A successful businessman and sound engineer, Robert Monroe is probably best known for his out-of-body travels. He is, without a doubt, the leading figure in the field. Monroe had no OBEs as a child. It wasn't until after he began experimenting with anesthesia and sleep-learning tapes that he began having OBEs. At first he believed he was suffering an unknown illness, and he sought medical attention. Further research led him to believe that he was having mystical experiences and he pursued them avidly. Years later, he perfected the ability to leave the body at will and travel anywhere in the physical dimensions and very far into the astral dimensions.

Monroe's first experience with OBE healing came when he uncovered a traumatic past-life memory. He was killed in a battle, and like Bruce Moen, the residual pain from the experience had apparently been carried over into his present lifetime, causing an unexplained pain in his abdomen. After uncovering the event, Monroe was pain free.

Stuart Twemlow MD examined Monroe for physiological abnormalities. Twemlow recorded a Galvanic Skin Response (GSR) which was highly unusual. Writes Twemlow, "Monroe had demonstrated his ability to move needles of sensitive voltmeters by waving his hand over them."[19]

As we have seen, a few of the above healings were the result of releasing the trauma from a past-life. Research into past-lives has shown this pattern in other cases.

Healed by Past-Life Therapy

One of the surprising results to emerge from past-life research is the physical healings that resulted from regressions. The use of hypnosis to recover memories of a past-life is not new, nor is the concept of past-lives. The evidence in support of reincarnation has been proven by the painstaking research of Ian Stevenson, who has compiled many hundreds of cases in which people have spontaneously recalled details of past-lives--details which upon research proved to be accurate and unknown to the witness.

The research showed that likes, dislikes, eccentricities, personality and phobias often transferred from one life to the next. In some cases, the trauma from the past life caused not only mental problems, but physical. Medical injuries and traumas in one life resulted in birthmarks, scars or illness in the next life. After recalling a past life, some patients began to report physical healings of illness.

Researcher Carol Bowman has documented several cases of past-life healings, including one involving her own son, Chase.

Regressed to a lifetime as a Civil War soldier, Chase recalled being shot in the wrist. In his current lifetime, Chase suffered from eczema on his wrist. Following the regression, the eczema, which had resisted other forms of traditional modern medical treatments, cleared up completely.

Another case is that of "Edward," age four, who complained of pain in his throat. The pain persisted and doctors eventually discovered a cyst that required immediate surgery. However, before surgery could be performed, four-year-old Edward told his astonished parents that he remembered being a French soldier named Walter. He remembered being shot in the throat. Edward told them he was only eighteen years old when he died. Even more amazing, Edward told them that the "shot" was gone. Edward was taken to the doctor who discovered that the tumor had completely disappeared. The doctor said that he had never heard of this type of tumor spontaneously disappearing, and that it would likely return. Ten years later, Edward remains perfectly healthy.[20]

Regardless of source, energy, and energy beams are a common theme in miraculous healings. Whether coming from a UFO, an alien instrument, or from an angel or saint, or during an out-of-body experience, witnesses universally describe highly energetic states. Miraculous healings come in many forms. Among the strangest are people who have been struck by lightning and cured of a wide variety of conditions. Many people are struck by lightning and killed each year. A lucky few, however, are healed of a long list of medical conditions.

Healed by Lighting

Consider what happened to Mary Clamser of Oklahoma City, Oklahoma. When she was nineteen years old, Clamser was diagnosed with multiple sclerosis. She suffered from the disease for more than twenty years, and her condition gradually became more severe. She reached a point where her legs became numb and she could no longer walk unassisted. Then, on August 14, 1994, Clamser was inside her home when she was struck by lightning. Although she suffered burns and other harmful side-effects, she instantly began a miraculous recovery from her multiple sclerosis. Feeling came back into her legs, and less than a month later, she began walking again. "I knew something had changed," Clamser says "I was so overwhelmed that I started to cry."

As it turns out, many people have been healed as a result of lightning. The cases are surprisingly numerous and have been well-documented throughout history. Pannos T. Pappas Ph.D. (Professor of Physics and Mathematics at the Technological Educational Institute, Athens, Greece) is one of the world's leading researchers into healings by lightning, and has compiled an impressive chronology of cases.

In 1776, Mrs. Wynne of Dublin, Ireland was facing possible surgery for a large tumor in her left breast. Wynne returned to her home. Lightning struck her home and went through Wynne's body, knocking her unconscious. Two days later, an examination revealed a softening and shrinking of her tumor. In a few weeks, it was gone. Wynne's physician, Dr. Georgius Hicks was impressed and reportedly healed two other women of tumors using electric shocks.

In 1806, Samuel Leffers suffered a stroke resulting in numbness, partial paralysis, vision loss and difficulty in speaking. A few months later, he was struck by lightning, knocking him out. When he woke up, he no longer needed glasses, and his skin tone improved.

In 1822, Martin Rockwell was ten feet away from a lightning strike and felt a brief paralysis, and a numbness lasting for almost an hour. His chest also felt burned. At the time, he suffered from asthma. Following the lightning strike, his asthma cleared up and never returned.

In 1846, an anonymous black woman (age seventy) was struck by lightning. Although she had gone through menopause twenty years earlier, she began to menstruate again, a condition which remained for the next three years.

The Lancet Journal reported on a case involving Reuben, a farmer in Yorkshire, England around 1850. The farmer was suffering from cancer of the chin and lower lip. While plowing a field, he and his two horses were struck by lightning. His two horses were killed, but Reuben not only survived, his cancer went into sudden remission. The senior surgeon at the Lloyd Cottage Hospital wrote to the Lancet Journal, "What seems to be the most astonishing feature in the case is the healing process which was set up in the lip and chin soon after the accident. The cancer gradually lessened, and in a few weeks every trace of the diseased structure disappeared, and for ten years he enjoyed complete freedom from his former suffering and signs of the disease."

As with the UFO healings, the lightning strike healings also extend to animals. In 1896, Mr. Graff (a hog farmer in Kokomo, Indiana) was transporting a load of pig carcasses, victims of cholera, when his wagon was struck by lightning. This caused one of the carcasses to become reanimated. The pig ran from the wagon. The farmer chased it down and captured it. The pig showed no signs of cholera and appeared to be healthy.

In 1899, Eli Forbes (who had lost the use of his left arm due to rheumatism) was struck by lightning, causing his left arm to straighten. He felt a surge of strength in the arm and discovered he was now able to use it normally.

In 1901, a farmer from Tupai, China was dealing with a litter of eleven pigs, each of whom suffered from paralysis in their hind legs. Then their sty was struck by lightning, knocking all the piglets unconscious. Upon awakening, their hind legs moved normally.

In 1908, James Gorsuch of New York was struck by lightning. At the time, he was partially blind and deaf due to childhood scarlet fever. During an electrical storm, he felt electrical sensations which restored first his hearing, and over the next few days, his vision.

In 1909, Mr. Beazley of Melbourne, Australia was struck by lightning. At the time, he suffered from rheumatic gout, and could walk only with difficulty and a cane. Following the lightning strike, his health returned to normal, amazing the many people who knew him.

In 1911, Mrs. Decker (who was sixty-five years old and deaf since childhood) was struck by lightning while in her home in

Connecticut. The strike left her sore and bedridden for several days. Incredibly, it also restored her ability to hear. "Her hearing is now so good that she is able to carry on a conversation in an ordinary tone of voice," wrote the *New York Times*.

Also in 1911, in Fargo, North Dakota, Dr. C.H. Geary was struck by lightning in his home. At the time he suffered from paralysis. Immediately following the strike, the movement of his limbs was restored and he quickly improved to normal health.

In 1912, Polly Harper of Harpersville, New York was sitting in a chair in her backyard when a bolt of lightning struck nearby, knocking her unconscious. At the time, she was chair-bound with chronic rheumatism. When she woke up a few hours later, her rheumatism was gone.

In 1915, Mrs. Charles A. Burdick of Berlin, Connecticut was struck by lightning in her home. Although it knocked her down, when she recovered, her rheumatism disappeared.

In 1916, H.F. Riley of Wilkes-Barre, Pennsylvania was struck by lightning, which ejected him from his chair. Upon awakening, he realized he felt no more pain. At the time, he had suffered from rheumatism for five years. Following the lightning strike, his condition disappeared.

In 1925, Mrs. John Devinney of Beverly, Pennsylvania had lost the use of her arm. As she sat on her veranda, she was struck by lightning, immediately restoring the use of her arm.

Also in 1925, Noah W. Miers (age 67) suffered from paralysis of his left arm. While camping in Bakersfield, California, he was struck by lightning, causing him to regain the use of his left arm.

In June of 1932, Thomas Young, a farmer from Dukedom, Tennessee was near-death from mouth cancer which had spread through his body. While reclining in a hammock, one of the trees it was tied to was struck by lightning. Young felt the bolt pass through him, tearing off his shoes. In the days that followed, his cancer shrank and disappeared.

In 1934, four-year-old Muriel Fearnley (who was blind from birth) was sitting on the couch of her London home when lightning struck nearby, causing her to lose consciousness. Upon awaking the next morning, Fearnley was able to see for the first time. Only a few weeks earlier, doctors had pronounced her condition incurable.

In March of 1936, Adeline Slover, who had suffered from arthritis for fifteen years, was struck by lightning, causing a reversal of her condition. "It flashed before my face and I fell back stunned," said Slover. "Then I began to shake all over...I felt strength surging into my arms and legs ever since...It was a miracle sent from heaven."

In June of 1980, Edwin Robinson of Falmouth, Maine (who was blind and deaf and disabled from a vehicle accident) was struck by lightning. Following the strike, his hearing and vision both returned, his partial paralysis went away, and the bald spot on the top of his head grew back with hair.

Consider this account from a lightning victim. "I was struck April 20, 2001. I have dealt with severe eczema on my hands for several years, but since the lightning strike my hands healed up almost completely."

In 2007, Sam Woodruff was struck by lightning. At the time he had just given up radiation treatments for lung cancer and was in a steady decline. After being struck by lightning, his appetite returned and he began to gain weight. Further tests showed no sign of any lung cancer.

In July 2009, Donald Marsolais of Cornwall was struck by lightning while taking shelter under a tree. At the time he suffered from paralysis on his left side due to a stroke three years earlier. Following the lightning strike, his paralysis was cured.

These are only a few of the many documented healings by lightning. As can be seen, there are enough cases to say that something strange is clearly going on.[21]

More cases of miraculous healings could be listed, but the point has been made. Healing can come from a wide variety of paranormal sources, not just UFOs. This is important to consider when assessing a miraculous healing case.

The parallels between the various miraculous healings and UFO healings are as obvious as they are astounding. Again and

465

again we see that light and energy is the mechanism being used to affect the healing.

When a witness describes being struck by a beam of light, levitated and healed--they could be describing a UFO beam or a lightning bolt.

When a witness describes being visited by a glowing figure who entered through a wall into their bedroom and healed them, they could be describing an extraterrestrial from another planet, or a human saint.

When a witness describes being pulled up a beam of light and into a bright room where they were healed, they could be describing a near-death/out-of-body experience, or a UFO abduction.

Some researchers are impressed enough by the similarities between various paranormal phenomena as to lump them all under the same source, an intelligence that manifests under various guises. Others maintain that these are separate phenomenon with striking similarities.

Whatever the explanation, it appears that UFOs are one of the major sources for non-conventional healings. Now that we have established that UFO healings are real, the next question is: what does this mean for us?

Conclusion and Analysis

Now that we have amassed a large database of UFO healing accounts, (309 cases!) the next step is to try and make sense of it all. First, let's take a look at the dates of the encounters.

While UFO healings have been documented for at least a hundred years, there are indications that they have occurred for even longer. James Gilliland, a researcher and contactee from Mount Adams in Washington state is most famous for showing UFOs to groups of people at his Washington ranch. The area around Mount Adams seems to be particularly conducive to UFO sightings. And possibly even UFO healings. Gilliland heard about legends from the local Native Americans, the Klickitat and Multnomah tribes. According to their oral traditions, there are "light people" who live in the mountains. The Native Americans would routinely take their sick and injured up to the mountains and leave them overnight. The next day they would return to find that they had been healed.[1]

The documented cases date from 1914 to 2018, a span of 104 years. Only a few cases predate the modern age of UFOs. An analysis of the number of cases by decade shows a slow but steady increase of accounts.

1910s (1 case)
1920s (0 cases)
1930s (2 cases)
1940s (7 cases)
1950s (19 cases)
1960s (21 cases)
1970s (42 cases)
1980s (67 cases)

1990s (71 cases)
2000s (28 cases)
2010s (32 cases)
Undated (19 cases)

The peak of cases in the 1980s-1990s, and the drop in the number of modern cases may be misleading in that it often takes witnesses a long time to report their accounts. Other influencing factors might be the waxing and waning of public interest in UFOs. Whatever the reason, healings occur regularly each year. The average number of cases is approximately three per year. But as most people do not report their UFO encounters, the actual number of cases is likely much greater.

An analysis of the locations of the healings reveals a worldwide distribution of UFO healing encounters. Thirty-five separate countries are represented. In the USA, at least thirty-five different states have generated UFO healing reports.

Afghanistan (1)
Argentina (2)
Australia (3)
Azerbaijan (1)
Bahamas (1)
Belgium (1)
Brazil (4)
Canada (10)
Canary Islands (1)
China (2)
Chile (1)
Columbia (1)
Denmark (1)
Dominican Republic (1)
England (12)
Finland (3)
France (5)
Germany (2)
Hungary (1)

Italy (2)
Japan (1)
Mexico (2)
Netherlands (1)
New Zealand (3)
Norway (2)
Okinawa (1)
Peru (5)
Puerto Rico (10)
Russia (15)
Scotland (2)
South Africa (2)
Spain (2)
Sweden (3)
Switzerland (1)
Ukraine (6)
Unknown (20)

USA (163) (AK [1], AL [1], AZ [1], CA [40], CO [6], FL [11], GA [6], IL [2], IN [1] IO [1], KY [2], LA [1] MA [2], ME [1], MN [1],MO [1], MS [2], NC [4], NE [1], NJ (7), NM (2), NV [5], NY [5], OH (5), OR [9], PA [5], SC [1], SD [1], TX [4], UT [1], VA [4], WA [2], WI [2], WV [1], WY [2]

The worldwide distribution of reports shows that ETs do not express a prejudice regarding who they heal, at least not based on geographical distribution. Nor, as we have seen, does age, race, religion, or education seem to be a factor.

More specifically, the healings themselves occur inside people's homes (about twenty percent); outside people's homes (about twenty percent); inside UFOs (about fifty percent); and inside hospitals (about eight percent.) These figures should be considered approximate as it appears that some of the house-visits and outside encounters may have involved missing time or an abduction, and may have occurred aboard a UFO. There are also many cases in which people reported no abduction or interaction with entities. They merely had a sighting, which somehow resulted in a healing. Impressively, a number of cases occurred immediately prior to scheduled surgery or while the witnesses were on their way to have medical treatment at the hospital. Two outlying cases (one in a restaurant and another in a church) show that healings can occur pretty much anywhere.

Which brings us to the question, who exactly is being healed? Unlike my 1996 analysis which found that sixty-four percent of healings occurred to men and thirty-six percent to woman, the new larger data base reveals a nearly equal distribution, with about fifty-three percent male and forty-seven percent female.

Age does not appear to be a factor. Cures have occurred pre-natally, and to infants, small children, teen-agers, and men and women, young and old. Some of the recipients to the healings were in their seventies.

A few factors do seem to influence who is being healed and why. The majority of healings have occurred to people with a history of UFO encounters. In other words, your chances of being healed are considerably higher if you are an abductee or contactee.

Experiencers are also much more likely to have *multiple* healings, sometimes simultaneously, sometimes over a period of time. Also important to note, there are a number of cases in which the people who were cured were friends or relatives of a contactee.

However, a history of encounters is certainly not a prerequisite as about one third of the cases involve people who have had no prior contact with UFOs.

Another surprising pattern that may be a factor in who is being healed and why, is the witness's profession or career. There is a wide cross section of vocations represented, however, there does seem to be an abnormally large number of professions which could be characterized as providing a service for the benefit of humankind. Doctors, environmentalists, human rights activists, social workers, teachers, writers, police officers, inventors, artists, entertainers, these are the types of people being healed.

Only a small minority of cases involve healings which were the result of a request or prayer for a healing. Daniel D asked for a healing and received it. An anonymous woman (an abductee) asked for her husband to be healed, and he was. A few cases involve people (who have no history of UFO encounters) who prayed earnestly for a healing and received one. These types of cases, however, are statistically rare. The majority of healings are done by the aliens on their own terms. In addition, many people who are abductees suffer from diseases that are *not* being cured.

Perhaps the most remarkable features about UFO healings are the huge number of them, and the wide variety of conditions healed. Below is a comprehensive list of the conditions healed as documented in this book.

Addiction (2)
Aids (2)
Aneurysm, cerebral (1)
Angioma (1)
Appendicitis (1)
Arterial Sclerosis (1)
Arthritis (21)
Asthma (3)
Blood clot (2)
Burn (5)
Cancer (40) (body (16); bone (1); brain (2); breast (1); cervical (1); Hodgkin's (1); lymph nodes (1); lung (4); ovarian (2); pancreas (2); skin (3); stomach (4) throat (1) uterine (1))
Chagas Disease (1)
Chemical sensitivity/allergy (1)
Crohn's disease (1)
Cold/Flu/Streptococcus (11)
Colitis (2)
Diabetes (1)
Diphtheria (1)
Eczema (2)
Epilepsy (1)
Eyes (19) (Blindness (2); color blindness (1); detached retina (1); glaucoma (1); injury (1) near-farsightedness (7); night blindness (1); disease (2); sty (1))
Fever (2)

Fibromyalgia (1)
Gallstones (1)
Headache/migraine (2)
Heart Disease (12)
Hemorrhoids (1)
Hernia (3)
Hip dysplasia (1)
Hypertension (2)
Hypoglycemia (1)
Infertility (5)
Injuries (76) (abdomen/chest (6); arms/hands (10); back/neck (15); body (14); head (3); legs/feet (23);
Intestinal Illness (17)
Kidney Disease (4)
Kidney Stones (6)
Leukemia (2)
Leprosy (1)
Liver Disease/Hepatitis (5)
Lung Disease, damage, hole in (15)
Mole, removed (3)
Multiple sclerosis (1)
Muscular Dystrophy (1)
Paralysis (2)
Pneumonia (5)
Polio (2)
Prostatitis (1)
Rheumatism (4)
Sinusitis (3)
Spider Veins (1)
Spine, curvature (1)
Stroke (2)
Suicide (4)
Toothache/new teeth (5)
Tuberculosis (2)
Tumor/cyst (14) (body (1); brain (3); breast/chest (6); head (1); lung (1); spine (1); uterine (1)
Ulcer (1)

Unknown/Undiagnosed Illness (5)
Uterine (2) (cramping (1) infection (1)
Wart, removed (1)
Yeast infection (3)

The above list shows us that there is no illness, injury, condition or disease that is too large or too small for the ETs to heal. Whether minor and annoying, or chronic and debilitating, or fatal--the ETs have found a cure. The most numerous cures involve injuries. Right behind that is cancer. These two conditions alone account for more than one-third of all cures. With some sixty different types of illnesses being cured, it's logical to conclude that ETs may be able to cure a much wider variety of conditions than is listed here.

While the vast majority of healings involve a single condition, this is not always the case. Almost ten percent of the cases involve multiple cures. There are about a dozen cases in which people have received multiple cures as the result of a single encounter. "Doctor X" was cured of an axe wound and partial paralysis. An anonymous Peruvian customs official was cured of myopia and rheumatism. Carl Higdon was cured of kidney stones and a tubercular scar on his lung. Vasily A. was cured of dental problems and a finger injury. John Hunter Gray was healed of cigarette addiction, and experienced more than twenty physiological improvements as the result of a single encounter. An anonymous farmer from Russia was cured of knee injuries and kidney stones. Vladimir Voronezhskiy was cured of colitis and gray hair. "Cory" was cured of knee issues and vision problems. An anonymous man was cured of hypertension, a detached retina and a crooked leg. David Perez was cured of lung problems, body pains and suicidal depression. "Rory" had an encounter which resulted in an improvement to both his diabetes and arthritis. "Donna" is the only person to receive multiple cures in one encounter more than once. She was cured of a toothache and curvature of the spine in one, and epilepsy and vision problems in another.

About a dozen people have been repeatedly visited by ETs and cured of separate conditions on multiple, separate occasions.

Without exception, these people are UFO contactees. Richard Rylka was cured of injuries resulting from an auto accident, a finger injury, a tumor, polio, and an ear infection. Eduard Meier was cured of injuries from a moped accident and twice of pneumonia. Helene Charbonneau was cured of cancer, and injuries due to a car accident. Connie Isele reports being cured of arthritis, uterine cramping and broken legs. Edward Carlos was cured of pneumonia, melanoma, and arterial sclerosis. "Harold" was visited multiple times and treated for a congenital heart defect. "Alicia Hansen" was cured of a cyst and injuries resulting from a car accident. "Linda" was cured of a yeast infection, stomach cancer, and breast cancer. Chuck Weiss was cured of lung problems, skin cancer, and two separate injuries. Jim Sparks was cured of the flu, and also received an apparent lung cure. Alberto Fernandez reports being cured of an eye injury and lung cancer. Lynnette was cured of a heart condition and a tumor in her lung. Lauren Kurth was cured of sinusitis and melanoma. The Twiggs family collectively report cures of lung cancer, asthma, a sty on the eye, back pain, flu, a scar from a C-section and colitis. A few cases also involve multiple family members. John Hunter Gray and his son, California abductees Linda and Sherri, "Douglas" and his mother, and two married couples all report cures.

While there are almost thirty cases of multiple cures, proportionally, this is still less than ten percent of the actual number of cures. Conversely, more than ninety percent of the cases involve a single incident with a single cure.

Interestingly, there are a few cases involving multiple cures to different individuals at the same time. One case involves four people being cured of the flu. Linda and Sherri were both healed at the same time, and Linda reports seeing many people being cured aboard a UFO. Another case in Spain involves the cures of four children in a hospital. And again, two cases involve a husband and wife who were both healed at the same time.

Not all the cures have occurred to humans. There is one case of an ET being cured, and seven of animals being cured, including two roosters, a horse and five dogs.

474

Another interesting fact is that at least seven of the cures were of injuries sustained during the UFO encounter itself. Charles Moody injured his back during his abduction and was cured of the condition. Bert Twiggs reports hurting his back aboard a UFO and receiving a cure. A young Chinese boy was taken aboard a UFO, given a cut, which was then cured. There are two other cases just like this involving anonymous witnesses. While attempting to flee from a UFO, "Tim" fell, cut his hand, and was then abducted and cured of the injury. Another woman gashed her leg during an abduction.

Also interesting is, not all cures are successful. Linda reports being cured of a yeast infection, which later recurred. Another witness received a healing of head injuries, but died shortly later. There are a few other cases involving cures which were successful, though the witnesses died of other causes not long after. One witness was cured of gallstones, but later the condition recurred. The vast majority of cures, however, appear to be permanent.

An analysis of how the cures are enacted reveals more patterns. The largest category involves some sort of onboard operation, often using alien instruments. Light beams figure prominently in many of these accounts. However, there are many cases in which people were cured apparently by the mere presence of a UFO, though the possibility of a missing time event in these cases cannot be easily discounted.

A smaller portion of the cures were the result of injections or orally ingested medicines. Some involve mind power, hands-on healing or apparent paranormal methods as opposed to technology.

Who is doing the healing? This question is not always easy to answer, as not all the witnesses were able to view the entities, or provided incomplete descriptions. Grays, Nordics, Praying Mantis ETs, Reptilians and humanoids of various types are all represented. The humanoid form is almost universal. Grays are by far the most common entity doing the healings.

A statistical analysis of the healings has revealed several interesting patterns, but it doesn't answer the big questions.

What are we to make of the fact that there are more than 300 cases of UFO healings, and likely a great many more? Why are aliens healing people? What does this say about their agenda?

The obvious and immediate take-away is that ETs are benevolent. They come in peace, bearing gifts of healing. Many cases support this assertion, as do many of the recipients of the healings.

But as we have seen, it's not all rainbows and lollipops. Many experiencers have suffered medically as a result of their encounters and have *not* been healed. Other experiencers suffer from naturally occurring human diseases and injuries, and they are not being healed. And even those who have been healed sometimes experience injuries or mental and emotional trauma due to their encounters.

Are the ETs healing humans with altruistic motives, or is there something in it for them? Is it "equipment maintenance?" Are their motives solely to keep their "breeding stock" healthy?

The only place we have to look for answers is to those who have experienced contact.

UFO healing cases undeniably reveal a window into the motives of the ETs, and it seems impossible to conclude otherwise than that in some cases, the ETs are benevolent. Certainly, many of the witnesses feel this way. They consider the ETs friends, or even family. They express nothing but gratitude toward the ETs and consider their lives enriched by their encounters.

Conversely, some experiencers admit being healed, but believe that their treatment at the hands of ETs is little different than how humans treat lab rats. They feel that the cures are not done out of kindness, but are motivated by the aliens' selfish desires to keep their human experiments healthy, only to ensure the successful production of hybrid babies and the ETs' pursuit of knowledge of the human body.

Notably, ETs have repeatedly told people very clearly that their agenda is to heal the person, to warn them of upcoming disasters and provide guidance. This is a very common message given to abductees and contactees, and many such cases appear in this book.

Ultimately, what we end up with is a bell-curve. On one end we have cases that appear to be entirely benevolent, done for altruistic reasons by truly friendly ETs. On the other end are cases involving emotionless grays who treat their human patients with a bedside manner that is arrogant at best and at worst, with little or no compassion for the wellbeing of the patient. However, even in these cases, there is no evidence of sadism or deliberate torture. Also, the fact that many of the people who are being healed are doing good work humanity also seems to indicate that ETs do care about humanity at large. The UFO-rescue cases also seem to show a benevolent side to the ETs.

But if this is true, if aliens do care about humans, and they have the nearly miraculous ability to cure a wide variety of illnesses, injuries and diseases, why aren't they doing so? At least fifty million people die each year, and yet the ETs are not intervening, at least not in a way that can be verified. It appears that they are healing only a very small portion of humans, and continue to keep their healing technology secret.

Ultimately, however, this is speculation. We still don't know how many people are being abducted, or exactly how common UFO healings are. But the chances are good that many more people are being healed than the 309 cases in this book. Even now I continue to uncover new cases. "Don" who was healed of body injuries in 2018 tells me he was also healed of a brain tumor. In the mid-1990s, he was taken onboard a UFO where he saw grays, praying mantis and other beings. They told him he had a brain tumor and that they would cure him. Don said he felt fine. "You would've gotten sick," they told him.

In addition, many uninvestigated cases have not been included in this book. I have received reports of healings of lupus, blindness, deafness, heart problems, infection from a tattoo, removal of warts and more, but for various reasons, was unable follow-up on the cases.

Also consider the following encounter involving "Rayna," her daughter and two friends. All four were together when they experienced a missing time abduction in Sedona, Arizona. Afterward, Rayna underwent hypnotic regression and recalled a typical abduction experience. Her daughter was too young to undergo hypnosis, but showed signs of remembering the experience consciously. "She used to take dolls," said Rayna, "and put them under a lampshade and say, 'I'm healing them.' She talked about white men who came in through the window..."[2]

But they're not healing everyone, and they're not giving up the technology either. In his book, *Breakthrough*, Whitley Strieber writes that he continually gets letters from readers requesting that he ask the aliens to cure them of disease. Writes Strieber, "Many's the night I'd spent praying for the desperate people who have sent me letters. 'Please, Mr. Strieber, I have stage-three Hodgkin's and three kids and no husband, please get them to save me.' 'My friend has AIDS, he's suffering in agony, call the visitors, get them to come.' 'I need medicine from the other world or I am going to die.'"[3]

Strieber was able to meet with "a fascinating witness from California who'd apparently had a cure in connection with her contact experiences.' However, as we have seen, most people are not being cured.

Following the publication of *UFO Healings* in 1996, I began to get letters and emails from people. Even today, I continue to be contacted by people pleading for me to put them in contact with aliens who will heal them. I wish I could.

Virginia Aronson has looked into the question and asks, "Why don't they heal everybody?...We just do not know the answer to these questions. Perhaps it has something to do with our individual soul's destiny on Earth, maybe it's simply a matter of luck."[4]

We have seen that there are patterns as to who is being healed and why. But still, why not more people?

One answer may lie with the fact that UFOs still maintain a policy of covert activity. There has never been open official contact with the public at large. Instead, ETs have continued to appear regularly across our planet in what appears to be a slowly escalating level of activity. This could very well be the result of humanity's slow spiritual growth. The prejudice and hatred displayed by people of all nations, the constant wars, the pollution of our environment, the greed and corruption of society...all of these are likely contributing factors preventing open official contact. In many contact cases, ETs have specifically mentioned these concerns. Because of this, healing activities may have to be limited.

Of course, the extraterrestrials are wiser than to cure all of humanity's diseases at once. Imagine the consequences. A sudden cessation of all diseases would likely result in over-population and starvation in many areas of the world. And just think what would happen if our military leaders were given healing technology. The ability to cure flesh wounds in seconds would only give warring countries a never-ending supply of soldiers. Or what if the healing technology was available only to the wealthy? In all likelihood, the consequences would be even worse.

The medical field is a billion-dollar industry. The people in power are not likely to give this up easily. Also, being handed all the answers would not help humanity to become independent and capable of solving their own future problems.

Regardless of motives and agendas, ET healing cases do reveal a fascinating glimpse into their amazing healing technology. This alone might be the single most important contribution of UFO healing accounts: their potential to improve our own limited understanding of human health and healing.

The ETs' use of light in healing is a good example.

The human use of light in regards to healing has enjoyed a steady increase of interest and study, and is now a recognized therapy for several conditions. Some researchers are already trying to use the knowledge of ET medicine for practical applications.

After reviewing the healing case of Dr. X (healed of an axe wound and partial paralysis) and the case of Ventura Maceiras (who grew new teeth after his UFO encounter,) researcher Bill Chalker writes, "If such effects are due to these light beams, then forensic evaluations of their effects at the biological level, via DNA testing and perhaps other biomedical analyses, may reveal striking information about the processes involved and the apparent technologies deployed. Knowledge of such a mechanism would be an extraordinary biochemical and biomedical breakthrough."[5]

Major George A. Filer, after researching UFO healing cases, was struck by the use of green lights in several cases, and decided to use this knowledge to do some research on practical applications of ET lights. "Picking up on these stories," he writes, "I have researched the concept of healing by light in various color frequencies. I have a history of colds and flu-like symptoms for virtually every year of my life that have never been prevented by flu shots or really prevented or helped by modern medicine. Discussing this problem with a UFO researcher, and with patent developer Curtis Cooperman, he suggested light treatment. Using a simple lime green light, I have gone more than a year without a cold. Using a lime green light whenever my wife or I suspect we're coming down with a cold or the flu, we have reversed the effects and stayed healthy."[6]

The above accounts involve healing methods inspired by alien technology. However, there are some indications that various world governments have actually obtained UFO healing technology and are actively using it.

One facet of UFO research that was ignored and debunked for decades is now a recognized part of the phenomenon. This happened with UFO healings, but it also happened with UFO crash/retrievals. UFO crashes date back more than a hundred years and come from across the United States and the world. If UFOs have truly been captured by various governments--*and this is what the evidence is showing us*--then our governments must also have the alien technology found aboard these craft. Remember, a strong medical theme runs through the majority of the abduction reports. Descriptions of alien medical rooms and instruments are very common. Therefore, whoever is holding crashed UFOs has this technology. The real question is: are they using it?

The answer appears to be, *yes!* In his book, *In League with a UFO*, Lou Baldin tells the story of a man he interviewed who claimed to be involved in the scientific study of the alien craft that was captured at Roswell. According to Baldin's source, the Roswell craft revealed itself to be so advanced that the scientists concluded it was "a living organism." When recovered, the craft had a gaping hole in the side of it. As the scientists studied the craft, they were surprised when it began to heal itself in a manner similar to the healing of a human flesh wound. "The skin or surface of the ship grew back over a period of days," writes Baldin, "...Once the ship healed, there was no sign of the original damage."

Inside the craft, the scientists reported other odd effects. Watches malfunctioned. The sense of smell and taste seemed to be adversely affected. "The other senses," says Baldin, "sight, hearing and touch, changed for the better. If a certain scientist wore glasses, he needed to remove them to see. It was the same with hearing. All sound was clear regardless of previous hearing abilities. Touch was sensitive to the point of being erotic."

The scientists concluded that the ship was interdimensional, and that entering it was like entering a higher dimension. Just being inside the UFO left them energized and mentally stimulated. Time passed differently inside and outside the craft. Also the craft was larger on the inside than it appeared from the outside. There were numerous other strange effects.

The scientists discovered many gadgets aboard the craft. Some defied their abilities to remove them from the craft, others they were able to remove.

Many of the gadgets turned out to have incredible medical applications. Baldin writes of a hand-held device which looked like a large, beautiful precious stone. "When this item was placed on a living body," writes Baldin, "it detected tumors, both malignant and benign. Once the tumor was detected, the alien object projected an image of the tumor on its screen-like surface. The projected image was so clear that it was like looking at the tumor itself. The object glided over the skin of the body without making contact. If tumors did not reside in the body, the object remained stationary and cryptic messages appeared on its surface. The object did not need to scan over the entire body to locate the tumor; it knew instantly where the tumor or tumors were as soon as the object touched the skin. If a tumor was detected, it levitated and moved to the tumor. When more than one tumor was present in the body, it identified the one it was close to, then moved over to the next closest one and presumably catalogued it too. Size of the tumor had no bearing on the order it would be identified. The scientists believed that it was mapping the location of each tumor and all pertinent information somewhere, but they never discovered how or where the information was stored, whether it was within the object itself, or if it transmitted the information back to the alien craft. Every tumor that was displayed on the surface of the object was accompanied by alien symbols, presumably identifying what type of tumor it was and where on the body it was located."

This incredible alien diagnostic tool was only one of many similar medical gadgets. There was another which could repair wounds, opening and closing the skin without sutures. Writes Baldin, "The scientists felt that many if not all the gadgets were related to or performed medical functions."

According to Baldin's source, the scientists tested and used the instruments to secretly heal numerous people, usually elderly patients from nursing homes who were not informed that they were being healed.

The scientists asked the ETs who survived the crash, since they have the ability to cure human illness and injury, why did they not help people? The ETs said that they couldn't answer the question because the healings were performed only upon order from their superiors.[7]

Baldin is not the only one making these claims. In his book, *Day with an Extraterrestrial*, William Tompkins claims that the TRW Corporation has developed "life extension pharmaceutical products that could cure any disease and physically age-regress people."

Michael Salla, author of *The U.S. Navy's Secret Space Program*, writes that there are "advanced healing technologies secretly developed in classified programs. Witnesses and whistleblowers have described advanced healing technologies used in secret space programs that can regenerate limbs and organs, and cure any disease."[8]

So there it is; apparently we have already obtained UFO healing technology. We've had it for more than eighty years, and it is still being suppressed.

The UFO coverup is no joke. While our own tax dollars are being used to debunk a phenomenon that the government knows fully well is entirely real, while witnesses are made to look as though they are hoaxers, stupid, crazy or hallucinating, while millions of people die unnecessarily of conditions that could likely be easily cured through the use of a hand-held instrument, our own governments have decided that only the power elite deserve access to this technology, or even the knowledge of it.

Of course, this is an untenable situation. With a UFO phenomenon that shows no sign of going away, and is instead, escalating, it becomes increasingly clear that open official contact will occur. At the same time, we see a strong trend toward disclosure.

As encounters continue, and as people become more aware of the UFO phenomenon, a turning point may occur. Trying to cover-up the existence of UFOs will be like trying to hide the sun. There are simply too many people having experiences for the cover-up to be maintained. Even now, whistleblowers are revealing their accounts, and various governments and high-level governmental officials have made startling admissions regarding the truth of UFOs and extraterrestrial activity on our planet.

I'm guessing that once the cover-up collapses completely, open official contact with ETs will occur. Then we can start a new age for humanity, an age of love and cooperation between all peoples and all nations, including extraterrestrials. Idealistic? Perhaps. Possible? Absolutely! Will it actually happen? We'll just have to wait and see.

Chronology of UFO Healing Cases

Case #001. 1914. Inverary, Scotland. Anonymous male is cured of a broken arm by a gnome-like figure.

Case #002. Mid-1930s. USA. Anonymous male (broadcaster) "dreams" he is abducted by ETs and is cured of tuberculosis.

Case #003. 1937. Hinwil, Sweden. At age six, contactee Eduard Meier is visited by a human-looking ET and cured of pneumonia.

Case #004. 1942. Philadelphia, PA, USA. Professor Edward Carlos (age five) developed severe pneumonia. He experienced an NDE/UFO encounter, during which he was healed.

Case #005. 1942. Halifax, England. During WWII, "Elsie" (an elderly woman) sees a UFO outside her window, then is visited by three helmeted figures in silver suits who heal her of jaundice.

Case #006. April 1945. Okinawa Island. Soldier Howard Menger was blinded by an exploding shell. While being treated in the army tent, he was visited by a mysterious nurse who healed him and restored his vision.

Case #007. Autumn, 1945. Lutto, Finland. Helge Lindros is blinded by an exploding shell during WWII. While in his home, Lindross was visited by three human-looking figures who cured him of his blindness, and a shoulder injury.

Case #008. 1945. Santa Clara, CA, USA. Three-year-old "Ted" is visited by a gray ET who cures him of crippling angioma.

Case #009. 1946. Camp Lee, VA, USA. Soldier is cured of bruises and a broken nose by a human-looking ET who visits him in the army hospital.

Case #010. 5/25/1948. Border of Germany and Luxembourg. Hans Klotzbach is taken aboard a UFO and cured of severe leg injuries by an unseen German-speaking entity.

Case #011. 1950. OH, USA. "Donna" (age three and a half) is cured of curvature of the spine and a toothache following a bedroom visitation by a mysterious being.

Case #012. 1951. Atlanta GA, USA. Fred Reagan (private pilot) collides his plane with a UFO and is abducted by ETs (who look like metallic asparagus) and is healed of cancer. He dies one year later in a state asylum for the criminally insane.

Case: #013. Early 1950s. Passaic, NJ, USA. Contactee, Richard Rylka (then a child) contracts polio in a public swimming pool. Following a bedroom visitation by ETs, he is cured. It is the first of many cures reported by Rylka.

Case #014. Early 1950s. New Brunswick, NJ, USA. Contactee Richard Rylka (then a child) suffers an ear infection and is visited in his hospital room by human-looking ETs who heal him of his ear infection.

Case #015. Early 1950s. Toronto, Canada. Contactee John Adams (age three) experiences an unexplained recovery from polio of the spine. He later goes under hypnotic regression and discovers that ETs are responsible for the cure.

Case #016. July 1952. Agawam, MA, USA. Marianne Cascio (age eleven) experienced an abduction by gray ETs from her home. Following the abduction, she was diagnosed with Stargardt's disease, and went totally blind. She developed a strong psychic sight, and experienced two periods during which her sight miraculously returned.

Case #017. 1952. NJ, USA. Ellen Crystall (author of *Silent Invasion*) was two years old when she experienced a mysterious miraculous cure of an undiagnosed intestinal illness. A psychic (who knew nothing about this) says she was healed by a UFO.

Case #018. Early July 1953. OH, USA. "Donna" (age six), is with a group of people when a UFO "flashes" at her, resulting in a cessation of her epileptic seizures, vision improvements, and an increase in awareness.

Case #019. 7/30/1954. MO, USA. Buck Nelson (a farmer) is struck by a beam of light from a UFO, healing him of neuritis, lumbago and poor vision.

Case #020. 10/2/1955. Victorville, CA, USA. James R. Stewart burned his hand by holding a burning flare. Seconds later, he was struck by a beam of light from a UFO, healing his hand.

Case #021. 1956. Fort Erie, Ontario, Canada. "Robert" is cured of juvenile arthritis in his neck and back by mysterious visitors in his home.

Case #022. 10/25/1957. Petropolis, Brazil. An anonymous female child is cured of stomach cancer by small humanoids.

Case #023. February 1958. Aston, Birmingham, West Midlands, England. According to contactee, Cynthia Appleton, an anonymous human-looking extraterrestrial burned his finger, then cured himself with a jelly-like substance.

485

Case #024. 9/27/1959. Coos Bay, OR, USA. Leo Bartsch is spontaneously cured of an undiagnosed arthritis-like condition on his left hand and arm. No UFO was sighted, though Bartsch believed something had passed over his home.

Case #025. 1959. Southern CA, USA. "James" (a doctor) is taken aboard a UFO and cured at age five of a head injury.

Case #026. 1959. Pleasanton, TX, USA. Two roosters are struck by a beam of light from a UFO, curing them of body injuries caused by a cockfight, as witnessed by Susan Nevarez Morton.

Case #027. Late 1950s. Eastern Transvaal, South Africa. Contactee, Ann Grevler is cured by a human-looking male ET of a gash on her leg.

Case #028. 1950s. USA. Anonymous five-year-old girl is cured by gray-type ET of genital injuries due to sexual abuse.

Case #029. 1950s. CA, USA. Linda injures her liver and is abducted and treated for her condition by ETs.

Case: #030. Early 1960s (approx.) Los Angeles, CA, USA. An anonymous twelve-year-old girl born with a congenital heart defect receives a bedroom visitation by a human-looking figure, curing her, a fact verified by doctors and X-rays.

Case #031. 3/10/1960. Callejon de Hauylas, Peru. An anonymous boy suffering from severe body injuries is taken by a white-skinned, human-looking, female ET aboard a landed UFO, and cured of his injuries.

Case #032. Summer 1960. Seattle, WA, USA. "Jeffrey" injures his neck in a serious fall. He experiences missing time, sees three UFOs and realizes his neck is no longer injured.

Case #033. 11/12/1960. Devizes, England. A horse (suffering from a disease in her hooves) is cured by a mysterious six-foot-tall figure using an advanced alien instrument, as reported by the horse's owner, Ivor Sercombe.

Case #034. 1961. Isla Verde, Puerto Rico. An anonymous woman is abducted into a UFO and cured of a hernia.

Case #035. 1962. USA. Alice Haggerty (stricken with childhood diphtheria) is visited by robed figures who take her aboard a UFO and heal her.

Case #036. 9/3/1965. Damon, TX. USA. Deputy Robert W. Goode is healed of a wound on his finger by a purple beam of light from a UFO.

Case #037. December 1965. Uddevalla, Sweden. Construction worker, Richard Hoglund encountered a landed UFO and humanoids. After communicating with them, the ETs cured Hoglund of kidney stones.

Case #038. September, 1966. Durhan, England. Electronics specialist Fred White is visited by an exotic human-looking doctor who heals him of a hole in his lung.

Case #039. 1/21/1967. Toledo, OH, USA. Mrs. Wolfe (a nurse), encounters a UFO which paces her car and sends down bright beams of light. Following the encounter, Mrs. Wolfe's skin condition clears up.

Case #040. 12/7/1967. Denmark. Hans Lauritzen (a UFO researcher) was on a UFO stake-out when he had a close-up encounter resulting in the healing of his liver hepatitis.

Case #041. 1967. Lima, Peru. Ludwig F. Pallman is visited in his hospital room and cured of kidney stones.

Case #042. March 1968. Valparaiso, Chile. Ricardo Castillo Trujillo (a janitor) encountered a landed UFO and humanoids who cured him of nearsightedness.

Case #043. 7/7/1968. Hushtosyrt, Chegem Gorge, Russia. Victor Kostrykin came upon a landed UFO and humanoid figures. He entered the UFO and was cured of a congenital heart defect.

Case #044. 11/2/1968. French Alps, France. "Doctor X." is struck by a beam of light from a UFO hovering outside his home, curing him of partial paralysis and an axe-wound on his ankle.

Case#045. 12/9/1968. Peru. An anonymous Peruvian customs official is struck by a violet beam of light from a UFO, curing him of nearsightedness and rheumatism.

Case #046. 1968 (approx.) Kentucky, USA. Jerry Wills is cured of a fever by gray-type ETs.

Case#047. 8/11/1969. Rouen, France. Ambulance driver, Jean Migueres is healed by a humanoid entity of injuries resulting from a vehicle accident.

Case #048. Late 1960s. Littlerock, AR, USA. Following a UFO abduction, "Mary," who suffered from an incurable disease (not described) is cured of the disease as the result of a missing time encounter.

Case #049. 1960s. New Brunswick, NJ, USA. Contactee Richard Rylka is healed of a crushed finger by human-like ETs who appeared in his hospital room.

Case #050. 1960s. CA, USA. "Harold" was born with a hole in his heart. During pregnancy, his mother was visited by a gray who used psychic healing on the fetus. Throughout the 1960s and 1970s, the entity returned to visit and abduct Harold to give him additional healings to maintain his healthy heart. At age 48, at the direction of his doctor (and the grays), Harold underwent heart surgery to close the hole in his heart.

Case #051. 1970. New Brunswick, NJ, USA. Contactee Richard Rylka experienced a car accident. He had a near-death experience, and saw ETs who told him that his injuries were fatal, and that they would intervene to save his life, which they did.

Case #052. 1970. Brooksville, FL, USA. A male witness, H.C., is taken aboard a UFO by four masked humanoids. Following the experience, his chronic asthma disappeared.

Case #053. 1970. Bahamas. Richard Hoglund is visited in his home by ETs who cure him of a brain tumor.

Case #054. 3/5/1971. Trenal, France. Radio technician, Gilbert Camus comes upon a landed UFO and three, giant, ant-like figures. Camus is struck by a beam of light, and is apparently healed of a liver ailment.

Case #055. 1971. Laguna Beach, CA, USA. Contactee Fred Bell suffers severe burns as the result of a pipe bomb attack. While in the hospital he claims that he was healed of his burns by a "receptor" necklace, a healing device given to him by the Pleiadeans.

Case #056. 1971. Mount Kiera, New South Wales, Australia. Sam (the pet dog of Danny Enderson) is cured of crippling arthritis by mantis beings.

Case #057. 1972. Dominican Republic. UFO hovers over a church, an entity appears in the church and cures a woman of stomach cancer.

Case #058. 12/30/1972. Argentina. Nightwatchman Ventura Maceiras is struck by a beam of light from a UFO. He suffers symptoms typical of radiation sickness. Following the encounter, he also grows additional teeth.

Case #059. 1972. CO, USA. An anonymous female suffering from infertility is visited in her bedroom by tall humanoid beings and is cured of infertility.

Case #060. March 1973. USA. Olga Adler is visited in her bedroom by a robed being who uses a metallic cylinder to cure her of chronic back pain.

Case #061. March 1973. Goias, Brazil. Bernadette Justiana Gomes (a housekeeper) is cured of Chagas Disease after her employer (General Paulo Ochoa, a UFO contactee) asked the ETs to intervene.

Case #062. 5/27/1973. Sao Paulo, Brazil. Dona Geni Lisboa is struck by a beam of light from a UFO and cured of hypertension.

Case #063. October 1973. Lehi, UT, USA. Debbie Roach is cured of an undescribed illness following a missing time abduction involving her entire family.

Case #064. 9/14/1973. Marseille, France. Denise B. is walking outside when she is struck by a beam of light, pulled into the air and has missing time. Upon return, her throat cancer is healed.

Case #065. 7/8/1974. Brooklyn, NY, USA. Columnist Brandon Blackman sees a UFO and is mysteriously healed of a cut on his finger.

Case #066. 10/25/1974. Rawlings, WY, USA. Oil field worker, Carl Higdon is hunting when he encounters a strange humanoid who abducts him into a UFO. Following the experience, Higdon is cured of kidney stones, and the scarring on his lung due to tuberculosis.

Case #067. 5/10/1975. Florence, KY, USA. Chuck Doyle is struck by a beam of light from a manta-ray-shaped UFO, curing his head cold.

Case #068. May 1975. Quebec, Canada. Helene Charbonneau, diagnosed with terminal cancer, is taken inside a UFO and healed by small humanoids.

Case #069. 7/12/1975. Dunedin, New Zealand. Four anonymous people (two males and two females) are in a public restaurant when time apparently stops and they are approached by a human-looking figure. All four people report being cured of the flu.

Case #070. 8/13/1975. Alamogordo, NM, USA. Sergeant Charles Moody injures his back while being abducted into a UFO by short humanoids. Onboard the UFO, the entities heal his back with a metallic instrument.

Case #071. 8/26/1975. Fargo, ND, USA. Sandy Larson, her daughter and her daughter's boyfriend encounter a UFO and have missing time. Following the incident, Larson's sinusitis is cured.

Case #072. 1975. New Smyrna Beach, FL, USA. Lynn Plaskett (a city councilwoman) is visited by a nineteen-inch, glowing, silver, disc-shaped object which hovers over her bed, sweeps over her body, and cures her of T-cell lymphoma.

Case #073. 1975. Bogota, Columbia. Juan Osorio is abducted into a UFO by human-looking ETs who cure him of cancer.

Case #074. 4/3/1976. Hinwil, Switzerland. Contactee Eduard Meier is healed by Pleiadeans (human-looking ETs) of body injuries from a car accident.

Case #075. 9/8/1976. Accopampa, Peru. An anonymous male encounters a landed UFO with occupants. One of the occupants touches the witness, healing him of arthritis.

Case #076. 1976. Molebka area, Perm Region, Ural, Russia. Vladimir S. encounters a UFO and human-looking ET. He is struck by a beam of light and is healed of severe back injuries.

Case #077. 1976. Brazil. A young girl, "Dirce," is visited in her backyard by a tall, strange-looking being who shined a light on her, curing her poor vision.

Case #078. 7/10/1977. Pinheiro, Brazil. Chicken and cattle farmer, Jose Benedito Bogeo is abducted into a UFO by human-looking ETs. Following the incident, he suffered from back pain, but also experienced a complete improvement in his eyesight, and no longer needed to wear glasses.

Case #079. 12/22/1977. Ensenada, Puerto Rico. Bernardo Vega is visited in his bedroom by three short entities who cured him of heart disease. His wife, who was ill and vomiting, also reported being cured.

Case #080. Mid-1970s. Florida, USA. Contactee, Anthony Champlain, is taken onboard a UFO and healed of arm injuries.

Case #081. March 1978. Canary Islands. "Henry" is visited by three human-looking ETs who cure him of intestinal illness.

Case #082. March 1978. Hinwil, Sweden. Eduard Meier is taken in full view of several witnesses aboard a UFO and healed of pneumonia.

Case #083. 7/17/1978. Cayey, Puerto Rico. "Carmela" is taken by short humanoids from her home into a UFO where she is cured of chronic kidney disease.

Case #084. 1978. Jao Pessoa, Paraiba, Brazil. An anonymous male is visited by two entities who offer to cure the man of a festering eye problem. Frightened, the male refused treatment from the ETs, who left by walking through the wall.

Case #085. 1978. San Luis Valley, CO. "Barbara Benara" is taken from her home by gray ETs and healed of cancer.

Case #086. 1978. USA. "Ana" is cured of a back injury by a uniformed occupant using a laser-like instrument.

Case #087. 8/30/1979. St. Eustache, Quebec, Canada. Jean Cyr (an army officer) and his family experience a series of low-level sightings over their homes, following which Cyr is mysteriously cured of multiple sclerosis.

Case #088. Summer 1979. Bayamon, Puerto Rico. Myriam is abducted by gray ETs and cured of bone cancer.

Case #089. 1979. Simferopol, Crimea, Ukraine. Faina Maksimovna sees a UFO outside her home and is visited in her bedroom by three tall humanoids who heal her of a thyroid tumor. Prior to the incident, she had prayed to God for a healing.

Case #090. 1979. Sturgeon Bay, WI, USA. An anonymous girl is taken aboard a UFO and cured of muscular dystrophy by human-looking ETs, (as reported by contactee, Dean Anderson.)

Case #091. 1970s. USA. "Star Traveler" is healed of a head injury by gray ETS, with whom he has many encounters. He also reports a healing of pleurisy.

Case #092. late 1970s (approx.) Las Vegas, NV, USA. Casey Claar is healed of a severe sunburn.

Case #093. August 1980. San Juan, Puerto Rico. Hector Vasquez is on his way to the hospital because of severe pain caused by kidney stones when a UFO appears, circles around his car, relieving his pain and removing his kidney stones.

Case #094. 11/19/1980. Longmont, CO, USA. "Michael" (an art teacher) is abducted into a UFO by gray ETs who enact a partial cure of his melanoma.

Case #095. 11/28/1980. West Yorkshire, England. Police Officer Alan Godfrey is cured of infertility as the result of missing time encounter with a UFO.

Case #096. 1980. Puerto Rico. Ivan Rivera Morales is abducted by gray ETs, taken to an undersea base and is cured of rheumatism.

Case #097. November 1981. Hubbard, OR, USA. Denise Twiggs is visited in the hospital room by human-looking ETs who speed up the healing of her caesarean section scar on her abdomen.

Case #098. 1981. England. "Ek Mau" (a five-year-old girl) is mysteriously cured of congenital hip dysplasia, and later attributes the cure to ETs due to a large number of UFO encounters and ET visitations throughout her life.

491

Case #099. 1981. Willamette Valley, OR, USA. "Marie," (a retired school teacher) experiences a miraculous cure of a stroke following a visit by tall faceless humanoids.

Case #100. July 1982. Catalina Island, CA, USA. "Mattie" is cured of eczema following a prolonged sighting of multiple, close-up objects.

Case #101. August 1982. IO, USA. Dagmar and her husband are taken aboard a UFO and given an examination, during which the aliens remove a mole located under Dagmar's arm.

Case #102. Summer 1982. Willamette Valley, OR, USA. "Douglas" is suffering from a severe streptococcus infection when he is visited in his hospital room by a strange-looking, female humanoid who cured him by injecting him with medicine.

Case #103. 1983. USA. Anonymous female is taken onboard a UFO and healed by three short figures of an infected cut on her hand.

Case #104. 2/28/1984. Farnham, England. An anonymous male is pulled from the scene of a car accident into a UFO where he is cured by several short gray-type ETs.

Case #105. September 1984. Bilbao, Spain. Jose Maria Arranz experiences a series of encounters with a seven-foot-tall entity, and is mysteriously cured of his back pain.

Case #106. 1984. Botucatu, Brazil. Joao Vicente is cured of a cerebral aneurysm after being given medicine given to UFO contactee, Joao Valerio (who obtained it from human-looking ETs)

Case #107. early 1985. Toronto, Ontario, Canada. "Veronica" observed a UFO land outside her home. Human-looking figures appeared in her room and took her aboard the craft and cured her of kidney pain. Their appearance transformed from human to gray.

Case #108. Summer, 1985. Vancouver, British Columbia, Canada. An anonymous female was meditating in her room to relieve her kidney pain when a tall humanoid appeared. The witness found herself aboard a UFO surrounded by seven-foot-tall humanoids who mysteriously cured her kidney problems.

Case #109. 1985. Obninsk, Kaluga, Russia. Marina Lukonina was visited by seven-foot-tall ETs who invited her aboard their ship and healed her of heart disease.

Case #110. 3/22/1986 Teocaltiche, Mexico. An anonymous six-year-old girl (stricken with cancer) is visited by a seven-foot-tall humanoid who cures her using two glowing tubes.

Case #111. 5/9/1986. Danville, PA, USA. An anonymous male and his family experience a missing time incident. Afterward, an undescribed body injury was mysteriously healed.

Case #112. 5/15/1986. Donetsk, Ukraine. Alexander Viktorovich is abducted from a train station by a human-looking figure who cured him of his back pain using touch.

Case #113. 12/27/1986. Milan, Italy. An anonymous male, (a celebrity), sees a UFO and several humanoid figures who invite him aboard their UFO. He declines, but reports that following the encounter, his lung disease disappeared.

Case #114. 1986. Florida, USA. An anonymous girl suffering from a brain tumor is visited by cloaked beings who heal her.

Case #115. 1986. La Jolla, CA, USA. Richard T is abducted into a torpedo-shaped UFO and examined by small humanoids. Upon his return, his paralysis is reversed, and the witness no longer needs to use a wheelchair.

Case #116. 1986. Lapland, Finland. Dr. Rauni-Leena Luukanen-Kilde (chief medical officer of Finnish Lapland and wife to Sverre Kilde, a Norwegian diplomat to the United Nations) is given first aid by a small ET immediately following a vehicle accident.

Case #117. 3/7/1987. Ping Wu, Szechwan Province, China. A family of three are taken inside a UFO. Bluish-skinned ETs cut the child's leg and heal it with a pencil-like instrument.

Case #118. June 1987. Drome, France. An anonymous male encounters a landed UFO and humanoids. He is invited aboard the craft, taken to an ET space-station, where is he cured of AIDs, and is then returned.

Case #119. 7/10/1987 Hollonville, GA, USA. "Reese" (who suffers from partial paralysis caused by a vehicle accident) is woken up in his bedroom by a UFO hovering outside. He experiences missing time. In the three months following the experience, his paralysis disappears.

Case #120. July 1987. Reno, NV, USA. Kate is cured of a uterine infection and cervical cancer by ETs.

Case #121. August 1987. Simferopol, Crimea, Ukraine. "Viktor" is out hiking when he experiences one-month-long period of missing time. He later recalls a complex prolonged encounter with ETs who cured him of an undescribed serious illness.

Case #122. 1987. Atlanta, GA, USA. "Alicia Hansen" experiences a head-on collision with another vehicle, and is taken from the scene of the accident into a UFO. Gray ETs tell her the accident would have been fatal. They cure her extensive injuries and return her to the scene of the accident.

Case #123. 1987. Afghanistan. An anonymous Soviet soldier suffers severe body injuries and is about to commit suicide by grenade when he is pulled into a UFO. Strange "people" cure him of his injuries, but cannot save his leg, which they amputate and heal.

Case #124. Mid-1980s. PA, USA. Edward Carlos is diagnosed with a melanoma. He undergoes surgery and experiences a remission, which he attributes in part to "energies transmitted to him by the abduction process."

Case #125. 3/20/1988. Richland Center, WI, USA. John Salter Jr. (aka: John Hunter Gray) and his son are abducted while driving. Onboard the UFO, they are examined by gray ETs who inject them with needles. Following the incident, Salter Jr. lost all desire to smoke and noted more than eighteen physiological improvements including improved skin tone, circulation, eyesight, hair and nail growth, disappearance of wrinkles, faster healing of cuts, weight loss and overall increase in health. His son also noted several improvements.

Case #126. 3/24/1988. New Iberia, LA, USA. Two people suffer a severe car accident and multiple injuries. One of the victims (the driver) was taken from the accident-scene into a UFO where a six-foot-tall, muscular, human-looking figure healed a portion of her injuries, and returned her back to the accident.

Case #127. May 1988. Sebago Cabins, NY, USA. Anonymous male is cured of arthritis-like condition in his legs while meeting with contactee, Sixto Paz Wells.

Case #128. 7/19/1988. Johannesburg, South Africa. "Diane" is cured of jaundice following an onboard UFO encounter.

Case #129. October 1988. New York City, NY, USA. "Fred" is taken aboard a UFO and sees a woman cut open and healed using a laser-like instrument held by a gray ET.

Case #130. December 1988. Watsonville, CA, USA. Ann DeSoto has a missing time encounter and wakes up with a strange mark on her hip. The arthritis in her hip is cured.

Case #131. 1988 (approx.) CA, USA. "Sherri" experiences an abduction where she is healed of a yeast infection.

Case #132. 1988 (approx.) CA, USA. "Linda" (Sherri's sister), experiences an abduction where (like her sister) is healed of a yeast infection. She also observes many other people being healed.

Case #133. 1988 (approx.) CA, USA. Linda is taken onboard a UFO and cured of stomach cancer. On a second occasion, she had a similar procedure done to her breast. Both events were recalled under hypnosis.

Case #134. 1988 (approx.) CA, USA. Anonymous man is cured of a stomach ulcer onboard a UFO by gray ETs (as witnessed by California abductee, Linda.)

Case #135. 1988 (approx.) CA, USA. Anonymous girl is cured of intestinal worms onboard a UFO by gray ETs (as witnessed by California abductee, Linda.)

Case #136. 1988 (approx.) CA, USA. Anonymous male is taken onboard a UFO and cured of bursitis by gray ETs (as witnessed by California abductee, Linda.)

Case #137. 1988 (approx.) CA, USA. Anonymous male is taken onboard a UFO and cured of arthritis in his hip, (as witnessed by California abductee, Linda.)

Case #138. 1988 (approx.) CA, USA. Anonymous man is healed of tumor aboard a UFO (as witnessed by California abductee, Linda.)

Case #139. 4/18/1989. Krasnoperekopsk, Crimea, Ukraine. An anonymous female suffering from heart disease is visited in her hospital moon by a human-looking male and healed.

Case #140. 7/5/1989. Atlantic City, NJ, USA. Richard Rylka is taken aboard a UFO and healed of a tumor on his forehead.

Case #141. 7/14/1989. Hubbard, OR, USA. Bert Twiggs is visited in his room by the "Andromes," human-looking ETs, who cure him of the flu.

Case #142. 8/7/1989. Pensacola, FL. After suffering a lightning strike, Katharina W. was taken board a UFO and healed by a gray ET of damage to her heart.

Case #143. Summer 1989. Kiev, Ukraine. Sergey K is recovering in a hospital from a stroke when he is visited in his hospital room by a tall human-looking figure who passes his hand over Sergey several times, curing him.

Case #144. 10/4/1989 Amsterdam, Netherlands. Tulip farmer Jan DeGroot encounters a human-looking ET in his greenhouse and experiences missing time. He wakes up to find that a large wart on his body is missing.

Case #145. 10/15/1989. Hubbard, OR, USA. Stacey, the daughter of Bert and Denise Twiggs is taken aboard a UFO and treated for asthma.

Case #146. 10/15/1989. Hubbard, OR, USA. Bert Twiggs is abducted aboard a UFO. While onboard, he injures his back during a fall. Human-looking ETs return Bert to his home and heal his back using a hand-held instrument.

Case #147. 12/15/1989. MS, USA. "Mae" (a waitress) encounters a UFO and has missing time. Following the incident, she is cured of severe arthritis.

Case #148. December 1989. Hubbard, OR, USA. Christopher, the son of Bert and Denise Twiggs was taken onboard a UFO with his family and cured of a sty.

Case #149. December 1989. Queens, NY, USA. Eddie Sosa is visited in his bedroom by five human-looking ETs who cure him of Hodgkin's Disease.

Case#150. 1989. Deming, NM, USA. Anonymous nurse is visited in her home by four short figures who heal her of vertigo using a box-like device.

Case #151. 1989. Sacramento, CA, USA. Connie Isele is healed of severe uterine cramping by gray ETs.

Case #152. 1989. Los Angeles, CA, USA. Licea Davidson is diagnosed with terminal cancer and given three months to live when she is abducted by ETs who give her painful operation, and cure her.

Case #153. 1980s (approx.) USA. A female abductee is taken aboard a UFO. She is cut open and healed using a pencil-like instrument.

Case #154. 1980s (approx.) Georgia, Russia. An anonymous factory worker was suffering a third heart attack when he found himself surrounded by grays. He passed out, and in the morning, all symptoms of his heart attack were gone.

Case #155. 1980s (approx.) Chicago, IL, USA. Doriel is visited by two human-looking ETs who cure her of infertility.

Case #156. 1980s (approx.) East Kilbride, England. An anonymous man is abducted by gray type ETs and healed of a tumor in his chest.

Case #157. 1980s (approx.) Puerto Rico. Willie Durand Urbina (a UFO researcher) is about to undergo surgery for a cancerous brain tumor when he experiences a miraculous recovery, followed by two UFO sightings.

Case #158. late 1980s (approx.) San Francisco, CA, USA. Chuck Weiss experienced a dramatic miraculous healing of lung damage caused by drug abuse.

Case #159. Late 1980s (approx.) Hungary. An anonymous woman experiences four abductions, resulting in her condition of cancer being cured.

Case #160. 4/15/1990. Island of Iona. Professor Edward Carlos was struck by a beam of light and experienced missing time. Under hypnosis he recalled seeing reptilian humanoids, white-skinned humanoids, and insectoid figures. The ETs used laser-like instruments to clear out blockages in Carlos's arteries.

Case #161. 6/20/1990. Sochi, Russia. Vladimir Vasilchenko encounters two female ETs who heal him of a boil on his finger using an alien instrument.

Case #162. Summer, 1990. Kolva Base, Verk, Komi, Russia. Vasily A. is abducted from his home and cured of a finger injury and dental issues by human-looking and gray ETs.

Case #163. 11/25/1990. Tula, Russia. Tatyana Grigorevna Gavrilina is taken into a UFO by a human-looking female, examined and then healed of stomach pain.

Case #164. 1990. Moscow, Russia. Military officer Mr. Moskalenko injures his leg after being attacked by a mysterious force. A strange man approaches and heals his leg using apparent mind power.

Case #165. early 1990s (approx.) Southwestern USA. An anonymous male is driving through the remote desert with his family. The car overheats and the male burns his hand. A mysterious "hospital" appears by the side of the road. The man is taken inside and healed by human-looking figures.

Case #166. early 1990s (approx.) Chicago, IL, USA. "Ann" is taken onboard a UFO where she is cured of a sinus condition with a wand-like instrument.

Case #167. early 1990s (approx.) England. Bob Rylance is taken by "little guys" from his bedroom and into a UFO, where he is cured of "a diseased part" of his stomach.

Case #168. early 1990s (approx.) Hubbard, OR, USA. Denise Twiggs is taken aboard a UFO and given an operation to remove a section of her intestines ulcerated by colitis.

Case #169. Early 1990s (approx.) Midwestern USA. "Eddie" is cured of colored blindness following on onboard UFO operation.

Case #170. Early 1990s. Harrison County, WV, USA. "Daniel" is taken aboard a UFO by gray and green ETs. During an abduction event, Daniel asked the ETs to heal his impacted wisdom tooth, which they did.

Case #171. early 1990s. Finland. A man suffering from a chronically enlarged liver is struck by a beam of light from an egg-shaped UFO, healing his liver.

Case #172. Early 1990s (approx.) Santa Rosa, Peru. An anonymous truck driver is cured of malignant stomach cancer following a close encounter with a UFO.

Case #173. January 1991. Ponce, Puerto Rico. A few days after being bit on the leg by a shark, Jose Maria Fernandez Maria sees a UFO close-up and the following morning experiences rapid healing of his wound.

Case #174. 9/28/91. Skogveien, Norway. Anonymous male is cured of chronic asthma during a UFO sighting with contactee, Arve Gjovik.

Case #175. 1991. Norway. "Natalie" is visited in her bedroom by a group of gray ETs who heal her of severe back injuries.

Case #176. 1991. Claremont, CA, USA. A woman is struck by a blue beam of light from a UFO, curing her of chronic back pain.

Case #177. 1991. Atlanta, GA, USA. "Alicia Hansen" is diagnosed with a cyst in her breast, which mysteriously disappears.

Case #178. December 1992. Virginia, USA. Beth Collings experiences a missing time abduction resulting in an improvement in her vision.

Case #179. December 1992. Virginia, USA. Anna Jamerson, friend of Beth Collings experienced a series of abductions resulting in improvements in her vision.

Case #180. 1992. Location unknown. Two people are cured of pneumonia during their abductions, as reported by David Jacobs Ph.D. in his book, *Secret Life*.

Case #181. 1992. Sacramento, CA, USA. Abductee Connie Isele wakes up to find three evenly spaced bruises on her arthritic knee. The arthritis is now gone.

Case #182. 1992. Southern CA, USA. "John" is visited by a gray alien, preventing him from committing suicide by gun.

Case #183. 1992. Location unknown. An anonymous man tests positive for AIDs, then experiences a few UFO abductions and tests negative for the disease.

Case #184. January 1993. Las Vegas, NV, USA. Contactee Frank E. Stranges is assaulted by MIB when human-looking ETs appear, take him into a UFO and heal his injuries with a cone-shaped instrument which emitted a blue light.

Case #185. 9/23/1993. Kokomo, IN, USA. Three days before a scheduled hysterectomy, Debbie Jordan sees a UFO and a gray ET and experiences missing time. Following the incident, a uterine tumor disappears.

Case #186. 1993. Fyffe, AL, USA. "Ron" had earlier missing time experiences and UFO sightings before experiencing a chainsaw accident which caused two broken ribs. He went to sleep and when he woke up, his ribs were healed, there was a burn mark on his shirt, and a pen in his pocket had been melted.

Case #187. 1993. Cambridge, OH, USA. "Neal" (Air Force Officer) wakes up to find burn-marks on his groin, and discovers his condition of infertility (the result of a childhood accident) has been healed. Outside his home he found strange burn marks on the ground.

Case #188. 1993 (approx.) Tbilisi, Russia. Boy is healed of knee injury by human-looking ETs.

Case #189. 1993 (approx.) Tbilisi, Russia. A man is cured of chronic back pain by friendly, human-looking ETs.

Case #190. 1993 (approx.) Tbilisi, Russia. An anonymous male is cured of a heart condition.

Case #191. 1992 (approx.) Tbilisi, Russia. An anonymous young female is taken aboard a UFO and cured of diabetes by human-looking ETs.

Case #192. 1/19/1994. Topanga Canyon, CA, USA. "Michelline" is cured by gray-type ETs of a hernia on her abdomen.

Case #193. 2/21/1994. San Francisco, CA, USA. Chuck Weiss is healed of severe arm pain by an invisible entity.

Case #194. April 1994. San Francisco, CA, USA. Abductee Chuck Weiss asks his ET contacts to heal him of tendonitis in his left middle finger. Days later, his tendonitis mysteriously disappears.

Case #195. June 1994. HI, USA. William Shelhart wakes up to find a triangular mark on his ankle. A second experience occurs involving a bright light and a new mark on his wrist, curing him of tendonitis in his wrist, and arthritis in his ankle.

Case #196. 7/12/1994. Williamsburg, KY, USA. While riding in a pick-up, Jay sees a UFO and experiences missing time. Following the encounter, he is healed of intestinal problems.

Case #197. Summer 1994. NC, USA. Jim Sparks is taken by gray aliens onboard a UFO and is shown a box which contains vials of a smelly, black liquid. He is told it was extracted from his lungs, and that it was a "gift."

499

Case #198. 9/12/1994. Midwestern USA. "David" is taken by gray ETs from his bedroom into a UFO and cured of undiagnosed intestinal difficulties.

Case #199. 12/13/1994. Burbank, CA, USA. On the day before surgery to remove a breast cyst "Morgana Van Klausen" has a UFO sighting followed by a bedroom visitation. Following the incident, the tumor is missing.

Case #200. 1994. LaGrange, GA, USA. "Lynnette" is healed by gray ETs of a softball-sized tumor in her right lung.

Case #201. Early 1995. Los Angeles, CA, USA. Jean Moncrief is diagnosed with a lump in her breast. She is visited in her room by entities and abducted. The next morning, there is a mark on her breast and the lump in her breast is gone.

Case #202. 8/17/1995. California, USA. Matthew is visited in his home by a gray who cures him of his knee pain.

Case #203. 9/3/1995. Davis, CA, USA. "Christina" is taken from her living room into a UFO where she sees a tall gray-type ET. She lost consciousness and woke up the next morning back in her home, cured of influenza.

Case #204. November 1995. Sacramento, CA, USA. Abductee Connie Isele is cured of broken legs in her hospital room by a tall humanoid.

Case #205. Late 1995. NC, USA. Jim Sparks is suffering from the flu when he is visited by two gray ETs who heal him of his illness.

Case #206. 1995. Murphys, CA, USA. "Dave" is taken from his home into a UFO and cured of leg injuries by gray ETs.

Case #207. 1995. New York City, NY, USA. Erica X., is abducted into a UFO. A gray alien cuts her leg with an instrument, then heals the cut using mind power.

Case #208. 1995. NE, USA. "Jill Wheeler" is taken from her home into an apparent underground base and is cured of a hypoglycemia-like illness by a nine-foot humanoid ET.

Case #209. 1995 (approx.) CA, USA. Anonymous woman reports the healing of yeast infection to researcher, Richard Boylan.

Case #210. 1995 (approx.) Los Angeles, CA, USA. Alternative health practitioner, Lavinia Ritkiss is visited by short humanoids who gave her a homeopathic cure for arthritis and other diseases.

Case #211. 1995. Sacramento, CA, USA. Chuck Weiss wakes up to find that a precancerous node on his face (which he had for years) is now missing. Because he has a long history of encounters, he credits the healing to ETs.

Case #212. 1995. USA. An anonymous female is cured of uterine cancer during an encounter. Previously, the woman experienced a healing of a yeast infection.

Case #213. 10/6/1996. San Antonio, TX. USA. "Andrew" experiences a missing time abduction from his home. Upon return, a large mole on his head was missing.

Case #214. 12/27/1996. San Antonio, TX, USA. "Andrew" experiences a missing time abduction during which he was cured of a painful kidney stone.

Case #215. March 1997. San Juan, Puerto Rico. "Carmina" (a clinical psychologist) is visited in her downtown office by a human-looking ET who cures her of a cyst in her left breast.

Case #216. June 1997. Borovye, Chelyabinsk region, Russia. A farmer taken aboard a landed UFO piloted by tall humanoids who cure of knee injuries and kidney stones.

Case #217. October 1997. West Covina, CA, USA. David Perez is beamed by a red-light from a UFO, curing him of suicidal depression, general body pains and lung problems.

Case #218. 1997. Lake Baikal, Russia. R. Slavskiy encounters a landed UFO and humanoids. He is taken onboard and cured of leprosy.

Case #219. 7/11/1998. Puerto Rico. An anonymous woman is visited in her bedroom by a human-looking figure who abducts her into a UFO where gray ETs remove a cyst.

Case #220. Summer 1998. Petrozavodsk, Russia. Igor Nikolayevich Petukhov (a farmer) experienced three separate encounters with a short humanoid outside his home, followed by an inexplicable improvement in his chronic heart disease.

Case #221. 9/28/1998. Angol, Chile. Gabriel Ortega Flores (age four) is being driven by his mother when they encounter a UFO and feel a blast of heat. Flores is suddenly cured of severe rheumatic fever.

Case #222. Winter 1998. Location unknown. Anonymous witness suffering from a severe respiratory infection has a "powerful dream" of being abducted and healed by a gray. Upon waking up, the witness enjoys a speedy recovery.

Case #223. 9/20/1999. Momoishi, Japan. While fleeing from a UFO, "Tim" falls, cuts his hand, and is abducted into the object, where he meets short grays who heal him of his cut.

Case #224. 12/20/1999. Denver, CO, USA. "Natalie" drives under a UFO and begins dreaming about being taken onboard. In the weeks that follow, her hair darkens and her spider veins quickly heal and disappear.

Case #225. 1999. Grand Tetons, WY, USA. Anonymous man falls down a cliff while mountain climbing, and encounters a blue-feathered being who cures him of broken legs.

Case #226. 1990s (approx.) USA. Contactee Joni Ferris is taken by ETs from her bedroom into a UFO where she is cured of pneumonia.

Case #227. 1990s (approx.) United Kingdom. An anonymous nine-year-old girl is taken by a praying mantis ET from her bedroom and into a UFO, where she is cured of an arthritis-like condition in her legs.

Case #228. 1990s. (approx.) USA. An anonymous woman suffering from acute arthritis in her shoulder is cured by a rod-of-light during a contact experience.

Case #229. 1990s. (approx.) Hubbard, OR, USA. Bert Twiggs is taken aboard a UFO and healed of lung cancer (a condition he was not aware of.)

Case #230. Late 1990s (approx.) AR, USA. A grandmother is healed of the flu by alien-looking figures.

Case #231. November, 2000. Gainesville, FL, USA. Jim Law is visited in his bedroom by gray ETs who cure his inguinal hernia.

Case #232. 2000. USA. An anonymous woman is taken from her home and cured by gray ETs of a severe blood clot.

Case #233. 2001. FL, USA. FDEA agent, Alberto Fernandez is visited in his bedroom by an entity who uses green light to cure him of a severe eye injury.

Case #234. June 2001. Virginia Beach, VA, USA. Dudley Delaney is cured of prostate problems following a UFO abduction.

Case #235. October 2001. Nizhniy, Novgorod Province, Russia. Oleg (a businessman) is visited in his home by a UFO and occupants who cured him of his atrophied legs.

Case #236. 2002. (approx.) Italy. While in the hospital suffering from cancer, a man is healed by three humanoid figures using a strange instrument.

Case #237. 01/07/2003. Ontario, Canada. Mary is paced by a UFO for several miles. Following the incident, a chronic heart murmur disappeared.

Case #238. 10/2/2004. Bristol, TN, USA. "Sidney" (a country western singer) has a close-up sighting with a UFO and missing time. Following the incident, a diagnosed brain tumor is gone.

Case #239. Early 2000s. Oakland, CA, USA. Alicia Flowers is abducted and told by the ETs that they were healing her of hepatitis.

Case #240. January 2005. Location unknown. Alison Anton was visited in her bedroom by a mantis like being who healed her eyesight using energy and light.

Case #241. 2005. Priestwood, Bracknell, England. Terry Walters is cured of back pain following a UFO abduction.

Case #242. 2005. Miami, FL, USA. Alberto Fernandez (an army officer, police officer and government employee) is cured of a cancerous lump in his lung while in the hospital x-ray room.

Case #243. 4/18/2006. Argentina. "E. R." (diagnosed with pancreatic cancer) finds herself pulled into a UFO where she is cured by five tall ETs.

Case #244. 5/4/2006. Denver, CO, USA. Businessman Stan Romanek is cured of knee injuries during a missing time incident.

Case #245. August 2006. Canada. E. A. Sabean is cured of chronic renal failure by short hooded beings. It was the third encounter she had with the beings.

Case #246. 2006 (approx.) Uxmal, Yucatan, Mexico. Salvador, is diagnosed with lung cancer and told by his doctors that his condition is terminal and sent home to die. Following a series of UFO sightings, he is cured by five entities.

Case #247. 1/8/2007. Cape Fear River, NC, USA. Chris Bledsoe is taken into a UFO and cured of Crohn's disease.

Case #248. Spring 2007. Gyanja, Azerbaijan. A woman (who was reported missing) has missing time and recalls being examined by humanoid figures. Suffering from a rare form of cancer, following the encounter, she was cured.

Case #249. 11/3/2007. Puerto Rico. Maria M. Rivera is taken from her home and abducted into a UFO and cured of ovarian cancer by gray ETs.

Case #250. 2007 (approx.) Southern, CA, USA. Craig Campobasso suffered a severe bowel obstruction and was rushed to the hospital for immediate surgery.

That night he experienced an unexplained healing. The next morning, x-rays showed that the obstruction was gone.

Case #251. 1/10/2008. Las Vegas, NV, USA. Anonymous witness who suffers from poor night vision encounters a UFO and experienced a dramatic improvement of his vision.

Case #252. 1/12/2008. Dubno, Rovno, Ukraine. Olga Voronezhskiy and her husband Vladimir were taken from their home into a UFO by short humanoids with large heads. Olga was taken to a chair and cured of chronic colitis. Victor's reported feeling increased energy and strength, and his hair went from gray to black.

Case #253. December 2008. Berlin, Germany. Diagnosed with a pregnancy and leukemia on the same day, Greta Brandt considers suicide, but is approached by two humanoids and taken inside a UFO where she is healed of leukemia, which was confirmed by her doctor.

Case #254. 12/30/2008. USA. "Thomas" encounters strange lights outside his home and returns from the encounter cured of a chest infection.

Case #255. 2008. Canada. An anonymous woman is visited in her hospital room by Praying Mantis ETs who attempt to cure her severe head injuries.

Case #256. 2008. Ocean City, MD, USA. An anonymous male suffering from cancer becomes mysteriously well following a series of close-up UFO sightings.

Case #257. February 2009. Andorra, Spain. Four children (all suffering from terminal cancer in the Pyrenees Children's Hospital) are visited in their hospital rooms by short humanoids and cured of cancer.

Case #258. September 2009. USA. "Cory" and his wife are taken by grays disguised as humans from their home into a nearby building where he is cured of knee problems. Cory also reports improvement to vision and sense of smell.

Case #259. Summer 2010. USA. "Michelle," diagnosed with breast cancer, is visited by gray ETs who cure her.

Case #260. 2010. Fresno, CA, USA. "Kathryn" is healed of hand pain by a beam of light in her bedroom.

Case#261. 2010 (approx.) Alaska, USA. "Belle" a Native American medicine woman is cured of an axe-wound by human-looking ETs.

Case #262. 2010 (approx.) AZ, USA. Gwen Farrell CHT is visited in her bedroom and healed of sinusitis.

Case #263. 2011. LaGrange, GA, USA. "Lynnette" is taken by gray ETs from her home into a craft and healed of a heart condition.

Case #264. 3/4/2012. Miami, FL, USA. "Nena" (the pet dog of Rey Hernandez) is visited by an ET and taken into a UFO and cured of arthritis and paralysis.

Case #265. 7/23/2012. Lehighton, PA, USA. "Michael Chambliss" sees a gray type ET and experiences missing time. Upon waking up, his broken foot is now healed.

Case #266. 8/2/2012. Warren, PA, USA. Joy Davies is taken inside a UFO and cured of arthritis. Her dog was also taken, and also became more active.

Case #267. 2012. FL, USA. Teri Lynge (Florida assistant state section director for MUFON) was visited in her bedroom by a short, scaly figure with compelling eyes. The being used a metallic instrument to cure Lynge of chronic abdominal pain.

Case #268. 2012. Location unknown. "Kay" (a UFO researcher and abductee) visits a channeler and requests a healing. She is later visited by gray ETs who cure her of fibromyalgia.

Case #269. May 2013. Kirkland, OH, USA. "Erin" undergoes two bone marrow transplants and is cured of leukemia. A photo taken of the girl shows a her being struck by a red beam of light, invisible to the photographer, causing speculation that she was cured by otherworldly methods.

Case #270. 6/9/2013. Manchester, NJ, USA. "Steven" is visited in his bedroom by a tall, white, glowing humanoid who healed him of an imminent heart attack.

Case #271. 7/4/2013. Asheville, NC, USA. Reverend Michael J. Carter is visited in his bedroom by a tall, human-looking figure who cures him of a severe blood clot in his leg using apparent mind power.

Case #272. 2013. MA, USA. Woman is visited by a gray alien in her bedroom and is healed of a knee injury.

Case #273. 2013. AL, USA. Ruth Simmons injures her leg during a UFO abduction by grays, and is healed by a Nordic using mind power.

Case #274. 2013. USA. An anonymous physician experienced severe bleeding following a wisdom tooth extraction. He passed out and woke up aboard a UFO being examined by a gray ET. The next morning, his wound was healed.

Case #275. 2013. UT, USA. Don Anderson is visited in his home by a humanoid who cures him of a chest cold by feeding him a strange medicine.

Case #276. 7/23/2013. USA. Alina Del Castillo is cured of infected cut on her toe by a violet-colored orb.

Case #277. 10/4/2014. Colorado Springs, CO, USA. Following a close-up UFO sighting, a man developed the ability to see with binocular vision.

Case #278. 2014. Belgium. "John" is visited by three entities in his bedroom who heal him of painful foot injuries.

Case #279. 2014. New Zealand. Lauren Kurth (a healer and contactee) is diagnosed with melanoma. She has an encounter and experiences a miraculous healing.

Case #280. January 2015. Marysville, WA, USA. "Marla" (suffering from a gallstone) wakes up to find a scar on her abdomen. A visit to the doctor shows that the gallstone is now missing.

Case #281. 2/25/2015. Winnipeg, Canada. Jim Schaefer (diagnosed with cancer of the lymph nodes) is healed after being targeted by a glowing orb in his home, which he filmed as it entered his body.

Case #282. 7/23/2015. Yonkers, NY, USA. "Rory" is visited in his home by an unseen being who improves his condition of arthritis and diabetes, and also enhances the health of his dog.

Case #283. 7/27/2015. Woodbury, MN, USA. "Yolanda" is about to rush to the hospital because of pain from an ulcer when she is visited by a being who heals her using a beam of light.

Case #284. 9/19/2015. Irvine, CA, USA. UFO researcher Mike Knox is visited in his hotel room by gray aliens and healed of a separated Achilles tendon in his left leg.

Case #285. 2015. Western ME. USA. "Sonya" was having regular contacts with green-skinned insectoid ETs when she experienced a visitation resulting in a dramatic improvement to her condition of glaucoma.

Case #286. 2015. Isle of Wight. Suffering from chemical and electrical sensitivity, "Camilla" visits a healer, and then is repeatedly visited by an invisible entity who cures her.

Case #287. March 2016. USA. "Katrina," a dog owned by Juju T. and suffering from "valley fever" is taken onboard a UFO and healed by human looking ETs.

Case #288. 2016. MS, USA. "Ron" (a computer programmer) is visited in his bedroom by grays and tall humanoids and healed of pain from spinal surgery.

Case #289. 12/1/2017. Knightsville, SC, USA. An anonymous woman is visited in her bedroom by a gray ET who heals her of a migraine headache.

Case #290. June 2018. Cape Cod, MA, USA. Don experiences a wave of sightings over his home, and is cured of disability and body injuries.

NOTE: The following cases are undated:

Case #291. Date unknown. New Zealand. Lauren Kurth is taken into a craft and healed of sinusitis.

Case #292. Date unknown. Victoria, Australia. An anonymous woman is taken inside a UFO and cured of back pain.

Case #293. Date unknown. Location unknown. Anonymous female is taken from her bedroom and healed of ovarian cancer.

Case #294. Date unknown. Location unknown. Anonymous gentleman is healed of back injuries onboard a UFO.

Case #295. Date unknown. Location unknown. Anonymous male is healed of back pain.

Case #296. Date unknown. Location unknown. Anonymous witness is visited by a gray ET and cured of a headache.

Case #297. Date unknown. Location unknown. Anonymous female with a history of abductions is healed of severe stomach pain by a blue light.

Case #298. Date unknown. Location unknown. Anonymous woman is healed of a chronic stomach condition by an ET using a rod-like instrument.

Case #299. Date unknown. Location unknown. Anonymous female is taken by gray ETs from her home into a UFO where she is cured of severe hemorrhoids.

Case #300. Date unknown. Location unknown. Anonymous witness is cured of asthma as the result of a bedroom visitation.

Case #301. Date unknown. Location unknown. Anonymous witness has tar-like substance removed from lungs and is warned by grays not to smoke marijuana.

Case #302. Date unknown. Location unknown. Anonymous witness is cured of infertility as the result of a UFO abduction.

Case #303. Date unknown. Location unknown. Anonymous female is visited in her bedroom by two "helpers" who remove a "suspicious growth" in her breast.

Case #304. Date unknown. Location unknown. Anonymous male is cured of hypertension, a detached retina and a "crooked leg" during an onboard UFO experience. His wife (an abductee) asked the aliens to heal him.

Case #305. Date unknown. Location unknown. An anonymous female discovers that her appendix has been surgically removed, however, she never had surgery.

Case #306. Date unknown. Location unknown. An anonymous witness who is seeing a psychologist to treat suicidal depression has UFO contact, causing the disappearance of her depression.

Case #307. Date unknown. Location unknown. An anonymous witness is cured of cancer by ETs, as reported by his neighbor.

Case #308. Date unknown. Location unknown. An anonymous male (a soldier) is cured of cancer by ETs, who told him the disease was parasitic.

Case #309. Date unknown (poss. circa 2007). Morenci, AZ, USA. A male abductee asks the ETs to heal his son of muscular dystrophy. The ETs provide vials of medicine which allegedly cure the son.

Footnotes and Sources

Preface

1. Dennett, Preston. *UFO Healings: True Accounts of People Healed by Extraterrestrials*. Millspring, NC, Wild Flower Press, 1996. (out of print.)

Introduction

1. Creighton, Gordon. "Healing from UFOs." *Flying Saucer Review.* Sep-Oct, 1969, Vol. 15, #5, pp20-23. See: http://www.fsr.org.uk/fsrmain.htm.
2. Triad UFO Conference, March 1994, Hotel Del Coronado, San Diego, California.
3. Jacobs Ph.D., David. *Secret Life: Firsthand Accounts of UFO Abductions.* New York: Simon & Schuster, 1992, p191.
4. ----. *Walking Among Us: The Alien Plan to Control Humanity*. San Francisco, CA: Red Wheel, Weiser LLC, 2015, pp17, 248.
5. Mack MD, John. *Abduction: Human Encounters with Aliens*. New York: Charles Scribner's and Sons, 1994, pp13, 45.
6. ----. Passport to the Cosmos: Human Transformation and Alien Encounters. New York: Crown Publishers, Inc. 1999, p14.
7. Fiore Ph.D., Edith. *Encounters: A Psychologist Reveals Case Studies of Abductions by Extraterrestrials*. New York: Doubleday, 1989, pp322, 334.
8. Clarke, Ardy Sixkiller. *Sky People: Untold Stories of Alien Encounters in Mesoamerica*. Pompton Plains, NJ: New Page Books, 2015, p276.
9. Bullard, Thomas. *UFO Abductions: The Measure of a Mystery*. Alexandria, VA: Fund for UFO Research. 1987, pp149-150.
10. Wright, Dan. "The Entities: Initial Findings of the Abduction Transcription Project--A MUFON Special Report, Part Two." *MUFON UFO Journal.* Seguin, TX: Mutual UFO Network, March 1994, #311, pp3-6.
11. Hernandez JD, MCP, Ph.D., Reinerio. "UFO Healings That Have Been Swept Under the Rug." *FREE*. The Edgar Mitchell Foundation for Research Into Extraterrestrial and Extraordinary Encounters. Website: https://www.experiencer.org/ufo-healings-that-have-been-swept-under-the-rug-by-reinerio-hernandez/
12. Blum, Ralph and Judy. *Beyond Earth: Man's Contact with UFOs*. New York: Bantam Books, 1974, p143.

13. Stringfield, Leonard. *Situation Red: The UFO Siege*. New York: Fawcett Crest Books, 1977, p72.
14. Vallee, Jacques. *The Invisible College: What a Group of Scientists Has Discovered About UFO Influences on the Human Race*. New York: E.P. Dutton, 1975, p21.
15. Beckley, Timothy Green. "Dean Anderson's Ten-Year Contact Saga." *UFO Universe*. New York: Condor Books, Inc. July 1988, Vol 1, No#1, pp6-7.
16. Steiger, Brad. *The Other*. New Brunswick, NJ: Inner Light Publications, 1992, pp148-149.
17. Huneeus, Antonio. "Close Encounters in Peru." *UFO Universe*. New York: GCR Publishing Group, Inc. Spring, 1994, Vol 4, No#1, pp52-54.
18. Filer, George. "Filer's Files: #37-2008." "Filer's Files: #36-2009." "Filer's Files: #27-2014." *UFO Info.Com*. See website: http://www.ufoinfo.com/index.html.
19. Thompson, Richard. *Alien Identities: Ancient Insights Into Modern UFO Phenomena*. San Diego, CA: Govardhan Hill Publishing, 1993, p128.
20. Rogo, D. Scott. *The Haunted Universe: A Psychic Look at Miracles, UFOs and the Mysteries of Nature*. New York: New American Library, 1977, p103, 108.
21. Boylan Ph.D., Richard J. and Lee K Boylan. *Close Extraterrestrial Encounters: Positive Experiences with Mysterious Visitors*. Newberg, OR: Wild Flower Press, 1994, p25.
22. Boylan Ph.D., pp22-24.
23. Lamb, Barbara and Nadine Lalich. *Alien Experiences: 25 Cases of Close Encounter Never Before Revealed*. Laguna Woods, CA: Trafford Publishing, 2008, p9.
24. Aronson, Virginia. *Celestial Healings: Close Encounters that Cure*. New York: Signet. Dec 1999, pp13-19.
25. Clelland, Mike. *The Messengers: Owls, Synchronicity and the UFO Abductee*. RichardDolanPress.Com: Richard Dolan Press.2015, p306.
26. Rodwell, Mary. Facebook post. Sept 2018.
27. Holloway BA, Ch.T., Karin Hoppe. "Techniques for CE-IVs: The Time Line." See: http://www.ufoinfo.com/news/techniques2.shtml
28. Cochrane, Hugh F. "UFOs: What We're Not Told." Website: https://www.ufocasebook.com/nottold.html. Spring, 1999.
29. Weiss, Chuck. *Abducted by Aliens*. http://abductedbyaliens.org/, p150.
30. Booth, B.J. "Do You Really Want ET to Call?" UFOcasebook.com. https://www.ufocasebook.com/ettocall.html
31. Johnson, Paula. "Can Ufonauts Cure Us of Aids, Cancer and Other Fatal Diseases?" *UFO Universe*. Jul 1988, Vol 1, #1, pp24-27.
32. Personal files/letter to author.
33. Leneesa. "Alien Healings." *UFO Experiences Blogspot*. See: http://ufoexperiences.blogspot.com/2005/10/alien-healings.html.

34. Chalker, Bill. *The Hair of the Alien*. New York: Simon & Schuster, 2005, pp205-206.
35. Cameron, Grant. *Alien Bedtime Stories*. It's All Connected Publishing, 2015, pp234, 272-273.
36. https://www.medicalnewstoday.com/articles/282929.php
37. http://www.who.int/news-room/fact-sheets/detail/the-top-10-causes-of-death

Chapter 1: Why Aliens Make Good Doctors

1. Bullard, Thomas. *UFO Abductions: The Measure of a Mystery*. Alexandria, VA: Fund for UFO Research. 1987, p11.
2. Druffel, Ann and D. Scott Rogo. *The Tujunga Canyon Contacts: Updated Edition*. New York: New American Library, 1980, 1988, pp26-27.
3. Druffel & Rogo. P55.
4. Druffel & Rogo. P312.
5. Fiore Ph.D., Edith. *Encounters: A Psychologist Reveals Case Studies of Abductions by Extraterrestrials*. New York: Doubleday, 1989, pp55-56.
6. Fiore, Ph.D., pp70-73.
7. Fowler, Raymond. *The Andreasson Affair*. Englewood Cliffs, NJ: Prentice-Hall, Inc, 1979, 152.
8. Fowler, pp53-55.
9. Fuller, John G. *The Interrupted Journey*. New York: Dell Publishing, Inc, 1966. pp155-156, 193-194, 196.
10. Hopkins, Budd. *Missing Time: A Documented Study of UFO Abductions*. New York: Richard Marek Publishers, 1981, pp80-81, 87-88.
11. Jacobs, David. *Secret Life: Firsthand Accounts of UFO Abductions*. New York: Simon & Schuster, 1992, p94.
12. Jacobs, p133.
13. Jacobs, p89.
14. Walton, Travis. *The Walton Experience*. New York: Berkley Publishing Corp., 1978, pp104-105.
15. NUFORC. http://www.nuforc.org/webreports/110/S110603.html
16. MUFONCMS. *Mutual UFO Network*. See: https://mufoncms.com/cgi-bin/report_handler.pl?req=view_long_desc&id=62117&rnd=
17. Ropp, Thomas. "Forget Roswell; Arizona's UFO Hotbed." *Newsday*. Melville, NY--Jul 6, 1997.
18. Dennett, Preston. *One in Forty: The UFO Epidemic*. Commack, NY: Kroshka Books, 1994, pp221-254.
19. Holzer, Hans. *The Ufonauts: New Facts on Extraterrestrial Landings*. Greenwich, CT: Fawcett Publications, Inc., 1976, p234.

Chapter 2: Medical Evidence

1. Fowler, Raymond E. *MUFON Field Investigator's Manual.* Seguin, TX: Mutual UFO Network, Inc., 1983, pp8, 131-133.
2. Good, Timothy. *Above Top Secret: The Worldwide UFO Cover-up.* New York: William Morrow & Co., Inc., 1988, pp303-304.
3. Good, pp197-190.
4. Lorenzen, Coral and Jim Lorenzen. *Abducted! Confrontations with Beings from Outer Space.* New York: Berkley Publishing Corp, 1977, pp114, 131.
5. Bowen, Charles. *The Humanoids: A Survey of Worldwide Reports of Landings of Unconventional Aerial Objects and Their Occupants.* Chicago, IL: Henry Regnery Company, 1969, pp234-236.
6. Beckley, Timothy Green. *Strange Encounters: Bizarre and Eerie Contact with UFO Occupants.* New Brunswick, NJ: Inner Light Publications, 1992, pp9-10; Steiger, Brad and Joan Writenhour. *Flying Saucers are Hostile.* New Award Books, 1967, pp23-24, 36-37.
7. Hopkins, Budd. *Missing Time: A Documented Study of UFO Abductions.* New York: Richard Marek Publishers, 1981, p22.
8. Hopkins, pp138.
9. Hopkins, pp201-204.
10. Sanchez-Ocejo, Virgilio and Wendelle C. Stevens. *UFO Contact from Undersea: A Report of the Investigation.* Tucson, AZ: Wendelle C. Stevens, 1982, pp40-46.
11. Good, pp98-99.
12. Steiger & Writenhour, p15.
13. Steiger & Writenhour, pp21-22.
14. Norris, Michael. "The First Annual Gulf Breeze Conference: Part II." *UFO Encounters.* Norcross, GA: Aztec Publishing, Vol. 1., #12, p7.
15. Leir DPM, Roger K. *UFO Crash in Brazil.* San Diego, CA: Book Tree, 2005, pp18-19.
16. Steiger & Writenhour, pp22-23.
17. Vallee, Jacques. *Confrontations: A Scientist's Search for Alien Contact.* New York: Ballantine Books, 1990, pp130-139, 217-223.
18. Vallee, pp124-125.
19. Hall, Richard. *Uninvited Guests: A Documented History of UFO Sightings, Alien Encounters and Coverups.* Santa Fe, NM: Aurora Press, 1988, pp231-232.
20. Schuessler, John. *UFO Related Human Physiological Effects.* Houston, TX, 1996, p16. https://www.scribd.com/document/36311975/Shuessler-UFO-Related-Human-Physiological-Effects-1996
21. Shelsky, Rob. *Deadly UFOs and the Disappeared.* GKRS Publishing, 2015, Pp270-271.

Chapter 3: Hands and Arms

1. Gross, Patrick. Urecat-UFO Related Entities Catalogue. Website: https://ufologie.patrickgross.org/ce3/1914-uk-inverary.htm
2. Green, Gabriel and Warren Smith. *Let's Face the Facts about Flying Saucers.* New York, Popular Library, 1967, pp85-86; Kandinsky. "Two Cops, a UFO and an Alligator." *Abovetopsecret.com.* See Website: http://www.abovetopsecret.com/forum/thread736671/pg1
3. Randazzo, Joseph. *The Contactee Manuscript.* Studio City, CA: The UFO Library, Ltd, 1993. (see chapter 11)
4. Beckley, Timothy Green. *Strange Encounters.* New Brunswick, NJ: Inner Light Publications, pp15-16.
5. Personal files/interview with author.
6. Steiger, Brad and Sherry Hansen Steiger. *Real Aliens, Space Beings and Creatures.* Canton MI: Visible Ink Press, 2011. p47.
7. Rosales, Albert. *Humanoids Encounters: The Others Amongst Us: 1990-1994.* Triangulum Publishing. pp258-259. See website: https://nanopdf.com/download/1990-humanoid-reports_pdf#
8. Weiss, Chuck. *Abducted by Aliens.* http://abductedbyaliens.org/. Pp13-14.
9. NUFORC. http://www.nuforc.org/webreports/077/S77185.html
10. MUFONCMS. *Mutual UFO Network.* See: https://mufoncms.com/cgi-bin/report_handler.pl?req=view_long_desc&id=27480&rnd

Chapter 4: Legs and Feet

1. Creighton, Gordon. "Healing from UFOs." *Flying Saucer Review.* Sep-Oct, 1969, Vol. 15, #5, pp20-23.
2. Good, Timothy. *Alien Update.* London: Arrow Random House, 1993, p75.
3. Vallee, Jacques. *The Invisible College: What a Group of Scientists Has Discovered About UFO Influences on the Human Race.* New York: E.P. Dutton, 1975, pp21-24.
4. http://www.cufos.org/HUMCAT/HUMCAT_Index_1969.pdf.
5. Editor. "Encounters with Aliens on this Day." *UFOinfo.com.* Website: http://www.ufoinfo.com/onthisday/March07.html
6. Rosales, Albert. *Humanoids Encounters: The Others Amongst Us: 1990-1994.* Triangulum Publishing.
7. Ramirez, Julio Victor. "UFOs in Puerto Rico: Thinks UFOs Cured His Leg." *UFO Experiences Blogspot.* December, 14, 2006. See website: http://ufoexperiences.blogspot.com/search?q=HEAL
8. Morrow, Helga. "The Sedona Chronicles." *The Missing Link.* Jan/Feb 1993, p17.
9. Morrow, Helga. "The Sedona Chronicles." *The Missing Link.* Jan/Feb 1993, p17.

10. Aronson, Virginia. *Celestial Healings: Close Encounters that Cure.* New York: Signet. Dec 1999, pp69-79.
11. Bryan, C.D.B. *Close Encounters of the Fourth Kind: Alien Abduction, UFOs and the Conference at M.I.T.* New York: Alfred A, Knopf 1995
12. MUFONCMS. *Mutual UFO Network.* See: https://mufoncms.com/cgi-bin/report_handler.pl?req=view_long_desc&id=49739&rnd=
13. Rosales, Albert. *Humanoids Encounters: The Others Amongst Us: 1999-1995.* Triangulum Publishing. Pp133-136.
14. Rosales, Albert. *Humanoids Encounters: The Others Amongst Us: 1999-1995.* Triangulum Publishing. Pp211-212.
15. Romanek, Stan. *Messages: The World's Most Documented Extraterrestrial Contact Story.* St. Paul, MN: Llewellyn Publications, Inc, 2009. Pp205-210.
16. Ufocasebook.com. Website: http://theufocasebook.freeforums.net/ http://ufocasebook.conforums.com/index.cgi?board=alienabduction&action=display&num=1251663765
17. MUFONCMS. *Mutual UFO Network.* See: https://mufoncms.com/cgi-bin/report_handler.pl?req=view_long_desc&id=51980&rnd=
18. Blackvault.com. http://www.theblackvault.com/casefiles/analysis-of-a-white-material-that-appeared-to-materialize-in-a-residence-in-the-presence-of-twin-experiencers-near-oxford-maine-september-2015/
19. Worley, Don. http://www.abduct.com/worley/worley58.php
20. Personal files/Interview with Author.
21. Burkes MD, Joseph and Preston Dennett. "Medical Healings Reported by UAP Contact Experiences: An Analysis of the FREE Data." *Beyond UFOs: The Science of Consciousness and Contact with Human Intelligence.* (Edited by Rey Hernandez, Jon Klimo Ph.D. and Rudy Schild, Ph.d.) FREE.org. pp397-400.
22. Clarke, Ardy Sixkiller. *Encounters with Star People: Untold Stories of American Indians.* Pompton Plains, NJ: New Page Books, 2012, pp106-110.
23. "Episode #32: What if We Interviewed Big Mike? Alien Abductions, UFOs. Whatifpodcast.com. http://whatifpodcast.com/ep-32-alien-abduction/.
MUFONCMS. *Mutual UFO Network.* See: https://mufoncms.com/cgi-bin/report_handler.pl?req=view_long_desc&id=71840&rnd=

Chapter 5: Abdomen and Chest

1. Rosales, Albert. *Humanoids Encounters: The Others Amongst Us: 1999-1995.* Triangulum Publishing. P56.
2. Twiggs, Denise Rieb and Bert Twiggs. *Secret Vows: Our Lives with Extraterrestrials.* New York: Berkley Books, 1995, p98.
3. Turner, Karla. *Into the Fringe: A True Story of Alien Abduction.* New York: Berkley Books, 1995, pp161-169.

4. Filer, George. "Filer's Files #37-2008." *UFOinfo.com*. See website: http://www.ufoinfo.com/filer/2008/ff0837.shtml
5. Personal files/interview with author.
6. Rosales, Albert. UFOs over Florida: Humanoid and Other Strange Encounters in the Sunshine State. Triangulum Publishing. 2017, p189.

Chapter 6: Neck and Back

1. NUFORC. http://www.nuforc.org/webreports/036/S36128.html.
2. Chorvinsky, Mark. "Our Strange World." *Fate*. St. Paul, MN: Llewellyn Worldwide, Ltd., Oct 1993, pp22-24.
3. Good, Timothy. *Need to Know: UFOs and Military Intelligence*. New York: Pegasus Books, 2007, pp323-325; Hall, Richard. *Uninvited Guests: A Documented History of UFO Sightings, Alien Encounters and Coverups*. Santa Fe, NM: Aurora Press, 1988, pp282-283.
4. http://www.caravaca.blogspot.com/; Atlanti, Sean. *Sean's Humanoid Sightings, 1801-2009*. Unpublished.
5. Personal files/interview with author.
6. Rosales, Albert. *Humanoids Encounters: The Others Amongst Us: 1980-1984*. Triangulum Publishing. p200.
7. Op cit.
8. Twiggs, Denise Reib and Bert Twiggs. *Secret Vows: Our Lives with Extraterrestrials*. New York: Berkley Books, 1995, p111-112.
9. Personal files/Interview with author.
10. Personal Files/Interview with author.
11. Morrow, Helga. "The Sedona Chronicles." *The Missing Link*. Jan/Feb 1993, p17.
12. http://ufocasebook.conforums.com/index.cgi?board=unitedkingdom&action=print&num=1037118993
13. Klimo Ph.D., John. "A Report on Phase III of FREE's Experiencer Research Study: The Results of a Qualitative Study." *Beyond UFOs: The Science of Consciousness and Contact with Human Intelligence*. (Edited by Rey Hernandez, Jon Klimo Ph.D. and Rudy Schild, Ph.d.) FREE.org.,
14. Burkes MD, Joseph and Preston Dennett. "Medical Healings Reported by UAP Contact Experiences: An Analysis of the FREE Data." *Beyond UFOs: The Science of Consciousness and Contact with Human Intelligence*. (Edited by Rey Hernandez, Jon Klimo Ph.D. and Rudy Schild, Ph.d.) FREE.org., pp443-443.
15. Lambert, Olivia. "With X-Files Hitting Our Screens, We Take You Through Australia's Scariest Abductions." *News.com*. See website: http://www.news.com.au/technology/science/space/with-xfiles-hitting-our-screens-we-take-you-through-australias-scariest-abductions/news-story/4be1cb8390b1b8355758a2e6e6ee8260

Chapter 7: Head Injuries

1. Fiore Ph.D., Edith. *Encounters: A Psychologist Reveals Case Studies of Abductions by Extraterrestrials.* New York: Doubleday, 1989, pp166-197
2. Traveler, Star. "'Clown Healers' from Reticulum." *Contact Forum.* Newberg, OR: Wild Flower Press. Mar/Apr 1995, Vol. 3 #? pp9-10
3. Anonymous. "Praying Mantis Account by A." Ufobc.ca. Website: http://ufobc.ca/Beyond/prayingmantis/prayingmantis-a.htm

Chapter 8: Body Injuries

1. Good, Timothy. *Above Top Secret: The Worldwide UFO Cover-up.* New York: William Morrow & Co., Inc., 1988, pp50-54.
2. Personal files/Interview with author.
3. Rosales, Alberto. *Humanoids Encounters: The Others Amongst Us: 1960-1964.* Triangulum Publishing. See website: http://www.galactic-server.net/rune/ufoheal4.html
4. Randazzo, Joseph. *The Contactee Manuscript.* Studio City, CA: The UFO Library, Ltd, 1993. (see chapter 11)
5. Stevens, Wendelle C. *Message from the Pleiades: The Contact Notes of Billy Meier, Vol. 2.* Tucson, AZ: UFO Photo Archives, 1990, pp251-258.
6. Rosales, Alberto. *Humanoids Encounters: The Others Amongst Us: 1980-1984.* Triangulum Publishing.
7. Johnson, Donald A. "Encounters with Aliens on This Day." *On This Day.* UFOinfo.com. (original source: Bob Gribble.) Website: http://www.ufoinfo.com/onthisday/May09.html
8. Ruehl, Franklin R. "Dr. Rauni-Leena Luukanen: They Saved My Life Three Times." http://ufoexperiences.blogspot.com/2007/01/dr-rauni-leena-luukanen.html
9. Personal files/Interview with author.
10. Rosales, Alberto. *Humanoids Encounters: The Others Amongst Us: 2010-2014.* Triangulum Publishing. p215.
11. Pfeifer, Ken. "Two Friends Alien Abduction After Car Crash." http://worldufophotosandnews.org/?p=5602
12. Stranges, Frank E. *My Friend from Beyond Earth.* Van Nuys, CA: I.E.C. Inc, 1981, pp43-47.
13. Raynes, Brent. "Reality Checking: UFO Healings?" *Alternate Perceptions Magazine.* Dec 2004, #86. See website: http://mysterious-america.com/realitycheckap12.html
14. Personal files/interview with author.

Chapter 9: Burns

1. Good, Timothy. *Earth: An Alien Enterprise.* New York: Pegasus Books, 2013, pp83-87.

2. Randles, Jenny. *Abduction: Over 200 Documented UFO Kidnappings Exhaustively Investigated.* Clerkenwell Green, London: Robert Hale Limited, 1988, pp70-72.
3. Bell, Fred. (as told to Brad Steiger.) *The Promise.* New Brunswick, NJ: Inner Light Publications, 1991, pp118-119.
4. Personal files/interview with author.
5. Personal files/interview with author.

Chapter 10: Colds, Flu, Fevers and Infections

1. Randazzo, Joseph. *The Contactee Manuscript.* Studio City, CA: The UFO Library, Ltd, 1993. (see chapter 11)
2. Randazzo, Chapter 2.
3. Stringfield, Leonard. *Situation Red: The UFO Siege.* New York: Fawcett Crest Books, 1977, pp63-69.
4. Rosales, Alberto. *Humanoids Encounters: The Others Amongst Us: 1975-1979.* Triangulum Publishing.
5. Lorenzen, Coral and Jim Lorenzen. *Abducted! Confrontations with Beings from Outer Space.* New York: Berkley Medallion Books, 1966, pp52-69
6. Unknown Country. "Insight Behind the News: Alien Healing." Website: http://www.unknowncountry.com/insight/alien-healing-0.
7. Fiore Ph.D., Edith. *Encounters: A Psychologist Reveals Case Studies of Abductions by Extraterrestrials.* New York: Doubleday, 1989, pp89-113.
8. Fiore Ph.D., pp114-131.
9. Twiggs, Denise Reib and Bert Twiggs. *Secret Vows: Our Lives with Extraterrestrials.* New York: Berkley Books, 1995, pp52-53.
10. https://nanopdf.com/download/1990-humanoid-reports_pdf#
11. Steiger, Brad and Sherry Hansen Steiger. *The Rainbow Conspiracy.* New York: Windsor Publishing Corp, 1994.
12. Leupold, Edwin H. "Deming Woman Recounts 50 Years of Real-life UFO 'Close Encounters.'" *Headlight.* Deming, NM: Jan 27, 1994. (See UFONS, Apr 1994, #297, p4.)
13. Personal files/interview with author.
14. MUFONCMS. *Mutual UFO Network.* See: https://mufoncms.com/cgi-bin/report_handler.pl?req=view_long_desc&id=6539&rnd.
15. Sparks, Jim. *The Keepers: An Alien Message for the Human Race.* Columbus, NC: Wild Flower Press, 2006, pp186-188.
16. Burkes MD, Joseph and Preston Dennett. "Medical Healings Reported by UAP Contact Experiences: An Analysis of the FREE Data." *Beyond UFOs: The Science of Consciousness and Contact with Human Intelligence.* (Edited by Rey Hernandez, Jon Klimo Ph.D. and Rudy Schild, Ph.d.) FREE.org., pp441-442.
17. Personal files/interview with author.
18. ETcontact-healingblogspot.com. "I Have an Implant in My Head." Website: http://etcontact-healing.blogspot.com/

517

19. Personal files/interview with author.
20. UFO Stalker. "Alien Encounter in Knightsville, South Carolina--Healing Visitation from Grey Beings." Dec 4, 2017. UFOMG! Out of This World News. Website: https://ufomg.com/2017/12/04/alien-encounter-in-knightsville-south-carolina-on-2017-12-01-040000-healing-visitation-from-grey-beings/
21. Kurth, Lauren. "Lauren Kurth: My Contactee Experience." You-tube. https://www.youtube.com/watch?time_continue=1&v=6QQGfrW2Di8
22. Burkes MD & Dennett, p443.

Chapter 11: Intestinal Healings

1. Crystall, Ellen. *Silent Invasion: The Shocking Discoveries of a UFO Researcher.* New York: Paragon House, 1991, pp5-6.
2. Wennergren, Kristina. "The Underwater UFO Base Visit by the Swedish 'Henry'--His UFO Experience from the Canary Islands." http://galactic.no/rune/henryufocontact.htm.
3. Potapova, Elena & Alexey K. Priyma. "The XX Century Chronicle of the Unexplained." *Tula Local Press,* 1999.
4. Fiore Ph.D., Edith. *Encounters: A Psychologist Reveals Case Studies of Abductions by Extraterrestrials.* New York: Doubleday, 1989, p105.
5. Fiore Ph.D., p105.
6. Dodd, Tony. *Alien Investigator: The Case Files of Britain's Leading UFO Detective.* London: Headline Book Publishing, 1999, pp107-108.
7. Twiggs, Denise Reib and Bert Twiggs. *Secret Vows: Our Lives with Extraterrestrials.* New York: Berkley Books, 1995, p188.
8. MUFONCMS. *Mutual UFO Network.* See: https://mufoncms.com/cgi-bin/report_handler.pl?req=view_long_desc&id=93425&rnd=
9. Culver, C. Leigh. "An Unforgettable Close Encounter." UFO Encounters. Norcross, GA: Aztec Publishing, Vol 2, #3, pp3-7, 29-30.
10. Cameron, Grant. *Alien Bedtime Stories.* It's All Connected Publishing, 2015, pp246-247.
11. Cameron, pp23-29.
12. "The Parallel World TV Program," Facts Newspaper. STB Channel. Kiev, Ukraine, June 20, 2008. www.ufostation.net
13. Lynge, Teri. "Alien Healing." Terilynge.blogspot.com. Website: http://terilynge.blogspot.com/2014/10/alien-healing.html
14. MUFONCMS. *Mutual UFO Network.* See: https://mufoncms.com/cgi-bin/report_handler.pl?req=view_long_desc&id=69560&rnd=
15. Klimo Ph.D., John. "A Report on Phase III of FREE's Experiencer Research Study: The Results of a Qualitative Study." *Beyond UFOs: The Science of Consciousness and Contact with Human Intelligence.* (Edited by Rey Hernandez, Jon Klimo Ph.D. and Rudy Schild, Ph.d.) FREE.org, p171.
16. Klimo Ph.D., p173.

17. Klimo Ph.D., p181.

Chapter 12: Alien Eye Doctors

1. Menger, Howard. *From Outer Space to You*. Clarksburg, WV: Saucerian Books, 1959, pp39-47.
2. Rosales, Alberto. *Humanoids Encounters: The Others Amongst Us: 1930-1949*. Triangulum Publishing. p277.
3. Sable, Patricia. "The Light from Within: The Strange Story of a UFO Abductee." *UFO Universe*. New York: Charlotte Magazine Corp, Feb/Mar 1991, Vol 1, #1, pp14-18, 66.
4. Humanoid Catalog. (HUMCAT) *Cufos.org*. See website: http://www.cufos.org/HUMCAT/HUMCAT_Index_1968.pdf
5. Blum, Ralph and Judy. *Beyond Earth: Man's Contact with UFOs*. New York: Bantam Books, 1974, p147.
6. Letter to author from Mario Rangel.
7. Gross, Patrick. See: https://ufologie.patrickgross.org/ce3/1977-07-10-brazil-pinheiro.htm
8. www.cpbufo.hpg.ig.com.br
9. Twiggs, Denise Reib and Bert Twiggs. *Secret Vows: Our Lives with Extraterrestrials*. New York: Berkley Books, 1995, p130.
10. Collings, Beth and Anna Jamerson. *Connections: Solving Our Alien Abduction Mystery*. Newberg, OR: Wild Flower Press, 1996, p76-77.
11. Collings & Jamerson, p76-77, 211, 271.
12. Bryan, C.D.B. *Close Encounters of the Fourth Kind: Alien Abduction, UFOs, and the Conference at M.I.T.* New York, Alfred A. Knopf, Inc., 1995, p26.
13. Burkes MD, Joseph and Preston Dennett. "Medical Healings Reported by UAP Contact Experiences: An Analysis of the FREE Data." *Beyond UFOs: The Science of Consciousness and Contact with Human Intelligence*. (Edited by Rey Hernandez, Jon Klimo Ph.D. and Rudy Schild, Ph.d.) FREE.org., pp413-417.
14. Anton, Alison. "ETs and Healing." *Etreunion.com*. See website: http://etreunion.com/
15. NUFORC. http://www.nuforc.org/webreports/068/S68957.html
16. MUFONCMS. *Mutual UFO Network*. See: https://mufoncms.com/cgi-bin/report_handler.pl?req=view_long_desc&id=64406&rnd=
17. Personal files/interview with author
18. Klimo Ph.D., John. "A Report on Phase III of FREE's Experiencer Research Study: The Results of a Qualitative Study." *Beyond UFOs: The Science of Consciousness and Contact with Human Intelligence*. (Edited by Rey Hernandez, Jon Klimo Ph.D. and Rudy Schild, Ph.d.) FREE.org, p172.

Chapter 13: Alien Dentists

1. Blum, Ralph and Judy. *Beyond Earth: Man's Contact with UFOs*. New York: Bantam Books, 1974, pp143-145; Stringfield, Leonard. *Situation Red: The UFO Siege*. New York: Fawcett Crest Books, 1977, pp72-74; http://www.cufos.org/HUMCAT/HUMCAT_Index_1973.pdf

2. Teets, Bob. *West Virginia UFOs: Close Encounters in the Mountain State*. Terra Alta, WV: Headline Books, Inc., 1995, pp26-27.

3. Burkes MD, Joseph and Preston Dennett. "Medical Healings Reported by UAP Contact Experiences: An Analysis of the FREE Data." *Beyond UFOs: The Science of Consciousness and Contact with Human Intelligence.* (Edited by Rey Hernandez, Jon Klimo Ph.D. and Rudy Schild, Ph.d.) FREE.org., pp394-395.

Chapter 14: The Integumentary System

1. Hall, Richard. *The UFO Evidence, Volume 2: A Thirty-Year Report.* Evanston, IL: Center for UFO Studies. Pp199, 267, 328-329.

2. Personal files/interview with author. (see also: Dennett, Preston. *Undersea UFO Base: An In-Depth Investigation of USOs in the Santa Catalina Channel.* Blue Giant Books, 2018, pp135-149.

3. Steiger, Brad. *The UFO Abductors.* New York: Berkley Books, 1988, pp62-63.

4. Salter Jr., John. "No Intelligent Life is Alien to Me." *Contact Forum.* Newberg, OR: Wild Flower Press, Vol 1, #1, pp1-3; Schmidt, Steve. "Friendly Aliens?" *Herald.* Grand Rapids, ND, Nov 11, 1989. (see also: UFONS, Dec 1989, #245, p6)

5. Tessman, Diane. "Three Amazing European Close Encounters." *UFO Universe.* Winter 1993, Vol 2, #1, pp62-64.

6. Clear, Constance. *Reaching for Reality: Seven Incredible True Stories of Alien Abduction.* San Antonio, TX: Consciousness Now, Inc., 1999, pp89-110.

7. NUFORC. http://www.nuforc.org/webreports/011/S11510.html http://www.nuforc.org/webreports/014/S14001.html

Chapter 15: The Liver

1. Fiore Ph.D., Edith. *Encounters: A Psychologist Reveals Case Studies of Abductions by Extraterrestrials.* New York: Doubleday, 1989, pp102-103.

2. Steiger, Brad. *The Other.* New Brunswick, NJ: Inner Light Publications, 1992, pp145-146.

3. Webb, David F. and Ted Bloecher. HUMCAT, Case #1971-39. Investigators: M. Tyrode and Fernand Legard. See also: http://www.ufoinfo.com/onthisday/March05.html

4. Steiger, Brad and Sherry Hansen Steiger. *The Rainbow Conspiracy*. New York: Windsor Publishing Corp, 1994, p40.
5. Garoutte, Aileen. "Dr. Alicia Flowers, Ph.D.--on the UFO Road Again." UFOexperiences.blogspot.com. https://ufoexperiences.blogspot.com/search?q=flowers

Chapter 16: The Kidneys

1. Good, Timothy. *Earth: An Alien Enterprise*. New York: Pegasus Books, 2013,pp165-180. http://galactic.to/rune/richardhoglundcontact_engl.htm
2. Pallman, Ludwig F. and Wendelle C. Stevens. *UFO Contact from Planet Itibi-Ra*. Tucson, AZ: UFO Photo Archives, 1986, pp96-101.
3. Steiger, Brad. *The UFO Abductors*. New York: Berkley Books, 1988, pp58-61.
4. Rosales, Alberto. *Humanoids Encounters: The Others Amongst Us: 1980-1984*. Triangulum Publishing. p380.
5. Sanchez-Ocejo, Virgilio and Wendelle C. Stevens. *UFO Contact from Undersea: A Report of the Investigation*. Tucson, AZ: Wendelle C. Stevens, 1982, ppf158-159.
6. Rutkowski, Chris A. *Abductions and Aliens: What's Really Going On?* Tonawanda, NY: Dundurn Press, 1999. Pp79-80.
7. Rosales, Alberto. *Humanoids Encounters: The Others Amongst Us: 1985-1989*. Triangulum Publishing. pp23-24. See also UFONs #263.
8. Clear, Constance. *Reaching for Reality: Seven Incredible True Stories of Alien Abduction*. San Antonio, TX: Consciousness Now, Inc., 1999, pp89-143.
9. Sabean, E.A. Strange: *UFOs and Aliens in My Life*. Navarone Books, 2010, Pp32-39. http://www.navaronebooks.com/

Chapter 17: The Heart

1. Leneesa. "Alien Healings." *UFOexperiences.blogspot.com*. See website: http://ufoexperiences.blogspot.com/2005/10/alien-healings.html
2. Leneesa. "Alien Healings." Also: Levitsky. "Victor Kostrykin-An Internationally Recognized UFO Contactee." See website: http://survincity.com/2011/12/victor-kostrykin-an-internationally-recognized/
3. Lamb, Barbara and Nadine Lalich. *Alien Experiences: 25 Cases of Close Encounter Never Before Revealed*. Laguna Woods, CA: Trafford Publishing, 2008, pp161-163.
4. Rosales, Alberto. *Humanoids Encounters: The Others Amongst Us: 1975-1979*. Triangulum Publishing, pp249-250.

5. Rosales, Alberto. *Humanoids Encounters: The Others Amongst Us: 1985-1989*. Triangulum Publishing. Original Source: Col. German K. Kolchin 'UFOs and Aliens: Intrusion on Earth,' Moscow, and Saint Petersburg, Sova Publishing 2007, quoting Fourth Dimension and NLO Yaroslavl #0, 2000.

6. Op cit.

7. Wilson, Katharina. *The Alien Jigsaw*. Portland, OR: Puzzle Publishing, 1993, pp127-129, 250.

8. Lecture by Michael Hesemann at 1994 UFO Expo West, Los Angeles, CA.

9. Mack MD, John E. *Abduction: Human Encounters with Aliens*. New York: Charles Scribner and Sons, 1994, pp348-368.

10. Morrow, Helga. "The Sedona Chronicles." *The Missing Link*. Jan/Feb 1993, pp-15-17.

11. Rosales, Alberto. *Humanoids Encounters: The Others Amongst Us: 1995-1999*. Triangulum Publishing. pp189-190.

12. Cameron, Grant. *Alien Bedtime Stories*. It's All Connected Publishing, 2015, p244.

13. Personal files/interview with author.

14. MUFONCMS. *Mutual UFO Network*. See: https://mufoncms.com/cgi-bin/report_handler.pl?req=view_long_desc&id=72524&rnd

Chapter 18: The Lungs

1. Stevens, Wendelle C. *UFO Contact from the Pleiades: A Preliminary Investigative Report*. Tucson, AZ: Wendelle C. Stevens, 1982, pp42-43.

2. Mack MD, John E. *Abduction: Human Encounters with Aliens*. New York: Charles Scribner and Sons, 1994, pp334-344.

3. Johnson, Paula. "Can Ufonauts Cure Us of Aids, Cancer and Other Fatal Diseases?" *UFO Universe*. Jul 1988, Vol 1, #1, pp26-27.

4. http://www.galactic-server.net/rune/ufoheal3.html (See also: Rosales, Albert, *Humanoids Encounters: The Others Amongst Us: 1970-1974*. Triangulum Publishing.

5. Stevens, 1982, pp240-241.

6. Rosales, Albert, *Humanoids Encounters: The Others Amongst Us: 1985-1989*. Triangulum Publishing. p84

7. Sparks, Jim. *The Keepers: An Alien Message for the Human Race*. Columbus, NC: Wild Flower Press, 2006, pp146-154.

8. Jacobs, David M. *Secret Life: Firsthand Accounts of UFO Abductions*. New York: Simon & Schuster, 1992, pp191.

9. Twiggs, Denise Reib and Bert Twiggs. *Secret Vows: Our Lives with Extraterrestrials*. New York: Berkley Books, 1995, pp112-113, 131-132.

10. Weiss, Chuck. *Abducted by Aliens*. http://abductedbyaliens.org/

11. Rosales, Albert, *Humanoids Encounters: The Others Amongst Us: 1980-1984*. Triangulum Publishing, p233.

12. Filer, George. "Filer's Files #43-2000. *Ufoinfo.com.* See website: http://www.ufoinfo.com/filer/2000/ff_0043.shtml

13. http://ufocasebook.conforums.com/index.cgi?board=alienabduction&action=display&num=1251663765

14. Burkes MD, Joseph and Preston Dennett. "Medical Healings Reported by UAP Contact Experiences: An Analysis of the FREE Data." *Beyond UFOs: The Science of Consciousness and Contact with Human Intelligence.* (Edited by Rey Hernandez, Jon Klimo Ph.D. and Rudy Schild, Ph.d.) FREE.org., p442.

15. Burkes MD & Dennett, p442.

Chapter 19: Arthritis & Chronic Fatigue Syndrome

1. Creighton, Gordon. "Healing from UFOs." *Flying Saucer Review.* Sep-Oct, 1969, Vol. 15, #5, p21. See: https://en.wikipedia.org/wiki/Buck_Nelson

2. NUFORC. http://www.nuforc.org/webreports/017/S17381.html

3. Johnson, Paula. "Can Ufonauts Cure Us of Aids, Cancer and Other Fatal Diseases?" *UFO Universe.* Jul 1988, Vol 1, #1, pp26-27.

4. Johnson, Donald A. "On This day." *UFOinfo.com.* See website: http://www.ufoinfo.com/onthisday/September06.html

5. Good, Timothy. *Unearthly Disclosure.* London: Arrow Books, 2000, 296-297.

6. Fiore Ph.D., Edith. *Encounters: A Psychologist Reveals Case Studies of Abductions by Extraterrestrials.* New York: Doubleday, 1989, p105.

7. Fiore Ph.D., pp105-106.

8. Randazzo, Joseph. *The Contactee Manuscript.* Studio City, CA: The UFO Library, Ltd, 1993. Chapter 3.

9. Townsend, Peggy R. "Close Encounters of the Watsonville Kind." Sentinel, Santa Clara, CA. Nov 11, 1993. (UFONS, Jan 1994, #294, p1)

10. Steiger, Brad and Sherry Hansen Steiger. *The Rainbow Conspiracy.* New York: Windsor Publishing Corp, 1994, p41.

11. Aronson, Virginia. *Celestial Healings: Close Encounters that Cure.* New York: Signet. Dec 1999, pp69-79.

12. Weiss, Chuck. *Abducted by Aliens.* P84. See website: http://abductedbyaliens.org/

13. Dennett, Preston. *Extraterrestrial Visitations: True Accounts of Contact.* St. Paul, MN: Llewellyn Publications, 2001, pp95-122.

14. Day, Chet. "Cure from Outer Space." *Chetday.com.* See website: http://chetday.com/aliencure.html
http://lovedriven.com/spacesyrup/

15. Translation (c) 2012, Scott Corrales, IHU. Special thanks to Raul Núñez and Ramón Navia-Osorio, IIEE) By Ramon Nava Osorio and Raul Nunez. "Healed by a UFO: the Flores Family Odyssey." See website: http://inexplicata.blogspot.com/

http://ufodigest.com/article/healed-ufo

16. Cliff, Martha. "'I Lost 12 Hours of My Life and I Have No Idea What Happened': People Who Are Convinced They've Been Abducted by Aliens Share Their Very Bizarre Stories." *Dailymail.co.uk.* See website. https://www.dailymail.co.uk/femail/article-4422478/People-abducted-aliens-share-stories.html

17. Leneesa. "Alien Healings." *UFOexperiences.blogspot.com.* See website: http://ufoexperiences.blogspot.com/2005/10/alien-healings.html

18. Thorne, Holly. "Aliens Cure Pennsylvanian Woman's Arthritis. *Themortonreport.com.* http://ufoexperiences.blogspot.com/2005/10/alien-healings.html

19. Marden, Kathleen. "The UFO-PSI Connection in My Own Life." *Alienjigsaw.com.* http://ufoexperiences.blogspot.com/2005/10/alien-healings.html

20. MUFONCMS. *Mutual UFO Network.* See: https://mufoncms.com/cgi-bin/report_handler.pl?req=view_long_desc&id=70219&rnd

Chapter 20: Infertility

1. Personal files/Interview with author.

2. *Visitors from the Unknown Television Movie.* Producer: Sharon Gayle. Director: Penelope Spheeris. Writer: Michael Grais. 1991.

3. Steiger, Brad. *The UFO Abductors.* New York, Berkley Books, 1988, p152.

4. NUFORC. http://www.nuforc.org/webreports/036/S36222.html

5. Burkes MD, Joseph and Preston Dennett. "Medical Healings Reported by UAP Contact Experiences: An Analysis of the FREE Data." *Beyond UFOs: The Science of Consciousness and Contact with Human Intelligence.* (Edited by Rey Hernandez, Jon Klimo Ph.D. and Rudy Schild, Ph.D.) FREE.org., p441.

Chapter 21: Tumors and Cysts

1. Good, Timothy. *Earth: An Alien Enterprise.* New York: Pegasus Books, 2013, pp165-180.

2. Rosales, Albert, *Humanoids Encounters: The Others Amongst Us: 1975-1979.* Triangulum Publishing, pp348-349.

3. *Studies of Abductions by Extraterrestrials.* New York: Doubleday, 1989, p105.

4. Randazzo, Joseph. *The Contactee Manuscript.* Studio City, CA: The UFO Library, Ltd, 1993. Chapter 11.

5. Robinson, Malcolm. "The International Page." *Missing Link.* May/Jun 1993, #126, pp18-19.

6. Personal files/interview with author.

7. Jordan, Debbie and Kathy Mitchell. *Abducted! The True Story of Intruders Continues.* New York: Carroll & Graf Publishers, Inc, 1994, pp257-260.
8. Hamilton, Bill. "A Case of Medical Intervention." MUFON UFO Journal. Seguin, TX: Mutual UFO Network. Aug 1995, #328, pp14-15.
9. Good, Timothy. *Unearthly Disclosure.* London: Arrow Books, 2000, p302.
10. Rosales, Albert. *Humanoid Encounters: The Others Amongst Us: 1985-1989.* Triangulum Publishing, p193.
11. Good, 2013, pp308-309.
12. MUFONCMS. *Mutual UFO Network.* See: https://mufoncms.com/cgi-bin/report_handler.pl?req=view_long_desc&id=80141&rnd
13. Personal files/interview with author.
14. Burkes MD, Joseph and Preston Dennett. "Medical Healings Reported by UAP Contact Experiences: An Analysis of the FREE Data." *Beyond UFOs: The Science of Consciousness and Contact with Human Intelligence.* (Edited by Rey Hernandez, Jon Klimo Ph.D. and Rudy Schild, Ph.d.) FREE.org., p442.

Chapter 22: Serious Illnesses & Chronic Diseases

1. Overstreet, Sarah. "Search of Space Conjures Up Spooky Stories." *News Record.* Miami, OK, Oct 27, 1992. (See UFONS, Dec 1992, #281, p11)
2. Rosales, Albert. *Humanoid Encounters: The Others Amongst Us: 1930-1949.* Triangulum Publishing, p197.
3. Fiore Ph.D., Edith. *Encounters: A Psychologist Reveals Case Studies of Abductions by Extraterrestrials.* New York: Doubleday, 1989, pp132.145.
4. Raynes, Brent. "Reality Checking: UFO Healings?" *Alternate Perceptions Magazines.* December 2004, #86. See website: http://mysterious-america.com/realitycheckap12.html
5. Op. Cit.
6. Randazzo, Joseph. *The Contactee Manuscript.* Studio City, CA: The UFO Library, Ltd, 1993. Chapter 11.
7. Adams, John. "To Whom It May Concern." *Missing Link.* Federal Way, WA: UFO Contact Center International. Aug 1992, #119, pp11-13.
8. Haggerty, Alice. "Abductee: USA." International UFO Library Magazine. Studio City, CA: UFO Library, Inc., Vol 2, 1991, p34; Jacobs, Ph.D., David. *Secret Life: Firsthand Accounts of UFO Abductions.* New York: Simon & Schuster, 1992, pp191-192.
9. Moxon, Megan. *Aliens Across America.* J & M Publishing, 2015. Pp13-15.
10. Uchoa, Paulo and Denise Ochoa Slater. "The Bernadette Healing Case." Lecture at Orange County, CA MUFON, August 18, 2010. See: http://www.mufonoc.org/the-bernadette-ufo-healing-case/

https://www.youtube.com/watch?time_continue=4088&v=T42_hqu-FNw

11. Humanoid Catalogue. *CUFOs.org.* See Website: http://www.cufos.org/HUMCAT/HUMCAT Index 1973 pdf

12. Randle, Kevin. *The October Scenario: UFO Abductions, Theories About Them and a Prediction of When They Will Return.* Iowa City, IA: Middle Coast Publishing, 1988, pp17-24.

13. Stevens, Wendelle C. *UFO Contact from the Pleiades: A Preliminary Investigative Report.* Tucson, AZ: Wendelle C Stevens, 1982, pp451-455.

14. Beckley, Timothy Green. "Dean Anderson's Ten-Year Contact Saga." *UFO Universe.* New York: Condor Books, Inc. Jul 1988, Vol 1, #1, p7.

15. Burkes MD, Joseph and Preston Dennett. "Medical Healings Reported by UAP Contact Experiences: An Analysis of the FREE Data." *Beyond UFOs: The Science of Consciousness and Contact with Human Intelligence.* (Edited by Rey Hernandez, Jon Klimo Ph.D. and Rudy Schild, Ph.d.) FREE.org., p406-412.

16. Unknown Country. "Insight Behind the News: Alien Healing." Website: http://www.unknowncountry.com/insight/alien-healing-0

17. Casellato, Rodolfo R., Joao Valerio da Silva and Wendelle C. Stevens. *UFO Abduction at Botucatu: A Preliminary Report.* Tucson, AZ: UFO Photo Archives. 1985, pp37-39, 194, 220.

18. Steiger, Brad and Sherry Hansen Steiger. *The Rainbow Conspiracy.* New York: Windsor Publishing Corp, 1994.

19. Atlanti, Sean. *Sean's Humanoid Sightings.* Unpublished.

20. MUFONCMS. *Mutual UFO Network.* See: https://mufoncms.com/cgi-bin/report_handler.pl?req=view_long_desc&id=23209&rnd=

21. Rosales, Albert. *Humanoid Encounters: The Others Amongst Us: 1985-1989.* Triangulum Publishing, p122.

22. Hind, Cynthia. *UFOs over Africa.* Madison, WI: Horus House Press. 1997. Pp143-176.

23. Rosales, 1985-1989, pp230-231.

24. Aronson, Virginia. *Celestial Healings: Close Encounters that Cure.* New York: Signet. Dec 1999, pp69-79.

25. MUFON CMS. *Mutual UFO Network.*

26. Bryan, C.D.B. *Close Encounters of the Fourth Kind: Alien Abduction, UFOs, and the Conference at M.I.T.* New York, Alfred A. Knopf, Inc., 1995, p20.

27. Morrow, Helga. "The Sedona Chronicles." *The Missing Link.* Jan/Feb 1993, pp-15-17.

28. Personal files/interview with author. See also: Dennett, Preston. *Inside UFOs: True Accounts of Contact.* Blue Giant Books, 2018, pp113-131.

29. Personal files/interview with author. See also: Dennett, Preston. *Extraterrestrial Visitations: True Accounts of Contact.* St Paul, MN: Llewellyn Publications, 2002, pp10-13.

30. Rosales, Albert. *Humanoid Encounters: The Others Amongst Us: 1995-1999*. Triangulum Publishing, p109.
31. Interview with author/personal files.
32. UFOcasebook.com. See: http://ufocasebook.conforums.com/index.cgi?board=worldwide&action=display&num=1414734205
33. Rosales, Albert. *Humanoid Encounters: The Others Amongst Us: 2000-2004*. Triangulum Publishing, pp78-79.
34. Garoutte, Aileene. "Remarkable Case and a Cure." *UFOexperiences.com*. See: http://ufoexperiences.blogspot.com/search?q=CURE
35. Burkes MD & Dennett, pp420-424.
36. MUFONCMS. *Mutual UFO Network*. See: https://mufoncms.com/cgi-bin/report_handler.pl?req=view_long_desc&id=74113&rnd=
37. Klimo Ph.D., John. "A Report on Phase III of FREE's Experiencer Research Study: The Results of a Qualitative Study." *Beyond UFOs: The Science of Consciousness and Contact with Human Intelligence.* (Edited by Rey Hernandez, Jon Klimo Ph.D. and Rudy Schild, Ph.d.) FREE.org, p172.
38. Burkes MD & Dennett, p442.
39. Burkes MD & Dennett, p442.

Chapter 23: Cancer Cures

1. Creighton, Gordon. "Healing from UFOs." *Flying Saucer Review.* Sep-Oct, 1969, Vol. 15, #5, pp20-21.
2. Buhler, Walter K.; Guilherme Pereira and Hey Matiel Pires. *UFO Abduction at Mirassol: A Biogenetic Experiment.* Tucson, AZ: Wendelle C. Stevens, 1985, pp139-141.
3. Lorenzen, Coral (Editor). APRO Bulletin, Tucson, AZ. January 1982, p5.
4. Mesnard, Joel (translated by Claudia Yapp.) "The French Abduction File." *MUFON UFO Journal.* Seguin, TX: Mutual UFO Network, Inc, Jan 1994, #309, pp10-11.
5. Johnson, Paula. "Can Ufonauts Cure Us of Aids, Cancer and Other Fatal Diseases?" *UFO Universe.* Jul 1988, Vol 1, #1, pp25-26.
6. http://unsolvedmysteries.wikia.com/wiki/Lynne_Plaskett
7. Romero, Luis Reyes. *Operacion Contacto.* See website: http://www.thinkaboutitdocs.com/1975-january-ufo-alien-sightings/
8. O'Brien, Christopher. *The Mysterious Valley.* New York: St. Martin's Pres, 1996, pp37-39.
9. Martin, Jorge. *Flying Saucer Review.* Vol. 43, #1.
10. Hall, Richard. *Uninvited Guests: A Documented History of UFO Sightings, Alien Encounters and Coverups.* Santa Fe, NM: Aurora Press, 1988, pp311-312.

11. Rosales, Albert. *Humanoid Encounters: The Others Amongst Us: 1985-1989*. Triangulum Publishing, p65.
12. http://www.nuforc.org/webreports/031/S31374.html
13. Jedd, Marcia. "What Do Aliens Want?" *Fate*. St. Paul, MN – Llewellyn Worldwide, Ltd. Jan 1997, 49-51.
14. Mack MD, John E. *Abduction: Human Encounters with Aliens*. New York: Charles Scribner and Sons, 1994, p46.
15. Lecture by Licea Davidson at 1994 UFO Expo West in Los Angeles, California.
16. Condon, Christopher. "World, Other Planets, Represented at UFO Congress in Budapest." *Budapest Week*. Budapest, Hungary, Oct 29-Nov 4, 1992. (See: UFONS, Feb 1993, #283, p13.)
17. Fiore Ph.D., Edith. *Encounters: A Psychologist Reveals Case Studies of Abductions by Extraterrestrials*. New York: Doubleday, 1989, p89-114.
18. Atlanti, Sean. *Sean's Humanoid Sightings*. Unpublished.
19. Corrales, Scott. "Voices of the Millennium: The Inexplicata Interview." http://www.ufoinfo.com/news/inexplicatainterview.shtml
20. Huneeus, Antonio. "Close Encounters in Peru." *UFO Universe*. New York: GCR Publishing Group, Spring 1994, Vol. 4, #1, pp52-54.
21. Druffel, Ann. *How to Defend Yourself Against Alien Abduction*. New York: Three Rivers Press, 1998, pp105-108.
22. Weiss, Chuck. *Abducted by Aliens*. See: http://abductedbyaliens.org/ Pp150-151.
23. Personal files/interview with author.
24. Twiggs, Denise Rieb and Bert Twiggs. *Secret Vows: Our Lives with Extraterrestrials*. New York: Berkley Books, 1995, p188.
25. Leneesa. "Alien Healings." UFOexperiencesblogspot.com. See: http://ufoexperiences.blogspot.com/2005/10/alien-healings.html
26. Burkes MD, Joseph and Preston Dennett. "Medical Healings Reported by UAP Contact Experiences: An Analysis of the FREE Data." *Beyond UFOs: The Science of Consciousness and Contact with Human Intelligence*. (Edited by Rey Hernandez, Jon Klimo Ph.D. and Rudy Schild, Ph.d.) FREE.org., pp417-420.
27. Chaves, Raul Oscar. (Translated by Scott Corrales.) "Argentina: An Operation by Strange Entities?" *UFOinfo.com*. See website: http://www.ufoinfo.com/news/argentinaentities.shtml
28. Clarke, Ardy Sixkiller. *Sky People: Untold Stories of Alien Encounters in Mesoamerica*. Pompton Plains, NJ: New Page Books, 2015, p280.
29. Sparks, Jim. *The Keepers: An Alien Message for the Human Race*. Columbus, NC: Wild Flower Press, 2006, pp214-215.
30. Rosales, Albert. *Humanoid Encounters: The Others Amongst Us: 2005-2009*. Triangulum Publishing, p211.

31. Good, Timothy. *Earth: An Alien Enterprise*. New York: Pegasus Books, 2013. See: http://www.phantomsandmonsters.com/2014/10/alien-healing-claims.html

32. MUFONCMS. *Mutual UFO Network*. See: https://mufoncms.com/cgi-bin/report_handler.pl?req=view_long_desc&id=11904&rnd=

33. "Aliens Cure from Leukemia." http://mysteries24.com/n4-5603-Aliens_cure_from_leukemia
http://www.unexplainable.net/ufo-alien/aliens_cure_leukemia.php

34. "Are Aliens Healing Children?" See website: http://www.myuforesearch.it/Aliens%20healing%20us.html
http://evidenciaovni2.blogspot.com/2009/06/aliens-curan-cuatro-chicos-de-cancer.html

35. "Alien Healing Claims." *PhantomsandMonsters.com*. See website: http://www.phantomsandmonsters.com/2014/10/alien-healing-claims.html

36. Moxon, Megan. *Aliens Across America*. J & M Publishing, 2015, pp149-152.

37. Kurth, Lauren. "My Contactee Experience." *Youtube.com*. See: https://www.youtube.com/watch?v=6QQGfrW2Di8

38. Burkes MD, Joseph and Preston Dennett. "Medical Healings Reported by UAP Contact Experiences: An Analysis of the FREE Data." *Beyond UFOs: The Science of Consciousness and Contact with Human Intelligence*. (Edited by Rey Hernandez, Jon Klimo Ph.D. and Rudy Schild, Ph.d.) FREE.org., p429-433.

39. UFOcasebook.com.
http://ufocasebook.conforums.com/index.cgi?board=alienabduction&action=display&num=1251663765

40. "Soldier Healed by Visitors." *Unknowncountry.com*. See website: http://www.unknowncountry.com/contactee-interview/soldier-healed-visitors

41. Holzer, Hans. *The UFOnauts: New Facts on Extraterrestrial Landings*. Greenwich, CT: Fawcett Publications, Inc, 1976, p70.

42. Good, Timothy. *Above Top Secret: The Worldwide UFO Cover-up*. New York: William Morrow & Co., Inc., 1988, pp303-304.

43. Goode, 1998, pp223-227.

44. Druffel, Ann and D. Scott Rogo. *The Tujunga Canyon Contacts: Updated Edition*. New York: New American Library, 1980, 1988.

45. Oldham, Bret. *Children of the Greys*. Murfreesboro, TN: House of Halo. 2013, p48.

Chapter 24: Health Upgrades

1. Davisson Ph.D., Dr. Darrell D. *Holographic Worlds*. 2013. P155.

2. Clarke, Ardy Sixkiller. *Sky People: Untold Stories of Alien Encounters in Mesoamerica.* Pompton Plains, NJ: New Page Books, 2015, p280.

3. http://www.ufoinfo.com/onthisday/May09.html

4. http://ufocasebook.conforums.com/index.cgi?board=tips&action=print&num 1108753265

5. Mack MD, John. *Passport to the Cosmos: Human Transformation and Alien Encounters.* New York: Crown Publishers, Inc. 1999, pp115, 248-249.

6. Sparks, Jim. *The Keepers: An Alien Message for the Human Race.* Columbus, NC: Wild Flower Press, 2006, p191.

7. MUFONCMS. *Mutual UFO Network.* See: https://mufoncms.com/cgi-bin/report_handler.pl?req=view_long_desc&id=79655&rnd=

8. MUFONCMS. *Mutual UFO Network.* See: https://mufoncms.com/cgi-bin/report_handler.pl?req=view_long_desc&id=38785&rnd=

9. Lamb, Barbara and Nadine Lalich. *Alien Experiences: 25 Cases of Close Encounter Never Before Revealed.* Laguna Woods, CA: Trafford Publishing, 2008, p128.

10. MUFONCMS. *Mutual UFO Network.* See: https://mufoncms.com/cgi-bin/report_handler.pl?req=view_long_desc&id=63748&rnd=

11. MUFONCMS. *Mutual UFO Network.* See: https://mufoncms.com/cgi-bin/report_handler.pl?req=view_long_desc&id=10361&rnd=

12. Joseph, Frank. "Readers Psychically Penetrate Infamous Area 51." *Fate.* Lakeville, MN: Llewellyn Worldwide, Jun 2003, Vol 56, No 9, Issue 638, p14-21.

Chapter 25: Even the Animals

1. Morton, Susan Nevarez. "They're Here--First Place." *Express News.* San Antonio, TX, Feb 26, 1989. (See: UFONS, April 1989, #237, p11.

2. Rosales, Albert. *Humanoid Encounters: The Others Amongst Us: 1960-1964.* Triangulum Publishing, p52.

3. Rosales, Albert. *Humanoid Encounters: The Others Amongst Us: 1970-1974.* Triangulum Publishing, p62.

4. Hernandez JD, MCP, Reinerio. "Preface." *Beyond UFOs: The Science of Consciousness and Contact with Human Intelligence.* (Edited by Rey Hernandez, Jon Klimo Ph.D. and Rudy Schild, Ph.d.) FREE.org., ppXXII-XXIII.

5. Personal files/interview with author.

6. Dennett, Preston. *Not from Here: Volume 2.* Blue Giant Books, 2016, pp92-104.

Chapter 26: Friends in High Places

1. Clarke, Ardy Sixkiller. *Sky People: Untold Stories of Alien Encounters in Mesoamerica.* Pompton Plains, NJ: New Page Books, 2015, pp248-252.

2. MUFONCMS.   https://mufoncms.com/cgi-
    bin/report_handler.pl?req=view_long_desc&id=13350&rnd
3. Dongo, Tom. *The Alien Tide*. Sedona, AZ: Hummingbird Press, p15. See:
    http://www.nuforc.org/webreports/060/S60351.html
4. Richter, Lillian. *Visitors Behind Our Stars*. Visitorsbehindourstars.com.
    2013, pp 4-20.
5. NUFORC. http://www.nuforc.org/webreports/042/S42859.html
6. Weiss, Chuck. *Abducted by Aliens*. See: http://abductedbyaliens.org/,
    pp160-161.
7. Ferrington, Tony. *Rescue in the Pacific: A True Story of Disaster and
    Survival in a Force 12 Storm*. Camden, ME: International Marine, 1996.
8. Personal files/interview with author. See: Dennett, Preston.
    Extraterrestrial Visitations: True Accounts of Contact. St. Paul, MN:
    Llewellyn Publications, 2001, pp123-138.
9. UFO   Related   Entities   Catalog.   (URECAT).   See   website:
    https://ufologie.patrickgross.org/ce3/1939-07-brazil-
    serradogordo.htm
10. Bord, Janet and Colin. *Unexplained Mysteries of the 20th Century*. New
    York: McGraw-Hill, 1990, p347.
11. Rosales, Albert. *Humanoid Encounters: The Others Amongst Us: 1955-
    1959*. Triangulum Publishing, pp182-183.
12. Personal files/interview with author. See: Dennett, Preston.
    Extraterrestrials Visitations, 2001, pp95-122.
13. NUFORC. http://www.nuforc.org/webreports/084/S84827.html

Chapter 27: Experiencers & Psychic Healing

1. Blum, Ralph and Judy. Beyond Earth: *Man's Contact with UFOs. New
    York: Bantam Books*, 1974, p150.
2. Mack MD, John E. *Abduction: Human Encounters with Aliens*. New York:
    Charles Scribner and Sons, 1994, p398.
3. Atlanti, Sean. *Sean's Humanoid Sighting and Research Catalogue: 1801-
    2009*. Unpublished.
4. https://www.reddit.com/r/UnresolvedMysteries/comments/66ybqn/i
    mj%C3%A4rvi_ufo_case_1970_finland/
5. Randles, Jenny. *Abduction: Over 200 Documented UFO Kidnappings
    Exhaustively Investigated*. Clerkenwell Green, London: Robert Hale
    Limited, 1988., p53.
6. Randles, p86.
7. Morrow, Helga. "The Sedona Chronicles." *The Missing Link*. Jan/Feb
    1993, pp16-17.
8. Bartholomew, Robert E & George S. Howard. *UFOs and Alien Contacts:
    Two Centuries of Mystery*. Prometheus Books, 1998, pp378-379.

9. Beckley, Timothy Green. *Strange Saga.* New Brunswick, NJ: Global Communications, 2005., p147.
10. Dvir, Adrian. *Healing Entities and Aliens.* 2003.
11. http://www.ufogreyinfo.com/aboutjudy.htm
12. Fiore Ph.D., Edith. *Encounters: A Psychologist Reveals Case Studies of Abductions by Extraterrestrials.* New York: Doubleday, 1989, pp89-114.
13. Hopkins, Budd. *Missing Time: A Documented Study of UFO Abductions.* New York: Richard Marek Publishers, 1981, pp51-88.
14. Strickler, Lon. "Alien Healing Claims." *Phantomsandmonsters.com.* See: http://www.phantomsandmonsters.com/2014/10/alien-healing-claims.html
15. Mack MD, 1994, p102.
16. Mack MD, 1994, pp238-239.
17. Worley, Don. See: http://www.abduct.com/worley/worley64.php
18. Lamb, Barbara and Nadine Lalich. *Alien Experiences: 25 Cases of Close Encounter Never Before Revealed.* Laguna Woods, CA: Trafford Publishing, 2008, pp9, 129-131, 133-135, 138-139, 170-172. (also personal files/interview with author)
19. Personal files/interview with author. See: Dennett, Preston. *Extraterrestrial Visitations: True Accounts of Contact.* St. Paul, MN: Llewellyn Publications, 2001, pp73-94.
20. Aronson, Virginia. *Celestial Healings: Close Encounters That Cure.* New York: Signet Books, 1999, pp238-258.

Chapter 28: Other Miraculous Healings

1. Boyd, Doug. *Rolling Thunder.* New York: Delta Books/Dell Publishing Co., Inc, 1974, pp14-23, 85-94.
2. Brown Jr., Tom. The Vision. New York: The Berkley Publishing Corp, 1988, pp213-215.
3. Eaton, Evelyn. *The Shaman and the Medicine Wheel.* Wheaton, IL: Theosophical Publishing House, 1982, p10.
4. Knight, J.Z. *A State of Mind: My Story.* New York: Warner Books, 1987, pp250-278, 366-367.
5. Vallee, Jacques. *The Invisible College: What a Group of Scientists Has Discovered About UFO Influences on the Human Race.* New York: E.P. Dutton, 1975, pp158-161.
6. Vallee, p150.
7. Trainor, Joseph (Editor.) "The Strange Case of Dr. Moscati." *UFO Roundup.* Vol. 10, #18, May 4, 2005. See website: http://www.ufoinfo.com/roundup/v10/rnd1018.shtml
8. Feirheiley, Don. *Angels Among Us.* New York: Avon Books, 1993, pp54-74.

9. Slemen, Tom. *The Angel of the Twelfth Night and Other Seasonal Supernatural Tales.* 2015, pp48-50.

10. Ring, Kenneth. *The Omega Project: Near-Death Experiences, UFO Encounters and the Mind at Large.* New York: William Morrow, 1992, p109.

11. Morse MD, Melvin with Paul Perry. *Transformed by the Light.* New York: Villard Books, 1992, 129-157.

12. Taylor, Albert. *Soul Traveler: A Guide to Out-of-Body Experiences and the Wonders Beyond.* Covina, CA: Verity Press, 1996, pp99-100.

13. Wilson, Terrill. *How I Learned Soul Travel.* Golden Valley, MN: Illuminated Way Publishing, Inc., 1987, pp103-105, 134.

14. Steiger, Brad. *In My Soul I am Free: A Biography of Paul Twitchell.* Golden Valley, MN: Illuminated Way Publishing, Inc. pp35-38.

15. Bruce, Robert. *Astral Dynamics.* Charlottesville, VA: Hampton Roads Publishing Co., 1999, pp487-488.

16. Hughes, Marilynn. *Odysseys of Light: Adventures in Out-of-Body Travel.* Norfolk, VA: Hampton Roads Publishing, Co, 1991, pp30-59; Hughes, Marilyn. *Crystal River Flowing.* Norfolk, VA: Hampton Roads Publishing, Co., 1993, pp67-68.

17. McKnight, Rosalind. *Cosmic Journeys: My Out-of-Body Experiences with Robert Monroe.* Charlottesville, VA: Hampton Roads Publishing, 1999, pp215-218.

18. Moen, Bruce. *Voyages into the Unknown.* Charlottesville, VA: Hampton Roads Publishing Co., 1997 pp111-122, 178-179 188-193.

19. Monroe, Robert. *Journeys Out of the Body.* New York: Doubleday Books, 1971, p279; Monroe, Robert. *Ultimate Journey.* New York: Doubleday Books, 1994, p114.

20. Bowman, Carol *Return from Heaven: Beloved Relatives Reincarnated within Your Family.* New York: HarperCollins Publishers, 2001, pp22-48

21. Paxton, Julie. "Struck by Lightning." *Fate.* St. Paul, MN: Llewellyn Publishing Co., April 1995. Vol. 48, #4, Issue #541, pp79-80; Pappos Ph.D, Pannos. "Therapy by Lightning." See website: http://www.panospappas.gr/lancet.htm

Conclusions and Analysis

1. http://www.oregonmufon.com/index.php/ufo-stories/107-ufos-at-gilliland-s-trout-lake-sanctuary

2. Coats, Rusty. "Believers Share Stories." *Bee.* Modesto, CA, Jan. 9, 1994. (See UFONS, Feb. 1994, #295, pp8-9.)

3. Strieber, Whitley. *Breakthrough: The Next Step.* New York: William Morrow & Co., Inc., 1988, p1.

4. Aronson, Virginia. *Celestial Healings: Close Encounters That Cure.* New York: Signet Books, 1999, pp289-290.

5. Chalker, Bill. *Hair of the Alien: DNA and Other Forensic Evidence of Alien Abductions*. New York: Simon & Schuster, 2005, p206.
6. Filer, George. "Filer's Files: #37-2008." *UFOinfo.com*. See website: http://www.ufoinfo.com/filer/2008/ff0837.shtml
7. Baldin, Lou. *In League with a UFO*. Leathers Co. Productions: Leawood, KS, 1997, pp13-50.
8. Salla Ph.D., Michael E. *The U.S. Navy's Secret Space Program*. Exopolitics Consultants, 2017, Pp275-276.

About the Author

Preston Dennett began investigating UFOs and the paranormal in 1986 when he discovered that his family, friends and co-workers were having dramatic unexplained encounters. Since then, he has interviewed hundreds of witnesses and investigated a wide variety of paranormal phenomena. He is a field investigator for the Mutual UFO Network (MUFON), a ghost hunter, a paranormal researcher, and the author of 23 books and more than 100 articles on UFOs and the paranormal. His articles have appeared in numerous magazines including *Fate, Atlantis Rising, MUFON UFO Journal, Nexus, Paranormal Magazine, UFO Magazine, Mysteries Magazine, Ufologist* and others. His writing has been translated into several different languages including German, French, Portuguese, Russian, and Icelandic. He has appeared on numerous radio and television programs, including *Coast-to-Coast* and the History Channel's *Deep Sea UFOs* and *UFO Hunters*. His research has been presented in the *LA Times,* the *LA Daily News,* the *Dallas Morning News* and other newspapers. He has taught classes on various paranormal subjects and lectures across the United States. He currently resides in southern California.
www.prestondennett.weebly.com
prestonufo@gmail.com

535

Books by Preston Dennett

The Healing Power of UFOs	Blue Giant Books, 2019
Not from Here, Volume Three	Blue Giant Books, 2018
Undersea UFO Base	Blue Giant Books, 2018
Not from Here, Volume Two	Blue Giant Books, 2017
Inside UFOs	Blue Giant Books, 2017
UFOs over Arizona	Schiffer Publishing, 2016
Not from Here, Volume One	Blue Giant Books, 2016
UFOs over Nevada	Schiffer Publishing, 2014
UFOs over New Mexico	Schiffer Publishing, 2012
Ghosts of Greater Los Angeles	Schiffer Publishing, 2010
Bigfoot, Yeti & Other Apemen	Chelsea House, 2009
UFOs over New York	Schiffer Publishing, 2008
Aliens & UFOs	Chelsea House, 2008
The Coronado Island UFO Incident	Galde Press, 2007
Human Levitation	Schiffer Publishing, 2007
Supernatural California	Schiffer Publishing, 2006
UFOs over California	Schiffer Publishing, 2005
Out-of-Body Exploring	Hampton Roads Publ., 2004
California Ghosts	Schiffer Publishing, 2004
Extraterrestrial Visitations	Llewellyn Publications, 2001
UFOs Over Topanga Canyon	Llewellyn Publications, 1999
One in Forty: the UFO Epidemic	Kroshka Books, 1997
UFO Healings	Wild Flower Press, 1996

Blue Giant Books
ISBN: 978-1984340702
226 pages

Undersea UFO Base

An In-Depth Investigation of USOs in the Santa Catalina Channel

For 100 years, strange activity has been occurring off the southern California Coast. Mile for mile, this area is one of the top producers of USOs (unidentified submersible objects) in the entire world. Drawing on firsthand testimonies from the Navy, Air Force, Coast Guard, police officers, lifeguards, residents and many others, Preston Dennett presents a compelling case for the possible existence of an undersea UFO base. Sightings of weird lights, anomalous glowing clouds, objects flying in and out of the water, mass UFO sightings, humanoid encounters--they're all here. More than ten years of research, presented here for the first time. The truth about this area can no longer be denied: something very strange is lurking in these waters.

- more than 70 cases of UFOs over the water.
- more than 70 cases of USOs in the water.
- original never before published cases.
- firsthand eyewitness testimonies from the Coast Guard, Navy and more.
- mass UFO sightings, some involving hundreds of objects.
- humanoid encounters, including abductions to an apparent base.
- An inside look at the History Channel's Deep Sea UFOs 1 & 2 & UFO Hunters.
- maps showing the location of all the activity.
- an in-depth exploration of the "Malibu Anomaly."
- photographs of UFOs and USOs, witnesses and encounter locations.
- original USO accounts from across the world.

Is there really an Undersea UFO Base off the southern California Coast? The evidence can be found inside this unique and groundbreaking book.

Blue Giant Books
ISBN: 9781539700029
175 Pages

Inside UFOs

While most UFO books are re-hashes of old cases, *"Inside UFOs"* presents the cutting edge of UFO research with ten all new original cases of extensive contact. A wide variety of ETs are presented, including various types of grays, Praying Mantis-type ETs, humanoids and Nordics. The witnesses are normal everyday people who suddenly find themselves in very unusual situations. The unique and unusual nature of the cases in this book will surprise even those well-versed in the UFO literature.

- A Navy Corpsman is invited aboard a UFO by his shipmate, only to meet fifteen-foot-tall friendly Praying Mantis-type ETs.
- A young child experiences an encounter with Nordic ETs that marks a lifelong series of contacts.
- A paperboy encounters a UFO and missing time, leaving him with an undiagnosed illness and a mystery that remained unsolved for years.
- An office-worker is confronted by a nine-foot-tall praying mantis, only to discover that she's also having contact with gray-type ETs too.
- a teacher stops on the road when a huge metallic sphere drops from the sky, and out steps a handsome-looking spaceman.
- A new mother is shocked to see an alien right outside her window, staring intently at her newborn son.
- a desperately ill housewife is transported from her home into an unknown base and cured by an eight-foot-tall orange-haired humanoid.
- A young farm-boy encounters UFOs on his family's farm, beginning a very close and lifelong relationship with ETs.
- A Navy Electronics Specialist has a complex UFO encounter aboard a Navy Ship, and is taught by the ETs about alternative energy sources.
- A nursing assistant has several missing time incidents culminating in a fully conscious encounter with gray ETs with an important message.

Why are the aliens here? What is their agenda on our planet? Are they hostile or benevolent? This book answers these questions and more, directly from the witnesses' themselves. This is not just another book about abductions by grays. This collection of true UFO stories shows how fascinating and bizarre ET contact can be.

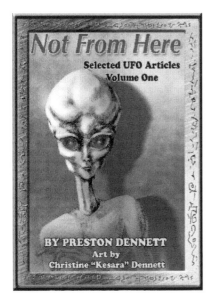

Blue Giant Books
ISBN: 9780692650219
229 pages

Not from Here: Vol 1

The first of three volumes, this book reveals the stranger side to the UFO phenomenon. Drawing on cases from across the world, it shows just how bizarre the UFO phenomenon can be. A wide variety of topics are covered.

Conversations with Extraterrestrials. In most cases, ETs are very tight-lipped. But in some rare cases, people have held conversations with extraterrestrials.

Phone Call from an Alien. UFO contact is much stranger than most people can imagine. Contact occurs in many ways, sometimes even by telephone.

UFO--Don't Shoot. When faced with the unknown, it is human nature to shoot first and ask questions later. But what happens if you shoot at a UFO?

Alien Zoos. Are there zoos onboard UFOs? The answer is yes, and they contain many strange creatures, some from here and some not from here.

UFOs over Graveyards. Why are aliens hovering over graveyards? These spooky accounts are both surprising and unsettling.

They Walk Among Us. Sometimes aliens are seen in the strangest places, including bookstores, convenience stores, buses, train-stations, casinos, schools, subways and more.

The Alien-Clown Connection. Alien screen memories come in many forms, but the alien-clown connection is one of the strangest of all.

The Intimidation and Murder of UFO Witnesses. Many UFO witnesses have learned the hard way that it can be very dangerous to be a UFO witness.

Exposed--Project Redlight. Not all UFOs are being piloted by ETs. In some cases, the pilots appear to be the U.S. military. Are we flying the flying saucers?

Mining Data on UFOs. UFOs appear to have multiple agendas, including an active interest in mines and the precious metals of our planet.

NOT FROM HERE

Selected UFO Articles
Volume Two

Preston Dennett
Art by
Christine Kesara Dennett

Blue Giant Books
ISBN: 9781532804588
211 pages

Not from Here: Vol 2

The UFO phenomenon is profoundly strange and complex. This series of books focus on the strange and unusual cases, the kind that don't fit the standard model of UFO contact.

UFO Investigator's Disease. a collection of cases in which UFO researchers become themselves investigated by UFOs. It's a clear case of the hunter become the hunted.

Aliens-R-Us. In some cases in which ETs tell people that the reason they were contacted is because they and the ETs are related.

The Incredible Shrinking Abductee. Sometimes people are affected by ET technology in ways that are mindboggling , including being shrunken down in size.

The Mystery of Angel Hair. It's a strange web-like substance emitted from UFOs. Nobody knows what it is or what it means. In this huge collection of cases, some surprising answers are revealed.

Extraterrestrial Gardeners. Aliens are conducting a comprehensive study of our planet. They are collecting samples of all kinds of plants, and affecting plants in bizarre ways.

UFO Rescue at Sea. It almost never happens, but in a few isolated cases, castaways lost at sea have been rescued by a UFO.

The Smell of UFOs. What do UFOs smell like? This is one of the largest collection of cases of UFO odors ever assembled. An analysis provides some surprising insights.

The UFO Breathing Pool. In one of the strangest of onboard experiences, abductees are placed inside a pool and made to breathe the liquid.

Alien Drinks. Sometimes people are given liquids by the ETs and told to drink them. The question is, why?

UFOs and Rockets. UFOs have been observed monitoring a wide variety of rocket and missile launches across the world. These cases show that ETs are keeping a very close eye on our explorations into deep space.

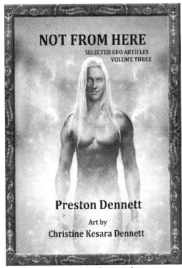

Blue Giant Books
ISBN: 9781719142748
183 pages

Not from Here: Vol 3

Diving deep into the heart of the UFO phenomenon, this volume (like the others) explores the weirder cases, the ones many UFO investigators don't like to talk about.

Caught in the Act. Although abductions number in the thousands or more, almost nobody ever sees an abduction happen. Or do they? The answer is yes, as these cases prove.

See a UFO--Lose Your Job. While seeing a UFO can be an exciting event, it sometimes comes with hidden dangers. Sometimes, seeing a UFO can even cost a person their job.

Alien Gifts. In very rare cases, aliens give people gifts, actual physical proof of their encounter. It almost never happens, but when it does, the results are astounding.

To Err is Alien. ETs are clearly more advanced than humans. But they are not perfect. Sometimes they make stupid mistakes.

Can We Contact UFOs with a Ouija Board? Usually used to communicate with spirits, there are now several cases in which the Ouija board is used to contact ETs.

UFOs over Prisons. UFOs are known to be attracted to nuclear power plants, military installations and other technological areas, including prisons. The question is, why?

Is Jesus an Alien? It's a question that's been asked many times, with few answers. There are now a number of cases in which people claim to have met Jesus aboard a UFO.

Is Bigfoot an Alien? Most UFO cases do not involve Bigfoot, and most Bigfoot cases do not involve UFOs. But in a tiny percentage of cases, these two phenomena perfectly intersect.

The Truth Behind Alien Anal Probes. Are people actually being anally probed by ETs? And if so, why? What exactly are the ETs looking for?

If You Build It. Abductees are often taken into the engine room of a UFO and told how it works. Some abductees have used their knowledge to actually build an alien engine.

Made in the USA
Middletown, DE
08 May 2022

65482967R00300